"A terrifying tale of the Lady Voracious of Canada and the boy she married who became Prime Minister." — **Kent Heckenlively, JD**, co-author of *Plague of Corruption*, *New York Times* bestselling author.

IN TRUDEAU'S KITCHEN

My Unexpected Journey with Power, Politics, and the Global Elite

JEFF BROWN

Inside Trudeau's Kitchen: My Unexpected Journey with Power, Politics, and The Global Elite
Copyright © 2025 Jeffrey Brown

Published by:
Trine Day LLC
PO Box 577
Walterville, OR 97489
1-800-556-2012
www.TrineDay.com
TrineDay@icloud.com

Library of Congress Control Number:

Brown, Jeffrey,.
–1st ed.
p. cm.

Epub (ISBN-13) 978-1-63424-533-3
Trade Paperback (ISBN-13) 978-1-63424-532-6
1. Brown, Jeffrey (1962-). 2. Autobiography. 3. Politics-Canada 4. Trudeau, Sophie (1975-). I. Brown, Jeffrey. Title

Credos is an imprint of TrineDay

First Edition
10 9 8 7 6 5 4 3 2 1

Printed in the USA
Distribution to the Trade by:
Independent Publishers Group (IPG)
814 North Franklin Street
Chicago, Illinois 60610
312.337.0747
www.ipgbook.com

For the billions of humans who have been abused by political power. I wrote for you, too.

For Barbara and Albert Brown, Frances and Bernard Perlove. Thank you for building me brave.

For Canada. Before it's too late.

OTHER BOOKS BY JEFF BROWN

Soulshaping: A Journey of Self-Creation

Ascending with Both Feet on the Ground

Love It Forward

An Uncommon Bond

Spiritual Graffiti

Grounded Spirituality

Hearticulations

Humanifestations

Where is God in all of this?: A Conversation

"Tyranny always masquerades as benevolence." ~*Jeff Brown*

Contents

Note to the Reader 1
Chapter 1: Setting the Stage 5
Chapter 2: Nothing to Hide, and Nowhere to Hide It 10
Chapter 3: Dancing in the Same Light? 15
Chapter 4: A Family Trip to Ottawa 26
Chapter 5: Meeting a Wildhorse 31
Chapter 6: Love Ride to Freedom 36
Chapter 7: A Sea of Accomplishment 45
Chapter 8: Obama Comes to Town 52
Chapter 9: Pam Grier 58
Chapter 10: I'm Here for You 69
Chapter 11: Instadrama 77
Chapter 12: Dim Sum 92
Chapter 13: Calling the Cops 98
Chapter 14: The Department of Justice? 106
Chapter 15: Glitches or Snitches? 114
Chapter 16: There's a Spider on the Pillow? 123
Chapter 17: Winkgate 149
Chapter 18: Humanifestations 161
Chapter 19: The Divorce 171
Chapter 20: Trudeaumania 183
Chapter 21: Zopi*clone* 205
Chapter 22: Re-entry Drama 209
Chapter 23: Jacordris Gregoire 215
Chapter 24: Left Atrial Enlargement 221
Chapter 25: Dudley Do-Wrong? 238
Chapter 26: Cross Border Stalking 254
Chapter 27: Smash and Grab 272
Chapter 28: Homecomings 283
Chapter 29: Final Thoughts: The Pen is Mightier than the Shadow Ban 301

Endnotes 315
Gratitudes 323
About the Author 325

Note To The Reader

It's difficult to write on a battlefield. As you will see, this book was written under the most strenuous of conditions. Vigilance and terror make strange bedfellows. As a result, I was unable to write it with the kind of nuance, insight, and creative flourish that I prefer. While stumbling through a labyrinth of fear and anxiety, the words were forming deep inside, but they sometimes had trouble breaking through to the surface. So, please bear with me as the story unfolds. It may read a little choppy and repetitious at times, but we get there. It's one thing to write a book after an experience has come to an end. It's quite another to write it while you are still on the battlefield.

People often ask me how this book can benefit them. I have many answers, all of which intersect with each other. First, In Trudeau's Kitchen puts words to a journey that many humans have experienced—the journey to survive political abuse of power. They have lived it, but few have had the opportunity to put the experience to words. As a result, much of the human story lays buried, longing to be shared. Little wonder nothing changes with respect to abuse of power. We're not letting the stories through that can change our world. By overcoming my resistance and telling my story, it is my hope that it inspires others to do the same.

Second, this book clearly captures and prepares you for the myriad ways that the new technologies are utilized to contain and control human consciousness. Not only to gain your favor politically, but to ensure that you get back in line if you dare to stray from your political affiliations. Like myself prior to 2019, most people can't even begin to imagine being manipulated on Meta and targeted by techno-terrorists and invisi-bullies. And yet, many of them will experience something like this. The spy world has dramatically changed and normalized. There are now hundreds of ways to gather data and manipulate consciousness. This book prepares the reader for the new world, so that they won't be caught by surprise as I was. In this way, I think of it as The People's Book—a Whistle-Blower's Almanac that gets you ready to protect yourself and shape the world to come.

Third, it's my view that the world will not change until we realize there is abuse of power on both sides of the political aisle. As a long time progressive, I was utterly certain that it was only the (allegedly) fascistic right wing that engaged in life-threatening intimidation and harassment practices. And then this happened, and I was forced to face the fact that the left often uses its seeming benevolence as cover for its own savagery. As it is, we live in a divided world. We can thank addictive "smart phones" and Meta's manipulative algorithms for that. You either align with the left, or with the right. As a result, we cannot find common ground and we spend an enormity of time hating on each other. This is precisely what the power-brokers want. If we are going to effect real change, we have to find the center together, and focus our shared energies on dismantling systems that abuse our humanity. This book provides a key piece of information—the issue isn't the left or the right. It's abuse of power, and it's everywhere.

I may never fully understand why this happened in my life. I have had a fairly clear idea of my bucket list for decades – my purpose, goals, and aspirations – and this was definitely not on it. The only way I can make sense of it is to imagine that there are two bucket lists. The first is the one that you carry around consciously – like a blazing torch. The second bucket list is the one that is held in the hands of Providence. It's not that I believe every challenging experience is written in the stars. Some things in this world are undeniably tragic. But there is something about this one that feels divinely influenced. The simple fact that I am still here to write about it – after a 4+ year onslaught of politically motivated terror, *and* a Near Death Experience – is miraculous. I can certainly attribute some of that to my warrior spirit, but there is something else happening here – something that defies reason. Creation had a hand in this. I'm sure of it.

And so did the soul. Before this happened, I had devoted most of my adult life to identifying something that I have come to call 'Soul-Scriptures' and 'Encodings.' Included among them are the archetypes (universal ways of being) and callings (offerings) that I believe each of us is here to explore and to actualize. With respect to my own path, I imagined myself an author of three longer self-help/spiritual books: *Soulshaping, An Uncommon Bond, Grounded Spirituality.* That is what I saw when I looked ahead. After completing Grounded, I wondered what was next. I vaguely sensed that there was something intense on the horizon, but I couldn't make it out. Now I understand why. I would have done everything in my power to avoid it. Instead, it crept up on me a little at a time, until there was no turning back.

As for those who walk beside me, I have sensed the presence of many ancestors on this journey. I stand on their shoulders, and they lift my weary spirit higher. This has felt particularly true in the last year. The most prevalent among them is my mother, Barbara Marcia Brown. Our tumultuous relationship helps me to understand why I was so triggered by many of these events (although I can't imagine anybody wouldn't be), but it also helps to explain my rowdy resilience. If my techno-terrorists had ever met her, they would have surely known not to pick this fight. Because they are nothing by comparison to the ferocity of Barbara Brown, God rest her soul. As I wrote this book, I often felt her near, reminding me that I wasn't just fighting for my life – I was fighting for everyone else's, too. Perhaps every whistle-blower is.

Note: When *italics* are used to first introduce someone, it is an indication that I am choosing to protect their identify by using a pseudonym.

I offer a few words from the pages to come:

I called my safe-keeper on the afternoon of Saturday, December 12 2020, to check on the time to meet for the binder drop-off on Sunday. He agreed to call back after checking on some timing details with his partner.

That evening, I was sitting on the couch chatting with my wife when my cellphone rang. It was 7:02 PM. The call display indicated that it was my friend calling from his home phone. But when I answered the phone, he didn't respond. I could sense that it wasn't a dead phone line. Someone was there; there was movement, the sound of someone breathing on the other end.

After I said hello twice, a woman very calmly said, "Hello."

"Who is this?" I asked.

No reply again, so I asked it more assertively.

She then replied with something like, "I suppose I should say that I am Pam Grier."

I assumed she was referencing the iconic American actress (unless she was referencing herself). I asked her why she was on my phone line – and she went silent again.

Shaken and confused, I hung up and dialed my friend. He confirmed that yes, he had called me.

And yes, he had heard me speaking. But he hadn't heard anyone else.

Yet the only person I could hear was the woman on my phone.

* * *

My friend the safe-keeper was a Toronto Islander. When I arrived at the ferry docks, I felt a looming sense of discomfort that quickly morphed into fright. It was a dark, misty pandemic night and very few people were around. Though I'd never been the type who worried about being followed, I found myself studying the people awaiting the boat to determine if they were Islanders or here for some other reason. I'd gone from feeling fundamentally safe and protected as a Canadian, to worrying about my well-being. If I had grown up in a despotic nation, I would have been prepared for this, but this was pristine Canada, the land of polite people and Dudley-Do-Right. There was no shadow here, right?

The boat arrived, and I stepped aboard with the binder. When I arrived on the other side, my friend was waiting for me, his trusted bicycle leaning against the fence. We embraced, and I handed him the binder. He quickly put it in the saddlebag, locked it down, and rode off into the mist. I stepped back onto the ferry and made my way home. Safe-keeping mission accomplished!

Thereafter, I was catapulted into a state of high anxiety. We were already in a pandemic lockdown, which felt inherently dangerous and uncomfortable. Compounding that, I now worried that the leader of my country perceived what I knew and what I had contributed as some kind of political threat. In the midst of it all, I found it difficult to regain my equilibrium. I began making personal videos to express myself and watched my generally gregarious nature fade away. I went to sleep anxious, woke up anxious. I was experiencing unfamiliar emotions that I had no language for and no capacity to release while in such a vigilant state. So much for feeling safer because of my proximity to power. Now I was living the other side of that equation – feeling more frightened because of that same proximity. And that is a whole different world.

CHAPTER 1

SETTING THE STAGE

Let me begin by going back in time. I was born in 1962 in Toronto, Canada, at a time when the reverberations of the Second World War were still very much alive within the collective. My parents – an attractive and morally righteous Jewish woman, and a handsome and charismatic Irish Catholic man – met in an elevator while working at Toronto's City Hall. They were drawn together by a flurry of good things: physical attraction, a shared love of music and film, and their mutual desire to live a life far removed from their painful upbringings. Dreamers both, they longed for the fantasy lifestyle that was being sold at the time: home ownership, suburban pleasantries, economic security. Unbeknownst to them and to many newlyweds of the time, the weight of their unresolved ancestral patterns would crash through the gates of their idyllic imaginings, replacing them with a trauma bond of horrifying proportions. With no real understanding of their issues and wounds, they could do little more than perpetuate them, spending much of their 21-year marriage at each other's throats. Sometimes, literally.

As a result, I grew up on a battlefield. Not a day went by where there wasn't some form of interpersonal conflict. Where other children might have shied away or obliged, I fought back, resisting and standing down abuses of power even while in my crib. Although I cognitively understood that it was more prudent to passively acquiesce, I just couldn't. For whatever reason, it was encoded in my mind that resisting tyranny – even with those I was born to – was essential for my survival. It made for an exhausting and excruciating childhood, yet something was gained. These acts of defiance became the bedrock – both energetically and with respect to my sense of self – for the achievements that followed.

Emboldening me to stand down aggression were the stories and symbols of war, shared by some of my closest relations. My Grandfather ("Beela") – truly my dearest childhood friend – had been a combat soldier in WW2, and he regaled me with grizzly tales that included the death of his best friend on a European battlefield. As did my Uncle Sidney – a celebrated Lancaster Bomber Navigator in WW2 – and my Uncle Manny – an air force photographer tasked with snapping pictures of airplane wrecks in the U.K. Driving their point home was a variety of war-time artifacts safely tucked away in my Grandmother's cedar chest. Among them were historical photos, medals and pins, and a small handgun that someone had brought back from Europe at the end of the war. Although we were a family of limited means – the closest we came to fame and fortune was my father's brief handshake with actor Gregory Peck on the steps of a Toronto office tower – we were nonetheless a proud and dignified lot, largely because of the wartime contributions made by my courageous kin. Clearly, standing down abuse of power was hardwired into my genes. As you will soon see, this will prove to be quite relevant on the road ahead. Because it is not only the traumas that we carry-forward from our ancestors – it is also the acts of heroic overcoming in the face of adversity.

Despite my fiery influences, it was no small thing to overcome daily conflict, particularly after I entered my teenage years. War is still war, and if there is no opportunity for restoration, you are eventually torn asunder, particularly when you grow up on a never-ending battlefield. What got me through was a saving-grace combination of loving grandparents, a cleverly constructed catalogue of coping strategies, and a series of moments that I can only refer to as glimmers of future possibility. From time to time – both within my dreams and in the heart of daily life – I had glimpses of myself as first a criminal lawyer, then a student of humanistic psychology, and finally an author. My conscious bucket list.

The legal imaginings were remarkably real. I would see Canada's most famous criminal lawyer, Eddie Greenspan, on television, and I felt this peculiar certainty that I would someday work with him. The interesting thing was that these glimpses didn't feel anything like wishful thinking. They were not the kind of escapist fantasies one conjures up to survive the unendurable – I was much too practical a boy to live in la-la-land. Working with him simply felt inevitable. I seemed to intrinsically understand where Eddie was coming from – both with respect to the presumption of innocence and the tyrannies of corrupted power. Although it seemed utterly impossible to imagine how this could happen in my hopelessly embattled circumstances, the very idea that there might be something good waiting for me at the end of this tunnel of misery gave me just the spark I needed to carry on.

Although I barely made it through high school – not even close to completing my grade 12 diploma, but somehow completing my grade

Chapter 1: Setting the Stage

13 with an 80% average – I had the audacity to apply to post-secondary institutions. Inspired by the success of the two renowned journalists in the family – Uncle Joe Perlove (*Toronto Star*) and cousin Jerry Gladman (*Toronto Sun*) – I applied for journalism programs at Carleton University and what was then called Ryerson Polytechnical Institute, along with several other universities. Much to my surprise, I got into most of them. Not sure whether to commit to a journalism career at age 19 or do an undergraduate degree, I settled on the latter. After all, Eddie Greenspan and I had a date with destiny, or so my youthful mind imagined. And law was supposed to be my first career. Writing, my last...

I went to McMaster University in Hamilton, Ontario, and completed a B.A. in Humanities (Political Science, with a minor in Psychology). To my surprise, I was then accepted into Canada's most prominent law school at the University of Toronto.

My first year was quite challenging. It wasn't the legal concepts that thwarted me. It was the dramatic gap between my rough-and-tumble beginnings, and the elite nature of the legal world. Surrounded by a whole host of students from some of Canada's most powerful families, my imposter syndrome dug its claws into me, undermining the intellectual acumen and legal prowess that lay buried below the surface. The tremendous reserves of energy I had expended reaching this stage, had required me to bury and repress a host of unresolved wounds and issues. Having made it to the other side, they were now summoned out of hiding.

I then took a leave of absence, devoting myself to healing from the challenges of early life. When I finally returned to law school for my second year, I was like a different person. I earned four A's, including one from a 'Practice of Criminal Law Course' with Eddie and (his brother) Brian Greenspan, and won the Law and Medicine Prize. In the summer between second and third year, I landed a job articling with Eddie after law school ended. Articling is a one-year apprenticeship that every Canadian law student is required to complete after they graduate. After they article, they move on to complete the Bar admission course, before being called to the Bar shortly thereafter.

My year with Eddie was anything but normal. I spent most of my year defending police officers. It began with research into charges against then Toronto Police Chief McCormick for 'war medals' pinned to his uniform. That was easy – I went to the library, found out that the Korean 'War' was actually characterized as a 'Conflict,' and soon thereafter, the charges were dropped. Next up, an Internal Affairs investigation into two Toronto cops.

Based on my performance on this matter, Eddie felt confident offering me the Melaragni trial, slated for the following January. Constable Anthony Melaragni and his partner Darren Longpre were charged after Melaragni shot and killed a car thief who had driven a stolen car at them in 1988. This case was no small thing for an articling student. It was a highly anticipated public trial, with an enormity of complexities and issues. After my intense childhood training camp, I was ready.

I diligently and rigorously prepped the case for many months, reaching an apex of focus that I had no idea lived inside me. When the virtually sleepless 3-month trial began, we were ready to kick ass. And kick ass, we did. With my cross examinations to direct him, my tuna sandwich pickups to feed him, and Eddie's natural courtroom panache and relational brilliance, we dismantled and destroyed the Prosecutor's Case. So effectively that, when it came time to present our defense, we didn't need to call the accused as a witness. Towards the end, I went back home and wrote 168 pages of jury address in four days and nights. The trial was soon over. But not before a violent riot ensued on the steps of the courthouse.

I spent the last weeks of my articles preparing a trial for an officer in Nepean, Ontario who was charged with Manslaughter.

By the time I was called to the Bar, and despite the very real temptation of signing an office lease with a group of my up-and-coming peers, I chose to step back from legal practice. It was the most difficult decision I would ever make. I was smitten with trial law, and a very real part of me longed to fight for people's rights in a courtroom for decades to come. But something else called me.

After devoting a considerable amount of time to working on myself – which included building a small home improvements business I owned, and a brief stint as a lawyer that confirmed my decision to leave – I moved onto the second goal on my bucket list: studying humanistic psychology at Saybrook University in California. I completed my Master's in Psychology in 2000. Soon thereafter, I began to work part time on my first book, *Soulshaping: A Journey of Self-Creation*. After finishing the manuscript in 2007, I received an offer from Namaste Publishing – the publisher of Eckhart Tolle's *The Power of Now*. I turned the offer down, and self-published my first edition of *Soulshaping* that autumn. The book then developed a small grassroots following, and I accepted an offer to publish from North Atlantic Books in California.

By the time the book formally entered the system in the summer of 2009, I had already begun to grow in social media. I was doing dozens of monthly radio shows and podcasts, and many of my posts and short writings were quickly becoming popular on Facebook. In September 2010, I wrote an inspired piece called 'The Apologies to the Divine Feminine (from a warrior in transition)' that immediately went viral, exponentially boosting my following.

In 2010, I left Toronto and moved to the country to write in peace. My calling to write was now on fire, and I wanted to remove all distractions so I could take my creativity to the next level. It worked out well. After moving to Rockwood, Ontario, I completed a wild spiritual documentary (*Karmageddon*) that I had co-produced with my best friend, *Samuel*. And I wrote like the wind, eventually forming my own small publishing business (Enrealment Press) so that I could bring my voice to the world on my own terms. After publishing two of my own books, I began to publish other authors as well. Among them were poet Victoria Erickson, sacred activist Andrew Harvey, and my (eventual) wife, Susan Frybort, whose poetry touched me deeply. I then expanded to launch my own online school – Soulshaping Institute – where I began to create and teach a spectrum of courses.

Although I was certainly not making a fortune, I felt deeply accomplished. It would have been enough to have simply survived my childhood. But to have then found a way to heal some of my personal and ancestral trauma, and become a lawyer, and then to become a published author who meaningfully impacted people's lives, lifted my spirits and gave me hope. Not simply for my own life, but for everyone's. Not to say that others don't have far worse circumstances to overcome – they surely do – but if I could overcome this much, I felt confident that many others could, too.

By the time Sophie Trudeau showed up in my life, I was living my life as a prayer for human possibility. I had made my life better, I was doing my small bit to make other lives better, and I figured that if we could just get enough of us on a healing and awakening journey, we could turn this troubled species around.

CHAPTER 2

NOTHING TO HIDE, AND NOWHERE TO HIDE IT

My journey with the Trudeaus began in the summer of 2015, months before Justin became the Prime Minister. My old friend, *Robin*, had gone to one of my favorite holistic centers – the Omega Institute in Rhinebeck, New York – for a yoga retreat. As it turned out, Sophie had also attended the same workshop.

To this point, I knew very little about Sophie and Justin. I was familiar with Justin's father – former Canadian Prime Minister Pierre Elliott Trudeau – but not with his son and his son's wife. I seldom read the news, and found the political world out of touch with the shifts in consciousness that many of us were aspiring to on a grass roots level.

Toward the end of the week, Robin called me to ask if I was okay with her giving Sophie some of my books. She had a pile of them in her van intended for a mutual friend on Long Island. This was not uncharacteristic for her. She was perhaps my biggest writing cheerleader, often passing my books to like-minded others. She sang Sophie's praises, and felt certain that she would resonate with my work. She was right.

At first, I resisted. After a number of years writing in the self-help field, I had grown to dislike the passing of my books to well-known people. It's not that I was opposed to them resonating with my work – I just didn't like the feeling of chasing them. It activated the part of me that had grown up in an economically peripheral family, always on the outside looking in. It somehow implied that I hadn't arrived yet, and needed their help. But that wasn't the truth. I no longer needed their help. I had things right where I wanted them.

But Robin did what cheerleaders do – she pushed me. So, in the middle of my busy day, I ignored my intuition and gave in. After all, I had to agree with her – this was a little different. We weren't chasing someone to get their attention. Sophie was right there. She had met her, and liked her, and it felt natural and unforced to give her the books. And she wasn't from

Chapter 2: Nothing to Hide, and Nowhere to Hide It

the self-help aristocracy that I had pandered to some years before – she was the wife of a Canadian politician. What harm could come from that? (Don't answer that.)

This was the first time that I ignored my intuition in this situation. It would not be the last.

Robin gave Sophie a few of my books. Included among them was my first book of quotes: *Ascending with Both Feet on the Ground*. Thereafter, I didn't give the passing of the books a second thought. I was busy writing and growing in social media, and *Enrealment Press* was demanding much of my attention.

On November 4, 2015, Justin Pierre James Trudeau was sworn in as Prime Minister of Canada. By the following spring, I was feeling a certain degree of alignment with the Trudeaus. His declared emphasis on open and transparent government, his self-proclaimed feminism, their public willingness to destigmatize mental health issues, and – I dare say – the fact that they were both yogis, left me feeling like we were on the same page. I had been stretching on the mat and writing about inclusivity, gender equality, and mental health issues for years, and never imagined that the things I believed in could be deemed significant by influential political leadership. It was truly exciting. Canada had just finished a conservative period with Stephen Harper as PM, Trump was rising in popularity in the US, and here was the aesthetically pleasing, liberal-minded, feminist-supporting, and seemingly genteel Justin Trudeau. Totally different energies that gave me a sense of hope.

On April 1, 2016, my wife and I went to Toronto to spend the day. When I realized it was April 1, I remembered my playful tendency to post outlandish things on my Facebook pages on April Fool's Day. In 2014, I posted that I had just been selected by NASA for inclusion on a 21-day rocket flight to the moon. In 2015, I posted that Obama had called me to tell me how much he, Michelle, and his secret service agents had enjoyed my book, *An Uncommon Bond*. You get the picture. And so, I found my way to a computer and put up the following post. In its own way, this would prove to be oddly prescient:

> It's been quite a day. Full of unexpected wonders. Got a call this morning from Canadian Prime Minister Justin Trudeau's office. Apparently, he read *An Uncommon Bond* and loved it deep. Seems he is planning to form a kind of consciousness soulpod to gather together and discuss the deeper implications of significant political decisions. He doesn't want to rely on practical feedback alone –

he wants to rely on the (alleged) wisdom of various authors and spiritual teachers. For some odd reason, he asked me to be one of them. I just had to say yes. First, we will do some yoga to clear out all the emotional debris, and then, after some dynamic meditation, the group of us will sit down and share our thoughts on some of the issues of the day. It's a brave new world...[1]

There was additional context for this. Long before, I had heard that Hillary Clinton had gathered with a group of personal development authors at Camp David. Included among them were Marianne Williamson, Tony Robbins, Stephen Covey, and the inimitable Jean Houston. It was my understanding that Jean's relationship with Hillary had continued thereafter, including consultations at the White House.

After I heard that, I'd said to my wife, Susan, that it would be fascinating if the Trudeaus gathered a group of like-minded Canadian writers to voluntarily consult on ways that a progressive consciousness could be integrated into their public interface. It wasn't something that I thought would ever happen, but it was fun to lean into on April Fool's Day.

That was the last I thought of it until February 7, 2017. On that fateful day, I was told that Sophie Gregoire Trudeau had posted a quote on her Facebook page from one of the books she had been given by Robin. It wasn't just any quote – it was a quote about transparency and truth. Looking back on it now, the irony is not lost on me:

> "We have nothing to hide, and nowhere to hide it. It just takes so much energy to bury our truths, and what can we reveal that hasn't been other's experience anyway. Our secrets aren't that unique. They are intrinsically human. Let's practice the art of radical transparency and shameless self-admission. Imagine truth circles in every community... "I admit..." and then we dance."   Jeff Brown, Ascending with Both Feet on the Ground.[2]

The quote was accompanied by a link to a Global News piece wherein Sophie discussed her former struggle with bulimia.

When I saw this, I felt delighted and strangely relieved. It certainly wasn't the first time that my writings had been shared by a well-known figure. But this felt different. This wasn't another author or a pop star – this was the wife of a world leader. And not just any world leader – the PM of the country I had grown up in. Suddenly, that very real part of me that never felt like a true Canadian, fell to the wayside, replaced with the very distinct feeling of *I belong*. I look back now and I find it incredulous

Chapter 2: Nothing to Hide, and Nowhere to Hide It

that a simple post by a stranger could hold this much significance. And yet, it did.

Feeling excited, I pressed SHARE. Sophie's post was now on my Facebook fan page: [3]

I lay down for a nap, but I was too excited to rest. I jolted out of bed, roused by the idea that I would try to connect with Sophie to see if she needed any help with volunteer writing. Although I was no longer someone who strongly believed in the Law of Attraction, I couldn't help but recognize that in last year's April Fools post, I had transmitted the intention to contribute. I couldn't imagine that she had seen that random post, but perhaps the universe had?

Even more significantly, I had recently re-read a Will L. Garver book called *Brother of the Third Degree*. The story revolves around a cadre of wise women and men who have found their way into places of power. While there, they quietly whisper in the ears of power-holders, surreptitiously wielding positive change. I was riveted by this book, both because it gave me hope for the kind of world I longed for, and because I found the idea of exerting a positive influence from behind the scenes utterly delightful. I'm not someone who longs for all the credit, but I am someone who wants to actualize his abilities for the higher good. The idea that I could quietly influence what I then perceived to be the Trudeau's benevolent mission, felt entirely right.

I contacted my friend Robin, to see if she had contact info for Sophie. She didn't, but she did have contact info for Sophie's friend – someone she had also met at the yoga retreat in 2015. She was happy to pass on a note for her to share with Sophie.

Writing the note was easy. Sending it was difficult. I remember the moment like it was yesterday. Perhaps we always do, when we make the mistake of ignoring our intuition. I was sitting in front of a computer at a Fed-Ex outlet in Toronto. I stared at the email, and my nattering intuition – like a little imp on my shoulder – piped up: *Don't do this*.

I deleted the email. Then I wrote it again.

I pulled my hands back from the keyboard and closed my eyes. I felt confused, oddly at war with myself. I searched for the answer – step toward, or step away? On the one hand, my genuine desire to make the world a better place, the feeling that I had now cracked the significance code and lifted my family along with me, and the feeling that the allegedly goodhearted Trudeaus were our great defense against the racism, sexism, and hatefulness that I thought was taking root in Trump's America. On the other, an all-knowing intuitive voice inside firmly said:

Don't do this. You spent your life trying to escape the bullshit of the world. You're in a good place now – you're in your writing zone. Don't fuck with it. Stay away from the political world.

And there was something else. I wasn't quite sure what it was. Something way deep inside and barely discernible was telling me that something here was not what it appeared to be. I was perhaps too blinded by my projections to understand it, but something didn't feel right. Something was askew.

I decided not to do it.

And then, just as quickly, I reached for the keyboard, and pushed "SEND."

My intuition had lost the day.

Soon thereafter, Robin informed me that her email to Sophie's friend had bounced back. Much to my surprise, I breathed a deep sigh of relief and replied: "No worries ... it's a sign. Not the right time. I will approach after this book is done..."

The next day, she informed me that she had also sent it to Sophie's friend on Facebook messenger.

It had been marked "read."

The strangest journey of my life had unknowingly begun.

CHAPTER 3

DANCING IN THE SAME LIGHT?

Soon thereafter (February 10), I received an email from Sophie Gregoire Trudeau herself:

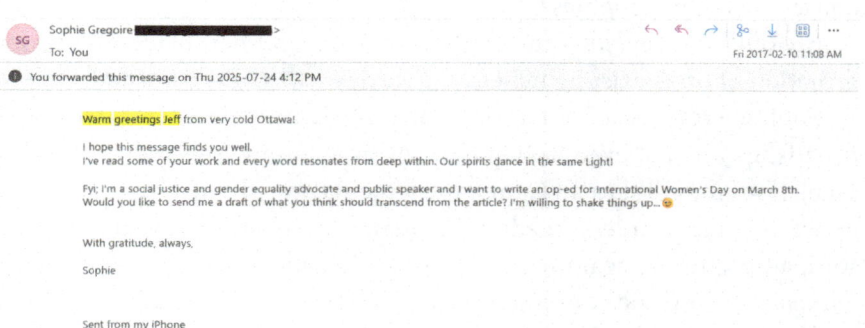

I was both pleased to hear from her, and a little taken aback by the tone of the email. It's not like I wasn't used to receiving emails from strangers that resonated with my writing – many authors get those – but this felt a little more assumptive and personal than usual. And, she was the Prime Minister's wife, which felt surreal.

My intuitive voice piped up yet again. It had some questions:

> Every word resonates from deep within? Really? Our spirits dance in the same light? Do they? How can she possibly know that? Hmmm…

It also had some suspicions:

> What's up with the timing of this article? Did she intentionally summon you by posting your work? Did she sense that you would try to connect and offer to help her? Did she see your April Fool's post last year? Sounds ridiculous maybe, but something doesn't feel kosher here.

In an effort to confirm or deny my wonderings, I read this email to 4 people I trusted and asked them what they thought. Although happy to support me, my wife was immediately uncomfortable with it: "Something's wrong with this picture." Robin said that it was simply a reflection of the effusive way that Sophie related. Samuel said that he wasn't sure.

And my oldest friend felt that it was a clear indication that Sophie was not into her husband and that she was fantasizing about me.

Nonetheless, I carried on. As I expressed to Sophie in my response, "It is such a rare thing for people in positions of influence to have the philosophies that you and Justin are putting forth. A rare opportunity to move the collective forward." The idea that I could utilize the connection with her to bring a helpful message through about gender equality, was simply too much to resist. Even if her boundaries might be a little questionable. And even if the reality was that I knew nothing substantial about her and Justin, and even less about the meaningful differences between liberal and conservative philosophies.

My *confirmation bias* – the tendency to interpret new evidence as confirmation of one's existing beliefs or theories – was fully activated.

Sophie wrote back with answers and ideas, and offered her "trust and friendship without even having met you as it simply feels right." She also asked if we should start an *I admit* movement through social media – a call to action to all genders to admit some of their challenges and mistakes. And, after quoting again from my book, *Ascending with Both Feet on the Ground* – "Truth or consequences as you say…" – she made a point of mentioning that "we should have a shot of tequila!!!! Lol."

I didn't need my intuition on this. The tequila reference made me uncomfortable.

Warning Flag #2.

We went back and forth sharing ideas related to the content for the article and the prospect of an *I admit* (or an *I apologize…*) movement. Sophie put forth the possibility that we collaborate (via their digital communications team) to launch the movement via Facebook on International Women's Day.

She also suggested that we get some amazing men involved, and perhaps some "well-known and liked personalities with great purpose like Emma Watson, Gloria Steinem…" And her "friends" Chantal Kreviazuk and Marianne Williamson. She also indicated that she was asking Justin if he could reach out to Jack Ma, Mark Zuckerberg, and Sheryl Sandberg. I was game and grabbed *I admit* and *I apologize* pages on Facebook that day.

While corresponding about the article, a strange interaction alerted me. Again, my commitment to the cause was still too strong to step away, but I found myself feeling mildly unsettled about what I perceived to be flirtatious, albeit cryptic, communications from Sophie. At the time, in the heart of my busy life, I didn't really stop to think about them, but I could feel my spidey senses tingling.

In an email dated March 1, 2017, Sophie signed off with the longest sequence of emojis I ever did see, one that included a peeled banana ready to be eaten, a bikini, a bottle of booze, a set of luscious red lips, and a martini to top it off! And with a strangely placed LOL at the end:

Not sure which emoji captured my intuition's attention, but that's all it took for my little voice to start chirping in my inner ear: *She wants to do more than dance in the same light with you, soldier. She also wants to eat your peeled banana on the beach. And don't be fooled by the deflective LOL at the end... she's trying to tell you something.*

Now, I'm perplexed that I didn't take it more seriously. Those sexy emojis really were inappropriate. I should have clearly expressed my discomfort. But the call to leverage purposeful work in the world again won out over my alarm bells.

While sending over more ideas related to the article, my dynamic with Sophie expanded to include Justin, which will prove relevant later. I emailed the following words on March 5, 2017:

> "A thought...
> I added in the last bit in the paragraph below for you to consider because I strongly feel that taking 'equality' to the next level has two elements. One is the focus on men getting involved, standing down inequality, recognizing the ways that patriarchy has also imprisoned them (the idea that no one wins). The other, which I feel must be integrated into the dialogue, is that women have been denied access to what men call (and celebrate as) the hero's journey. The stuff Joseph Campbell and to some extent Robert Bly wrote about, where men go off to the woods, or into an isolated spiritual retreat, or towards great adventure, in quest of their life's purpose/meaning/excavation of their gifts and callings. There is so much celebration of this, and yet, women have not had this path celebrated by society-at-large. Some of it has to do with the disgusting fact that they have been unsafe alone in the world/in the wild, and some of it has to do with the need to focus initially on basic equalities (vote, equal pay, respect for their bodies etc.) before getting to the next stage. All these basic equalities will have to fought for, on this bloodied planet, for many more centuries, but I also feel it's important to focus on women's right to explore their individual

path/purpose and to be supported in and celebrated for that courageous journey.

As advocates for gender equality, we wanted to write to you on International Women's Day, to celebrate the profound steps our society has taken to champion women's rights and to be treated as true equals. To speak our voices and to be heard. To enhearten the collective. To shape our democracy. To break and exceed the limitations that have been placed on the kind of work we can do, the extent of our political participation, the ways our bodies are supposed to look, *and our access to the pathways of expression that reflect our unique gifts and callings."*

That evening, she responded:

> Omg Jeff. I just read this to Justin and he's in tears. The hero's journey you are referring to is the philosophical and spiritual back bone of his whole election campaign.
> Thanks for sharing... 🙏

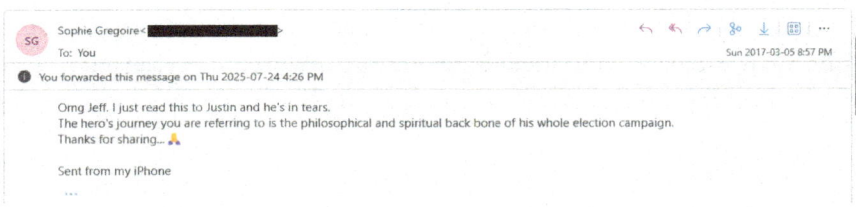

When I read this, I felt even more compelled to support their mission. After all, it was my mission too. We were spirits dancing in the same light. Or so I imagined at the time.

After working on various drafts, the article – now a joint op-ed with Caroline Riseboro of the Canadian non-profit Plan International Canada – was published in the Toronto Star system on March 7, 2017.[4] I felt proud, and ready to move onto the launching of the *I admit* movement.

Soon thereafter, I wrote Sophie an email that again captures the depths to which I was projecting onto these two people, without even knowing them. It's difficult for me to read this now:

> Of course, this is the nature of the heroic journey, yes? Stepping out before the world and owning your vision and your mission. Mission position, as a way of being. What you and Justin are attempting to do, and accomplishing, is remarkable. So many go into politics- and into self-help/spiritual writing, as I have found out often- because they are primarily motivated by egoic and finan-

CHAPTER 3: DANCING IN THE SAME LIGHT?

cial ambitions. It is a rare thing to see individuals in positions of great authority who are heartfully motivated by a profound vision of possibility for humanity. It's brave, and it may be the only thing that will save us. Someone has to paint a picture for humanity to walk towards, or we will stumble into the abyss as a species and never return. Keep up the Go(o)d work, both of you. It makes this old Canadian proud.

And yet, my pesky voice of concern continued to surface, this time related to the *I admit* and *I apologize* movements that Sophie had suggested.

Despite my letting her know that I had claimed the Facebook pages, and asking her about it on more than one occasion, she never replied. I also wrote her with a number of questions and ideas related to both movements. It was as though the whole conversation had never happened. I wasn't attached to the movement, but the silence confounded me. Because of my preexisting bias, I made the assumption that Canada's 'Leading Lady' (a term sometimes used for the PM's wife) was just a little bit excitable, and had to be reined in by Justin or the Prime Minister's Office (PMO), when certain plans or visions didn't align with the political world. I made the further assumption that she was too embarrassed to tell me that her idea had been stonewalled by the powers-that-be. An optimistic assumption, on my part.

My intuition didn't buy it. It piped up again, with a theory of his own: *She had no intention of developing that movement with you. She used that – and the name-dropping of some of the famous people that her and Justin know – to bait you, so that you would continue to volunteer your writing and your wisdom. Things that she sorely lacks. You are being played, my friend, by a master manipulator. And she's got you by your best intentions.*

I ignored my cynical sidekick, and carried on yet again. After all, I had reached that stage in life when you imagine yourself beyond being conned. And the simple truth is that – at this stage – I didn't much care what she was up to. What mattered was that our message reached the world. If she was the vehicle for it, so be it. I'd put up with most anything.

Soon thereafter, I sent Sophie all of my books – excluding *Ascending with Both Feet on the Ground* which she had originally quoted from – and my wife Susan's two poetry collections, *Open Passages* and *Hope is a Traveler*. I also sent a copy of Joseph Campbell's *Hero with a Thousand Faces* for Justin. Some of these books would prove thematically significant as my story unfolded.

My confirmation bias was bleeding out everywhere.

***

On June 3, 2017, Sophie again shared a quote from *Ascending with Both Feet on the Ground* on her Facebook page. It was accompanied by some words of her own, and a very sweet picture of Justin, and two of their children, Ella-Grace and Hadrian. Included in the caption was another quote from my work:

> The faster we run, the more determined is the Universe to slow us down. The more embedded our methods of self-distraction, the more agitating the truth-aches calling us back to authenticity. The more eagerly we race to the sky, the more intense the lessons that bring us back to earth. The Universe has no interest in our flight from reality. It wants us right here. Nowhere else… but here. -Jeff Brown, Ascending with Both Feet on the Ground.[5]

On October 11, we exchanged emails. In hers, Sophie mentioned that she was in DC on an official trip with Justin. And that she had quoted me "in some speeches I gave: humanness and spirituality must come together!" I felt elated. An inclusive spirituality had made its way to Washington! A few sentences later, she offered to make a contribution to the book I was currently writing – Grounded Spirituality: "Let me know if you need my help maybe for a foreword for your book." I responded favorably, imagining her a generous person who wanted to reciprocate for my generosity of words and ideas for her public interface. How kind.

Soon thereafter, Sophie wrote back that she would go to the Team (read: The PMO) when the manuscript was ready, to confirm if the Foreword was a go. I didn't particularly care if it was approved – I had an inkling that my grounded spirituality predecessor, author-activist Andrew Harvey, was the right person to write the Foreword – but I was pleased nonetheless. I expressed my delight in a subsequent Facebook post…[6]

My earnest intuition had other concerns: *It's no accident that she plants the idea of writing your book Foreword, right after telling you she quoted your words in Washington. There is an unstated transaction happening here. She gets to use your wisdom in exchange for some future offering that may or may not transpire. It's called 'future faking.' And you don't see what is happening because you are so 'honored' by the possibility that the 'Leading Lady' of Canada may write it.*

JEFF BROWN
October 11, 2017

I am delighted to hear that Sophie Gregoire Trudeau was quoting some of my words about grounded spirituality today, while speaking to panels on an official visit to Washington with the Prime Minister. You know we are making progress when grounded and humanizing spirituality becomes part of the political and cultural narrative. While there are many challenges ahead for all of us who long to humanize this planet, we are making progress…

CHAPTER 3: DANCING IN THE SAME LIGHT?

She knows exactly what she's doing. She's using her position to string you along, just like she did with the name-dropping around the 'I admit' movement. Sure-fire way to keep you feeding her ideas, at least until the book comes out. You are being played, brother. This is one seriously ambitious 'Leading Lady.'

Both I and my confirmation bias were still inclined to ignore those thoughts. It was certainly possible that this was Sophie's game, but I chose to give her the benefit of a doubt for now.

I continued to write her with various ideas, as they came through me. For example, on the afternoon of October 19, I was sitting in a library working on *Grounded Spirituality*, and sent Sophie a lengthy email that included a stream of thoughts about something that I was calling "sacred advocacy." She responded soon thereafter. Included in her rather effusive response were the following words: "I hope we get to meet one day!":

> "Jeff,
>
> I have read your "passages" over and over again…
>
> People are ready to hear this. It's time.
>
> I'm not only moved by all of it; I live it everyday.
>
> The truth behind your words resonates and echoes.
>
> I want to work with you! Build with you! Let's all be each other's building blocks….so the mountain rises higher
>
> and those who come after us will see farther….
>
> Please continue to send; it's a gift every time.
>
> I hope we get to meet one day!
>
> Hugs,
>
> Sophie"

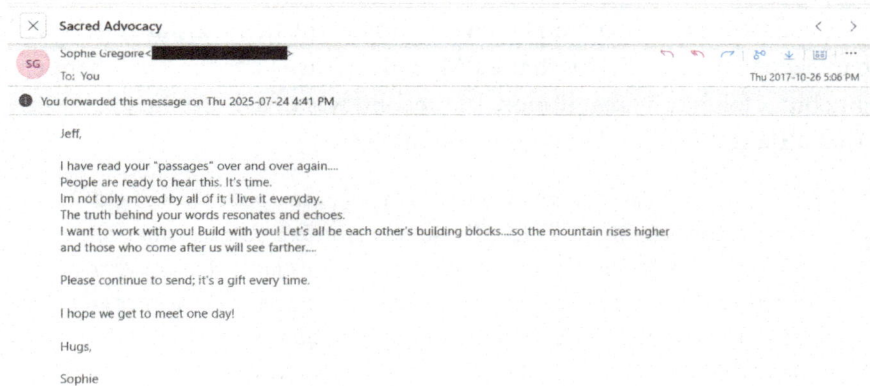

21

A few weeks later (November 23, 2017), I sent her a lengthy piece that I had just written called 'Praises for the Trauma Speakers.' The contents of this would prove significant, soon enough. In it, I included the following words:

> In the survivalist world that we come from, the most traumatized individuals were the most shamed and shunned. It was survival of the 'fittest', authenticity and healing be damned. If you could punch your way through the pain and accumulate, you were deemed a success. It didn't matter what your inner world or personal life looked like, so long as you championed the material world.
>
> It is time for a world that champions the survival of the truest. That stands down the accumulators and elevates the authenticators. A world where success is not measured by our ability to out-achieve our neighbour, but by our ability to remain heartfully connected to each other. That honours those who have the courage to feel and acknowledge their victimhood, to share their painful story, to invite all of us to self-reveal. That celebrates those who are brave enough to own their uniqueness in the face of judgment and ridicule. This is the only world that can last.

Early the next morning, I received what would prove to be a significant email from her …

> "Jeff,
> I'd love to meet you in person.
> I just finished reading Canada's apology to LGBT that my husband will read to the country next Tuesday.
> Every word dances with what you just wrote. It exposes our flaws as a country but also the opportunities we have to heal and grow.
> Let me know if an Ottawa visit could fit in your plans at one point…
> In humanhood, Sophie."

I had two reactions when I read this email. The first was sheer delight. I had been invited to visit with the PM's wife. I wasn't attached to it happening, but it felt like a great honor. The second was of a more sinister nature. That little shit inside of me had some things to say:

> *You do remember that you wrote what might have been the first published Apologies to the LGBQT community in 2016. It wouldn't surprise me if Justin got the idea for his whole performative apology series from your viral Apologies to the Divine Feminine from 2010. After all, it's noted on the front cover of the book Sophie quotes from: Ascending with Both Feet on the Ground. Are you seeing a pattern, yet?*

Chapter 3: Dancing in the Same Light?

I'm not a petty person. Even if they had gotten the idea for their apology series and, specifically, the Apologies to the LGBQT, from me, it wouldn't have bothered me. We all have to get our ideas from somewhere, and it's not as though they were plagiarizing my exact words. Besides, I was too smitten with the idea of visiting with the Leading Lady to much care. The little voice had more to say:

> It's no accident that she invites you to Ottawa in the same email that she informs you he is reading an Apology to the LGBQT community. Damn, she's good. And it's not the first time, dodo bird. We've seen this transactional pattern before. Are you and Sophie dancing in the same light Jeff, or are you just being worked from the shadows?

I ignored him, yet again, and carried on. I let Sophie know that I would be going out that way at some point this winter, and provided a link to my initial *Apologies to the LGBQT*.[7]

She responded to my trip mention, yet said nothing in response to the link that I shared. Interesting.

A few days later, Justin did his trademark tearful performance while reading something that the Canadian Broadcasting Corporation (CBC) called the "historic apology to LGBT Canadians."

I do admit to feeling slightly triggered by the use of the word 'historic.' If historic means the first, then this was simply untrue.[8]

Sophie and I began 2018 on good terms, connecting a few times about a possible meeting in Ottawa. On January 19, she suggested doing a video series with me to support the evolution and enlightenment of other men. I knew that she had already filmed one video dialogue with Canadian author Rupi Kaur in 2017. I emailed back that I was open to the idea. We discussed a possible time frame (April) after their imminent India trip and subsequent March break.[9]

On February 9, 2018, she wrote to tell me that she had made introductory remarks in Montreal – at an event where Michelle Obama would speak – and that "some words are inspired by you!"

I read through it quickly, and saw the reference to something I had shared with her on November 23, 2017 (survival of the fittest vs. survival of the truest) and also something that looked familiar to me from Epictetus ("You become what you give your attention to."):

> We become what we bring our attention to. On devient ce que l'on consomme! *Next time no one is watching and you're alone. Observe the inner conversation that takes place within you, Are you patient,*

23

compassionate and tender towards yourself? or are you constantly trying to change something about you that you feel is wrong or not good enough. This conversation serves as your daily life ground from which you interact with others... For too long, it's been all about the survival of the strongest and the richest and the fittest.... but friends, we are not only witnessing but living this moment in our shared history when real change for the common good is ignited by the survival of the Truest, the Authentic, the compassionate and the open-hearted.

Looking back, I remember scanning this and not feeling annoyed by the failure to reference me as the wordsmith behind the survival of the fittest/truest concept. I hadn't actually stated that *anything* I shared with her could be used without attribution, but I think I was too excited about the words reaching an engaged audience to concern myself with author credit issues. That would soon change.

Not surprisingly, my intuition piped up:

She said "Some words are inspired by you." That's not exactly right. It's more literal than that. The survival of the fittest/truest dichotomy is both your concept **and** *your actual words. Pay attention, brother.*

Soon thereafter, I sent her a long list of quotes for their soon-to-be fabled India trip. In it, I explicitly stated, "If anything resonates, feel free to modify them as you need...." My recollection is that there was an initiating email from her about an India speech, but that email cannot be found.

A few days later – Valentine's Day, 2018 – Sophie shared another of my writings on her Facebook page. This one was from my book, *Love it Forward*:[10]

"Everything real comes through the heart. When it is truly opened, everything secondary falls away- egoic glory, fame and fortune, substitute gratifications. The heart doesn't care about such things. It doesn't hold it against you if you don't own your home, achieve your goals, have a perfect body. The heart doesn't care what you have earned or accumulated. No matter our seeming differences, we are all the same when the heart gate opens. Deep feeling levels the playing field. Love is the great equalizer."

I re-shared it proudly on my Facebook page, but again I wondered... Is this an expression of appreciation for helping her, or an attempt to pacify me in case her using some of my material ever became an issue? The latter didn't make sense in this context, since I had sent this quote in the India collection and explicitly told her she could use it. Not yet knowing her

Chapter 3: Dancing in the Same Light?

well, it was difficult to decipher her underlying motivation. And difficult for me to discern if these seemingly generous postings of my work were actually a smokescreen for a potentially far broader usage of my work worldwide than I would be comfortable with. Such were the rumblings and churnings of thoughts just beneath the surface.

On March 8, Sophie connected me with her colleague Dunerci Caceres to coordinate our anticipated video recording. As I would find out, Dunerci is an "Executive Assistant" in the PM's Office. We had a few interactions – including a brief phone conversation to solidify details – and agreed upon April 25, 2018 as our go-to date for the dialogue Sophie had requested.

On March 28, I was somewhat taken aback by an email from Sophie with the subject line: "Thinking of you." It was excerpts from six pages of Rainer Maria Rilke's book, *Letters to a Young Poet*. At various points on five of the pages, Sophie had underlined key excerpts. Included among them were these words noted below:

> "The creative experience lies so unbelievably close to the sexual, close to its pain and its pleasure, that both phenomena are only different forms of the same longing and bliss. If one could say "sexuality" instead of "lust"...."
>
> "But it seems that this power of his is not always entirely genuine and not without assuming a pose."
>
> "full of adultery and confusion, far from the true destinies of man." Beside this excerpt, she had written "lack of clarity authenticity" etc.

Although I had been emailing about the awakening man – the subject of our anticipated video dialogue – the more sexually emphasized aspects of the excerpts threw me. I remember receiving the email, and not quite knowing what to do with it. Even if it was not deliberately suggestive, it still felt inappropriate, particularly when coupled with the 'Thinking of You' subject line. I was a married man, she was a married woman, and she was married to the Prime Minister of Canada for God's sake. And I had never even met her, so I didn't have the benefit of knowing her well enough to not take these kinds of excerpts the wrong way. The whole dynamic made me somewhat nervous. Don't they teach interpersonal boundaries in Leading Lady school?

But again – yet again – I chose to ignore my doubts and carry on. I regret this now. If previous suspicions had failed to deter me – *this* clearly should have been my point of departure.

CHAPTER 4

A Family Trip To Ottawa

I decided to leave for Ottawa a few days before the taping of my dialogue with Sophie Trudeau at their home – Rideau Cottage. Since my first book was published, I had done hundreds of radio shows and podcasts, but very little on-camera work. I was nervous and wanted to make sure that I had my lines so solid that nothing could distract me. I was speaking for my whole lineage, after all. I wanted to make them proud.

My vehicle was a banged-up Dodge Ram, so I booked a rental Jeep in Georgetown, Ontario. When you grow up on the outside looking in, you always worry you'll be seen as a fraud when you get invited into the center. It had been years since I'd struggled with those feelings, but the idea of pulling up to the Prime Ministerial home in a dented and rusty truck brought them to the surface. I wanted to show up like I belonged.

The weekend before, Susan and I drove into downtown Toronto to purchase two gifts for Sophie – a t-shirt, and a hat that said "Truth Speaker."

After months of being cocooned in my writer's world, I was concerned I would look pale on camera, so I'd been visiting a tanning salon. The last time I was there, I asked about self-tanning lotion. The attendant recommended a small sixty-dollar bottle. I snapped it up. Just before I left for Ottawa, I smeared a bunch of it on my face, upper chest, hands, and arms.

On the morning of Monday, April 23, I drove to Georgetown to pick up my Grand Cherokee. All tanned up with some place to go, I was ready to kick ass. But when I got there, they didn't have the SUV that I'd booked. What they did have was a giant black Yukon, the kind of vehicle used to chauffeur dignitaries around. I was no dignitary, but I was driving to meet one. Apropos. I planned to stay at a downtown Kingston hotel on Day One and then drive to my Ottawa hotel the next day. Sophie and I would meet for the lunch and video dialogue on Day Three.

I had never driven an SUV this size before. I crawled in for the long drive to Kingston. Soon after pulling onto the highway that cuts through North Toronto, I was overcome with emotion. Familiar childhood roads took me back to challenging scenes from early life. The night my father's Pontiac Strato Chief was seized for non-payment. The time we were arguing so intensely that we failed to notice we had driven through a red light at Bathurst and St Clair. My mother's secretarial office above the bowling alley at Glencairn Avenue. Our typical Sunday afternoon visiting up to six relatives at Branson Hospital. That embarrassing moment at Bayview Village Mall when we chose the only affordable – and surely most unsightly – bar mitzvah suit imaginable. My father laying on the couch for months, too depressed to get off his ass and find yet another job. My beloved grandmother's umpteenth visit to St. John's Convalescent Hospital. My mentally challenged cousin Gloria riding the bus up and down Bathurst Street to visit a whole team of doctors about her latest medical concern. I loved that woman most of all.

I was by no means feeling sorry for myself. If anything, I was marveling at the remarkable contrast between those life experiences, and this pristine moment of triumph. A member of the rough and tumble Brown clan going to the PM's house to have his ideas showcased to the country? It felt both entirely surreal and like some kind of ancestral healing.

My ride down memory lane continued all the way to Kingston. I pulled up to my downtown hotel in the early evening only to find that my massive Yukon was too tall for their underground garage. It seemed the entire downtown core prohibit downtown parking. Across the street was an outdoor parking lot, but paying for it required that I download something called an app. Beyond my technology grade.

In the hotel, someone suggested the hospital parking lot a few miles away. Apparently, they had the ceiling space to accommodate a Yukon. I drove there with some measure of concern: what would happen if I couldn't find a place to park? Would I have to stay up all night driving my Yuk around? That would surely ruin my sleep in Ottawa, and then I'd arrive for camera day in a zombie-like stupor.

When I finally found the garage, there was no one there to ask if the ceilings could accommodate my Yuk. So, I took my chances and crawled my way through the mostly barren parking lot to an upstairs spot.

In the hotel room, I noticed my face was orange. I called my wife to ask her if I'd fucked-up with the self-tanner.

"You're only supposed to leave it on for a few hours," she said.

It had now been six hours since I'd applied it. I half-jokingly asked her if there was an anti-tanner I could buy to restore my skin to flesh tone. Nope. I was going to the PM's house orange.

When I was young, there was an episode of the Mary Tyler Moore show called 'Put on a Happy Face' that had stuck with me. In the episode,

Mary was nominated for a prestigious "Teddy" award. But she was not in any condition to attend the event. She had a nasty cold, a sprained foot, a hair bump, and a stained dress. It felt like foreshadowing. As I lay down on the bed praying for a good night's sleep, I wondered if this was my Mary Tyler Moore moment.

I woke up early and made my way to the parking lot to get the Yukon. After a brief scare when I couldn't find it, I realized it was right where I'd left it. As I turned onto Hwy 401 east, I felt proud and grateful for all my relations who'd come before. I thought of their economic and health challenges, their penchants and proclivities, their idiosyncrasies and neurotic tendencies, the countless ways their patchwork of efforts had given me just what I needed to reach this stage of triumph and overcoming.

As I turned onto highway 416 to Ottawa, the nation's capital, it was as though they were all with me in the Yukon, huddled together, applauding me onward. Good thing I'd rented such a big vehicle 😊. I was doing my small bit to validate their efforts, to take the whole ancestral lot of them to the next level, to celebrate our lives as one imperfectly frayed human tapestry. And it was clear to me: I wasn't engaging with the Trudeaus because I wanted personal power. I was seeking healing – for all of us. We were now, officially, significant as Canadians. Some families only need one generation to discover that feeling. Others, hundreds. We had needed four, and now here we were – worthy Canadians out for a family drive.

Orange-tan man pulled into Ottawa, ready to rock. I found my way to my old-school Hotel, the Business Inn. My suite was like the perfect Manhattan writer's apartment, one I didn't want to leave… ever. I considered doing a 'Jewish dry run' – a drive to an event location before the big day, so you don't arrive late when it matters – but I thought it might make me nervous. I was doing the 'pretend it isn't happening' thing so I could get a good night's sleep, and I wanted to spend a few more hours going over my notes and memorizing some of my punchy dialogue lines. I intended to make my country – and my family – proud.

At some point, I lay down to reflect on something that was niggling at me. Call it a remote rumbling. That little voice inside had some concerns. I knew what my intuition was referencing – those sexy Rilke excerpts Sophie had sent me with the subject line, "Thinking of you." When combined with my subterranean concerns about other things she had expressed, I was left wondering if I had been invited there for reasons other than bringing my voice to the world. To be brutally honest, the little voice inside wondered if the PM's wife had a thing for little ol' me. It seemed preposterous, but stranger things had happened. I let the voice fully express its concerns and then muzzled it. Keep calm and carry on.

Much to my surprise, I slept well. I got up early and went for a walk in Ottawa. Having grown up in a roaring lion like Toronto, Ottawa felt like a soft and sleepy baby cub. I stopped in at a neighborhood café to review my video notes yet again. I don't normally read over my notes this frequently, but something told me I better do it while I had the chance.

At around 11 o'clock, I packed up my room and got in the Yukon to make my way to the PM's house. I was a little early, so I circled around Ottawa and then drove toward the Parliament Buildings. I'm not sure what I was thinking – I actually had no idea where these people lived. And I'm not sure what they were thinking – nobody had told me where the Rideau Cottage actually was. I thought I would just head toward Sussex Drive, find the official PM's residence that the Trudeaus had rejected, and there would be a cottage right beside it. But before I could realize my mistake, I had made the wrong turn and ended up on the long bridge to Quebec. So much for not using GPS. Mary Tyler Moore fuck-up day, here I come. Goodness, I didn't even know that Quebec was right across from Ottawa. I figured out a way to turn back around and crossed back into Ontario wondering why I hadn't prepared myself better. I am a Virgo, after all. I'm always prepared.

I drove around until I found someone to ask for directions. They had no idea where the PM lived either, but they pointed me in the direction of a gendarme stationed somewhere "up that way." I turned onto Sussex and then into a long driveway with a booth at the end. As I pulled up, I hit the horn. A portly man was asleep inside. He jumped up, eyes now wide open. He was not pleased.

"Sorry," I said, "I didn't realize how loud the horn was." I told him where I was heading, and, clearly irritated, he handed me a colorful tourist map. Like the kind they give you on a bus tour. It was both comedic, and a little worrisome with respect to national security. He circled the location where I was supposed to go and curtly informed me that I couldn't come in to turn around. I had to back all the way up.

Sorry to wake you, soldier.

I then turned right on Sussex and followed the circle around to a large thick gate.

As I pulled up, I experienced a moment of anxiety. Maybe this surreal event – going to the PM's house to be filmed while talking with his wife – was a figment of my imagination. Before I could convince myself it wasn't, a sturdy gendarme approached me, and with the kind of warmth I had seldom encountered in law enforcement, gestured for me to enter.

"Mr. Brown, come on in…"

I drove in, surprised they hadn't frisked me. Nor had they done anything to check inside or underneath the vehicle. In fact, other than a brief phone call with Dunerci Caceres to confirm the event weeks before and a quick request for my license plate just before the event, I didn't receive a single call or letter from law enforcement or the PMO before my arrival. I wasn't complaining, but between this and the  sleepy gendarme, I felt a little concerned for both the Trudeaus and the nation.

I drove through another iron gate and promptly turned down the wrong road. When I finally recalibrated, I spotted the house and pulled the big black Yukon into the driveway. Sophie Gregoire Trudeau and her intensely soulful gaze were waiting there to greet me. I was a tad taken aback.

I grabbed my cue cards and stepped out of the car into her warm embrace.

CHAPTER 5

MEETING A WILDHORSE

Sophie and I entered Rideau Cottage. We appeared to be alone in the house. She quickly showed me around the main floor. It was a comfortable, down-to-earth home for a PM and his family. Nothing pretentious or stately about it.

Soon enough, Sophie's tirade of sexual and marital frustration began. I had been in thousands of homes in my years in home improvements, but I never had an encounter quite like this one. The first lady was highly activated, and eager to share.

I believe it began with passion fruit in her hand.[11] Sophie spoke rapidly, while her hand moved the piece down her arms etc. I paraphrase: "Why can't Justin turn to me to meet his needs at the end of his day? Why can't he rub this passion fruit down my body? Why can't he lick it off of me? Why must he go in the other room to read science fiction?"

Despite squirming with discomfort, I tried to regain control of the situation by offering some words of wisdom. I advised her not to take it personally. I pointed out that he was not just going to work – he was the Prime Minister, and a young and inexperienced one at that. If he needed to decompress and gather himself when he came home, so be it.

At some point in her tirade, we entered the kitchen. Against the back wall was a very inviting kitchen table with a myriad of family pictures on the wall. It was easy to feel at home, here.

Sophie proceeded to share a whole host of details about their relationship at a pace and intensity I could barely assimilate. Her monologue included details of their first date. Justin had gotten her number long before, but had not called. "Why didn't he call, why didn't he call…?" And then, when he finally did, he picked her up in his deceased brother's dusty vehicle. She wasn't pleased. At some point on the date, he cried and said she was the one. She made a face and a sound to indicate she had a cynical view of this. She shared details about her extra-marital affair, which she said he'd discovered, that she'd only gotten halfway through reading my soulmate love story, *An Uncommon Bond*, "Because I don't have anything like that… I can show you the page where I stopped reading…"

"No," I said. I didn't feel comfortable with her showing me the excerpt in case it was a sexual one; She informed me that, before meeting her, Justin had preferred younger girls or women (I don't remember which word she used). Based on the way she said it, I assumed she meant noticeably younger than him, but she didn't clarify and I didn't ask. She also informed me that all they do now is fight and had done so for a long time. I suggested finding them a therapist, which I attempted to do later. She added that since becoming the Leading Lady she'd had a recurrence of her bulimia.

In a passionate and defiant tone, she shared how the team (the PMO) always wanted to contain her. She told me she couldn't be contained, and that I should call her "Wildhorse" because of her generally wild and expressive nature and her insatiable sexuality. She then went on to say something to the effect of needing a black and a white guy at the same time, to satisfy her.

Then came the most confusing moment for me, as if this whole conversation wasn't jarring enough. For the second time, I jokingly referenced that I was Jewish in the context of, "I don't drink alcohol. I have a Jewish liver."

Visibly annoyed, she said something to the effect of, "Why do you keep saying you are Jewish? Why do you need to say this?"

I didn't know if her reaction was a reflection of how she felt about Jews or merely a gap in the projection she had about who I was. I definitely felt like she had a number of 'ideas' about me that weren't rooted in direct knowledge. And, of course, so did I, with respect to her. We didn't know each other at all. And now, here we were, engaged in a startlingly intense and fast-moving conversation that would have made even the Buddha flinch.

Whatever assumptions I had made about our regal Leading Lady and her perfect family life, had been quickly dispelled. If I had known what I was stepping into, I doubt I would have felt so honored on my drive to Ottawa. The whole idea that this was a great family healing was predicated on the idea that the people living in the PM's home had it together. Not to say that Mrs. Trudeau wasn't likeable – she certainly was in a friendly, hyper kind of way – but the person I encountered was clearly living in a gilded cage, and a sexually dissatisfied one at that. She either needed to be rescued or properly fucked – or both.

Chapter 5: Meeting a Wildhorse

Throughout her monologue, she would remind me (or herself):

"Fifteen years, Jeff, fifteen years. I know I chose monogamy ... and I love my children. But this is not easy."

At some point, we had another hug in the kitchen, but I stepped away when I saw the look in her eye. I didn't quite know how to interpret it, nor did I want to find out.

* * *

When we finally sat down for the lunch that had been prepared for us, I felt relieved. Soup and sandwich had never looked so good. Throughout her outpouring, I had been trying to hold onto the key terms I would use for the video dialogue. But it was near impossible. Perhaps with her mouth filled with food, she would ease up and I could remember why I was here.

I felt even more relieved when two energized women from the PMO arrived: Dunerci Caceres, the PMO executive assistant I had been dealing with, and Marie-Pascale Des Rosiers, a PMO special assistant in communications. After Mrs. Trudeau proudly declared she had stolen Dunerci from another government position, Dunerci shared her thoughts on a book of mine she was reading ('Love It Forward'). The three of them then discussed some of the many speaking opportunities Mrs. Trudeau had to choose from. Although she was not formally a part of the Canadian government (unlike in the US, where the First Lady is a government employee), it was entirely evident that she was inextricably woven into the PMO. This wild horse was a fully engaged member of the team.

Three men arrived to set up for the video dialogue in the living room. At some point, I went to fill a glass with some of the kombucha that I had promised to bring, and spilled it on the kitchen counter. Mrs. Trudeau helped me clean it up. Not normally clumsy, I felt both shaken and stirred by my time with this unexpectedly wild horse.

When we finally sat down to shoot the video, the microphone didn't work with my roll-top sweater, so Sophie eagerly suggested fetching one of Justin's shirts. That felt entirely weird and I said no. I went outside to the Yukon to get a denim shirt I brought. On the way back, I stopped in the washroom to change, doing all I could to ground myself and reconnect with the words I wanted to share on camera. It wasn't easy. The images Sophie had shared were streaming through my mind. We had probably only spent about sixty minutes alone, but it felt like I had spent the whole day monitoring children at a day care. Or perhaps more appropriately – taming wild horses at a rodeo. I dusted myself off and carried on.

We filmed for about forty-five minutes, after which they shot a commercial with her for an event she was perhaps going to do in Cambridge. When we were done, I met their daughter, Ella-Grace, who had just gotten home from school. She was as charming and polite as a kid could be.

And then my inner voice said *Get the hell out of here!* I didn't want to encroach on their family time, but it was far more than that. I felt uncomfortable staying at the house for much longer, in case the PM came home and I met him – and worse, shared a meal with him – all the while knowing this private information about his life. I knew too much. What if he found out what she'd told me? Dudes don't tend to like it when other men know about their wife's sexual history and frustrations. Not to mention, this dude was the PM!

Simply put, it felt dangerous to hold all this information. It really was none of my business. Mrs. Trudeau had overstepped by sharing such intimate details with me. Something about her sloppy boundaries had me wondering if she was a triangulator – using third parties to serve a relational purpose in her marriage. I had no idea what that purpose might be, but I absolutely did not want to get sucked into someone else's dysfunctional relationship vortex.

When I let Sophie know that I had to go, she handed me the passion fruit to give to my wife. I got the feeling she was struggling between her impulses, and wanting to be a good person. We proceeded outside to the porch to take some pictures and then she instructed Dunerci and Marie to go inside while I started the car. Sophie came over to the passenger side. I lowered the window and we exchanged an uncomfortably long soul-gaze moment. As she stared into my eyes, I wondered if I should invite her to get in the back so that I could drive her some place. Anywhere but here – her gilded cage.

After leaving the compound, I drove around for a long time trying to ground myself after the most bewildering afternoon of my life. I had been holding myself very tight to get through the experience and my entire nervous system had been drained to the bone. I was wired, tired, and more than a little confused. I had been planning to drive halfway home, and then do the rest the next day. Now I was compelled to get me and the passion fruit home, quick. 😊

As I drove, I reflected. Quite apart from my immediate concerns for our country – anyone who has been in a combative relationship knows how hard it is to retain focus while working – I was dismayed by the gap between the Trudeau's media-friendly family optics and the reality of their life together. Who was the imposter, now?

Chapter 5 : Meeting a Wildhorse

Marriages go through all manner of challenges over time, but there was a level of intensity to Sophie's frustrations that begged the question: Was this marriage a real one, or just a political marriage? Either way, maybe people had a right to know what's going on here. Was this uncontained and frankly emotionally immature woman capable of meeting her responsibilities as Canada's Leading Lady? What would happen to her if she continued to live under this amount of pressure and frustration? And what about her husband? Was he equally uncontained and immature? Was he in way over his head as the leader of this great country? What had I and we gotten ourselves into?

I wondered why I'd been so eager to place them on a pedestal. I'd been overcome with so much emotion on my drive to Ottawa, and for what? For whom? Sure, they resonated with things I believe in, but I didn't even know these people. My perceptions were all projections and imaginings. What was it within me that was so willing to see myself and my family of origin as something less than these people? Why had I been so honored by an invitation from people I had yet to meet? Why do we make such assumptions of grandeur about people we don't even know? Where do these projections come from in our individual and collective psyche? And, perhaps most importantly, how much of our potential doesn't get actualized because we devote so much energy to looking up to celebrity strangers? Inherent in the assumption that they are something special, is the assumption that we aren't. What within us doesn't get fulfilled as a result?

CHAPTER 6

LOVE RIDE TO FREEDOM

After Ottawa, I settled back into my busy life and awaited the video. Despite the surreal nature of my time with Mrs. Trudeau, I felt a certain affection for her. There was a sort of familiar feeling – like a niece or a dear old friend. At the same time, my uncertainties were becoming more pronounced, as flashbacks to the kitchen scene continued to enter my awareness. I look back on this time as something akin to what happens when you are in the initial stages of sobering up about a personal connection you've made. There are a variety of good things that keep you there – in this case, the still existing belief that we were on the same progressive mission, and that there was good work to be done – but you can no longer pretend it's all love and light. It just isn't.

Nonetheless, I felt a strange sense of protectiveness over Mrs. Trudeau. Her outpouring was something more than salacious. It was worrisome with respect to her state of mind. I felt inclined to stick around as a grounding force. The more adults in the room, the better.

We continued to relate in positive terms. I sent her a recommendation to a Naturopath, and she emailed me a playful audio message where she imitated the sound of a horse. I began to call her "Wildhorse" in many of our emails. She referred to me – in one instance – as "Stallion of Deep Discovery."

The video we shot was assembled by the PMO, and it was put up on Mrs. Trudeau's Facebook and Instagram pages on July 25, 2018.[12]

She began to follow me on Instagram. I shared the video with my followers, still proud that my words and ideas had been embraced in the great halls of power. Somewhat surprisingly, my pages barely grew as a result of the video. Being politically affiliated is a kind of zero-sum game. Some join you, some leave you, and you end up roughly where you were. Even more surprisingly, I could barely recognize the version of me that appeared with Mrs. Trudeau in the video. He seemed somewhat elderly, and spoke far slower than I normally do. And he was pale as a ghost. I had unexpectedly found the solution to my orange skin issue. Spend an hour alone in Sophie Trudeau's fiery kitchen, and you will be so drained of life that your skin will pale.

Chapter 6: Love Ride to Freedom

On August 15, 2018, Mrs. Trudeau put up a Facebook post that included an image of my wife's book, *Open Passages*.[13] Soon thereafter, I sat down to watch a video that Mrs. Trudeau's team had shared on her Facebook page.[14] She was being interviewed by author Liz Plank at the C2 Conference in Montreal. At around 5:40-6:00 minutes, she referenced the quote I had shared with her the year before, and that she had previously included in a speech. It concerned the distinction between *the survival of the fittest* and *the survival of the truest*, fundamental to my understanding of two very different ways of being in this world: survivalism vs authenticity. Something about seeing it spoken live without attribution landed differently than it had in written form. It was perhaps fair to say that my not making an issue at a previous time implied it was okay for her to continue to use my words. Yet I felt sick to my stomach watching her speak it as though it was her own.

I then took some time to watch other speeches shared on her Facebook page. And there it was again, in a speech at the Y7 summit months before.[15] This time, she first referenced a famous Winston Churchill quote but she did not reference me as the source of her subsequent idea. I felt sick to my stomach again. My intuition piped up: *Why is it so important for her to appear to be the creator of this particular idea? What would be lost by referencing a Canadian author in this moment? What kind of strange situation have you gotten yourself involved in – one where you are giving generously and forgetting to protect your own hard-earned creations?*

Nonetheless, I carried on. After all, we had to keep the progressive train going! But my intuition was getting to me, slowly… but surely.

Soon thereafter, I emailed Mrs. Trudeau to see if she was comfortable with my sending approaches and responses that might serve them in the next election campaign. She indicated that they were "always welcomed." On September 22, 2018, I sent her a lengthy electoral notes document for the PM's political interface. I had begun sending ideas through earlier in the year, but this document was much more detailed. Mrs. Trudeau wrote back that she had printed off my ideas and points of discussion – and that she would read them through and share them with the PM. I am not sharing these details for an egoic reason. My tangible step in this direction would prove significant with respect to the ways things unfolded between us.

On October 10, I sent Mrs. Trudeau an email about the Foreword for my book *Grounded Spirituality*, which she had offered to write. The manuscript was now complete. In the email, I let her know that the book might be politically risky for them due to its contents, and that it was not a problem if it wasn't a fit. I was being both protective of them, and also protective of the book. As noted earlier, Andrew Harvey had offered to write a Foreword, and I was feeling more confident he was the right person for the job.

I sent the manuscript to Sophie, and received an email from Dunerci Caceres from the Office of the Prime Minister on October 29, indicating their regret at not being able to write the Foreword because of the book's opinionated content. Secretly relieved, I let them know that this was the right decision.

At the same time, I hearkened back to what my intuition had suggested when she first offered to write the Foreword. Was Sophie Trudeau, in fact, a future faker? Did she offer to do things later so I would keep sending her words and ideas now? If so, was I the only one she did this with, or were there others? And, were the previous flirtations part of a pattern too? Was she flirting with me in an effort to groom me to be of service to her? Was I the only one?

On December 2, 2018, Mr. Trudeau made the news in the oddest of ways. Celebrities had gathered in Johannesburg for the Global Citizen Festival: Mandela 100, a charity concert honoring Nelson Mandela a century after he was born. During the event, Justin tweeted to The Daily Show anchor Trevor Noah – the host of the festival – that Canada would give $50 million to *Education Can't Wait*, an organization that funds education for children impacted by conflicts, natural disasters, and other crises:

> "Hey @Trevornoah - thanks for everything you're doing to celebrate Nelson Mandela's legacy at the @GlblCtzn festival. Sorry I can't be with you - but how about Canada pledges $50M to @EduCannotWait to support education for women & girls around the world? Work for you? Let's do it."[16]

Trevor Noah expressed his amazement as Trudeau's tweet was shown on a big screen at the concert.[17]

Canadian political pundits were nowhere near as positive. His pledge – and the attention-seeking way that he communicated it – quickly drew criticism from Conservative party leader Andrew Scheer: "Taxpayers need a defender, not somebody who throws their money around to be popular with celebrities"[18] and others, including Toronto-based lawyer and former Liberal Chief of Staff Warren Kinsella who called Trudeau's tweet an "appalling" way for the decision to be communicated, "to an American-based TV host, no less."[19]

Chapter 6: Love Ride to Freedom

This particular event was somewhat significant for me, because it was the first time that I experienced real doubts about Justin Trudeau himself. I had no firm evidence to justify it, but I couldn't help but wonder if this man – who I already knew was publicly representing his marriage in a way that wasn't entirely congruent with its realities – was someone obsessed with fame – and more specifically – being accepted by the popular kids. It was not as though he had become famous based on his talents and abilities. He had won primarily because he was Pierre Elliott Trudeau's son. I wondered: Who actually lives below that luscious hair? Was this an adult man capable of running a trillion-dollar economy, or an out-of-his element kid who felt left out at the cool kid's Johannesburg gathering, and had to make his presence known? Was he a man in service to humanity, or a boy in service to himself?

My inner voice was less generous: *You would think being the PM would be good enough to gratify any holes in the kid's ego, wouldn't ya? Well, it isn't. He's a lost boy seeking validation. You best get off at the next station. I see a collision in your future and there's going to be a shitload of twisted wreckage. You got on the wrong train, brother.*

On December 9, I initiated an email thread to let Mrs. Trudeau know that I had included her in the acknowledgements section at the back of Grounded Spirituality. Given the book's content, I wanted her confirmation that it was acceptable to include her name.

She responded favorably, indicating that it wasn't necessary to go to the team for a personal gratitude in the book. Wildhorse was making an executive decision!

In the same thread, I also let her know that if she needed a volunteer writer to help them win the next election, I was available.

At the time, both my gratitude and my willingness to help them felt like a heartfelt reflection of my highest imaginings about her and her husband's mission. But there was about something else, too. Trump was right on our doorstep. We had to win! We had to fight the progressive fight for the sake of humanity! Again, I knew virtually nothing about Conservatism, and even less about the actual intentions of Justin Trudeau. Like so many of us with a lingering bias, I had no understanding of the forces that were truly at play here.

A few weeks later, Susan and I went on a vacation to the Turks and Caicos islands. Both when we landed in Providenciales, and when we returned to Toronto, I had the most interesting experience. To this point in my life, I had often felt a kind of low-grade worry whenever I crossed a border. My sense was that the anxiety emanated from my Jewish origins, and a variety of additional life experiences with figures of authority and abuse of power. But this time, all of my usual border anxiety had vanished. I was cool as a cucumber. And I knew why. It was because I was connected to the Trudeaus, and felt protected on an international level. Not that I'd contact Sophie if I had to pay duties 😊, but if something ridiculous happened, I certainly would.

Over the holidays, I reflected on how I was now moving through the world as a result of my proximity to power. There was definitively some underlying discomfort about all that had been shared with me, but there was generally a noticeably greater degree of freedom in my movements than I had previously experienced. I felt more relaxed in the world, knowing that they would likely have my back if trouble befell me.

While I liked the way that this felt, I was also appalled by it. What a strangely barbaric world we live in – one where many of us only feel safe when we have gained power's favor. One where we literally move through the world differently when we are affirmatively connected to or indispensable to the so-called elite. After thousands of years, I would have hoped that we'd have found a less barbaric paradigm to comfort and secure us.

As much as I longed for a world that is fueled by service to humanity, it was entirely evident that we aren't there yet. Not even close. Our relationship to power is still the predominant paradigm that triggers or soothes our nervous system. And if a privileged white man was living with a somewhat anxious baseline about power, what were POC carrying? Women? Transpeople? Anyone who was not likely to ever gain the favor of power? Bottom line: How do we co-create a world where our nervous systems are calibrated to service to humanity – not to power?

＊＊

While still in the throes of this personal exploration of power, I received an email from Mrs. Trudeau. Dated January 30, 2019, she let me know that she was e-connecting me with Mathieu Bouchard (a lawyer in the PMO), someone who works closely with the PM on the creation and editing of his speeches. She indicated that she had spoken with Mathieu and was asked to put me in contact with him.

I emailed Mathieu a few times and did not hear back. I also emailed Mrs. Trudeau and texted Dunerci at the PMO to let her know that I hadn't heard back. No reply from any of them. I assumed that the SNC-Lavalin scandal – and the firing of Chief of Staff Gerard Butts etc. – had something to do with them possibly deciding to tighten up and not bring outsiders in. But I cannot say for certain what actually happened. And I do admit to finding it quite rude. I had no attachment to contributing to the PM's speeches at this time, but was more perturbed by the silence, something already familiar to me from our prior interactions with the *I admit* movement. It's such a contradictory way of relating for people who are allegedly bringing a compassionate relational message to the world.

Lavalin would prove somewhat prescient with respect to my unfolding story. At the heart of this scandal was Jody Wilson-Raybould, a half Jewish and half Native Canadian lawyer who was the first woman ever chosen to be Justice Minister in Canada when Mr. Trudeau was elected in 2015. Wilson-Raybould's unwillingness to "find a political situation" in the criminal prosecution against Lavalin (read: influence a Deferred Prosecution Agreement), despite various efforts by Mr. Trudeau and the PMO to pressure her, was soon followed by her being shuffled to another Cabinet position as Minister of Veteran Affairs. She resigned from the Cabinet soon thereafter. As did fellow liberal cabinet minister Jane Philpott, over the government's handling of the affair. Following a series of hearings, Michael Wernick – Clerk of the Privy Council and someone who pressured Wilson-Raybould during a phone conversation – announced his early retirement. Trudeau was later found to have contravened Section 9 of the federal Conflict of Interest Act by improperly pressuring Wilson-Raybould. The Conflict of Interest Act endeavors to prevent conflicts between private interests and the public responsibilities of appointed government officials.[20]

At this time, my bias was such that I was utterly sure that Wilson-Raybould was a disgruntled and ambitious employee who was angry about being demoted. And, it was perfectly appropriate for a political party to pressure an Attorney General that they had selected as to how to approach particular cases. Despite my legal training, it did not occur to me that there is and always must be a clear and inviolable boundary between the party's political agenda and the judicial system that should never be encroached upon. And it did not occur to me that Mr. Trudeau could be an abuser of power. No way, no how! Not Baby Face!

Early in February, I emailed Mrs. Trudeau more in the way of detailed electoral thoughts. I was aware that there would be an election this year, and feeling inspired to share fresh ideas and insights. She replied in kind, indicating that we were on the same page and that she had tried to express the same message to her husband and the team.

That same day, Mrs. Trudeau emailed me to express that she had been writing some poems that she wanted to share with me. I let her know that it was fine to send them.

The next day (February 6, 2019), Mrs. Trudeau's team put up a poster image on her Facebook and Instagram pages that highlighted a quote from one of my books: "It all comes down to truth- truth *or* consequences," with my name noted on the bottom.[21]

On February 16, she began to email through her poems. I hadn't expected her to send love poems. Two of them felt potentially significant to me, in the context of my dynamic with her:

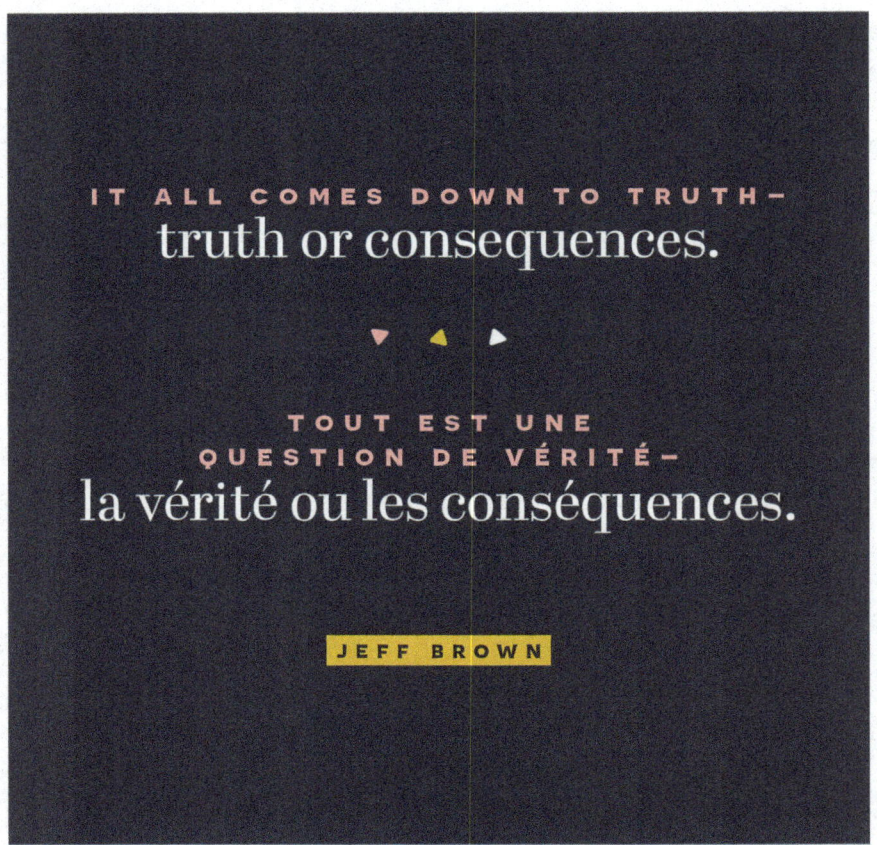

The first, *Sacred Love*, included the following words:

Why,

why do you run away from me?
Your eyes look down on hundreds of pages
While I'm your true manuscript.

Chapter 6: Love Ride to Freedom

Look up… this is our love story
Dive into my eyes
Look in deeper
This flame won't burn you
it will feed your heart beat

We've got sacred love
Sacred is our bond
Let fly the sacred dove
Beyond and above
We've got sacred love
We've got sacred love.

The second, 'Love Ride to Freedom,' ended with these words:

I've moved and soaked my mind.
I've felt the winds under the cedar tree.
I've roamed the land.
Of the wild and free.
And we both will stand on guard for thee.
But promise me you'll never leave this lifetime without making love to me…
Don't ever leave this lifetime without making love to me…

When I read 'Sacred Love,' I quickly wondered if it was written for me, because of the reference to a book manuscript. But I sent back writing feedback, as I had with most of the others.

When I read 'Love Ride to Freedom,' I had the distinct sense that it was written to me, for me. Of course, I couldn't be sure, because of the often cryptic way she communicated, but for a variety of reasons, I wondered. As a result, I chose not to respond to the piece. She then emailed it again a few days later. Wrongly or rightly, I interpreted the re-send as confirmation that she wanted me to know, by this gesture, that this piece was for me and that she wanted to be sure I saw it.

At this point, I had become fairly expert at ignoring anything that felt notably flirtatious, but I do recall feeling a next level degree of nervousness this time. I recalled Mrs. Trudeau telling me that her husband had found out about her affair. I don't remember whether she shared how he found out, but I wondered if she was closely monitored. She was Wildhorse after all, and if my experience in her kitchen taught me one thing, it was that she was probably perceived to be a political risk on the daily.

This was one mare that they simply couldn't control. And if she was being watched, it was certainly possible that her emails were being read. If so, then my Prime Minister was aware that she was sending love poems my way. Whether they were about me or someone else didn't even matter. That they were coming my way couldn't be a good thing.

I sent Mrs. Trudeau birthday wishes on her April 24 birthday. She shared that she would lean on my wisdom from time to time in the electoral season ahead. Things were just getting started. Here we go…

CHAPTER 7

A SEA OF ACCOMPLISHMENT

In the early days of autumn's federal election, I sent a number of suggestions and electoral ideas through Mrs. Trudeau for the campaign. Included among them was an email that emphasized the importance of drowning various criticisms of Mr. Trudeau's performance "in a sea of accomplishment." In other words, don't bother answering any unreasonable questions thrown at you by the opposition. Instead, offer a list of all that you have accomplished. Mrs. Trudeau confirmed that she had shown this email to her husband, and that he was aligned with it.

As yet another testament to the intensity of my confirmation bias, my wife and I spent one afternoon at an annual neighborhood street festival – the Cactus Festival. Included among the vendors at the festival was a Federal Conservative Party booth. Just before going, I had been made aware that the party had previously made an effort to change the age of pension from 65 to 67. This infuriated me, and fed into my biased belief that the Conservatives were cold-hearted elites with no regard for the working person. And so, right then and there, I gave the Conservative party candidate a piece of my mind, certain that I was standing on moral high ground by supporting the Liberals.

In early September, Netflix released an episode from Hasan Minhaj's series "The Patriot Act."[22] Hasan had come to Ottawa to interview Mr. Trudeau. Quite apart from the obvious question as to why the supposedly busy leader of Canada was bothering to be on a popular American show – there was this moment that stayed with me and struck me as significant.

During the interview, Minhaj directly challenged Trudeau on issues such as his administration's decision to purchase the Transnational Pipeline, their failure to hit their climate goals, and their deal to sell arms to Saudi Arabia. While pushing Trudeau on the latter issue, Minhaj referenced the idea that the Saudis were watching the show. Trudeau very soberly and seriously said this, "I'm sure they're keeping their eye on you." I wasn't sure why this moment struck me at the time, but it did. It felt like something a dictator would threaten – not the alleged savior of the progressive world. And it again led me to wonder.... Who lived below Justin's soft and seemingly hesitant demeanor? Who was this man, really?

On September 4, Mrs. Trudeau sent me an email with the subject header "FYI from our government!" It was some part of a report on various gender-equality related conversations signed by then Minister for Women and Gender Equality, Maryann Monsef. In a subsequent email that morning titled 'Last paragraph,' which focused on engaging men and boys in the empowerment of women and girls she wrote me this: "Is life leading you towards getting engaged politically? Just putting it out there..." I interpreted this as a prompt to action. That is, for me to consider becoming formally involved with the political world in a working capacity. Over the last few years, I had occasionally wondered what that might look like, but it made little sense in the context of my vaster creative callings. It could also potentially create conflicts-of-interest with my pre-existing publishing and teaching businesses.

Nonetheless, somewhere around that time, I began to volunteer in my local community of Dundas, Ontario (delivering flyers, dropping off pizzas) with Cabinet Minister Filomena Tassi's election team, both because I was still hopeful about Justin Trudeau, and because I wanted to get a closer look at politics. What was this world I had stepped into?

On September 18, 2019, I was hit with the next glitch in my pro-Justin Trudeau matrix. On that day, Time Magazine released a picture of the PM wearing brownface makeup to an Arabian Nights theme party at the private school where he was teaching in 2001. That night, Justin was interviewed on his campaign plane about the Arabian Nights costume. He responded that he didn't think it was "racist at the time." When asked if there were more incidents of this, Trudeau acknowledged that he had worn blackface "make-up" in high school to sing "Day-O," a Jamaican folk song performed by African-American singer and civil rights activist Harry Belafonte.[23]

The next day, while being interviewed on the steps of the Manitoba Parliament, a reporter reminded Justin of what he had revealed to them on the plane the night before and asked this question: "Have you since been made aware of or remembered other instances and, if so, how many?" After pausing and stumbling in his trademark style now familiar to Canadians, he provided an indirect answer: "I am wary of being definitive about this because the recent pictures that came out, I had not remembered. And I think the question is how can you not remember that?... The fact is, I didn't understand how hurtful this is to people who live with discrimination every single day..."[24]

Chapter 7: A Sea of Accomplishment

> My intuition chimed in: *He doesn't want to tell us how many other instances he remembers, because he's not yet sure how many will surface. That's called damage control. And Dude, seriously, look at the way this guy evades a direct response. You can almost hear his brain clicking as he scans his files for the politically opportunistic sound bite. He must really believe people are stupid.*

A third example of the Prime Minister with darkened features emerged – a video from the early 1990s with Trudeau in blackface, raising his hands in the air and sticking out his tongue.[25]

My inner knowing wasn't entirely wrong, but I was focused on a different issue. Not whether the man could remember how many photos were taken, but how often he actually engaged in these racist practices? Was this an occasional thing, or a persistent pattern? I had grown up watching American vaudevillian Al Jolson do blackface for a living, and had always found it repulsive. It didn't take a genius to realize that it was racist. If black people had done whiteface, they would have been quickly lynched.

On September 22, 2019, I went with my wife to see Justin at a campaign event in downtown Hamilton. It was my understanding that he was going to speak. I was actively supporting someone I had never met or witnessed live, and I wanted to see how I felt about him in person. Sophie knew that I was going, and wrote me that I "must go to him. He's an amazing Hugger." She let me know that she had told Justin I would be there.

When he finally arrived, he strutted across King Street, and the crowd began to race towards him. There seemed to be nothing in the way of crowd control to tame this mob of energized Liberals. He began to grab people's phones to take pictures with them, something you would imagine a rock star doing, not a hard-working PM. I walked towards him with my wife, and I just didn't have a good feeling about him. His eyes appeared dull, dead, wooden – more like a marionette than a person. A puppet, rather than a sovereign leader.

My wife had a few pictures taken with him. Suddenly, a group of impassioned people came charging towards us – like a herd of wild horses – demanding a picture. They carelessly rammed into Susan, knocking her to the ground. My heart choked in fear. She had been recently diagnosed with a visual disability, and had some difficulty gauging distances. I quickly reached down to lift her off the ground. We stayed a little longer and when it became clear he wasn't going to speak, we left to drive home. Susan recalls that my face in the car was one of great disappointment. Not because he hadn't spoken, but because of the clear gap between what I had hoped for, and what I had witnessed and felt.

* * *

Over the course of the next days, I could feel myself wanting to disconnect from Mrs. Trudeau and her political world. Latent lingering doubts were already there, but they were now growing stronger. In this case, the tipping point was a meaningless email that she wrote me, but there was a host of underlying issues. I was out of my element in their world – and I knew it.

On September 27, 2019, I wrote my first termination of friendship email to Mrs. Trudeau. She responded with some intensity, and made a point of reminding me that she wasn't going anywhere and that I still had her trust. I wasn't exactly sure what the latter meant in a context where I was disconnecting, but so be it. Interestingly, she also included the following words in her response. This would prove relevant later:

> "I've always sent your wise and insightful comments to my hubby and even the team more than once. It's always been well received."

I became next-level nervous. It may have been the first time that I woke up and realized that this was not a normal situation, where you put boundaries in place in a personal connection, and they are simply respected. This was the PM's wife, and they lived in a political world that was all about optics and power. The event a few days earlier – when my wife was knocked harshly to the ground – was a perfect metaphor for the dangerous nature of the world I had stepped into.

It is one thing to be trained to work on the political battlefield, but quite another to be an untrained civilian close to the fire. I was just a writer who liked to volunteer his services. I wasn't built to hold Prime Ministerial marital secrets, nor to have to worry about whether a Leading Lady's flirtations were putting me at risk. In a strangely metaphorical way, I felt like a dirty little secret, even though there was never anything sexual between us. And like most secrets, there was nobody in the room that I could talk with about my concerns.

And so, for a variety of reasons (peace of mind, among them), I decided to remain connected. Despite my misgivings about her and her husband, I still wanted them to win this election. It wasn't that I despised conservatives – I had actually voted for them on various occasions – but I had heard – rightly or wrongly – that the conservative candidate Andrew

Chapter 7: A Sea of Accomplishment

Scheer had two Trumpians on his team. At this stage, I still knew nothing about the very complex American political zeitgeist.

I continued to send electoral ideas through to Mrs. Trudeau. Included among them was the suggestion that they put up a social media post that emphasized either two <u>or</u> three particular streams of political focus. I provided examples. It struck me as important to not simply rely on fast-moving debates and sound bites to articulate your priorities, but to express them in clear, bullet points in longer lasting social media imagery. My recollection is that they chose the third option, and put up a related post soon thereafter.

I later found a wording error in one of their Facebook posts and let Mrs. Trudeau know by email. She passed it on to the team, and they corrected it soon thereafter.

A strange thing happened when I went to see Mr. Trudeau at a campaign stop one more time just before election day. I arrived a little bit late, and so did Mr. Trudeau's buses. As I turned into the parking lot, the lead bus almost collided with the back of my Jeep. Perhaps my intuition was more prescient than I had imagined.

I parked and went into the fire hall where he was going to speak. I really wanted to see how I felt about this man when he did something more than take pictures. I waited for him to enter, and listened closely as he spoke. He seemed somewhat nervous as he spewed his talking points. And quite young. Not physically young, but emotionally young. At the same time, he felt fresh, focused, and solid. I found it difficult to reconcile these two impressions. Almost like there were two parts to him that hadn't met each other yet. I left the building yet again unsure as to who he was.

On election night, some members of the local team used my house as a base for their electoral activities. Filomena Tassi, then Minister of Seniors, dropped in and brought us some of the best Italian pizza I have ever eaten. Soon after the team left, I turned on the television and found out that the liberals had won a minority government. I was quite excited. But then, moments before the Trudeaus stepped on the victory stage, I received a strange email from Sophie that quickly turned my delight into dread:

> "And the wild horses hold the wisdom… but let's remember we don't << own >> it. So proud to be allies together…"

It was immediately obvious to me that this email was a somewhat cryptic reminder that my political contribution was 'for the world,' and not about me. In other words, keep quiet about what you sent us. I was taken aback by this email – I already knew to keep quiet. It wasn't just the words – it was the precise timing of them. It certainly did not make me feel particularly safe to know that the last thing the PM's wife wanted to express before they stepped on the winning stage, was a reminder to me to remain silent. It seemed evident that my termination email on September 27, 2019 had made her nervous and concerned that she couldn't trust me. (Note: This would be confirmed in a phone call on December 8, 2020, and in an email with her on Dec 11, 2020). It also seemed evident that she perceived that the nature and/or impact of my contribution could be a political problem for them if revealed. Feeling both deflated and concerned, I chose not to respond to her silly email.

What had I gotten myself into?

Over the next weeks, I made an effort to make sense of her experience. That is, to understand why my previous termination email might have led her to make the assumption that I was then going public. Do all politicos react this way when people disconnect, or just the ones that have something to hide? Who was Sophie Trudeau, really?

Later in November, I went back to the Turks and Caicos for a vacation with my wife. We returned late Sunday evening November 24 at Toronto's Pearson airport. Hours later, I received an early morning email from Sophie, saying hello and inquiring into us having a phone chat. The email had no subject heading, which is unusual for her, as is an email sent by her before 9 a.m. I couldn't put my finger on it, but the email felt like it was nervously written. And perhaps not even her idea? I then had a thought I have never had before. I thought the timing of the email right after I had re-entered the country was not mere coincidence and wondered if someone ping my passport? Did they know I'd arrived at Pearson last night? I am a reasonable person, not prone to paranoid thinking, but something felt off. As though someone was irrationally concerned that I was meeting with Eastern European miscreants and sharing state secrets while eating grouper on the beaches of Providenciales 😊. I mean, it seems like a ridiculous kind of concern under normal circumstances, but if she was so worried about me that she wrote a harried email moments before stepping on the winning stage in front of the world, it wouldn't surprise me if they were concerned about what transpired while I was outside of Canada for a week.

I responded positively to Mrs. Trudeau's email in the hopes of calming her down in case she or they were concerned. I then received a text a little over an hour after my response, from Dunerci Caceres asking for my

Chapter 7: A Sea of Accomplishment

address so they could send me a "Christmas card." It's worth noting that they hadn't worried about sending me a card the two previous years of my active engagement. I became a little more concerned. Was the PM's office wanting to know where I live? Or, wanting to make me aware that they *would know* where I live? It all felt a little too orchestrated for my liking. Nonetheless, against my better judgment, I texted back my address.

I subsequently received two Christmas cards from the Prime Minister's Office. I suppose one card wasn't enough to make whatever point they were trying to make.

CHAPTER 8

OBAMA COMES TO TOWN

Mrs. Trudeau and I began 2020 with positive email interactions. I was feeling mildly uncomfortable about the whole question of monitoring and sometimes wondering what they might be doing with my address information, but it just felt simpler and safer to remain positively connected. Again, the events in the autumn had really underscored the fact that they have power, and left me feeling somewhat afraid to fully disconnect. I don't actually think that the PMO should be writing citizens to ask for their home address, particularly if they are anxious about them. But there was nothing I could do about it now. It was a done deal.

On January 14, Mrs. Trudeau emailed me to share that she had been invited to speak in Toronto, prior to the Economic Club's hosting of Barack Obama. She sent me the parameters of the speech, and asked me to write it in her uniquely cryptic way: "Heeeeeeeeigh!!!! Neighhhhhhh!!! Just a mind teaser if you wish to toy with the idea…" I responded favorably, and quickly wrote a speech about 'Conscious Capitalism.' Sophie sent it to the team and let me know that "the substantial content is great and I'll be using it!" She sent me the modified speech, and spoke it on January 23, before Obama spoke his.[26]

The pandemic began soon after. On March 13, the PMO announced that Mrs. Trudeau had contracted COVID-19 while away in London, England, at a WE Day charity event. A few days later, actor Idris Elba, the Hobbs & Shaw star, discovered he had contracted the virus while shooting a new film – after a WE Day charity event on March 4 during which he and Mrs. Trudeau had taken a picture together and hugged. In a video he shot on or about March 16, he shared that he had been exposed to someone who had tested positive on March 13 and that he too had tested positive. He also uttered these words: "This is serious. Now is the time to really think about social distancing, washing your hands…. Transparency is probably the best thing for this right now."[27]

When I heard this, I couldn't help but wonder if there was more to this story than met the eye. The reference to "transparency" certainly left me wondering if he was talking about Mrs. Trudeau's behavior and/or marriage. It is certainly possible to get COVID from a shared photograph, but I remembered the frenzied nature of Mrs. Trudeau's sharings in her kitchen, particularly her referencing the idea of fucking a black and a white guy at the same time. I couldn't help but wonder if the "hug"' on March 4 was just a hug. Was that truly the extent of their personal contact, or did Sophie also get all frenzied in his personal space? Nothing that Idris said suggested otherwise, and I am surely no psychic, but I wondered why he felt the need to tell us that he'd had contact with someone who tested positive, and to essentially name her. I mean, if someone tests positive, we already assume they had some form of contact with someone who tested positive, don't we?

In the months that followed, we continued to maintain amicable relations. Included among them was my gifting her my writing course, and her subsequently sharing various writings about her life with me. She also let me know that she wanted to do more for the world and asked me for ideas. I emailed through a number of additional ideas. Included among them was the suggestion that she write a book about her own story – one that normalizes emotional health issues, and celebrates human connectiveness and overcoming.

In the heart of an email thread, Mrs. Trudeau surprised me by letting me know that she missed me, and signing off with the words, "Your faraway nearby Sophie xx." I responded playfully in my response, including these words: "Dear faraway nearby. It is nearby faraway here..." But I remember feeling myself tense right after sending it. Not because it was nefarious to be playful, but because I felt concerned – yet again – that the Prime Minister's wife's tendency to flirt with me, was a dangerous game. It was one thing to continue to support their progressive messaging even if I had my doubts about their personal integrity, but quite another to add the concern that her powerful husband was aware of her questionable personal communications with me. I also wondered, given the nature of human patterning, if I was the only one who she referred to as her "faraway nearby." I somehow had my doubts. Wildhorse may well have had a whole gaggle of stallions of deep discovery that she was corresponding with.

In June, I decided that I wanted to look a little closer at how I was feeling about my connection to the Trudeaus. I knew that I would soon get busy developing a teaching model and podcast in 2021. Before I focus on long-term projects, I often put some time aside to get caught up on practical things, and to sort through any personal loose ends. Doing this allows me to be fully present when I sit down to write. I like to create from a clear slate.

At this time, I was feeling discomfort about the prospect of being tracked or monitored, and wanted to take a closer look. Again, I have never thought about this kind of thing before, but something didn't feel right. The question of passport tracking was still with me, as was an underlying concern that they had used my address to monitor me. My mind kept drifting to the belief that they likely wanted me to know that they would have my address when they requested it for their double Christmas card extravaganza. It doesn't take a genius to realize that the government doesn't need to ask you for your home address. That alone felt like an act of intimidation, quite apart from any issue around monitoring. In normal circumstances, I would probably not care about such things, but this context was anything but normal. I had helped these people, and the possibility that I had been, or was being, monitored didn't sit well with me. I understand that many people would not have been bothered by something like this – perhaps even expecting it from the political world – but it really troubled me. It had taken a fair amount of energy to work on things for her – and to personally process the events of our video day – and I didn't take kindly to the way she responded to my attempt to disconnect.

I was thinking about contacting a lawyer to talk about it, but because of the magnitude of the implications, I felt reluctant to disclose my concerns. Yet, I felt compelled to take some form of action. So, whenever I had a spare moment, I began by simply gathering all of the email correspondence with Sophie. My intention was to sit down and read it sequentially and cohesively, and once I was done, decide if I wanted to remain connected to Canada's Leading Lady. As I reflected, I began feeling more inclined to disconnect. I already had a series of doubts, but they strengthened as I read through the documents with a more pointed focus. In my fast-paced life, I had a tendency to skim them, and then get back to work. This time, I read them slowly and deliberately, allowing myself to feel into them. I was particularly struck by the tenor of some of the emails. I also discovered some relevant emails missing from my Hotmail account: the Rilke excerpts, the Wildhorse audio imitation, the letter from the PMO about the book Foreword, the last-minute email sent by Sophie before they stepped onto the winning stage in 2019. The absent emails concerned me. I do not have a habit of removing relevant emails from my account.

I also found that the Facebook post that I am near certain that the team had shared on Justin's page during the election, was no longer there. I did not screenshot it back then, so I cannot definitively prove it, but I clearly remember it. And although there is nothing illegal about them removing a post, it could suggest that they went into clean-up mode after my disconnection email during the 2019 election. Maybe it had shaken them even more than I realized. This exacerbated my growing feeling of concern.

I then arranged to speak with a prominent Canadian criminal lawyer, who I had an indirect connection with. I let him know about the missing emails, and I focused on the issue of passport monitoring. He confirmed that it would not be legal to do that. He also asked me if I was intending to go public. I remember feeling startled by that question, both because I was still loyal to the Trudeaus despite my doubts, and because the last thing I wanted was a public shit-show.

And yet I wanted to know if anything had happened that shouldn't have happened. I knew that I could not definitively prove that emails had been removed, because it is technically possible that I accidentally deleted them, but I did wonder if there was any way to determine if there had been any passport pinging or other forms of monitoring instigated. I appreciate that being pinged wouldn't have bothered many people under the same circumstances, but it really bothered me.

I made myself aware of the Privacy Act. The Privacy Act grants citizens the right to ask various government agencies to provide information they have on file about them. So, I began to write various government agencies just to see if there was anything on file related to me. I heard back from CBSA (Canadian Border Service Agency) and Passport Canada, both indicating that there was nothing of note. I was subsequently encouraged to write CSIS – the Canadian Security Intelligence Service – and received what I would come to learn was their typically cryptic response. Because they have a statutory exemption with respect to revealing personal information, they neither confirm nor deny that there is something on file related to your request. I found that glaringly discordant.

In September, Mrs. Trudeau and I had some emails about a possible trialogue with her, me, and an author friend of mine that she was familiar with. I was not attached to the conversation – I had recently recorded a conversation with my friend – but I thought it might be fun.

She also sent me a pre-publication piece she had written, and asked me to share my thoughts. I interpreted this as a request for an edit, and wrote back to ask her when she needed it back by. She replied: "ASAP! We're in politics." At this time, I was in that strange place where your positive and negative feelings about a person are about equal. You still feel hooked in – and yet your doubts about them and, in this case, the world they are embedded in – have grown much stronger. In any given moment, you could respond to them from a very compassionate and playful place, or feel yourself wanting to disconnect altogether. That's exactly where I was.

On November 10, 2020, I submitted a Privacy Act Request to the RCMP (Royal Canadian Mounted Police) to see if they had anything on file related to Sophie Trudeau and I. It was my understanding that, because they protect the Prime Minister and his family, they would be the most likely on-book organization to have knowledge of the situation I was exploring. My request for information included, but was not limited to, pinging and monitoring for the ten years prior. I received a confirmation that they had received my request, and then a subsequent email indicating that they needed 30-days more than the usual 30-day timeline due to Covid.

By late November, I became clear that it was time to disconnect from Sophie Trudeau and her political world. I wasn't harboring ill-will towards her, but it no longer felt right to remain connected. I had entered the connection with the best of intentions, but it no longer felt aligned. It was time to move on. The tipping point was her not getting back to me on the trialogue we had discussed – reminiscent of her not getting back to me in 2019 about the *I admit* movement. But it was far more than that. Included among my reasons: fatigue with her cryptic communications, concerns about future faking and flirting/grooming practices, possible plagiarism of words and ideas, discomfort with her poorly boundaried personal sharings, uneasiness about her response after I attempted to disconnect in 2019, a disrespect for the apparent incongruity between the Trudeaus' optics and their reality, the desire to terminate the occasional tensions in my own marriage that resulted from this intense situation, and a genuine need to extricate myself from the chaotic political world and return to a clarified creative space. The best way I can describe it is that I was breaking through my ill-informed personal and political confirmation bias, and seeing things for what they were.

Because I have a strong aversion to ghosting people, I pondered communicating my intention to disconnect directly. I even discussed the possibility of having a lawyer write a disconnection email for me, because I saw her intense reaction to my disconnection email in 2019, and wondered if it would be better for a lawyer to send the email for me. I consulted a lawyer friend to discuss the situation, and to see if he would be comfortable doing me a favor and writing a termination letter for me. He agreed to write it, but felt it might be better if I pay someone with a bigger name and more clout. It was the first time in years that I had thought about the need for clout to actualize a goal. I rejected the idea, and decided that I would do it myself. The idea that I had to pay a lawyer to terminate a personal connection felt ridiculous to me. It no longer does. He was right. It might have saved me a whole heap of trouble.

CHAPTER 9

Pam Grier

On December 5, 2020, I had a morning phone call with a trusted friend who lives in Toronto. I asked if he would be comfortable holding onto a binder of the correspondence between me and Mrs. Trudeau, just in case anything untoward ever happened to me. Canadians don't usually think like this, and I certainly never had before, but I felt some degree of unease. My fear was not rooted in anything as tangible as a direct threat. It was subtler than that – more of an intuitive hit that this situation was not entirely secure. My friend agreed to be a "safe-keeper." I was confident he was trustworthy – not someone who would share things publicly. We agreed that I would give him the binder the following Sunday (December 13, 2020), when I was planning to be in Toronto.

That afternoon, while sitting in the parking lot of a Staples in Ancaster, Ontario, I wrote Mrs. Trudeau my second email stating my intention to disengage from our relationship. It was, admittedly, not my best piece of writing, but it captured the essence of my desire to disconnect:

> … And please do me a small favour. I have reason to believe that your husband has had some monitoring done, of me. I may be mistaken, but I don't think so. I know that the boundarying email I wrote during the election freaked you out, and I am sorry for that. It was nothing for you to worry about. I was a true ally to both of you. I just wanted you to win. But I made a mistake, when I began to send electoral ideas. I was naive about what I was stepping into, and wish I could take it all back. So, please lets part on kind terms- I only wish the best for you- and ask him, if he is monitoring me on any level, if he could kindly stop. Blessings, Jeff.

About two hours later, I received a response:

> Hi!
> Jeff…. What do you mean by monitoring?
> That's quite odd…
> Is everything all right on your side?
> You should not regret anything you've ever sent my way. Even the

Chapter 9: Pam Grier

email where you said we weren't friends anymore because of the medication you were taking! Lol.

Why do we need to part? I'm confused.

Hugs
S

Mrs. Trudeau's reference to medication relates to a story I had shared with her about a difficult experience I'd had with a sleep aid in the fall of 2019 and early 2020. After my wife and I had moved in 2019, in the heart of my overwhelm, I began to take 'U-Dream,' a product that had become quickly popular in the holistic community because it was so effective. After some months, I experienced a broad array of physical symptoms and emotional reactions (i.e. generalized anxiety, agitation and impatience) that could only be explained by the sleep-aid. When I went online, I discovered that it had just been banned by Health Canada, because of the extreme impact it was having on users. The FDA had also publicly discouraged people from purchasing it.[28]

As it turned out, it had purportedly been spiked with a variation of a psychotropic medication (Zopiclone) etc. I quit cold turkey and then went through a very intense and uncomfortable withdrawal phase. I do not do drugs, or drink, so I had no understanding of withdrawal processes and tapering.

In any event, I had informed Mrs. Trudeau of this experience in the spring of 2020. In fact, I attributed my attempt to disconnect on Sept 27/2019 to the effects of the drug. At that time, her response was compassionate. But, in her email response above, she mocked my experience. I couldn't help but wonder if she had already pre-organized her damage control response in the event that I made another attempt to cut ties. Or, perhaps she had tossed it in after receiving my email. Either way, it was clear she wanted to remind me of something that could embarrass me. I have since learned this is quite common in the political world – a concerted effort to discredit someone who has gone public, or whom they fear may one day go public. The intention is to imply that you are unstable, or that you have a hidden agenda. In this case, I was particularly annoyed by this response, not simply because it was obviously insensitive, but also because I had supported these people and believed I deserved better. So, I reacted accordingly, in the subsequent email:

> You are LOL'ing what happens to a person who is taking an herbal sleep-aid that contains a psychotropic medication they don't know

is there? There is nothing LOL about any of that nightmare. But, I do now believe that it was- in that email- a bit of a truth serum. Kind of like when some people drink, and they tell the truth. Do you know what I mean? There were a number of things that were bothering me about our dynamic, that came to the surface. I regret writing it at that time, but there was truth to it.

As for how I am doing right now, I have never felt more stable or centered.

How about you? How is your mental state Sophie? You doing better than when last I saw you?

You got a lot from me. I gave it generously.

Let's leave it all, right there. I don't trust either of you.

Goodbye.

I have since been told this is called "throwing down the gauntlet." Whether I realized it or not, the duel was on.

Mrs. Trudeau responded minutes later, acknowledging her own challenges with sleep medication, something I was already familiar with from previous emails. She also claimed she hadn't been laughing at me in the previous email, which I did not believe. I'd learned some time ago that whenever Mrs. Trudeau adds an LOL to the end of a sentence, it often means that whatever was expressed right before it, was quite intentional.

We then had an email dialogue around some of the things that were bothering me (i.e. concerns about the non-accreditation of my work, not following up on suggested activities, the question of monitoring). I didn't actually want to resolve our friendship, but I felt afraid of what might happen if I didn't engage with her.

The next morning, I received the following email from Wildhorse:

> Jeff,
> I couldn't sleep last night. This hurts.
> Would it be possible to talk, you and I, before putting an "end" to this bond? I gave you my trust almost blindly because I felt safe with you from day one. But this is not just about me.
> Let me know when is a good time?
> With deep sincerity,
>
> Sophie

Deep sincerity? If she was such a deeply sincere person, why not simply respect my right to disconnect from her? Nonetheless, I felt bad that she hadn't slept and was having such a strong reaction to my emails. Despite my misgivings, I was fond of her, and I had no interest in causing her suffering. At the same time, I understood what "But this is not just about me" meant, and it was worrisome. She was clearly referencing her husband and his political career. Her reaction underscored her paranoid assumption that my wanting to disconnect, would somehow pose a threat to that. Of course it wouldn't. I simply wanted nothing more to do with them or their political world. If I had intended to make trouble, I certainly wouldn't have drawn their attention to my departure.

I agreed to a phone call. Not out of genuine interest, but because I felt afraid not to. Before chatting a few days later, Mrs. Trudeau included the following seductive words in an email to me: "I'm holding on to the bone … and the bond! Lol." (Let's not get into which bone she is referencing, okay :)? The whole situation was just plain absurd. Again, yet again, who were these people? And how could they possibly be running a country?

On Tuesday, December 8, we had a twenty-three-minute talk. With a newfound awareness of the need for self-protection, I taped the call. This was the first and last time we had ever spoken on the phone. During the call, she made a point of insisting there had never been a "they," with respect to her, me, and the team ("So there was never a they Sophie and Jeff um how were they working, it was you and I…"). In other words, there was no bridge from me through her to Justin. I interpreted this as a premeditated effort to protect her husband by denying any possible connection between my contributions and his politics. The fact that it was important to her to emphasize this in our call, only served to confirm my anxiety after my first attempt to end our relationship in 2019. Whatever I had been told or sent, and whatever I might have contributed, was clearly not supposed to become public knowledge. During the call she made other surprising personal admissions. For example, about her struggles with seeing things as "imminent danger." She acknowledged her sleeping challenges and indicated she was working with a naturopath to lower her cortisol (the fight or flight stress hormone). She also indicated that she was riding horses and had tried barrel racing" to "get the wild out," which was helping prevent paranoia and anxiety from setting in.

I brought up some of my monitoring concerns, such as her early morning email sent almost immediately after I returned to the country in 2019, followed soon after by the PMO's request for my address. She called the timing "synchronicity." On two occasions, she emphasized the idea of moving forward with our connection, and not looking back: "I would like for us to build trust from here, from now on… and never have to go back to what has been said, or felt before..." She also stated: "That's not enough for me. I don't want you to just say 'I don't have a hate on for you.' If you're willing, I would like us to build on where we are now." She was greatly relieved when I agreed to remain connected. I opted to be particularly amenable on the call, because I didn't like the alternative: living in fear of the politically motivated actions they might take if they saw me as a threat. Clearly this was a world that did not play by the rules of healthy interaction, and she was not the type of person – at least in this context – to say *thank you for your service* and let you go quietly.

On Friday, December 11, I emailed Mrs. Trudeau. I had the sense that my 2019 disconnection email had worried her, and had led to the 'keep quiet' email she'd sent me right before they had stepped on the winning stage when they won the 2019 election, as well as her emails sent weeks later about having a talk and/or my coming to Ottawa. In her reply, she agreed with this and confirmed that she had been worried.

On that same day, I had another conversation with my friend, in which he confirmed he was still willing to be the safe-keeper of the binder. We agreed to talk Saturday to confirm the time to meet on Sunday. I distinctly remember using the word 'binder' during this conversation. And it's important to note that I am not a collector of binders. Weeks before, when I had printed out all the correspondence, there were too many pages to keep in a loose pile. So, I put them in a binder.

That evening, after speaking with my friend, I went for a drive and reflected on the week's events. In a way, it was simple. I had tried to get away from Mrs. Trudeau and her political world, and she had kicked up a fuss. For my own peace of mind, I had agreed to remain connected. The intensity of her response on the two occasions I had tried to separate from her left me feeling concerned about what might happen if I severed all ties. In a law-abiding world, I wouldn't worry about such things, but clearly hers was a world where the normal human rules didn't apply.

This left me in quite a conundrum. If I remained connected to her, I would assure my self-preservation. But then I would be living a lie. If I lived my truth and cut all ties, I might have to deal with undesirable consequences. I wasn't thinking about *dire* consequences – at least not yet – but I intuited that something intense might come my way. It was just how the whole thing felt. For most people, the decision would have been a no-brainer. After all, we make all kinds of compromises in our lives for the purposes of self-preservation. But it was a little different for me. I had devoted much of my adult life to honoring my truths, however inconve-

Chapter 9: Pam Grier

nient they might be. I wrote extensively about honoring one's truth and sacred purpose, taught it in my classes, and embodied it to the best of my ability. I was so into the question of truth on one's path that I had created a term – truth-aches – that referred to the myriad troublesome symptoms we experience when we aren't fully living and walking our path. Yet here I was, selecting diplomacy over truth because the latter was so bloody inconvenient.

Just before arriving home, I actually pulled over to make a video that reflected my inner conflict.[29]

I slept on it and woke up determined to leave things as they were. It wasn't ideal, but I had a whole list of creative things to focus on in the new year. Any part of me that wanted out, or that contemplated going public about possible monitoring and other issues, would have to take a backseat to my peace of mind. Besides, I figured once I got lost in my projects, I would probably stop caring about this situation. If something significant came back from my RCMP Privacy Act request, I would then decide what to do with that information. In the meantime, it was better to just leave things be.

I called my safe-keeper on the afternoon of Saturday, December 12, to check on the time to meet for the binder drop-off on Sunday. He agreed to call back after checking on some timing details with his partner.

That evening, I was sitting on the couch chatting with my wife when my cellphone rang. It was 7:02 PM. The call display indicated that it was my friend calling from his home phone. But when I answered the phone, he didn't respond. I could sense that it wasn't a dead line. Someone was there; there was movement, the sound of someone breathing on the other end.

After I said hello twice, a woman very calmly said, *"Hello."*

"Who is this?" I asked.

No reply again, so I asked it more assertively.

She then replied with something like, "I suppose I should say that I am Pam Grier."

I assumed she was referencing the iconic American actress (unless she was referencing herself). I asked her why she was on my phone line – and she went silent again.

Shaken and confused, I hung up and dialed my friend. He confirmed that yes, he had called me. And yes, he had heard me speaking. But he hadn't heard anyone else.

Yet the only person I had heard on my phone was the woman.

63

(Sidenote: What is even stranger – or perhaps prophetic – is that when I first answered the phone, I had said something like 'Espionage Central', not because I am a psychic and knew somebody would be on my phone, but because I was being playful about us handing off a binder at a boat in the night. I had probably watched too many 'Homeland' episodes. My friend picked up on the energy of it and told me afterwards that he playfully responded with something like 'Agent 59330.')

* * *

Based on the preceding facts and events – particularly the intensity of Sophie's response to my attempts to break things off during the previous week – the only thing that made reasonable sense was that after I'd attempted to sever connections with her, someone was put on my phone to listen in for political purposes. It seemed logical to conclude that the wiretapper had heard one or both of my calls with my friend (December 11 and/or 12) where I'd mentioned a binder of correspondence. They couldn't stop me from handing it to a safe-keeper, so I believe they showed up on our final phone call before the meeting, in the hopes it would frighten me (or him) into not handing it over. The woman on the phone had not been threatening or aggressive, but she'd clearly been determined to make her presence known.

It's important to note that this was not one of those crossed line incidents that occasionally happened between neighboring landlines in the 70's, when you could vaguely hear other people talking. The voice on the other end was precise and clear. This was also not a situation where someone had accidentally called me, while trying to call someone else. It was my friend's landline number that had shown up on my phone, and the woman on the line had not asked who I was, or acted in any way surprised to have reached me. She'd been calm and deliberate, and it had struck me as obvious that she knew who I was.

When I used to work in home improvements, thousands of phone calls a year would come through my cell. In all that time, I had never once answered a call from someone other than the person whose phone number had appeared on my call display. The possibility that this had happened accidentally – at the precise moment I was orchestrating an exchange of valuable information – seemed remarkably unlikely. While this is not something I can definitively prove, nothing else makes sense to me. It was not a spoof call, where someone pretends they are someone else calling your number. My friend actually did call, and could hear me. The incident felt strangely similar to the cryptic way Mrs. Trudeau had often communicated with me. In other words, where things expressed or experienced often meant something other than what they appeared to mean. This is not to say that Mrs. Trudeau had ordered this phone interception. But it is to say that after nearly four years of interactions, one comes to recognize the way the political world makes its point.

It may be useful to point out that in my disconnection email with Mrs. Trudeau on December 5, 2020, I included the following words in reference to her husband: "and ask him, if he is monitoring me on any level, to kindly stop."

I began to wonder if those words played a significant role in what had occurred – if the knowledge that I was uncomfortable with monitoring (who wouldn't be?) had intensified the decision not just to monitor me, but to make sure I was aware of it. I don't know who ordered this particular phone interception. Many individuals and organizations benefiting from a liberal government would have had a reason to frighten me into silence. Of course, how they would have known about my efforts to disconnect with Mrs. Trudeau was beyond my imagining. Somebody, somewhere, must have told them. More on these questions later.

I immediately contacted some of my closest friends to let them know what had happened. My mind churned with doubts and fears about handing over the binder Sunday evening. I felt intimidated by the phone interception – just as someone had intended – and concerned that I was in danger. I couldn't think of any way my actions could be seen as illegal, but they didn't have to be illegal to ignite a counter-response from politically motivated wrongdoers.

Nonetheless, I decided to proceed. I was standing down abuse of power in my own crib. I was certainly not going to stop now. If they wanted to arrest me on the charge of binder passing 😊, have at it, motherfuckers. If nothing else, the phone "incident" was confirmation that my instincts had been right all along. This dark, unconscionable political world was not for me.

My friend the safe-keeper was a Toronto Islander. When I arrived at the ferry docks on Sunday evening, I felt a looming sense of discomfort that quickly morphed into fright. It was a dark, misty pandemic night and very few people were around. Though I'd never been the type who worried about being followed, I found myself studying the people awaiting the boat to determine if they were Islanders or here for some other reason. I'd gone from feeling fundamentally safe and protected as a Canadian, to worrying about my well-being. If I had grown up in a despotic nation, I would have been prepared for this, but this was pristine Canada, the land of polite people and Dudley-Do-Right. There was no shadow here, right?

The boat arrived, and I stepped aboard with the binder. When I arrived on the other side, my friend was waiting for me, his trusted bicycle leaning against the fence. We embraced, and I handed him the binder. He quickly put it in the saddlebag, locked it down, and rode off into the mist. I stepped back onto the ferry and made my way home. Safekeeping mission accomplished!

Thereafter, I was catapulted into a state of high anxiety. We were already in a pandemic lockdown, which felt inherently dangerous and uncomfortable. Compounding that, I now worried that the leader of my country perceived what I knew and what I had contributed as some kind of political threat. In the midst of it all, I found it difficult to regain my equilibrium. I began making personal videos to express myself and watched my generally gregarious nature fade away. I went to sleep anxious, woke up anxious. I was experiencing unfamiliar emotions that I had no language for and no capacity to release while in such a vigilant state. So much for feeling safer because of my proximity to power. Now I was living the other side of that equation – feeling more frightened because of that same proximity. And that is a whole different world.

On December 20, 2021, I posted "…is feeling unsafe" on my personal FB page.[30] As the feelings associated with this experience swirled inside me, I realized I needed to express myself. Not just at home, but also publicly. I am a relational writer by nature, and after years of leaping from experience to expression in social media, public outreach is in my blood. As I would find out, sharing any part of this publicly would come at a cost. On the one hand, it made me feel momentarily safer, but on the other, much less safe overall. It wasn't much of a stretch to assume that whoever had tapped my phone would also see what I shared on social media. This was the beginning of what would prove to be a four-year-plus tug-of-war between expression and repression.

Even if I could never formally prove that someone had ordered my phone tapped for political reasons on the night of December 12, 2020, I still felt like I had been abused by power due to Mrs. Trudeau's efforts to keep me connected to her circle. Although some wouldn't think that being asked to remain connected could be an abuse of power, it can be construed as one when the person asking is intimately connected to someone in a position of political authority. In this case, the wife of the leader of a

G-7 nation, who was irrationally concerned that my attempt to disconnect was a threat to their political lives. That is when "asking" becomes pressuring. Just the insistence to remain connected can be – and certainly was experienced by me – as an act of intimidation, simply because of the context. It's not like I didn't know who she was married to.

I decided to get a second phone. I didn't feel comfortable using my usual phone, nor did I feel comfortable using email. I began checking email using Tim Horton's Wi-Fi, a popular coffee shoppe chain, and repeatedly changed my password. And I began to wonder about things I never would have considered before. For example, one day I noticed a cable company truck parked outside my house for hours. Later that day, my neighbors confirmed that the repairman had been in their house for hours and had been quite miserable about it. They presumed his misery was related to having to work during Christmas week. Later that night, I noticed something strangely new on my Wi-Fi. Suddenly, there was a Hamilton city guest account showing up as "My network" on my phone, and another Hamilton data account as well. We are nowhere near the locations where these would organically arise, i.e. a library. My first thought was that I was now under internet surveillance as well, and they were somehow using the Hamilton city system to accommodate it. This was probably not true, but what was true was that I had entered into a new perceptual reality: one where I had to determine if and how I was being monitored, with very little in the way of direct information. The challenge of distinguishing legitimate threats from meaningless "synchronicities" (there's that word, again!) would soon become the norm in my strange new world.

The remaining days of December were the first time in my life I experienced terror. It was kind of like the feeling you get when your home has been broken into, or your car is stolen, but worse. With a surveillance issue, you never know if the lawbreaker is still there – and they have the power to fuck with your life in unimaginable ways. The idea that my calls were being monitored felt demeaning, but it was far more than that. That phone interception had real-time consequences. With my rising cortisol levels, I had a few incidents of palpitations and pain moving up and down my arm that felt quite perilous. I developed a greater appreciation for what people experience when they flee a country where abuse of power runs rampant.

The only thing that comforted me – and simultaneously informed my experience – was watching a video that related to the SNC-Lavalin scandal in 2019.[31] In it, former Attorney General Jody Wilson-Raybould had wisely recorded a conversation with Privy Council Clerk Michael Wernick, wherein he quite persistently and nervously pushed her to change her mind and go the DPA (Deferred Prosecution Agreement) route rather than prosecuting SNC. He made it clear that Mr. Trudeau was determined and firm on this, and that Trudeau was in a mood about it. He also indicated his concern about a collision (there's that word again) between her and the Prime Minister. The call went on for some time, until Wernick finally realized he wasn't getting anywhere and ended it.

During the conversation, Wilson-Raybould stood her ground, insisting she wasn't changing her mind, and that she was protecting both the PM and the Constitution by refusing to surrender her prosecutorial independence. She made it clear that she was concerned about going through a "Saturday night massacre," a reference to the night when the US Attorney General et al. lost their jobs during the Watergate scandal. She also said something that confirmed my worry about the way Mr. Trudeau operated: "I'm not under any illusion about how the PM has and gets things he wants …." She seemed to know what she was talking about.

Whereas before, my pro-Trudeau confirmation bias had led me to doubt Wilson-Raybould's credibility, I now saw the situation for what it was: a brave and honorable woman fighting for what was right and true, before a bullying and lawless prime minister and his network of minions. And though my situation seemed different, it was in some ways quite similar. For example, Mrs. Trudeau's determined effort to persuade me to remain connected felt similar in its motivation to Wernick's attempt to pressure Wilson-Raybould to make a choice that preserved the PM's political goals. Mrs. Trudeau was protecting her husband's political world ("But this is not just about me") from a perceived threat. And the fear that both Wernick and Wilson-Raybould exuded about the wrath of Trudeau was not unlike the fear I felt when I agreed to remain connected – and certainly the fear I felt after the intimidating phone interception.

Are we detecting a pattern yet?

Interestingly, my phone interception had actually occurred on a Saturday night. My own little Saturday night massacre.

CHAPTER 10

I'm Here For You

On January 1, 2021, I parked outside of the Tim Hortons in downtown Dundas to check my emails and change my password. I was sitting in a cold car, feeling particularly nervous and uncomfortable, when I saw and opened an email from Mrs. Trudeau. In it, she had included a cartoon avatar of herself celebrating the new year, and added these words: "Thinking of you! It's going to be a deeply transformative one!" I had no idea what the latter sentence meant, but wondered if it was her way of telling me that she was going to finally divorce her husband. Whatever it was, I responded favorably: "Thinking of you, too. I sure hope so Sophie. It's certainly not feeling very good right now. Blessings to your every moment..." I responded this way because I was afraid, not because I actually felt like blessing her. In trauma terms, I was now officially fawning, a psychological term that describes unconscious people-pleasing behaviors and responses to perceived threats in an attempt to diffuse potential danger.

A few days later, I received an official Prime Ministerial Xmas card from Sophie and Justin, postmarked on December 17, five days after the phone interception. In it, she references the two Christmas cards I told her I had received the year before when we spoke on the phone. Two cards in 2019 that I believed reflected their nervousness, and now another in 2020, that I suspect reflected it, too. The envelope was marked with her husband's name and referenced his Parliamentary office in Papineau, Quebec.

Not long before, my wife and I both received letters from the Canada Revenue Agency, requesting funds related to our 2019 personal taxes. What was interesting is that the postmark date on those letters was also December 17, 2020. They were not wrong with respect to the funds owed – my accountant had forgotten to add a particular T-5 total to my personal earnings – but I found the timing, and the contrasting tenor of the letters, quite interesting. I couldn't help but wonder if this was another "synchronicity", or if I was being presented with two simple options: (1) remain positively connected, or (2) we gonna fuck wit you...

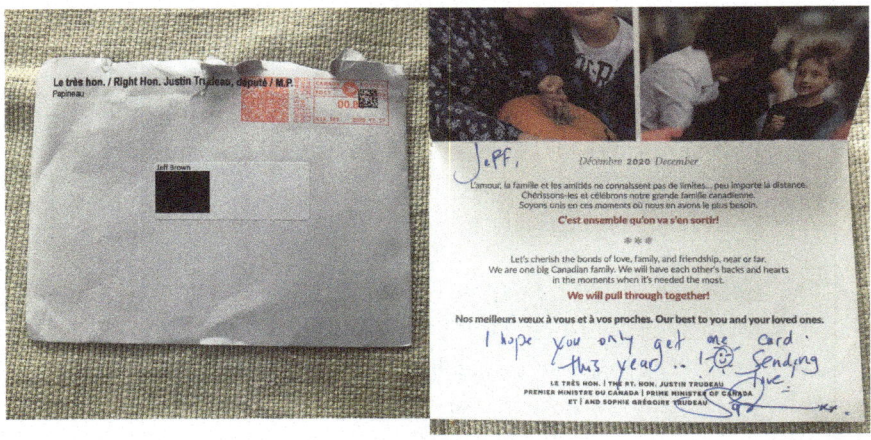

So, what to do? I spoke to friends, some of whom suggested that I just let it all go. Stop feeding it my attention, and it would eventually just fade away. I really heard them, and I felt their care, but I didn't feel inclined to let it go yet. I certainly wished that I could, but I am just not built that way. I understood that I couldn't prove that Mr. Trudeau, who I now playfully referred to as the *Prime Sinister*, put someone on my phone, but I had no doubt that some politically motivated wrongdoer did. I looked into the possibility that the phone thing was some oddly timed accident, but nobody I spoke with – including busy people who were on their phone thousands of times each month – had ever answered their cell phone to a familiar caller and found someone else there, waiting for them, and then addressing them directly. And neither had I.

My need to express myself asserted itself to a limited extent. I longed to go public with all the details, but I was reluctant. Not because I couldn't stand in the fire, but because I was concerned about the consequences for the country – many of my fellow Canadians were being financially supported by this administration during the pandemic – and for my wife – a brilliant, sensitive poet with an eye condition that worsened under stress. So, the words found their way in a form familiar to me as an author. I began to share my broader conclusions about abuse of power and fawning in social media. I had to do something constructive with this experience. For example, on January 2, I posted these words on Facebook:[32]

> Perhaps the greatest impediment to the world that I want to live in is the "abuse of power." We are slowly getting better at recognizing and confronting it in its most obvious forms. But this is not enough. We cannot stop there. Because it is even more dangerous in its subtle and invisible forms. There are "Invisi-Bullies" everywhere, hiding be-

hind their minions and using them to do their unjust bidding. These Invisi-Bullies often exist in powerful places, and rely on various manipulative tactics to affect their goals. They play all kinds of games to orchestrate their narcissistic ends. Without making a determined effort to look beyond the obvious, we will never see the ways that they operate. And without whistle-blowers, without sacred activists, without people making brave decisions in the face of tyranny, we will never move the needle toward a truly humane world.

Our relationship to power is a complicated and seductive one. We must do everything we can to acknowledge and loosen its inner and outer grip. We must work hard in the deep within to make a conscious distinction between our malevolent and benevolent intentions, and to ensure that we are not motivated – in our personal lives, in our business relationships, in our politics – by a narcissistic quest for power. We must be sure to ground our actions in the rule of law, and to honour each person's right to live with dignity. Only then will we co-create the world of possibility that will serve us all. Only then can we save our species from its own trappings.

And on January 9, also on Facebook:

> As I look back on my life, there is one thing I have consistently despised: abuse of power. Abuse of parental power, abuse of economic power, abuse of spiritual power, abuse of political power. I don't care if it comes from the right, or the left, or the centre. Abuse of power is always a crime against humanity. And there is no chance that we will heal the rifts between us, or co-create the inclusive world I long for, until it becomes extinct. There is nothing more compassionate than hating injustice.[33]

Also, on January 9, what appeared to be a fake account messaged me on one of my Facebook pages: "You messed up real bad. You are on the list. Better spend time with the family." Synchronistic timing? I think not. And soon thereafter, I put up another post:

> I recently had an experience, where I found myself 'fawning' in an effort to avoid abusive consequences from people in positions of power. This experience has helped me to more fully empathize with those who have lived in fascistic countries and had to placate power in order to remain safe. And, even more so, to understand the experience of many women who have had to 'fawn' over those they dislike, because of their fear of attack. No human should ever have to disown their true feelings, because they fear degradation or abuse. Ever.[34]

But it wasn't enough to stand alone, shouting into the void. I needed someone in the system to bear witness to what I was experiencing. It wasn't just the strange phone occurrence that bothered me. It was also the heat that was put on me to remain connected to Wildhorse. So, I reached out to a journalist from a major Canadian news outlet. She connected me with her editor, who then agreed to an off-the-record meeting.

I met the editor in Toronto's High Park, on a frigid January day. We sat on a shabby wooden bench, both wearing our masks. It was just plain weird. I felt unusually tentative, both because of the anxious and confused state I had been in for some weeks, and because I was still at a place where I wasn't certain that I wanted to share this story publicly. I definitely needed to talk with media, but I still had a strange loyalty to the Trudeaus and their politics, despite everything. Nonetheless, I shared as much of the story as I could in just short of an hour. I didn't bring a copy of the binder – I was not yet sure if I wanted anyone to ever read it – but I did bring one of the Christmas cards I had received, just to confirm that I had been connected to them.

The editor was very pleasant, and startled by the story. They used the word "crazy," which they politely apologized for later, to describe either it, or me, or both. I took no offence, because I understood how off-the-wall-crazy this story is. It's messy, and its human, and at a time where millions of people were sure that authority was out to get them – she told me that her emails are flooded daily with stories that exude paranoia – it's difficult to ingest.

At the same time, this was the first time that I had to consider the possibility that people wouldn't believe me. When you have experiences that you know to be true, you don't naturally assume that people will doubt you. But doubt you they will, especially if there are events that are not taped or filmed or directly eye (or in this case, ear) witnessed. My wife and friend heard me, but they did not hear "Pam Grier." Only I did. And so, the gaslighting had begun…

The editor expressed interest in seeing the binder, but didn't push me. We left it that they would consider the story, I would think about going public, and we would touch base again soon. One significant thing that they asked stayed with me: "Why didn't you call the police after the phone interception?" I said that there was no point because I believed that the event was politically motivated, and that it probably involved the highest levels of law enforcement. In other words, nobody was going to admit it. And, I couldn't imagine that my phone company was going to tell the local police that I was under surveillance. If it was on the books (judicially ordered), or off them, they either aren't going to say or they aren't going

Chapter 10: I'm Here for You

to know. But it did get me thinking. So, I contacted my lawyer friend and asked him if he would read the binder of emails between myself and Mrs. Trudeau, and listen to our (taped) phone call. Then he could determine if there was any legal basis for a wiretap. He agreed.

In addition, I contacted a well-known 'security expert,' who connected me with someone who had knowledge of how CSIS operates. Without realizing it, I was at the beginning of my informal education about yet another world I knew nothing about: the security and surveillance world that exists within <u>and</u> outside of our formal government agencies.

In our phone call, he made it very clear that much of what CSIS does is off the books. In other words, they utilize non-CSIS employees to engage in surveillance-related activities. He also indicated that the method employed here – having someone interact with me on my phone in a way that only I could hear – was unusual and not something that he imagined CSIS would engage in if they were trying to manage a risk. He also indicated that, if it was CSIS, they don't have to go through the phone company to do this. They have their own paths of easy access.

The most important thing he said was that calling the cops was likely a waste of time. He contended that even if I could convince a police officer to bring this to a judge to get some kind of warrant for information from my cell provider – they wouldn't have it. And even if they did, it would get shut down from above.

Nonetheless, I did call the local Hamilton Police and chose not to respond to the officer's return call. Who can be trusted to help you, when someone at or near the top of the power chain is wanting to keep you frightened and contained?

On January 25, 2021, I had a 49-minute off-the-record call on my second phone with a very credible Canadian journalist. It's important to note that when I got this phone, I provided my real name and address. I had no knowledge of burner phones at the time, nor did I know anything about voice recognition software. The journalist was affiliated with a conservative news outlet. He had no issue with believing the story, and he was eager to get his hands on the binder. He indicated that he would speak to a long-trusted local colleague about picking it up. He also mentioned that he too believed he was under surveillance. It didn't seem to faze him, perhaps because it was something that came with his journalistic territory.

Soon thereafter, he texted me that he had a Toronto colleague, who he had known for 20+ years, who was willing to come to Dundas to pick up the binder. I resisted and wrote back that I was waiting on my lawyer.

I wasn't ready to hand the emails over to anyone, and certainly not a conservative. Not that I had any real understanding of what a conservative actually was, but my confirmation bias was still somewhat intact. As I said before, I didn't feel ill-will towards Mrs. Trudeau – I just wanted nothing to do with her. And truth be told – the idea of remaining silent terrified me, *and* the idea of going public truly terrified me. I was now living in the heart of a full-fledged double bind.

And then it got strange again. Only a few hours after speaking with the journalist, I received my first email from Mrs. Trudeau since January 1 – 24 days earlier. It was an unusually forthright, intimate, and connective email that she made a point of mentioning she was writing from *her bed*. This left me wondering if someone was listening to my media phone call *and if* she was sent to seduce me back into a positive connection. Apart from the obviously inappropriate nature of the content, I interpreted the words "Action for justice and compassion," as her way of telling me to be compassionate in my assessment of previous events. In her words:

> "Hello depth-seeking soul…
>
> I'm sitting on my bed running through a copy of *Love it Forward* that you had given me a while back. You are in my thoughts. Let us never be afraid to dive into deep soul waters… as this ultimate act of intimacy reminds us of our own divinity. So many beings are afraid on the planet… only because they were never shown or taught to believe that they are already connected to the Universal Force, or God, or whatever conception or non-conception of the magic of Life they hold.
>
> Now is time for more reflection and action.
>
> Action for justice and compassion.
>
> I wonder what shapes your "ink" is taking on "paper"… are you inspired? Blocked? Flowing?
>
> In togetherness, Sophie."

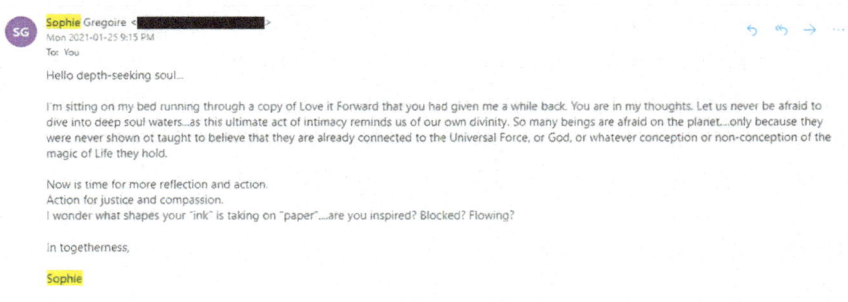

Chapter 10: I'm Here for You

I didn't actually want to respond, or to fawn, but silence seemed to trigger my worry. So, I responded a few days later, honestly, if somewhat indirectly. I suspected she knew what I meant...

Blocked indeed. I am so disappointed in people I believed in that I don't feel like doing much of anything. The world has become a very strange place, and I don't feel like writing a thing.

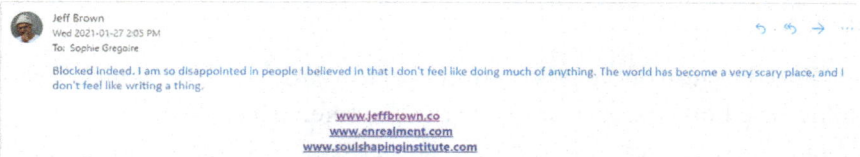

Hours later, she wrote me an email response that I perceived to be quite manipulative. In it, she endeavoured to remind me that there is no evolution without crisis, and encouraged me to clear any emotional debris that I am holding onto because I am a << clearer >> who is needed at the board so that others can flow, too. In other words, learn from what's happened, and get back to your calling to write. She signed the email: patient love, Sophie. It is important to note that she does not ask me who I am disappointed in, or why I am scared. Perhaps because she knows...

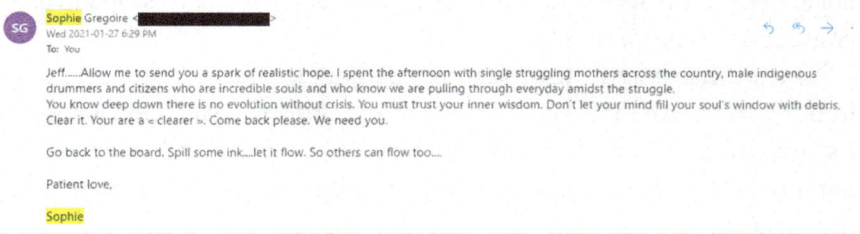

Now it gets even stranger (or more obvious, depending on your perspective). I had decided, at some point, that I wanted to talk with three journalists. I wanted to get a sense of three different perspectives, and understand how these kinds of stories were approached. I had a quick Facebook interaction with someone I had known from McMaster University who had written for the Hamilton Spectator. He suggested I connect with a particular journalist from the Spec. I left him a message early week, and he called back and left a message. I then called him from my second phone on Thursday January 28 around 1 PM. He responded that he wanted to talk but that he had a call now, and would call back between 130-2 PM.

I then received an email from Mrs. Trudeau at precisely **1:31 pm**:

Both because of the precise timing of the email, and that which it contains (the book excerpt of mine that she references which is essentially about not being reactive; the suggestion that she is here for me and that I am safe; the quickly written fumbled sentence {"May you allow the warmth loving hand..." etc.), I again came to the conclusion that she was aware I was engaged in media conversations, and wanted to claw me back. In other words, she knew something about what was going on with my phones. After all, she had already responded to my "Blocked indeed" email, and now she comes back, right at this key moment, to tell me I am safe, protected, and loved. Wrongly or rightly, I perceived this as a kind of a "Hail Mary," an over-the-top attempt to pull me back from the media edge. I did not respond to the email. I was finally ready to stop fawning, consequences be damned.

The journalist and I then met in a parking lot behind a grocery store in Burlington. We sat in our cars and chatted through the open windows. I shared my story, and found him to be very grounded and receptive. We left it there for now. I was still feeling cautious, confused. Not feeling like myself at all.

CHAPTER 11

Instadrama

In early February, I met with my lawyer friend. He had read the binder. When asked if there was a legitimate basis for a judge to grant CSIS or any other agency permission to wiretap, his response was clear: "Unequivocally no." Of course, that's not to say that there hadn't been an illegitimate basis. More than likely, it meant that the phone event was initiated "off book" – or it was granted by a misled judge i.e. a perjurious affidavit sworn to the effect that I *had* done something wrong.

With wrongdoing confirmed, I then turned my attention to passing the binder to a media outlet off-the-record. Without that information, I saw no other way for them to understand what would possibly motivate someone to get on my phone to intimidate me. Context was necessary. At the very least, I was wanting someone in the 'system' to read my story and hold onto the details of my experience. I thought about it, and felt most comfortable passing it to the editor I had sat on the bench with in High Park. Something about their cautious and sensible nature led me to trust them, as had the words uttered by the journalist who recommended them. And so, we agreed to meet at a downtown Toronto street corner, on another cold winter's day. The editor pulled up right on time, and I dropped the package on the front seat. They agreed to contact me after reading the documents.

Soon thereafter, I took the ferry to Toronto Island and took back the binder I had passed to my friend for safe-keeping. As the potential implications of the phone event landed within me, I became more and more concerned that I had unknowingly stumbled into a dangerous situation. And, if I was reading this right, that meant my 'safe-keeper' wasn't necessarily safe. I understand that this is not something Canadian's usually worry about, but it struck me as highly unlikely that the surveillance ended with the phone call. Perhaps if I had taken the bait, and backed off from handing the binder over, but not if I had forged on. I just couldn't shake the feeling that the monitoring lived on in some form, or another. Why wouldn't it, if someone was trying to protect political power, particularly if that power only had a minority government?

And then I turned my attention – in what little free time I had in my busy life – to explore the question of what to do about this. I hadn't been around the legal world for three decades, and had few lawyer connections, and no understanding of how to explore or report what appears to be politically motivated wrongdoing. Where does one turn in a strange situation like this? I began to reach out, usually by email, to a myriad of individuals who I thought might be helpful. Some responded and were open to interactions. Included among them: litigation lawyers, a former Prime Ministerial Chief of Staff (not with the current administration), a sitting Senator in the House of Commons, a retired Police Inspector that I had known for years. I also interacted with my longstanding defamation lawyer, who indicated that he wasn't getting some of the emails sent from my Hotmail account. He informed me that this hadn't happened in all his years of practice.

Others weren't open to talking, because they had no expertise in this area. Some simply didn't respond. And those I did speak with had their own opinion. Some said to let it go, others said to bring it through media, another said that I could possibly sue for a new tort–"seclusion intrusion"–a law that allows individuals to seek compensation for breaches of privacy–but that I would have to definitively prove who had ordered "the incident." Another suggested writing a fictional book about my experiences–something I explored now and then but that never felt right. Either I was going to bravely bring this story to the world, or I was going to find a way to let it go. The idea that I would turn this situation into an economically beneficial book opportunity didn't feel right. For sure, it would be rightful, and there had already been damages, but that was not a motivating factor for me. I had entered the dynamic with Mrs. Trudeau with a desire to serve, and even though I had come to lose respect for both her and her husband, I didn't want to write a book unless I had no choice. If I brought this forward, it would be as an act of service – to myself, in an effort to feel safe through public revealing – and to the public, because they surely had a right to know what was going on with people living off of them. Even if Mrs. Trudeau was not a formal employee of the government, she was deeply intertwined with the PMO, had one staffer (or more?) working directly under her, and she was fed, housed, protected, and driven about on the people's dime.

The one thing that I did want to do was to remove all remnants of Sophie Trudeau from my main website (jeffbrown.co). She was noted in my main website bio, my audio course landing page bios, and in the video section where our dialogue was most prominent. I had showcased the video – and included her in my bio, not because it was economically beneficial (as noted earlier, being politically affiliated is not to one's advantage) but because it had meant so much to me to have my words and ideas embraced in the halls of power. I was proud of it all, and yet, I was now horrified by those affiliations. What was once a source of pride was now a sense of deep remorse. But there was a problem with removing all the references. I was bringing forth my story during a pandemic, when a flurry of people were flooding the media et al. with their personal stories concerning abuse of authority. My website references of Sophie Trudeau might actually prove my legitimacy to those I had contacted about the story. If they saw that there was some solid history between me and Mrs. Trudeau, they might be more inclined to connect. I left it all up there, for now.

One of the people I spoke with suggested that I look to the RCMP as the possible culprit, because, again, their job is to protect the PM from real or perceived threats. So, I initiated a second privacy act request on March 15, 2021 (concerning the period from November 10, 2020 to present) to see if they had anything on file related to me. I had not yet received information relating to my initial request, but I was still hopeful that there was integrity somewhere to be found in the systems that protect us.

At the same time, I was riding a raucous river of feelings related to all of this. Like nothing I had ever known. I couldn't seem to find a way to lower my cortisol levels, despite regular massages and a number of psychologically restorative tools in my toolbox. My sleep was poor, and I was too tense to get on the yoga mat and stretch my body open. I was able to meet my basic working responsibilities, but my creatively spontaneous nature was nowhere to be found. Vigilance and terror make strange bedfellows.

I wasn't the only one who had difficulty processing these events. A number of friends that I spoke with were blown away. One, a powerful and successful professional, nearly crumbled to the ground when details of the story were shared. Others were so uncomfortable that they quietly retreated from our long-standing friendship. Some made it clear that it was too close for comfort because of their own histories with abuse of power. It wasn't that they didn't believe me – it was that they did.

Simply put, something about this messy story brought up everyone's inherent fear of power. Despite the fact that we lived in something called a "democracy," it was clear that – when push came to shove – nobody actually felt truly safe. And I couldn't help but think that the pandemic played a role in compounding people's general fear and mistrust. Because the last thing anybody wants during a time of great crisis, is to doubt the sturdiness of the man in charge. I could even feel the resistance within myself. From a purely psychological perspective, I experienced a need to believe that Trudeau had nothing to do with the incident. A very real part of me still wanted to believe that he was the man for the job.

One thing that was coming clear was just how *unbraved* we are a species. By unbraved, I mean that we are too terrified to honor our intrinsic value and speak truth about power. Whether we had actual experiences with political leadership, or had been conditioned to fear power by experiences with other abusers of authority, or it was woven into our DNA as a result of our ancestral lineage, we were one frightened humanity. No wonder nothing seemed to change worldwide with respect to the games played by the so-called elite. Most of us were hiding our light under a bushel of fear. Myself included.

The double bind continued to plague me. I would write things that I wanted to publish, and then quickly back off, too frightened to tell the story, yet too defiant to keep it all to myself. On a few occasions, I sat down and recorded elements of my story on Zoom. I found temporary comfort in the telling of the story. But there was no lasting comfort to be found, as I would only venture so far in the re-telling before retracting, due to my fear of consequences. The effect of the various events, combined with whatever personal and ancestral experiences I'd had with authority, left me frightened about what these evildoers would do next. I continued to bounce back and forth between repression and expression, like dancing to a broken record. One persistent step forward, one persistent step backwards, leaves you exactly where you were when you started. It is haphazard and chaotic, riddled with equal parts confusion and confidence. It's little wonder that people living inside of a double bind often get physically ill. The body is not built for this level of inner conflict and confusion. It is built to move in one direction or another, but not both at the same time.

Throughout this experience, and certainly by the time I sat down to really write this book, I understood that I was standing inside of something that was not just about me. It was about *all of us*. And particularly for the billions of people who had been abused by power in their lives – especially those who were not in a position to do anything about it. I felt a responsibility to go on. For myself, to be sure. But I also felt an obligation to go on for others. If a privileged white man couldn't see his way through this complex maze, how could we expect anyone else to? Even if "the incident" was not ordered by the Prime Minister, it was certainly ordered by someone. And that someone had overstepped their boundaries. It was my responsibility to get to the bottom of it, one way or another.

At some point, I sought out therapeutic support. It didn't take a genius to realize that I had PTSD. It showed up in my ongoing discomfort on the phone (Is my line tapped?), in the house (Is this house probed?), and in the anxious part of me that was waiting for the next shoe to drop. And, more classically, in my inability to relax on the couch where the phone had rung, in difficulty concentrating, in lack of interest in activities I usually enjoyed, in cataclysmic nightmares, and in having real difficulty holding the space for friend's personal challenges. I tried my best but I couldn't settle into their stories, while mine was so unsettled. Somehow, everything they talked about felt insignificant by comparison to my own pressing circumstances. Try as I might to regain my footing, I simply couldn't will it into being. I was someone who had been consistently grounded and decisive for years, but something about these particular events hit every button I had – even buttons that I never knew existed.

Any part of me that imagined that PTSD is something that you could pull yourself out of with the force of will, was entirely mistaken. I understood that not everybody would respond to a phone event and its related context in this way, but I also came to understand that trauma is a subjective experience. How an individual responds to an event is entirely dependent on who they are, their life experiences, and how they are internally organized. In other words, if someone says that they were traumatized by an event, they were traumatized. It doesn't mean they were necessarily wronged, but it does mean they felt traumatized. It's that simple. It makes no difference if we can relate to their experience, or if it fits into culturally approved trauma categories. What matters is that the person identified their experience as a trauma. I certainly identified "the incident" as a trauma, no matter how calmly 'Pam Grier' spoke to me. Because I knew what was behind it.

It's also worth noting that my anxiety wasn't entirely rooted in these precise events. I also had an underlying feeling that there was more to this than met the eye. In other words, that even if I backed off forever, these wrongdoers still wouldn't be done with me. One way or the other, they were going to make sure that I paid for my rejection of Mrs. Trudeau and her world, and for refusing to be intimidated into silence after "the incident." After all, who rejects (seeming) royalty?

I contacted a therapist that I had worked with years before, and we began weekly sessions. She was a capable talk therapist, and we worked our way through the events. In an effort to make sense of my response, and to explore a solution, we focused our attention on a method called "parts work." That is, identifying those parts of me that were firmly affixed to a certain event, and those parts of me that were inclined to let it go. Despite her noble efforts to persuade me that it was the feisty 14-year-old part inside of me that was holding onto this, I didn't budge. Because my protective 14-year-old wasn't merely a fractured aspect that had come into being to defend myself and others – he was actually a reflection of my true archetypal nature. It was no accident that I couldn't sit quietly when abused by power. I was born to stand it down.

* * *

My inner voice continued to insist on being publicly shared – posts, videos, comments on various pages. It wasn't necessarily in my best interest – expressing things publicly might just incite the wrongdoers to act out – but my expressive nature still couldn't contain itself. Nor could my belief in my right to candid and free expression. There were many moments when I would feel tempted to repress words that were rising into expression, and I would think of someone I knew who had suffered the consequences of repressing their rightful anger at those who had abused them. I would literally envision them trapped inside of their own unique double bind, and feel emboldened to speak my truth.

Some of the words that came through me during this phase of my journey are depicted below. If I couldn't extract justice, I could at least speak some personal truth and extract some semblance of wisdom. Something good had to come of this nightmare:[35]

> Sincere apology changes everything. Not politically motivated apologies, not agenda-driven apologies, not apologies rooted in fear. Genuine apologies. The kind that come right through the heart. The kind you can't help but make. The real ones.

> No one living in a democracy should have to live in fear of their political leadership. No one should have to worry about abuse of power directed at them from above. No one should have to fawn or cower before a bully or an invisibully. No one should have to wonder what will happen to them next. If they are, they are living in a fascist state.
>
> JEFF BROWN

CHAPTER 11: INSTADRAMA

Jeff Brown
March 24, 2021 · 🌐

I am relieved to report that I have severed all of my political associations. It was not easy. I stood firmly in support of Justin Trudeau's agenda, and Sophie's offerings. I will not be supporting either, again. I will also not be supporting my local liberal MP in the likely pandemic election. Nor will I be pivoting toward anyone else in the Canadian political world. That stage in my life is over. Stepping in that direction was a terrible mistake on my path. I was naive, and I should have trusted my intuition. I will not make that mistake again.

Jeff Brown
April 13, 2021 · 🌐

I have fought all my life for the light. Not the light bereft of darkness, but the light that is not ruled by it. It would be counter-productive, and antithetical to my commitment to the collective, to cower before the darkness at this stage of life. I have been preparing my whole life for the next courageous step. It has arrived in an entirely unexpected form, but so be it. We don't get to choose everything on our own. Sometimes the path is woven into being by forces within, and beyond us.

In an effort to move some of my anger through me, I contacted a Bioenergetics Therapist that I had trained with some years ago. Bioenergetics[36] is a body-centered psychotherapy that is premised on the idea that mind and body are functional reflections of each other. Our behavioral issues and personality defenses are perfectly mirrored within the body, manifesting as chronic muscle tensions and obstructed expression. To support healing and integration, the client engages in a series of physical exercises that energize the body, enliven the breath, soften blocks and holdings, and unearth the emotional material that is trapped inside. When repressed memories arise, the client is encouraged to explore and express them in visceral ways, including tantrums, crying, hitting, punching, kicking, spontaneous movements and sounds.

I knew that the feelings about this situation were building up inside my body. I felt a burning need to go to my basement and pound the Bioenergetics cube – a Bioenergetics cube is a foam structure that sits on the ground that one hits with a baseball bat or tennis racket, or with their feet or hands to move anger, rage and other emotions. The process usually begins with a variety of physically grounding and breathing exercises to ensure moving from a rooted and connected place within. Once grounded, the person begins to hit the cube, and to express any words or sounds that accompany the release. I had come downstairs to hit the cube often, but had found it difficult to fully let loose in my hyper-vigilant state.

Laurel helped me to find my voice. A masterful Bioenergetics practitioner, she understood the necessity for strong physical release, to reduce the tension I was holding, and to energize and empower me to carry on. When asked if she believed that I had to bring this story public, she exclaimed "yes!" with conviction. Because she was privy to something often lost in our Un-Braved world: the direct relationship between courageous self-expression <u>and</u> the living of an energized and empowered life. This is the very nature of buried emotions. When we repress them, we diminish and deaden our life force. When we express them, we bring ourselves back to life.

Laurel and I also engaged in a number of Tension & Trauma Releasing Exercises (TRE). Created by Bioenergetics therapist David Berceli, TRE® is an innovative series of exercises that assist the body in releasing deep muscular patterns of stress, tension, and trauma.[37] The exercises safely activate a natural reflex mechanism of shaking or vibrating that release muscular tension, equalizing the nervous system. When this vibrating mechanism is activated in a safe and controlled environment, the body is encouraged to return back to a natural state of balance.

TRE allowed me to get below the anger, and to come into contact with the grief and confusion that sourced it. It also brought me into contact with a vaster perspective. When you are in a state of hyper-vigilance, your whole consciousness is living in a linear state. On a sensory level, you can only take in that which serves your quest for safety. Most everything else is omitted from your moment-to-moment awareness. The shaking mechanism in TRE broke through that vigilance, and brought me back to a more expansive consciousness, if only for a while. From that perspective, I could again remember that there was a reality and a perspective beyond this anxiety-riddled framework. There was a path of relief waiting for me. I just had to find my way through.

With body-centered therapies to bolster me, the expressive little scrapper inside me began to take public revealing to the next level.

On May 11 2021, I put up a 'story' on Instagram that referenced an experience I had with the spouse of a political leader, one where she

Chapter 11: Instadrama

shared private details about her marriage, and herself. I referenced the importance of boundaries. It's important to note that Mrs. Trudeau has followed me on Instagram since July, 2018. And that a 'story' is not a permanent post on IG, but remain up for a limited period of time…

> I once spent some time with the spouse of a political leader. She shared all kinds of private details about her marriage, and herself. Shocking things that I didn't want to know, things that were none of my business. I never felt entirely safe holding that information. I worried that he would one day find out what I knew. There is something to be said for asking someone, before you share dangerous information with them. Give them the option, before it comes flying out of your mouth. Boundaries keep everyone safe, in this reactive world.
>
> JEFF BROWN

Soon after I put up the story, I received my first email from Mrs. Trudeau *in more than three months*, inviting me to talk:

I chose not to respond to her email. With respect to what prompted it, I'm no formal statistician, but I am an odds guy. It struck me as highly likely that she had read, or had someone monitor the story I had just put up, and that this was what inspired her to suddenly reach out. Members of the public would not know who my post was referencing, but she would. I did not respond because I was no longer in a fawning state, and had no interest in another coercive political conversation. What I did do was try to figure out which account was reading my story either as her, or for her. Her name was not on the list of people who had read my 'story,' nor had I ever noticed her there.

I investigated, and found an account that was following me and reading some of my stories. There was no way of knowing for sure given that there are many unnamed accounts on IG, but it felt like the kind of fake account a political person (or someone monitoring for them) would use to follow various accounts so the public won't know who they are following. It was private, with a generic name, zero followers, and yet it was following 188 accounts.

I decided to further investigate by requesting to follow it. Private accounts require permission to follow. When requested, they have a few options – reject, ignore, block, or accept the ask. In this case, they did none of the above. They immediately left Instagram. Now I know this doesn't definitively prove that it was Mrs. Trudeau, and I also understand that it is probably not illegal to be watching someone's posts and story if you are worried about what they might say publicly, but the idea that Canada's Leading Lady, while living in a home with the PM, is possibly watching (or having a friend/corporation/government agency watch) your every word, doesn't feel particularly safe, especially in this context.

Soon thereafter, I contacted the Ethics Commissioner of Canada to look into the possibility of reporting some of the events to them. I asked a few questions, received a few answers, and decided not to go that route at this time. I had been told that if the Ethics Commissioner felt it appropriate, he could refer the case to the RCMP to investigate. But given that the RCMP had still not properly responded to either of my Privacy Act requests, I was not feeling particularly trusting of them. I did give some serious consideration to writing another termination email to Mrs. Trudeau, though. I wrote a prominent law firm to inquire if they could write a formal termination letter to Mrs. Trudeau, but before I could hear back, I was onto the next step. There is no clear blueprint for how to proceed in a strange situation like this.

Chapter 11: Instadrama

Then things got weirder. On May 17, 2021, I posted this on my Instagram...[38]

> I have no capacity to engage in conversations that aren't entirely truthful and brave. I love courageous conversations that clarify confusion and heal the rifts. Where everyone makes admission and owns their mistakes. Cryptic, misleading, politically staged conversations are an insult to everyone's intelligence. And a waste of everyone's time. Real talk, or no talk at all.
>
> ## JEFF BROWN

A few days later I received the strangest Direct Message (DM) from a relatively dormant IG account not known to me.[39] The main image appeared to be a woman with a fake beard that concealed part of her face. Here is the content of the conversation. My responses are in italics…

> You're a disgusting pig who should be in jail.
> *Jail for?*
> Before answering, I'd like to know if you're willing to acknowledge knowing who I am and why? Without this honesty, we'd only be perpetuating the cycle of dishonesty, which would be a further waste of both our time.
> *I do not know who you are from your name or image. Why don't you tell me?*
> Do you know who I am?
> *I answered that already*

Don't know who I am or was it that you don't know who I am based on my name or image?

Both

Please clarify

Are you claiming that you don't know who am based on my image, name, or anything else that might become recognizable?

I don't want to play these games.

You know who I am. Word games you might win doesn't change this fact. Seriously, be grateful for the time and attention I gave you and then fuck off.

Grateful.

What do you mean that? Are you implying you're grateful? If you are, why the implied message? Why not proudly claim and declare that?

You'd rather play word games.

What's your real name?

Omg, seriously fuck off.

Based on the threat (not unlike the stranger threat communicated to me on Facebook in January), the sentence "Be grateful for the time and attention I gave you and then fuck off," and the timing right after I put up a post about cryptic, misleading, politically staged conversations a few days earlier, I wondered if it was one of the Trudeaus (or a minion) using someone else's page to communicate with me. Page commandeering was said to be quite common on Meta. But how could I know?

So, I posted the image on one of my FB pages and asked people if the image behind the beard looked familiar. Without being prompted, a number of people said it looked like Sophie Trudeau. I also posted a query with the image on my Instagram. Soon thereafter, someone who followed me there informed me that they had written one of the people following the page to see if they knew who owned it. The latter claimed that it was owned by her schizophrenic aunt who she had very little contact with. So, I let it go. But I always wondered how the 'Aunt' who contacted me, would be writing me with things that seem so specific to the things that were transpiring. After all, I had refused to respond to both of Mrs. Trudeau's last emails to me – end of January, and the week before. The domineering writing style didn't feel like Mrs. Trudeau (although she uses the adolescent OMG frequently in emails) but it would not surprise me if it was someone trying to protect the Trudeau's politic. If so, then I have to wonder if the 'person'

CHAPTER 11: INSTADRAMA

who contacted the 'niece' was real, or if both they – and the niece – were also part of this deflection game.

As I would soon find out, this kind of conundrum would become a very real part of my life. The question of who is making contact – and why – pervades much of this story, except when I make a big step towards public revealing and then they come out and show themselves much more clearly. This will become much more obvious in the following chapters.

(Sidenote: As I will reiterate later, I went back in 2024 or so and my FB and IG postings asking if people recognizing the pic, were removed. Not by me. And the profile was gone altogether, until quite recently when it was back again...)

Soon enough, Mrs. Trudeau did what wild horses do – she broke through the gate and again got in my face. On Saturday evening, June 12, I felt empowered to create and post a video on IG.[40] The video mentioned that I was finally feeling ready to come out from the shadows to talk about something that I had been struggling to reveal. <u>About one hour later</u>, I received an email from Mrs. Trudeau confirming that the video had been sent to her by her rockstar friend:

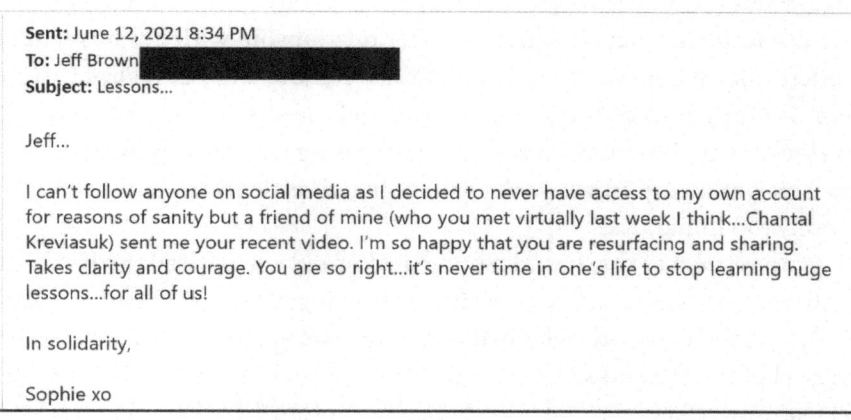

Sent: June 12, 2021 8:34 PM
To: Jeff Brown
Subject: Lessons...

Jeff...

I can't follow anyone on social media as I decided to never have access to my own account for reasons of sanity but a friend of mine (who you met virtually last week I think...Chantal Kreviasuk) sent me your recent video. I'm so happy that you are resurfacing and sharing. Takes clarity and courage. You are so right...it's never time in one's life to stop learning huge lessons...for all of us!

In solidarity,

Sophie xo

Mrs. Trudeau's quick response to this video led me to believe that she was in a state of high anxiety about me and feeling concerned that I was going public. And the words expressed in the email only served to intensify my worry. By this time, I'd had enough of feeling monitored, or, at the least, being a point of attention by someone living in the Prime Minister's residence. I wanted to be free from all ties. I then sent Wildhorse my third (and final) attempt to terminate on June 13, 2021. I'm not sure I could have been any clearer:

> **From:** Jeff Brown ▮▮▮▮▮▮▮▮▮▮▮▮▮▮▮▮
> **Sent:** June 13, 2021 9:42 PM
> **To:** Sophie Gregoire <▮▮▮▮▮▮▮▮▮▮▮▮▮▮▮▮>
> **Subject:** Re: Lessons...
>
> Sophie. This is the last time I will write you. I am writing to reiterate what I expressed in December. I do not want anything to do with you, or your political world. It is unkind and unfair, and it is not for me. I gave from my heart, and my heart now says no. When you reach my age, you will understand how clear things become. Respect my request, precisely as you would want others to respect yours if you had made it. Please do not bother to respond to this email. Respect my boundary and leave me be. Sincerely, Jeff

My recollection is that I then stopped following Mrs. Trudeau on Instagram. I was finally feeling a little stronger and more empowered again after months of fright and a myriad of PTSD symptoms.

It's a difficult thing to describe – particularly if someone carries the assumption that the 'Leading Lady' of a country is an emotionally mature adult – but I honestly felt like I was dealing with some combination of mob boss – words like *solidarity* led me to wonder – and a reactive teenager, who somehow imagined that we were merely having an easily resolved high-school spat. I hearkened back to that moment in her home when she disclosed intimate details about her relationship with her husband. I understand that he was just 'Justin' to her, but did she not realize that he was also the leader of a G-7 nation? And that the effect of having someone married to the PM worried about you exposing her publicly, would scare the shit out of any citizen? Was she too narcissistic to appreciate this, or merely too immature?

With respect to the 'friend' Sophie had noted who shared my IG video with her, she was a well-known Canadian singer named Chantal Kreviazuk (properly spelled) who had begun following me on Instagram some weeks before. When I saw that, I admit to wondering if she had been sent to read my posts or to be a bridge of resolution between me and Mrs. Trudeau. Soon after following me, she shared some of my writings, and asked me to do an IG live with her. *After* doing the live, she wrote me that she had checked out my bio, and saw that I was connected with her friend, Sophie Gregoire Trudeau.

When I found out she was the one who passed my video to Mrs. Trudeau that Saturday night, I wrote her and accused her of monitoring me for Mrs. Trudeau. She thoroughly denied it. It seemed like an odd kind of video to share with Sophie right after it went public, if you didn't know *something* about this context. But the truth is that it is impossible for me to know. I do know that I had also written Chantal some months before, with a question related to a song I had co-written with Laura Sgroi ("Our Love is a Virus"[41]). And that may well have been the very organic reason she connected with me months later. The very active sharing of my work may well have been a function of the fact that she checked it out and it resonated. And the passing of that video to Mrs. Trudeau was perhaps little more than a sharing rooted in their apparently mutual interest in truth-speak.

Either way, Chantal played a significant role in this story. Because the passing of the video led to a sequence of events that finally severed me from Mrs. Trudeau and her political world. Free at last, or so I imagined at the time.

CHAPTER 12

Dim Sum

Thereafter, I felt emboldened to go public. Not with just some of it, but all of it. And I would again come close, sharing pieces of my experience with my followers, in video form. For example, I put two videos up on Instagram that came very close to a full reveal. On June 14, I published a video[42] called "Thawing out after a difficult experience" that spoke of my emotional process with respect to these events. In particular, I spoke to the ways that undigested trauma lives itself out in our physical body and permeates all areas of our life. In the second video "Trauma is a subjective experience," I discuss a number of things, including the relationship between my male conditioning and my PTSD. That is, my own internalized judgments about having such a strong subjective response to these events.[43]

And then the fear would return to stop me, along with something else. I had this idea in my head that I wanted help from the system itself. Before these events, I would not have looked to the system to help me. I knew its inherent limitations, and I had a longstanding tendency to take my empowerment into my own two hands. But I was weakened and I experienced the phone interception – and various earlier and subsequent events – as a denial of my personal rights as a Canadian. Call me naïve, or unduly optimistic, or just plain masochistic, but I kept hearing myself say, "I want my rights back," in the back of my mind. I wanted my right to privacy back. I wanted my right to free speech back. I wanted the return of my rights to life, liberty, and security of the person. My grandfather and uncles had risked their lives for our natural-born rights during WW2, and I wanted them back. And, I wanted the violation of those rights to be acknowledged and returned by the system itself.

Soon enough, I contacted the editor that was holding my story. We had been in periodic contact since early February. At first, when I became concerned for both mine and my wife's health and decided to let this go. Then, when I notified them that I wanted to continue. They had read the binder, and were allegedly giving themselves time to process their thoughts. I was fine with that, given that I too was processing these experiences. Something about it simply being in the hands of media was enough for me back then, although I did take notice of the fact that they did not respond to a series of emails – and did not get back to me when they said they would on a few occasions.

In any event, now that I felt ready to shift from off to on-the-record, I reached out. We had a phone conversation, and they agreed to speak with their higher-ups to see what they thought. A few weeks later, they indicated that they couldn't publish this story because of Mrs. Trudeau. I didn't quite understand what that meant, but I did ask to meet so I could retrieve the binder. We met in a downtown Toronto neighborhood and had a good talk. And then they said something that helped me to understand what was going on here: "Justin deserves another term because of his performance during the pandemic."

I didn't know which of his performances they were referring to, but there it was. In a nutshell, whether a citizen's situation gets turned over to an investigative journalist, takes a back seat to an editor's political perspective. This shouldn't have surprised me. This was the same person who told me that their decision to publish various things was not based on what engaged the public (i.e. what they click on), but on what was actually good for them. In other words, not what the public *was* interested in, but what they *should* be interested in.

The question is obvious: Who is qualified to make that decision and shape society? Surely not a politically motivated editor, unless they can definitively prove that they are the great Seer we have all been waiting for. If not, then it's probably best to investigate all reasonable allegations – left, right, or center. And, if they carry weight, to publish them so that the people living in the democracy can decide for themselves whether the story is meritorious. Because no one is more qualified to determine public interest than the people themselves. If the people click on it, it is in the public interest. End of story.

This was my first, but surely not my last, experience with story suppression and the politicization of media. And not the last time I had to consider the question of whether certain media outlets actually hold onto a story, not because they may one day publish it, but because they want to be sure that it never reaches the public's awareness. Neutral, unbiased, investigative journalism is becoming extinct in our society.

I wrote and mailed a letter to the Privacy Commissioner of Canada to see if they could influence the production and release of what I had requested in my two Privacy Act requests re: RCMP on November 10/2020, and March 15/2021. One of the Privacy Commissioner's functions is to initiate an investigation when government agencies refuse to provide the requested information in a timely manner. To this point, I had received nothing in the way of a meaningful response. My letter was received by them on June 29, 2021, and an investigator tasked with the file soon thereafter.

I then made a series of efforts to reach out to a variety of journalists. Some I connected with, and then backed off. Some backed off from me. I continued to dialogue with a spectrum of other individuals about the potential directions I could take. One of them was a famous Canadian whistle-blower, who gave generously of his time. He was particularly astute with respect to Canadian media, and made it clear that no Canadian media outlet would ever run a story like this about a PM or a PM's wife. He seemed to know what he was talking about. He wasn't the only one to communicate that view. A well-connected Canadian journalist said the same thing, and when asked if my life was in danger in this situation, the journalist answered affirmatively.

One night, my wife had a dream that perfectly reflected the state that I was in. In it, I was going from door to door on my street, trying to get somebody, anybody, to help me. It was symbolic of course, but it did feel true to the disempowered nature of my experience. Except that I wasn't actually knocking on my neighbor's doors. I was knocking on the doors of strangers, many of whom were part of a system that wasn't designed to go out on a limb for a fellow stranger. At least not for one that wasn't aligned with their politics.

I continued to share my unfolding thoughts in written and video form, on Facebook.[44]

On July 22, 2021, I spoke off-the-record about this situation with a sharp-as-a-tack Canadian investigative journalist, on my alternate phone. We had a very detailed conversation, one where they

Jeff Brown
July 24, 2021

This has been the most difficult and confusing 8 months of my adult life. I have relied on a giant toolbox of techniques and resources, and it has not been enough. Sometimes, things happen that cannot be met by our skillset. They require skills that we have not yet developed. A situation that has continued to be uncomfortable, has NOT abated, and continues to challenge my patience. Some people don't know when to stop. It is my prayer that the situation finds its way to a sweet harbour, but I have my doubts. They say that you find out who your real friends are, when crisis comes. This has been my experience. People have arrived from unexpected places and been a great comfort to me. Thank you. And, all the while, the lessons keep on coming. I am built for lessons, and for finding my way through challenging landscapes. All support is welcome as I traverse the strangest terrain imaginable.

expressed a desire to explore my story, despite confirming that their media outlet was also unlikely to bring any story that intertwined with the personal life of a PM. Unlike in the US – where the personal details of a leader's life are always considered newsworthy – Canadian media contains it, perhaps imagining that the sordid details of a leader's life are inimical to our polite nature. Nonetheless, this free-thinking journalist made a commitment to explore the details.

The call happened from 1 pm to 2:11 pm. At 1:59 pm, right as we were winding down the call, a Liberal party text was sent through to my phone from the phone number 365-650-4053: "Hi, it's Amy with Justin Trudeau's liberals. Can we count on your support in the next election, whenever it arrives?"

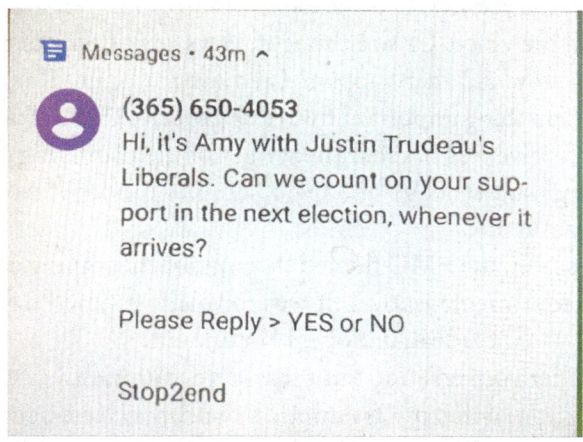

"Justin Trudeau's Liberals?" What, does he own the joint?

I saw the text right after the call ended. It's important to note that this is the same phone I had used to speak with media in January, calls that were interestingly timed with subsequent emails from Mrs. Trudeau. Interestingly, I now had this new phone and number for about 30 weeks, and I had scarcely received any texts on it (and certainly not the liberal party texts that were going around some time ago). And I had seldom used this phone, and never added this number to any phone lists of any kind, and certainly not a Liberal party list. Yes, I get that the phone text at the end of my call with the journalist can be labeled "synchronicity," but it seems highly unlikely. I believe that it is far more likely that someone politically motivated was listening to me on this phone, heard the things that were shared, and that the journalist expressed an interest in pursuing the story, and sent this text as yet another way of trying to intimidate me into silence by letting me know they are there. Given that Mrs. Trudeau was so concerned about public revealing prior to the phone interception, it makes complete sense to me that whoever was playing these games with me now had even more reason to frighten me into silence. Because I hadn't backed off.

I bounced back and forth between righteous anger and misguided attempts at forgiveness. I didn't actually want to forgive Mrs. Trudeau, but my now worn-out nervous system did. I was exhausted, and unconsciously seeking some form of relief. One night, after watching and crying to the brilliant Nick Cage film, *Pig*,[45] I made a forgiveness video and put it up on Instagram. I figured that, one way or the other, either Mrs. Trudeau or her minions would watch it, and we could all move on. But then I woke up in the morning, angry at myself for even considering forgiveness in this situation. I deleted the video. Or so I thought. Days later, to my dismay, I found it still there – how did that happen? I removed it again. If nothing else, I had learned something important from this debacle. That is, that sometimes people feign forgiveness because the weight of their suffering is simply unbearable. They want to let go and live again. But it doesn't work if the forgiveness is inauthentic.

A few days later, the PMO floated the possible beginning of an election campaign to four media outlets. It was formally initiated days later – on August 15 – when Trudeau dissolved Parliament.

I had another conversation with the same journalist I had last spoken with. They indicated that my assumption that it may have been the RCMP on my phone was unlikely to be true. I had been making that assumption as of late, because the RCMP had refused to provide a proper reply to my two Privacy Act requests. It was the journalist's view that this was not something the RCMP would do, and that I should call "the incident" into the RCMP division that focuses exclusively on potential wrongdoing by Members of Parliament. I wasn't quite ready for that, but what I was ready for was to connect with former RCMP officers, to see what they thought about this situation. I went online and located three of them that were now in the private 'security' field.

The first, I emailed about the wiretap. He was very succinct and clear that it wouldn't have been the RCMP. He also said that I should be reporting "the incident" to law enforcement.

The second person was fascinating. I emailed him with a bit of context, and he was good enough to arrange a meal with me in Toronto's Chinatown on August 18, 2021. I arrived early, and staked out the street corner like the amateur sleuth that I was. As it turns out, he was staking me out at the same time, but in a far more professional way – from the window of the drug store across the street. After we met, he took me to an old-style Chinese restaurant. Some of the best dim sum I have ever eaten.

I shared details of my story, and he shared fascinating details of his long history with law enforcement. This guy had seen it all. He suggested that I sue, or that I write a fictional book based on my experiences. I again ventured to ask the question: Is my life at risk? He responded that I was lucky a brick hadn't landed on my head. He seemed to know what he was talking about. He also revealed how easy it is for skilled professionals to penetrate and disable your house alarm, and to quickly install audio probes in the house. According to him, they enter with a painter and a drywaller, so they can quickly cover over any holes they had to drill. When I asked why he was helping me, he responded that he done some bad things in his time, and now he wanted to do good things. I believed him.

He also confirmed that the RCMP was very unlikely to have initiated the phone interception in December, both because they have no allegiance to political power, and because they were too protective of their pensions to risk being involved in anything like this. If it had been the RCMP, I should have received the required letter after the wiretap is concluded. In Canada, it is legally mandatary that the person under formal surveillance is notified after it is complete. He also indicated that the other RCMP officer that I had contacted – the one who firmly said that I should contact law enforcement about the phone event – was very credible and trustworthy. This leaned me in the direction of finally calling it in. When it came time to pay for our dim sum, he wouldn't let me. I was grateful for my time with this generous man.

The next day, I had a Zoom from home with the third investigator – a former RCMP member who had once run their wiretap office. I shared details of my story, and then it got weird. His mood changed after I mentioned the Trudeaus, and he firmly asserted that I should contact Mrs. Trudeau to let her know that I was not going public with anything. This was not something I had any interest in doing – I was not going to kiss Trudeau ass – but his intense reaction was notable. It was almost like something was personally at stake for him. When we were done, he insisted that I don't pay him for his time. Nonetheless, I sent him an e-transfer.

CHAPTER 13

CALLING THE COPS

I searched online for the RCMP department that deals with Members of Parliament and emailed them. Although I wish I had taken this step earlier, I was operating from a misunderstanding of who may have been responsible for tapping my phone, and I just wasn't ready. But I had enough of living like this. I simply did not feel safe as a Canadian. It was impacting every facet of my life: my physical and emotional health, my marriage, my sleep, my creative and professional life.

On Friday August 27, a RCMP Constable called me. We had a good talk. I laid it all out for him, and he informed me that the rule is that allegations of wrongdoing have to be called in locally first. If local police need help, they will then contact the RCMP. He asked if he could check with his supervisor and call me back.

Soon after, I received a call from him. He stated that they concluded that I should first report this to the police in Ottawa because it was arguable that the initiating event occurred there (my visit to Trudeau's home). He also noted it would likely come back to his RCMP division – because they do have a team who investigate wiretaps and hacking.

So, I called the Ottawa police force. They responded – for jurisdictional reasons – that I should first contact my local police.

I called the Hamilton Police that evening. To my surprise, I heard back from an officer a few minutes later. Because I didn't want to share many details on the phone, we agreed to arrange a time on the weekend for someone to come by, or for me to visit the precinct. Hours later, while we were sleeping, the house alarm went off in the basement and startled us awake. This was the first time it had gone off for no apparent reason since it was installed two years prior. And it wouldn't be the last time it went off at key moments in this story.

The next morning, two Hamilton officers and a Social Worker arrived at my door early. I was surprised to see them. We all sat down at the dining room table, and discussed the situation. The social worker informed me he was making a note that I was of sound mind, something they had to

Chapter 13: Calling the Cops

confirm before considering an investigation. They were eager to get their hands on a copy of the binder, so I agreed to put together a USB stick for them in a few days.

Early the next morning, the house alarm went off again for no *apparent* reason. It wouldn't go off again until 2022.

This occurrence felt similar to the phone interception. Events often seemed to serve a dual purpose: to let me know that they are there (whoever *they* are), and to also make me afraid or rattle me. Interestingly, they were elements still difficult to pin down or precisely identify. But that seemed to be part of *the game*. Create smoke and mirrors. Instill doubts and confusion. Baffle. Confound.

A few days later, one of the officers arrived at our home quite early in the morning to pick up the USB stick. I think this was the first time in nine months that I felt safe in my own home and as a Canadian. Because you can trust the cops, right? Sure you can. 😊

In the weeks that followed, I made a few calls to the Police precinct to check in on any new developments. At first, I was told that the matter had been handed to two detectives – neither of whom called me back. It was then passed on to a man named Detective Sgt. Knapp. I proceeded to leave him a few voice messages. I heard back from him sometime between September 18-22. It was an odd conversation. He seemed harried and impatient, and told me something to the effect that the RCMP wasn't going to reveal to them if I was under surveillance. When I suggested preparing a summary of the binder for him, so he wouldn't have to read hundreds of pages, he agreed but said "there is no hurry." I made the assumption that there wasn't a rush because they were so busy during the pandemic. But now I am more inclined to see this conversation as an indication that something had already transpired in the case, that shifted them from quite eager ... to not interested.

Despite the officer indicating that there was no rush, I emailed him the summary of the binder contents on September 27. He did not respond.

* * *

On Thursday September 30, 2021, I posted one of my abuse-of-power political writings on Instagram.[46] The next day, I included a familiar piece about not wanting to participate in cryptic, misleading political conversations.[47]

That same day, things got bizarre on Instagram again. I noticed that a page in the name of Xavier James Trudeau (Justin's eldest son) had just begun following me on Instagram. It appeared to be a recently created account, with a picture of Xavier as its main profile image. The account used the Liberal party website as its visible off-link and included the oddest message (for a kid) in the caption below it: "My goal is to create a life that I don't want to take a vacation from. You are never too old to set a new goal or to dream a new dream." It struck me that an adult might be contemplating a transition to a more balanced lifestyle – but a 12-year-old?

The account had also posted an image – Justin with all 3 of the kids on a beach in wetsuits. The caption underneath read: *Always love surfing with my family.*

Based on the history of bizarre happenings on IG, I wondered if this was yet another strange attempt to communicate with me, or scare me into silence. Not from the kid – but from the (seeming) adults playing these games with me. After all, Trudeau has just won a minority government, but was not yet sitting again as the Prime Minister. Had my posts about abuse of power triggered the protection team, yet again? Or was this just some random person playing games on the internet?

I inquired further and it seemed that the Trudeaus had flown to Tofino, B.C., on Thursday, September 30 for a vacation. The Prime Minister's publicly posted daily schedule indicated that he would spend the day in private meetings in Ontario, yet he was spotted with his family on the beach in B.C.[48]

As it turns out, September 30 was the very first National Day for Truth and Reconciliation in Canada. This new federal holiday honors thousands of indigenous children who were forced to be assimilated into Can-

Chapter 13: Calling the Cops

ada's state-backed residential school system. Leaders of the Tk'emlups te Secwepemc Nation – located near the site of the former Kamloops residential school, where the unmarked graves of 215 children were said to be discovered in May – told Canadian media that they had written twice to Mr. Trudeau requesting that he visit their community on Thursday. He didn't, and was hit with considerable criticism for it in the week to come.[49]

I took a closer look at the Instagram account over the course of the day, and it seemed clear that the creator of this page had chosen to follow 89 accounts, most already followed by Sophie and Justin's pages. This would make it look more credible as a legitimate Trudeau page, and of course, putting the pic of Justin and the Liberal party link would be immediately visible.

Before I went to bed on October 2, 2021, I put up an IG post with the young Trudeau boy's supposed account, AND I tagged Sophie Trudeau and the account owner, asking them to confirm if it was really Xavier.[50]

When I woke up that morning, there were various comments on my post, including a direct message to me (and a comment on the post) from what appeared to be Xavier sent from his real account[51] letting me know that this account following me was fake, and that he had reported it. I also had some messages from people indicating that the fake account owner had also been posting on my wall, trying to save face by disagreeing with comments – that no child would write such words about being "never too old to dream."

When I looked again, the fake account was gone from IG. The deletion was not likely because the account was a bot (they don't self-remove), or because people had reported it. It is my understanding that they usually remain up for days and weeks after being reported. So, the fake account owner must have removed it. I interpreted this as fear of exposure. Even if the fake account was not in any way connected to the Trudeaus, just the fact that they responded so quickly to this tag made me uncomfortable. In general, tagging any political person's page would seldom elicit a response, and certainly not such a rapid one. Mrs. Trudeau had specifically told me that she was disengaging from social media. And the fact that the real Xavier James Trudeau appears to have been sent right onto my wall to tell me that the fake account wasn't him, made me equally as uncomfortable. Strange goings-on, on the I-Gram.

Yet again, I considered letting this entire situation go. I was utterly exhausted from 10 months in a fight-or-flight hormonal response, and well aware of the perils associated with what I had walked my way into. And, I felt more isolated than I had in decades. Not to say that I was all alone

– but the vanishing act recently performed by some of my closest friends was impossible to miss.

Nonetheless, I couldn't stop. I was propelled forward by some strange and unknown force. I wasn't clear if it was a heroic or a foolish journey at this stage, but I knew that I had no choice but to walk it.

So, I continued to look for the just right reporter to investigate my story. One afternoon, an article in the Toronto Star newspaper caught my eye. It was about the Pandora Papers, and it was co-written by an investigative journalist named Robert Cribb. I searched his name on YouTube, and watched a three-minute video with him talking about the importance of quality journalism in our society. I liked him. Although I knew that the Toronto Star was a Liberal leaning newspaper, I had a sentimental attachment to it. My beloved Uncle Joe Perlove had written sports for them for years, and the Star had been the newspaper of choice for my family thereafter.

I reached out to Cribb on October 3. I heard back from him the next day. We had an in-depth phone conversation, and I sent him a variety of details soon thereafter.

On October 13, 2021, I called the Liberal party to look into whether my suspicions regarding the context for the July Liberal Party text were accurate. I recorded the phone call. I gave the person I spoke with the number of my alternate phone where I received the text. He confirmed that this number was *not* on the list where they send political texts. This confirmed my belief that my call with the news person was likely monitored and that the text was deliberately sent as yet another way of letting me know they are watching me. I continued to note that these indicators were usually somewhat faint, but got stronger when they hear, see, or read about me doing something that ignited their fear of being publicly revealed. In other words, when I make a big step forward, my invisi-bullies emerge from the woodwork and become more VISIBLE.

The next day, I emailed Detective Sgt. Knapp to confirm that he had received the binder summary I sent in September. I also alerted him to the fact that I had "found relevant evidence of the prior illegal surveillance on my second phone." I was referring to the Liberal Party text. I also left about a half a dozen messages for him in the month of October. No reply to anything.

I began to feel concerned about why I wasn't hearing back from the cops. They had seemed so eager to get their hands on this information, and then they go MIA. I began to pore over the criminal code with an eagle's eye. Not because I had done anything wrong, but because I was worried about being falsely accused of wrongdoing by a politically influenced and data-manipulating detective. I then reached out to a friend who was a true afficionado of the Criminal Code. We discussed the situation, and we both agreed that there was no legal basis to charge me. It was the *illegal* basis that continued to worry me.

Robert Cribb and I arranged to meet for the first time in front of the public library in the Toronto Beaches. As I drove there from the Hamilton area, I found myself envying the people who raced past me in their cars. Not to say that their lives were easy, but most of them probably didn't have an extra layer of terror hanging over them. The whole idea that I was driving to Toronto to share details of my Trudeau-related experience felt surreal. And, given the persistently hyper-stressed state of my body, it felt utterly real at the same time. The body knows when there is peril, and it can't be fooled.

Cribb and I went on a long walk down to the beach and along the boardwalk before sitting down at a picnic table. I felt very comfortable with him. He reminded me of the journalist (Bob Woodward) that Robert Redford played in the film 'All the President's Men.' We shared a variety of things with each other, and drew up an initial game plan. I granted him exclusivity to the story, and got down to business. Included on my to-do list was a cause-and-effect document that I subsequently emailed on October 27. We were off to the races.

Included in Cribb's sharing was something quite shocking. Something he said that The Star had recently heard from the RCMP. It actually took me a few minutes to digest it. I shared it over the years in phone conversations with friends, and often suffered for it in the form of cut-off calls and intensification of threats. (When later asked when that info was going to become public knowledge, Cribb said "where there's smoke, there's fire.")

At some point in November, I met my Chinatown Investigator contact for another round of dim sum. Same restaurant, except this time he let me pay. Just before we parted on Dundas Avenue, he looked me square in the eyes and firmly stated: "Don't trust ANYBODY with this. And, if you get into trouble, contact me." Of course, I was still at the stage where I was wanting to trust somebody with this, but his words stayed with me and proved to be prescient.

I leaned into the idea of writing a book about these experiences. My agent suggested that I put together a book description, which she would share with a small and select group of publishers. I could feel the longing to write my story taking root inside – I wanted my voice back after looking for help in all the wrong places – yet I was resistant to writing a whole book. Both because I was still too emotionally engaged with the material, and because I still found the idea of making money from this experience off-putting. Not that I didn't deserve some. In the time I had spent on this, I could have created a whole bevy of helpful and lucrative courses. Yet I still couldn't shake the idea that I wanted help *within* the system, itself. If only I could get the support I needed, I could save myself the time of having to engage in a long writing process, and just get on with my life.

At the same time, I had some idea of what I was up against. After all, I'd been informed by those "in the know" that the Canadian media would not disclose this story.

I quickly put together a book description for my agent and prepared a little area in my house for my next book – not one I ever had envisioned on my book-writing bucket list.

On November 30, 2021, I received a formal letter from the Office of the Privacy Commissioner of Canada (OPCC). In it, I was notified that the RCMP had chosen not to fulfill either of my Privacy Act requests ("Deemed Refusal") and that my requests were – in the view of the Privacy Commissioner – "well-founded." In other words, they had done all that they could to get information, and no information was forthcoming. The RCMP could have said any number of things – that nothing appeared in relation to my name, that my request was incomplete. They chose to say nothing at all. Why?

In the letter, I was also made aware of the option of appealing their refusal-to-provide information. In other words, I had an opportunity to explore it further, if I was willing to initiate an application for judicial review at the Federal Court of Canada.

On December 10, 2021, I emailed a prominent local law firm to see if they could help with the appeal. On the same day, I had a lively phone call with another lawyer, and he indicated that he could help me to prepare and bring the application. I had no experience with the Privacy Act, nor with the notoriously daunting Federal Court, and I didn't have the energy to learn about and engage in a complex court process. Yet how could I get answers, if I didn't try?

On December 16, 2021, I received two strangely timed and unexpected emails from the RCMP. They were suddenly impelled to respond to my requests, weeks after their refusal had opened the door to a Federal Court Appeal. (Had someone heard my phone call with the lawyer about proceeding?) The first email related to my now 13-month-old initial Pri-

Chapter 13: Calling the Cops

vacy Act request. The other, to my 9-month-old second request. In both emails, they requested I send an email confirming that I had received the information. Attached to each was a letter indicating that they had conducted a search for records in "Ottawa, Ontario," and they were unable to locate any that related to my request. There was nothing on file in my name, and that included my conversations and emails with the Constable I had connected with in August.

Ninety minutes after I received the RCMP emails, I drove toward Rockwood, Ontario, north of Hwy 401 on Guelph Line. Moments after I passed the Petro-Canada gas station on the right, I noticed there was a vehicle behind me, closing in quickly, with very bright lights. It appeared to be some kind of a large white jeep. As it drew menacingly close, I turned quickly into the entrance to Brookville Park on the right, and then immediately swung around to turn towards Guelph Line.

The ominous white vehicle turned into the driveway only seconds after I did – without pre-signaling – and it sped straight in. I must have tricked it by turning back towards Guelph Line. As it passed, I noticed it was a makeshift model I had never seen. Kind of like a patch-worked Hummer, but it didn't seem to have all the usual markings. Whatever it was, it was a vehicle that you could not miss. It was evident that it was determined to get my attention, and/or intimidate me. Once back onto Guelph line, I watched for it in my rear-view for some time, but didn't see it come back out from the park. Impossible to say if this was all just a coincidence, but it didn't feel like it. It felt deliberate and intentional.

In the weeks to follow, I met with two Conservative publishers. Both were interested in my story. One of them was already talking about a July publish date, and he was eager to proceed. I quite liked him, but I took a step back. There were logistical reasons for this. I needed to talk things through with lawyers, and my wife had a biopsy scheduled for a small lump on her arm for January 21. Suddenly, that eclipsed all my other concerns.

On December 30, I sent my final email to Detective Sgt. Knapp. I wished him happy holidays, and again informed him that I had confirmatory evidence of wrongdoing re: the Liberal Party text. I also informed him that other strange things had happened since sending him the summary, and that I was considering the Privacy Act Appeal in Federal Court.

I again received no reply. I then decided to let go of the Hamilton Police trajectory. I was tired of games of all kinds, and I was much too tired to chase them.

CHAPTER 14

THE DEPARTMENT OF JUSTICE?

I backed off on the book and prepared my appeal. I didn't care about the suspicious RCMP emails I had received a few weeks earlier. The letter from the PC granted me a right to appeal, and that was sufficient for me.

The application was formally filed on January 7, 2022 (#T-35-22). I named the Minister of Public Safety (Marco Mendocino) and the RCMP Commissioner (Brenda Lucki) as respondents. I briefly referenced the Trudeau context, but focused primarily on the RCMP's refusal to provide.

After filing an application of this sort, the next step is for the Department of Justice (DOJ) – who represents the respondents for the Attorney General (AG) – to file a Notice of Appearance, which simply means that they will engage the process I have initiated. I am told this is usually a simple formality, but in this case they contacted me to give them permission to file it late. I granted it.

The next stage was for me to serve an affidavit of supporting facts within thirty days of my initial filing, due February 7. They then had thirty more days to serve theirs on me, followed by twenty days to organize a mutual cross-examination process. When that was complete, I had the option of assembling all the previous documents and filing it with a memorandum of fact/law with the Federal Court Registry. The DOJ then had some time to file theirs. Finally, we would make our submissions before a judge.

On January 26, I was sent a late payment notice from Revenue Canada concerning one of my small businesses. I had inadvertently submitted a Source Deduction payment – the amount of money withheld from employee payroll – one month late. They fined me the maximum amount possible – 10% of the late amount, or $1,615.96.

It was a strange time in Canada. The Freedom Convoy – protests to oppose mandated COVID-19 vaccines for cross-border truck drivers – had arrived in Ottawa on January 29 and appeared to be settling in for the long haul. Trudeau appeared to be too busy twiddling his thumbs to properly engage them or hear their concerns. Strangely enough, I felt em-

Chapter 14: The Department of Justice?

powered by these hard-working freedom fighters. Not because I agreed with their position on vaccines, but because I believed that their real impetus for mobilizing a movement was related to Trudeau himself. He certainly justified their suspicions about him, when he referred to them as a "fringe minority" on January 26,[52] a characterization consistent with his unfounded and hateful description of anti-vaxxers as "very often misogynistic and racist" on December 29, 2021.[53] So much for being the inclusive Prime Minister.

Only hours before I was set to file my affidavit, I made the decision to remove a whole sequence of sections that included the interactive context between Mrs. Trudeau and me. I had a right to include it, and it would certainly provide a potentially helpful context for my Privacy Act requests, but I backed off. I still included a bare-bones reference to the Trudeau context – but nothing more.

Interestingly, I received an emailed letter from the lawyer for the DOJ just before I was to file the affidavit. In it, the lawyer let me know that my Privacy Act requests should have included more context, and he proposed a "practical solution." He wrote: "If the application is discontinued, my client would prioritize the response to a new access of information request… If the application is not discontinued, we will need to bring a motion to strike." He also informed me that the emailed letters I had received in December, which indicated that there were no records in Ottawa, nullified my right to have brought this judicial review. He cited two cases to support his contention.

Nonetheless, I chose to file my affidavit. After the threat-to-strike letter, I certainly didn't trust them to facilitate an honorable response to another Privacy Act request. It was very clear that the DOJ was determined to fend me off. Somebody, somewhere, did not want me to file an affidavit of facts.

Perhaps most importantly, I didn't trust what had happened back in December. Like so much of this story to this point, I couldn't definitively prove my suspicions, but the fact that I received those two 'Nothing in Ottawa' emails (with an obvious grammatical error, suggesting they may have been quickly written) soon after reaching out to lawyers, *and* that I'd had an intimidating automotive experience soon thereafter, had my red flags waving. As I would soon find out, claiming that there is nothing on file on 'Ottawa' is meaningless, and no less vague than my initial requests. There are a number of potentially relevant information banks to scour. Amateur hour, at best.

Fuck cowering in fear. Now, I was pissed off. I then put up a post on my Facebook personal page that reflected my anger. It would not surprise me if this was read by people who were influencing the response to my appeal:[54]

> "It has been quite a week. Among other things, I am engaged in a Canadian Privacy Act appeal process, related to my attempts to get full disclosure from the RCMP of surveillance/monitoring related events in two distinct time periods. The RCMP did what is called a "deemed refusal" with respect to those requests, which essentially means that they refused to respond. As a result, I launched an appeal process, which includes affidavits, cross-examination, and the right to appear before a federal judge to request RCMP disclosure. I am currently at the affidavit stage. About an hour before I was to file it on Thursday, the Department of Justice emailed me with a threat to bring a motion to quash my entire application. I could feel this coming, right before it arrived. Although the Dept of Justice is supposed to be a neutral government agency, uninfluenced by political considerations, we saw in the Lavalin matter in 2019 that attempts are made to influence them. In this case, it is very clear to me that someone out there does not want my rightful appeal to continue. And doesn't want my affidavit- with relevant factual details- to enter the public record. It has been filed, but it has not yet been issued. My suspicion is that they will try to find a reason to block it. It is precisely this kind of abuse of power that keeps me alive to this situation. There is nothing I disdain more than abuse of power. Nothing."

I subsequently emailed correspondence to the DOJ firmly challenging the lawyer's legal position, and questioning the motivations behind his threat. I waited to receive their motion to strike. It never came, although I do wonder if it would have, had I included all the contextual details in the affidavit.

What did arrive was an emailed letter dated February 21, 2022, again indicating that if I discontinue my application and submit a new request with the relevant details and dates included, my request would be prioritized. This didn't make sense, given that they could simply prioritize finding that information within the context of this application. In terms of legal strategy, I surmised this was being suggested so that any information that came through from me in the cross-examination related to these facts, would then be reportable by me and/or the media. They didn't want

Chapter 14: The Department of Justice?

that. They wanted this gone. I responded by making it clear that we could make further delineations of details within the context of this appeal – rather than starting over.

In other words, I said no.

* * *

Now and then throughout the month of February, Cribb worked on an article about this for The Star. He emailed me with a series of fact checks and wording requests, and I happily provided them. The idea that I might finally get some help, calmed me right down again. But, despite his best efforts, The Star's editor(s) chose not to publish it at that stage. Cribb told me that he fought hard for it. I believed him. He had spent days reading all the material related to this situation, and had every reason to want it to go to press. At some point, I suggested that he partner up with one of the investigative journalists I had spoken with. I had a feeling that this person could get the information he needed. My understanding is that he did reach out to that journalist, but it didn't come together.

The DOJ served their affidavit on March 7. Among other things, they contended that my requests were too vague to be able to reasonably respond to them. Strange, because if that were true, then why had the RCMP gone to the trouble of searching Ottawa and reporting that they were unable to locate records that related to my request? And why had the DOJ then contended that those emailed 'findings,' nullified my right to appeal? Either the requests were too vague and there was no way to search, or they weren't. They couldn't have it both ways.

We now had twenty days to organize our cross-examination process. On March 10, the DOJ responded to an email by letting me know that he had no intention of cross-examining me on my affidavit, and indicating that the cross-examination would be "by way of video conference," available on the afternoons of March 25 and 28. It is worth noting that the latter date is one day later than the 20-day limit, so the DOJ was fine with granting an extension beyond the 20-day period prescribed in the rules.

I proceeded to request a court reporter recommendation, and he provided one. I wrote her, inquiring into whether it would be possible for others to attend the cross-examination, as Cribb had requested to attend. I was unaware at this time that observers are not permitted. A few days later, the DOJ informed me that they had changed their mind, and that the cross-examination "should be in writing. This would also, of course, save the significant expense of booking with a court reporter and preparing a transcript." Nice guy, doing all he can to save me some bucks. I protested this adamantly. I wanted to cross-examine someone under oath and whose responses I could respond to in real-time. I was also made aware that cross-examination in writing is easier to control, because the lawyer can instruct his client not to respond to various questions, and there is no opportunity to debate that refusal with the witness present.

On March 16, I asked my web designer to remove the reference to Sophie Trudeau from my main website bio. It had initially felt significant to have her there, but it now felt hypocritical. Not long afterwards, I also had her name removed from my audio course landing page bios. The one thing that I did leave up for now was the link to our video dialogue. I was still mindful of the fact that it might serve me to keep it there, in case someone I reached out to for help with the situation did further research to confirm my connection with her.

That same day, I wrote counsel to arrange the time for the date he suggested – March 28, 2022. He responded the next day by reiterating that "cross-examination in writing was entirely adequate and appropriate in these circumstances." He also informed me that he would be out of the office until March 22. I wrote back on March 23, again insisting on a proper cross-examination. I also asked him to help me to arrange a case conference with a federal judge, where we could discuss his assertion about the adequacy and appropriateness of written cross-examination.

I wrote back on March 28, again asking him to help arrange a case conference with a judge. I finally heard back on March 29 – the day after the last date he had originally suggested for cross-examination. In his response, he reminded me that my case was without merit, and that the time allotted for cross-examination had now expired. He also made me aware that the deadline for the delivery of my application record – the package that includes all case documents and a memoranda of facts and law was April 19. In other words, there would be no cross-examination and we would move onto the final stages of the case. Can you stay stonewall?

I then wrote an email challenging him on what I perceived to be improper behavior in this matter. He then backed off. He wrote back a few days later, informing me that the Federal Court Rules "have always allowed you to pursue in-person cross-examination. Although you are out of time to do so, we are willing to entertain in-person cross-examination at an appropriate court reporter's office in Toronto within a reasonable time." Ironically, he failed to mention that option while insisting on written cross-examination only. He also indicated that although I was now "out of time," he would be amenable to consenting to a motion for an extension of time. Generous feller. He concluded his email with the kind of absurd utterance that could only instigate laughter: "I have not made it a point until now but I must object to your continued attacks on my integrity. They are uncivil, unfounded and insulting. They also have no impact on the positions taken in this litigation. I will continue to address you with the respect that all people deserve and I would hope you can do the same." Gaslighting, anyone?

I was tired. It's not like I didn't have a full-time job, and then some. I did, and wrestling with law enforcement and the judiciary was not serving me. My cortisol levels had been high for now over a year, my wife was feeling more and more depleted (although luckily her biopsy was not cancerous), and I was concerned that I was on the verge of collapse. For some time, I had imagined this whole situation as something akin to David vs. Goliath, but it was getting clear that it was far more imbalanced than that. Even if I accepted that counsel was doing his job in a manner that is just and fair, it was clear that the system itself was not set up to provide the information I sought. I began to contemplate discontinuing my application.

On April 3, 2022, I put up a post on my Facebook personal page that indicated I was considering writing a book about these experiences. Again, I tend to lean towards book-writing for the purposes of safety and self-expression, when it becomes clear that I am not going to get any help within the system itself. Writing was a way to regain my power. These were the words I used:[55]

> "As I step closer to the possibility of writing a book about my Trudeau-related experiences, I am utterly blown away by how deep our fear-of-power conditioning goes. In a true democracy, nobody should be afraid to speak truth about power, truth to power, truth. But so many people I know, are automatically terrified by the very prospect of such a book. It's as though we have all inherently accepted that there is no true democracy, no real rule-of-law, no possibility of fair play in our politic. And that my faith in an integral and honourable politic, is naive, ungrounded, laughable. It may well be, but I can't imagine how we will make it right, if nobody steps out from the shadows to speak their truth."

Almost immediately after the post was live, Mrs. Trudeau appeared to have stopped following me on Instagram. This only confirmed my worries around being actively monitored by someone in the political world.

I soon followed suit by blocking her on Instagram. I had been afraid to make that move before, but now it felt safer. We were finally on the same page.

On April 13, I made a new Privacy Act request of the RCMP. Because the DOJ had indicated that my original requests were too vague, I made a much more detailed and contextually specific request. That same day, I also made a more specifically detailed request of CSIS than the one that I had initiated in 2020.

I also submitted Privacy Act requests to the Privy Council, and Shared Services Canada, which delivers digital services to Government of Canada organizations. Both requests proved fruitless. With respect to the Privy Council, they made it clear that "the Office of the Prime Minister is excluded from the Privacy Act, their office is not subject to document retrieval." In other words, a citizen has no way of gaining access to what transpires within the top office of government. How very strange: that which transpires in an office that exists entirely in servitude of the people, cannot be accessed by any of the people being served.

I received a response from the RCMP on May 9, 2022 that indicated that there was nothing on file. They noted that they conducted a search for records in National Division Records and Specialized Police Services. The DOJ had included in their affidavit a long list of branches that can be searched. I wasn't satisfied with this response, so I wrote them back to inquire if they had checked a variety of other listed branches. The following was their response. It would soon prove quite relevant:

> "Good afternoon Mr. Brown,
> For this request, searches were conducted in National Division which includes the policing of protected individuals such as the Prime Minister and his family and Specialized Policing Services which covers searches done in the RCMP operational databases. For example, searching names regarding occurrences. No records were located.
>
> All wiretaps require legal authority and would be connected to an RCMP investigation. As we stated, no investigative files were located, therefore, no wiretap information related to yourself was found. An additional search in our operational database was done today, to confirm the results already received, and no records were located."

That next weekend, my wife and I went for a bike ride in nearby Ancaster. This was the first day since the phone interception on December

12, 2020 that I felt relatively normal while moving about in the world. The word "normal" had a very different meaning for me since this all began. I had my daily responsibilities, and then I had this heavy burden weighing on me, overwhelming my consciousness and keeping my nervous system in a perpetual PTSD loop. For this day at least, I remembered what it was like to just ride my bike.

Around this time, I received a typically vague response from CSIS (dated May 4, 2022) which indicated that they had searched Personal Information Bank CSIS PPU 045, a collection of records related to individuals investigated for national security concerns or who came to their attention incidentally while carrying out said responsibilities. These were the results:

> The Governor-in-Council has designated this information bank an exempt bank pursuant to section 18 of the Privacy Act. Further to subsection 16(2) of the Act, we neither confirm nor deny the existence of the requested information. If the type of information described in the bank did exist, it would qualify for exemption under section 21 (as it relates to the efforts of Canada towards detecting, preventing or suppressing subversive or hostile activities), or 22(1)(a) and/or (b) of the Act.

On May 26, 2022, I exercised my lawful right of complaint by mailing an investigation request to The Privacy Commissioner of Canada. It was my hope that they could somehow find a way to gain access to information as to whether any of the troubling events had been orchestrated by CSIS.

CHAPTER 15

GLITCHES OR SNITCHES?

In June, I came in even closer to the possibility of writing a book about my harrowing, disorienting, and inane past two years. I had requested support from every Canadian system, but my call had not been answered. For the purposes of Susan's and my safety, and also because I believed that Canadians had a right to know, my literary agent and I were again exploring the possibility of getting a book deal in place. I have my own publishing business, but I preferred the idea of doing it with support from a more mainstream publisher. My agent suggested that I speak to a well-known author from the US named Kent Heckenlively (*"Plague of Corruption: Restoring Faith in the Promise of Science"* etc.) because of his experience with writing book proposals and speaking truth to power.

We had a very dynamic phone call on the afternoon of June 7. I spoke on my main cell phone – the same one I had used for the original phone incident. We discussed my situation and he strongly suggested that I write a book outline that focused on this as a "Hero's Journey" calling out governmental abuse of power and corruption. It was a very insightful and encouraging conversation. I had little doubt that it was also monitored – due to what happened hours later on Facebook.

Early that morning, I received a Facebook 'Community Standards' violation notification related to a post that I had put up on my business page right after the pandemic began. I saw it around 9 AM on June 8, but it showed that it was sent through to me just after midnight. It was a post that was being widely circulated on Facebook in March, 2020, and included some of the positive news about the virus. It was later proven that the news was probably not entirely accurate, but at the time we were all looking for hopeful news, so I had shared it.

Your post goes against our Community Standards so only you can see it. See options.

Of course, the post is not the relevant issue. The relevant issue is that only hours after my phone call with an anti-vaccine author, regarding me writing a candid disclosure book, this two-year-old virus-related post suddenly gets flagged. A logical conclusion is that it was specifically scouted by a professional with a specific agenda – to construe evidence of a virus-denial post. A general follower would not be able to locate this old post unless they spent hours on a computer scouring my wall to find something posted more than 2 years ago. There are well over 1000 posts in the way.

It's important to note that I have been working inside the Facebook system since 2007, and only once do I recall there being a community standards issue on my account. In that situation, I had posted a comment on the page of JP Sears, and after someone reported it, I appealed and won. That's it. In my view, the odds that this happened arbitrarily are similar to the odds that the person on my phone December 12, 2020, was accidental. Infinitesimal.

I was given the choice of challenging the account flagging – something I was very unlikely to win with any post deemed anti-vax/virus – or accept it. So, I accepted it, which means I now had one mark against me in the FB system. Three strikes and you're out.

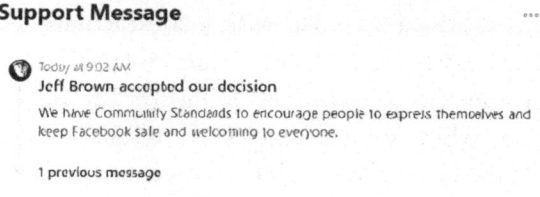

If I was interpreting this maneuver correctly, it was – like so many events before and since – intended to serve a dual purpose: (1) To let me know that my call with the anti-vaxxer about writing a book was monitored. In other words, that my privacy had been invaded yet again; (2) To threaten me with dire consequences of writing a book about the Trudeaus, such as loss of income. My livelihood was largely dependent on social media. It was my primary vehicle for communicating my many offerings: books, classes, sessions, etc.

If you are doubting the reasonableness of my interpretation of this event, I ask you to suspend judgment for now. There is much more of this kind of mind-fuckery to come.

Not long after, the house alarm began to go off in the middle of the night. It happened 12 times between June 17 and August 19, 2022. It was always the same window alarm at around the same time in the night. Most noteworthy, it always correlated with some kind of significant action: speaking on my main phone with a friend about the situation, social media posts that related to the situation, interactions related to writing a book. It was as if the alarm was meant to be my warning bell: "Stop talking, or else." In addition, my phone was abruptly disconnected a number of times when speaking with friends in regard to my situation with the Trudeaus. It was becoming almost predictable.

On July 2, I drove over to the town dump to drop off some garbage. Right after I pulled up to the bin, the truck that was behind me in line pulled up beside me. The driver informed me that there was a swastika fingered into the dust on my back window. I took a look, and so it was. Embarrassed, I quickly wiped it out. What is interesting about this, is that I do not have a mezuzah or any other symbol of Judaism on or near the front door of my home. Nor do I participate in anything related to the Jewish community in my town. Other than a few neighbors, nobody even knows that I am Jewish. So, I called a long-time Jewish townsperson to see if she had ever heard of swastikas being left or drawn on people's property here. She replied – no. Synchronicity, or perfectly in-synch?

On July 19, I received an email with a contractual offer to publish a book about these experiences on my main Hotmail account. The offer came from a prominent Conservative publisher. The working title was *In Trudeau's Kitchen: My Close Encounter with our Sociopathic Global Elites.* Like clockwork, the house alarm arbitrarily went off hours later.

Despite having an encouraging sense about both the publisher and editor, and the prospect of feeling more secure through a public revealing, I took a step back from signing the deal. It is hard to explain, but I had a nagging feeling that something else had to happen first. I wasn't sure what it was, but my intuition told me to wait. It's one thing to write a book after an experience has come to an end. It's quite another to write it while you are still on the battlefield. I asked the publisher to let the story continue to unfold. They agreed to wait.

Over time, I had noticed that my Instagram page in particular appeared to be growing at a much slower pace than it previously had. Later in July, I made an effort to boost a post (create an ad) for my most popular download course – The Abandonment Wound Healing – from my laptop. There had never been any issue with boosting this course before. But this time, the FB sensor blocked it, claiming that it was an "invalid image." It wasn't – it was a picture of me standing in Lake Ontario that we took for the main course landing page. And it had been utilized many times without an issue. Glitches or snitches? If the latter, it struck me as likely that someone at Meta was abusing their power. Not just because they were potentially doing the bidding of someone protective of Canadian political leadership, but because they are a public company with a fiduciary duty to their shareholders to maximize profits. If someone working there was deliberately obstructing my capacity to make a living, it is very likely that they were also breaking the law.

I also began to notice a message regularly appearing and blocking me when I attempted to respond to innocuous DMs on Instagram. This gaslighting theme – implying that I was the threat while threatening me – was just getting warmed up.

On August 18, I visited with Robin (the person who first gave my books to Mrs. Trudeau) to see if any of the missing emails, previously noted, were in her email account. I had made it a habit of sending some of the most interesting emails between me and Sophie to her. We were able to locate a number of the emails that had been missing from my Hotmail account in 2020. They included the email from Mrs. Trudeau that contained alluring excerpts from a Rilke book with the subject heading "Thinking of you"; the frightening email she sent me just before the Trudeaus stepped on the winning stage in the 2019 election; the email from Sophie's assistant – an Executive Assistant in the PMO – that expressed their regret about not being able to write a Foreword for my *Grounded Spirituality* book; and an email wherein Sophie had attached a playful audio of herself doing a (Wild)horse imitation. Although I did not knowingly remove any of my email correspondence with her, I accept that it is possible that I did so accidentally, while sending them to my friend. As it stands, there are still a few others that I recollect that are missing.

The next curious event occurred on August 31. As noted earlier, you may recall that British actor Idris Elba came out publicly right after the pandemic began, to hint that Sophie Trudeau had perhaps given him Covid while they were at a WE Day event in England. I suspected that whatever happened – a story not explored deeply by mainstream media – was still lingering as a worry for the Trudeau camp.[56] In any event, I resonated with some of Elba's quotes and writings. On August 31, 2022, I posted an Elba quote on my very active Facebook page (then close to 500,000 followers).[57]

This appears to have caused alarm, based on what immediately followed. Hours later, what appears to be a recently constructed fake account in the name of a white man named JOHN IDRIS (Idris is a predominately black name), messaged my wife with a "hello" (and then another "hello") on her business page. It was from a recently constructed profile with virtually no apparent activity. The profile also had an interesting image of a Phoenix Rising in the background, and the caption contained a message: "Self-respect."

Again, I'm an odds guy. The odds that some white guy with the name 'John Idris' just happened to write my wife with a "hello" only hours after I post an Idris Elba quote, felt quite remote, particularly in this context. It was my belief that this was intended to warn me that I was being watched, and to intimidate me into silence. I was still at a stage where I found these intersecting and interrelated occurrences very confusing. (I no longer do.)

And then it got even more suspicious. Flash forward a few days after the Elba post and correlating profile. My wife and I were having a heated discussion regarding her reluctance to publicly share about these events, and her personal experience of the situation that had consumed our lives the last few years. From the beginning, she was concerned about the emails Mrs. Trudeau sent to me, but she chose to support me nonetheless, casting aside her doubts in favor of bringing some of my ideas into the world on a greater scale. This particular day, I was feeling frustrated and reactive at her reticence, specifically because I believed – wrongly or rightly – that we would be safer with a greater degree of public revealing. It was unreasonable to expect this of her, but I was feeling quite powerless and wanted someone to speak up and advocate for me. I knew we would be stronger as a unified force. This was the basis of my argument.

She then received the following comments from what appeared to be a newly formed account on a post she put up on her Facebook business page. I can assure you, there is no contextual connection between the content of her post and the message below. It is my view that the wording of the latter essentially confirms that someone was listening in the house. I do remember that our phones were both turned on, and in proximity to where we had our discussion. Even more interesting to me was the parallel between the crest image in the John Idris picture, and the image of this other fake account: same Phoenix Rising or Thunderbird. I can extrapolate that this was orchestrated so that when I see their post, I will receive the clear warning that neither is an "accident." They are here, there, everywhere. It is all connected.

Below is the comment written on the post. Notice that the minor grammatical errors suggest that this may not be an English-speaking person writing this. More on the possible ethnicity of our cyber-stalker later...

> "You will not stimulate that thought, yes we are aware of what could happen but don't you trigger panic. Sometimes just sometimes its best not to look a aggressive dog in the eyes and look the other way, it will stop barking. So please for now do not pour oil in the fire, it maybe wiser to be aware of the consequences of such actions. He wants you to press that panic button just dont do it, meanwhile try to find solutions in privacy."

Prior to Susan receiving that warning, I had begun to notice a steady flow of emails suggesting that someone was attempting to log into my Facebook account. They were not coming directly from FB, although I did receive them on the primary Hotmail account that is connected to my Facebook profile. Around the same time, I also noticed a steady flow of fake emails related to Revenue Canada in the inbox of my same Hotmail account.

That same week, there was a consistent stream of fake Facebook account warning emails on my main website email address with subjects such as: 'Page Violation,' 'Facebook Copyright Issue', 'Your ad has been reported', 'You have 2 copyright strikes, and we'll have to disable your ad account/page', etc. They came from a variety of differently constructed email addresses. This pattern had actually begun on August 25, 2022, when both my wife and I received *identical warnings* – via our website email addresses – of shutting down our Facebook pages. Neither address receives emails from our Facebook accounts, which means that someone made the effort to locate each of our websites to send us the same warning, likely in the hope that at least one, if not both of us, would see it. From the perspective of the battlefield, it made sense. If they couldn't strong arm me into surrendering, they could intimidate my wife to push me to surrender.

Things had clearly escalated.

These triggering emails would now become my constant companion.

In the weeks and months that followed, I also couldn't help but notice a broad array of strange occurrences and disparities related to my Facebook and Instagram pages. For example, I had begun searching through old postings inside my Facebook business page in order to pull excerpts for my next quotes book – *Humanifestations*. Suddenly, it became impossible to go back beyond 3 years. That had never occurred before. Then the "Publish" button disappeared, making it impossible to re-post from those archives. A number of people messaged to alert me to the fact they weren't receiving my posts on my FB business page, and that there was no longer a "Follow" button. People also messaged me on Instagram to inform me that they weren't receiving and/or couldn't share my posts. I checked my settings and there were no formal blocks – nothing had changed. On one occasion, I actually put up a post inquiring into whether people were able to share my posts. A number of people responded that they couldn't share. One person stated that he had tried three times that week, and only now – after I posted about this specific issue – could he share a post. When I attempted to respond to DMs, the "Try Again Later: We limit...." warning would often appear. It seemed like this was something more than the usual glitches.

In the midst of the pressure-cooker, I again felt a strong compulsion to let the whole situation go. If I was right that there was a connection between my politically inspired nightmare and someone at Meta obstructing my livelihood, then this was possibly enough pressure to kill me. Perhaps that was the goal?! After all, I was almost 60 and this was not a good time to spend years in a chronic fight-or-flight state.

It's very difficult to convey what it was like to live and function in everyday life, with this situation gripping me. Based on conversations I'd had with a variety of people about this situation, it was very possible, if not likely, that my phones, emails, house and car were monitored. When you become aware that you are likely under surveillance, the whole complexion of your life changes. You stop talking on the phone, because it is difficult to contain your desire to talk about what is happening with friends. You stop speaking your mind in your car, in your home, on social media. You stop sharing candidly over email. You stop love-making. You stop connecting with your soul. You no longer feel authentically human. And, as you will soon see, that's when they send all the fake friends and rigged situations to try to get something on you. When you are isolated and vulnerable. Their whole game works in stages.

Although I had become a shell of my former self, I was not a lifeless one. Lifeless would have been more comforting. Instead, I became a highly activated, super-charged shell, riddled with anxiety, discomfort, and spiked cortisol levels. Like a vat of bubbling acid, I was all churned up – with no way to release. How could I express myself in a way that was cathartic, when most every interaction was tainted with the awareness of potentially being watched?

At the same time, a kind of fierceness was burgeoning deep inside. I was getting more and more determined to fight harder. Both my fear and my fortitude were growing in equal measure. And – in the midst of the chaos – it was beginning to dawn on me that, maybe, just maybe, this entire situation was somehow meant-to-be. Not because I believe that every horrifying experience is a gift orchestrated by the universe – I certainly don't believe that – but because it somehow made sense in the context of my own bodacious life, one where I had chosen to fight for my right to the light time and again. This crucible was strangely familiar.

As I fell deeper into the darkness that surrounded this painful isolation, I kept finding some light to hang onto. It came in the form of brave music. I couldn't get enough of Nick Cave's profoundly spiritual work, Matisyahu, the HU, Judah and the Lion, and a remarkable series of tracks called 'Soaking in his Presence' (Yeshua) that I began writing to on YouTube. In every case, I felt a call to something deeper, truer, more magnanimous than the lowly vibration of malfeasance that had now permeated my once dignified life – and surely the lives of billions before me. I had worked so hard for my little bit of glory, and I wanted it redeemed. That was the core lesson I had imparted to others in my writing: never hide your blazing light under a bushel of shame. Your story is your glory, always. Could I practice what I preached under the most difficult circumstances?

On September 6, another unsettling incident occurred. I was sitting on my front porch in late afternoon, casually chatting with a neighbor. A few random people strolled by on their way home from work. Just a normal day in our quiet small town, until my attention was jarred by a man who made a pointed effort to lock eyes with me. This was clearly not a friendly neighbor, saying hello. He was a towering and physically fit white male in his 30's with bulging muscles and a stone-cold stare. An equally strong and bulky dog – possibly a Pitbull – yanked on his leash. The man then moved his searing, laser-focused gaze to my door, scanning the area with intensity. It was not like someone who had never seen my house – it was like someone who wanted me to see him staking out my house. In the almost three years since the phone interception, I had not noticed any physical presence intent on intimidating me. I had become skilled at sifting, scrutinizing, and discerning experiences through a sensible filter, and discarding them as mere *possibilities* – if there was a basis to do so. But this incident felt different.

Interestingly, when I later checked our security camera record, he wasn't there. I saw the people passing before him, and I saw the people passing after him. But I did not see him. It was like he was never there.

All part of the game. Intimidating experiences, with little evidence to prove them.

CHAPTER 16

THERE'S A SPIDER ON THE PILLOW?

On September 29, Robert Cribb and a well-known Private investigator who I will refer to as *Walkie Talkie (WT)* came to my home. We sat down at my dining room table, and had an insightful discussion about the situation and possible steps forward. At some point, I mentioned what had happened with the Hamilton Police. WT was startled. It was incomprehensible to him that I had reported a situation so substantial, and didn't hear back, now 13 months later. He assured me he would further investigate the circumstances, through his personal connections. He knew the Chief from his policing days in Toronto. Soon thereafter, we agreed that both I – and the Star – would also reach out to the Hamilton Police to see what had transpired.

Hours later, again in the middle of the night (and for the first time since August 19), the house alarm blared, jolting us from our slumber. And again, the night after that. Clearly, someone, somewhere, was alarmed by our conversation at the dining room table.

I called into the Hamilton Police on October 7, leaving my name and number for Officer Burke – the young officer notated on the file and who I had handed the USB stick to in 2021.

I did not get a response. I called back a few times the following week. The representative on the phone assured me that they would write an email to the Constable and Detectives on duty to call me back.

No reply.

Hours later, I received several fake Meta account warning emails, sent to my website email address. In addition, I received uncharacteristic emails citing: "Unusual traffic from your computer network" when online at home, a malware and 161 hacked files warning related to my main website. Then there was the creme de la crème – another incident I actually predicted would occur.

After the meeting with Cribb at the house, an official letter from the official Revenue Canada arrived. It was dated October 11, and it contained a request for $782.69 for something allegedly owed by one of my companies. I called my accountant, and he wasn't even sure what it was related to.

I also had a strange experience one day while attempting to open my Apple account on my I-Phone from my home wi-fi. The message: "Your Apple Device is being used to sign in to a device near Ottawa, Ontario." Had my phone been paired with someone's in Ottawa? (Of course, it had.)

In mid-October, a new game began. I began to receive regular notifications in my Facebook account from fake business accounts implying that my account would be suspended for various improprieties. These would become a remarkably regular part of my Facebook life in the months – and year(s) – to come.

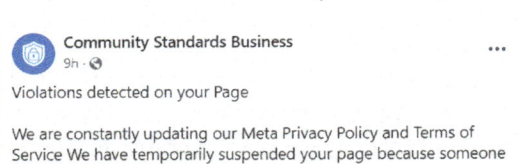

It was becoming clear that the synchronicity argument wasn't measuring up. Not because synchronicities don't happen – of course many people receive trickster notifications and emails of this kind – but because there were simply too many impeccably timed, situation-responsive events to fall under the umbrella of synchronicity. This was no longer a situation where there was an occasional happening. This was now a situation that was both coordinated, concentrated, and persistent, particularly when I made any step in the direction of public revealing. These incidents became even more active, and sometimes arrived in clusters, after I did something that ignited concern about me going public.

One thing that was crystal clear was that my surveillers were in a double bind, too. Their disparity was related to how obvious they could be with respect to letting me know they were there. If indications were of a more subtle nature, it would be difficult for me to prove it was them. But, in that case, they also risked that I wouldn't notice it. Thus, they would fail to achieve their goal of intimidating me. And yet, if it was too obvious, I would surely notice it, but it would then be much easier for me to prove their wrongdoing.

They should have just stopped.

Chapter 16: There's a Spider on the Pillow?

I finally received a call from Hamilton Detective John Barron on October 17. He acknowledged that the file was still open and that he had taken carriage of it. He asked to obtain an updated summary of events. I informed him that I would put it together within the next week. I then called him right back to ask about the USB stick of relevant emails and information I had given Constable Burke in 2021. On that stick were hundreds of emails between Wildhorse and I – and some of my commentary.

I asked him specifically where the USB stick was.

He indicated that he did not know. He asserted he would try to find out where it was. I asked him directly if it would have been given to the Trudeaus.

He replied "no."

On October 26, WT emailed me, requesting that I promptly call him. My recollection is that we discussed relevant aspects of the situation. He specifically asked me whether I had been vetted before going to the Trudeau house in 2018. He had previously asked this same question when he visited my home weeks earlier, and was startled by my reply. When he asked the question again, he was equally startled: I had not been directly vetted before entering the Trudeau home. I also noted that my vehicle (the rental Yukon) and I, personally, were not checked when I arrived at their home. WT found it unbelievable that the RCMP didn't have knowledge of my 300+ emails with Mrs. Trudeau. They are tasked with protecting the PM and his family, which means being aware of most everything that happens in their lives and on their devices.

On October 27, Cribb notified me by email that the Hamilton Police had confirmed that my complaint was formally filed and that it is an open matter.

On October 28, WT reached out again to have a phone conversation. In that meeting (and in a subsequent email), he stated that he required email evidence of my three efforts to disconnect from Mrs. Sophie Trudeau, and a recording of the phone call on December 8, 2020, when she encouraged me to remain connected. He needed concrete evidence that I was the one who had attempted to disconnect. He stated: "I can't get into why I need it on the phone, but I will explain after it happens… I need the 3 emails with dates and the audio texted to me so I can play it for somebody…" He also requested a transcript of the phone call. He indicated that he needed all of it before Tuesday morning, November 2. I affirmed I would have it to him by the end of the coming weekend.

That same day, I received a letter from the OPC related to their investigation into CSIS's refusal to provide a meaningful response to my Privacy Act requests. Because CSIS is granted a national security related exemption in the act, whereby they do not have to reveal whether information exists, their unwillingness to provide was deemed proper, and my complaint was therefore *not* considered to be "well founded." At the same time, I was reminded that I had a right under Section 41 of the Privacy Act to apply to the Federal Court of Canada for review of the decision of a government institution to refuse to provide access to personal information. If I intended to appeal, I had 45 days from the date of receiving this letter to do so. I had to decide if I wanted to proceed.

On October 29 or 30, I had a quick meeting with Cribb at a Starbucks in the Toronto Beaches. He had requested a copy of the material I was providing to the Detective. I handed him a USB stick with the two most recent detailed updates. He then revealed to me the "working theory" as to why the Hamilton Police had retreated last year. Based on the initial stages of WT's inquiries, the theory was that the Hamilton Police had been informed by the RCMP that I had been stalking Mrs. Trudeau.

I informed him of what I was preparing for WT. In a subsequent email response, he suggested I also provide WT with the love poems, as well as anything else that illustrated the flirtatious nature of Mrs. Trudeau's engagement with me.

It now dawned on me why WT wanted concrete evidence that it was me who was trying to disconnect from Mrs. Trudeau. And why the police department abandoned the case in 2021. It was because they believed that *she* was at risk. Little did they know that our questionably boundaried Leading Lady had behaved in inappropriate ways. That *she* was actually the national security risk.

If this working theory was accurate, it was no surprise to me. Mrs. Trudeau had already tried to characterize me as an unwell person after my second attempt to disconnect, referring to the sleep-aid I was taking. We all know that it is standard practice in the political world to go on the offensive when confronted with allegations of wrongdoing. Again, if they don't say you're crazy, they say you have an agenda or ulterior motive. You're either mad, or you're bad, or you're both. In that business, they call it "damage control." I prefer to call it "truth control," one of Mr. Trudeau's only noteworthy political skillsets.

What most surprised me was that local police had accepted it at face value. I understood that it was probably standard practice to check in with

Chapter 16: There's a Spider on the Pillow?

the RCMP – the law enforcement agency tasked with taking care of the PM and his family – to see if they had any knowledge of events. But to not confirm the veracity of the information they received by contacting me directly or checking the documents that I provided, felt like a radical breach of authority, one that left my wife and I suffering needlessly for an additional year. In Canada, local police are a provincial responsibility and the RCMP is under federal jurisdiction. The Hamilton Police do not work for the RCMP, nor should they be beholden to them. Their primary responsibility is to their local citizens. Not only had they failed to contact me, they had not even returned the evidence (the USB stick) that I had provided. And I was certainly left to wonder if that stick – with all my evidence and my personal commentary – ended up with the Trudeaus or whichever politically motivated individuals are involved in this situation. Something was suspicious here, particularly so given that the RCMP had claimed to have no information related to me and the Trudeaus in the Privacy Act requests I had submitted. How is that possible if they were telling the Hamilton Police that I was stalking Wildhorse? In my mind, it looked like a glaringly obvious cover-up. Someone was protecting political interests.

Around November 5, Det Barron came to get USB stick #2. It encompassed various details, including recent summaries of events. I asked him a series of questions about why it hadn't been investigated last year and about the location of the original stick. My recollection is that he said the stick was either lost or retained in the place where they keep evidence. He apologized and admitted that they "dropped the ball" last year with respect to the investigation. He also said that he is no longer on the file – it had been moved to the Intelligence branch. Finally, some intelligence on the job!

On November 28, I received a call from Hamilton Police Detective Nathan Rowan, from Intelligence/Organized Crime, indicating that the file had just been forwarded to his office. He informed me that he was reviewing the new USB files that I had given Detective Barron. He indicated that he had wanted to connect today to touch base and to let me know they hadn't forgotten about me. He also said that I needed to come in to give a formal statement – he would arrange it for next week or thereafter. I asked him what happened to the missing original USB stick with all my voluminous evidence. He said that he had further investigated, and that my report last year had gotten stuck between two units for approximately a year. It was a "screw-up" that never got dealt with, but that it had now gone up the chain of command and was something that had to be dealt with ASAP. He said that there were "no strings behind it." It was just a matter of "people not doing their jobs…" When I directly inquired if the stick had gone to the Trudeaus, he explained it was originally put in "property," and then signed out by the detective who had been assigned the case for review. He then "misplaced it." The new stick I gave to John had also been submitted into property before he took it out to review. In reference to Detective Sgt. Knapp, he indicated "that officer… I couldn't see him doing anything untoward… he just screwed up…" He informed me about an email chain with him and Knapp, and said they also corresponded by phone. Knapp said he checked his entire desk and couldn't find it. Detective Rowan assured me he would keep on him about it. I deliberately asked him about the stalking accusations directed towards me. I wanted to make him aware that I was privy to this information and that it was important enough for me to mention it.

I got off the phone and breathed a deep sigh of relief, like maybe… just maybe… justice would be done. For this moment at least, things were good in the hood.

At the same time, I wanted to continue to pursue other avenues. After what I had been through with the police, I wasn't going to limit my efforts to them. So, I turned my attention to the Federal Court Appeal – do it or don't do it? Last year's appeal of the RCMP damn near killed me. Was it worth it, again?

I called WT to see what he thought. I wanted to know if some of these various shenanigans could have been orchestrated by CSIS. Because if he was absolutely certain that they bore no responsibility, then I would consider not proceeding. He was very clear in his response. *Yes, it could be them. Don't doubt yourself now. Keep doing what you're doing.* He also indicated that the Hamilton Police were interested in the case. He pointed out that the delay on the investigation is a ploy he is familiar with when there is "wrongdoing…. if there was no wrongdoing, if they knew right off the bat there was nothing here and didn't happen they would have notified you after two or three months…" I asked why they didn't follow up to inform me they couldn't help me. He replied that "they were told not to… by the RCMP… RCMP went to them and said there's nothing there blah blah blah… and then they were probably told to just let it go, don't bother with it anymore… to me that's a sign they are hiding something…"

I shared what Cribb had told me about the RCMP telling Hamilton Police that I was stalking Sophie. WT responded: "They're not going

Chapter 16: There's a Spider on the Pillow?

to second guess the RCMP... you know the best defense is to go on offence... to create a story about you... when I heard THAT also, I knew... like why would they even bother with that... it's not true." Later in the conversation, he confirmed: "I knew it was bullshit..." And, "Hamilton's keen, I can tell you that..." As always, he was being careful about what he shared on the phone: "When I see you next, I'll tell you what happened in Hamilton and who I saw." He said that he thought I would hear back from the Hamilton Police in the New Year.

After this valuable phone meeting with WT, I contacted the Privacy Commissioner and spoke with someone who felt that my best course of action with respect to CSIS was to report these events to the National Security and Intelligence Revenue Agency (NSIRA) – a credible organization responsible for ensuring that national security agencies, including CSIS, are complying with the law and that their actions are reasonable and necessary under the circumstances. Basically, the NSIRA ensures accountability. I checked in with the NSIRA and they informed me I had to first write a letter of complaint to David Vigneault, the Director of CSIS, wherein I should specify my allegations. If I did not receive a response from him within 60 days, or if I was not satisfied with his response, I could then submit my claim to the NSIRA. I wrote Mr. Vigneault soon thereafter.

On December 8, I received word from my Co-producer that a documentary that we had made ('*Karmageddon*') had been unexpectedly rejected by Amazon Prime Video. We had begun the submission process in November, and it was our understanding that the film would be accepted after we completed a few technical steps. We completed them, and were waiting to see the film made available. In the meantime, we had a very optimistic conversation from our cell phones about the potential income we would generate from such a wide platform. Suddenly, with no explanation, the film was rejected. Strange.

The NSIRA option wasn't enough for me with respect to CSIS. After all, I had already seen how easily truths are covered up by people in positions of power. I would only trust a judge. So, I put together a 48-page Federal Court application, citing David Vigneault, and Marco Mendocino, the Minister for Public Safety, as the respondents (this was later corrected to the appropriate respondent in these actions – The Attorney General of Canada). Because the lawyer in last year's RCMP appeal had asserted that I was to provide clear context in an application of this kind, I included *many significant details* from my email and phone interactions with Mrs. Trudeau. This also felt like the wisest thing to do given that I was threatened with a motion to quash last time. If I was going to face such a motion, I was going to at least ensure that the judge knew the context that they were quashing.

In my application, I endeavored to articulate an argument that challenged the CSIS's exemption to reveal that is laid out in the Privacy Act. It's not that I didn't agree with it in most contexts – those tasked with the great responsibility of protecting our nation's security do need to know that they can operate in secret *when appropriate* – but that doesn't mean that there shouldn't be some system of oversight in place, protecting against the misuse of the system by dishonest complainants or other wrongdoers. Given that my situation involved allegations of wrongdoing subsequent to my efforts to personally disconnect from the Prime Minister's wife – nothing that, on its face, is a national security concern – it did seem reasonable to me that a judge should be able to take a look to see if there was anything questionable in the personal information bank. Not every context and circumstance should be exempt from scrutiny in a democracy. It's my view that the absence of some mechanism whereby a judge or other neutral figure can further investigate a situation like this, is a violation of section 8 ("search", which includes wiretap), 15 ("equality"), and 7 ("life, liberty, and security of the person") rights under the Canadian Charter of Rights and Freedoms. These violations of my rights are not a reasonable limit that can be demonstrably justified in a free and democratic society.

In essence, I was asking the court to find some of the sections of the Privacy Act that shield CSIS from public revealing unconstitutional. It would be one thing if we could ensure that there is *never* wrongdoing in government agencies, but because we should never make a *presumption of perfection* about anyone in a position of authority, we must always ensure that there is some way for citizens to determine if wrongdoing or misuse of power has occurred. Dudley Do-Right is a wonderful (albeit naive) aspiration, but Dudley Do-Wrong must always be accounted for.

* * *

I woke up on the morning of December 12, which was ironically, the two-year anniversary of the phone interception, to drive to the Federal Court in Toronto to file the Application. It was a cold Canadian morning and I felt frightened. I was going to court to file an application that included a variety of details related to my interactions with the PM's wife. I was

Chapter 16: There's a Spider on the Pillow?

certain nobody had ever filed anything quite like this on the public record in the Canadian court system. It was deeply unsettling. I had entered into my dynamic with Sophie Trudeau in an effort to make the world a better place. Was reporting the subsequent wrongdoing going to make the world a better place?

As I drove the highway, I felt a compelling desire to turn back. This was just too much – how would my tired old body survive this pressure-cooker? I had a burning desire to call a friend, any friend, to talk it through. But the likelihood that my phone was tapped prohibited that option.

I then did what I had done dozens of times in the last two years: I looked over at the drivers in the cars around me. I looked at them, and I imagined their own struggles with abuse of power in their lives. In this way, I knew that I was not completely alone. I meditated on their lives, my life, all of our struggles with power, and then repeated the mantra that had accompanied me for most of the last two difficult years: "If a privileged white man doesn't speak truth about power, how can we expect anyone else to..." Whatever the outcome, by asserting my right to exist, I felt that I was also asserting everyone's right to exist. I wasn't just fighting for my life. I was fighting for everyone else's too. It was for all of us who have suffered systemic abuse of power while on this planet. And let there be no doubt – that is most of us.

I drove on and pulled onto Queen Street in Toronto, I turned off my phone and placed it in the glove box. I then parked a number of blocks away from the court, in case my phone and car were tracked. As I walked the street, I thought of a best friend who worked close by. I wished he was here. Times had changed. I had to do this one alone.

Summoning my deepest reserves of courage, I walked the block to the Federal Court building, and made my way upstairs to file my documents. One copy for me, three copies for the court and the Department of Justice. I was the only person in the large waiting area. Strange. After some minor issues, I paid my fee and the documents were stamped and filed. My story was now a number – T-2602-22. It was forever part of the public record. In some small way, I felt like I existed again. And, in another, I felt appropriately terrified. Was I a fool, or a hero? I was also angry. Did they really have to put someone on my phone two years ago? Couldn't we have just parted in peace? Was this level of chaos worth it to any of us?

I trudged back to the car. As I drove home, I thought about what would happen next. Power doesn't take kindly to being exposed. As I had already seen, even the idea of it, turns them foul. I thought about it, and figured that one of two things would rapidly occur: either I would receive a significant warning from META about a post I put up, or another funds request from Revenue Canada. One way or the other, there would be repercussions for daring to stand my ground.

That assumption was correct. A mere few hours later, I received the next level of warning to disable my Facebook account. This time, for a post I had put up a few days earlier. A very popular satirical post about the New Age that I had posted dozens of times before, and that had been shared tens of thousands of times over the years with nary a complaint. This was now the second time this had happened this year. And again, it had happened almost immediately after I made a strong step towards public revealing. There was no doubt in my mind that it was connected.

I appealed the decision. A few days later I received a response that indicated that they were not able to review it due to staff shortages. In the same notification, they stated: "If your content goes against our community standards again, your account may be restricted or disabled."

And so it was. I now had a persistent and anxiety-provoking account warning staring me in the face. Not only did it leave me on precarious ground with respect to my once free expression on Meta, but it also made me less likely to run ads for my future online courses because I now had the looming concern that I would be removed by the platform either before or during the course. If so, I would have to refund all the students their payments, while never being able to retrieve the amount spent on the ads. I was fucked.

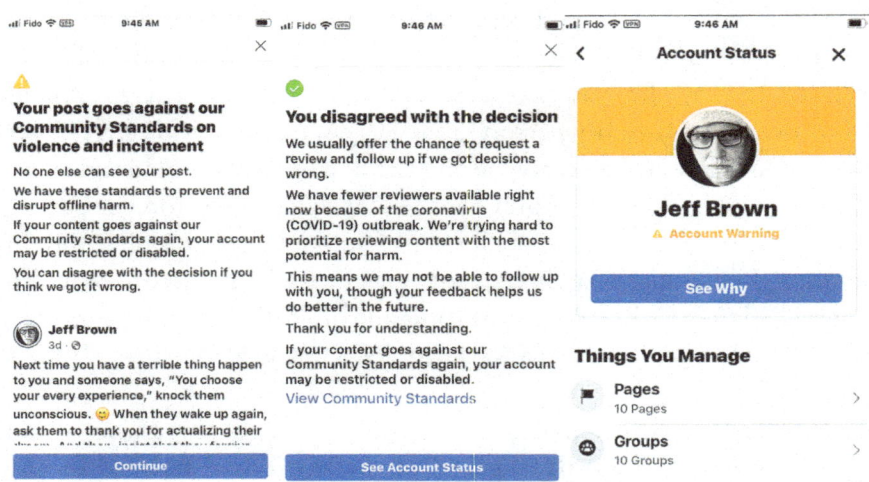

Chapter 16: There's a Spider on the Pillow?

It was quite a brilliant move by whoever was behind it. Not just because it frightened me with respect to expression and livelihood, but because it meant that I would also be less likely to put up a post with a link to my 48-page Court application on my Facebook or Instagram pages, for fear they would suspend me. I had no intention of doing so, but I would be very surprised if this wasn't part of their strategy. After all, I had somewhere around 700,000 followers on Meta's apps.

At the same time, it was a foolish strategy. Every time these fuckers did something to threaten my livelihood, they stoked the fires of my determination. When you leave someone who comes from nothing feeling like they have nothing left to lose, they fight even harder for their rights. If your goal is to back them off, then back off yourself and maybe, just maybe, they will decide to let it all go. But not if you keep intimidating them.

After fighting tooth and nail for my rights as an infant, I was well-equipped to continue. And despite the fact that my mother and I had a challenging relationship, I had no doubt that she loved me, and that she would want me to continue to fight this battle. We both hated bullies, after all, and we both felt a responsibility as Jews, to stand down any and all significant abuses of power. I understood the detrimental consequences of my resistance, but truth be told, I had always said that I would rather die a warrior's death, than live a coward's life. Longevity of life means little if you have surrendered your dignity to abusers of power.

One of the interesting things that confounded me about the timing of the Facebook warning was how quickly they were alerted that I had filed the document. When it happened last June, it was easy to know what I was up to because I had spoken on the phone to the anti-vax guy. But I hadn't done that today, and I didn't remember talking about this on my phone for some time. Having said that, I had surely talked about this in my home, worked on the document on my computer at home and in public libraries, and emailed various drafts to myself along the way. If I, and others, were correct that I was under all manner of surveillance, then it wasn't difficult for them to know. Still, I wondered. Did someone tell them? If so, who?

Energized and enraged, I then made the firm decision that if I was removed from Facebook, I was going to release all the documents to the public. I also put up posts on my Facebook business and personal pages on December 17,[58] to let others know that I was likely to be booted off of FB, and informing them of the likely connection between my activities behind-the-scenes, and the two warnings I had received. I pinned the post to the top of both pages for all to see. I invited my followers to find me elsewhere if I was removed. I had opened a Substack account months earlier, and posted a link to it in the comments. Thousands came over to follow me there that weekend. I was grateful, and reminded by this gesture of the power of the people. Although I had put the writing of the book on hold again, I had also made the firm decision that if this latest investigative attempt with the police led nowhere, I was going to fully commit to writing the book. I had the strangest feeling that the only way that I would ever get justice was if I turned away from the system altogether, and turned towards humanity. The system had one more chance.

A few days earlier on December 13, both I and a friend who I spoke with regularly on the phone – a friend who had borne witness to my phone cutting off on various occasions after I revealed information about the Trudeaus – began to receive desperately written emails from someone with a variety of ever-changing names. In all cases – they also referred to themselves with the name *Limestone*. On one occasion, my friend received an email from someone with yet another name who claimed to be writing on "behalf of Limestone." At first, they were sent to her website email address. Then days later, to her private email that is not publicly known. In the emails that I received, "Limestone" was making accusations about their phone being compromised, government victimization, false identities, gaslighting etc. One email arrived with this visible subject line: "If you knew what has been going on with my phone for 2 and 1/2 years."

The game was on.

* * *

I emailed Detective Rowan on December 13 with an update of some recent events. I received an email back on December 16, letting me know he would review the documents and be in touch as soon as possible.

Toward the end of the month, I had yet another challenge with boosting a post. This had become a regular happening on Facebook, but it had now spread to Instagram. Blocks to my livelihood:[59]

> **jeffbrownsoulshaping** How very interesting. When I attempt to 'boost' a post here on Instagram, I am prevented from doing so. And this image persistently comes up. It is my understanding that Instagram is part of a publicly shared corporation. I wonder how those shareholders will feel about people being blocked from running legitimate advertisements. We already know how Congress feels about 'shadow bans'. What about advertising blocks?
> 13 seconds ago

> **Try Again Later**
> We limit how often you can do certain things on Instagram to protect our community. Tell us if you think we made a mistake.
>
> Tell us
>
> OK

Chapter 16: There's a Spider on the Pillow?

Over the holidays, I experienced an unexpected peace that I hadn't known in a long time. I began to sleep through the night again, and to take better care of my body. The very idea that I might get investigative support calmed and equalized my system. This sense of relief emanated from my interactions with the newspaper as well. Cribb had informed me that The Star was likely to publish the story if the Hamilton Police confirmed an active investigation. He had already written and fought for the story, while I was in my court process with the RCMP in 2022, but they had chosen not to publish at that time. It was different now. The story was on the public record. I had laid out many of the details in my privileged, reportable court application. They just felt that they needed something more for the purposes of "credibility." That is, they needed the cops to formally investigate.

It's important to note that the Toronto Star is the primary liberal newspaper in Canada. If Trudeau had lost the support of the Star's predominantly liberal base, he was probably finished politically. It is hard to imagine that anything would frighten the Liberal party more.

On January 9, I received a friendly email from Detective Rowan, apologizing for the late notice, and inquiring into whether I could come in to the station the next morning, January 10, 2023, to give my formal statement.

I drove to the police precinct to give my statement. I was brought into a comfortable room, with a camera on the wall, with an officer from the Major Crimes Department named Troy. I probably should have brought a lawyer, and/or taped it, but I felt secure at the time. My mistake.

The officer assured me that I could relax, be informal, and simply tell my story. He indicated that he had booked the whole day for this. For three hours, I shared the intricate details of the story. I may have looked at the binder of details once, but most everything was straight from memory. At the end, he asked some basic questions, and we discussed investigative paths. He indicated – quite appropriately – that their job is to distinguish between criminal allegations that they can investigate, and things that they can't. We agreed that the phone interception was a criminal allegation that could be investigated. I also suggested that they contact the Liberal Party about that phone text to see if the person who sent it has any memory of who told them to send it at that particular time. Troy liked that idea and said he hadn't thought of it. He indicated that they welcomed investigative ideas.

Then Detective Rowan entered the room, and requested we speak in private. He brought me into another room. He was visibly agitated. In fact, I have never seen a cop this nervous. I paraphrase, "Mr. Brown, you aren't taping me are you?" I reassured him that I wasn't. He then addressed the missing USB stick. "Mr. Brown, we don't know what happened with that stick. Knapp was very busy, with many active cases. He figures he may have just overwritten those documents on the stick with other documents." This explanation seemed highly improbable to me – there were volumes of documents that would have to be overwritten. I again directly inquired if there was any chance it could have been given to the RCMP or the Trudeau office. He replied "No," and defended Detective Sgt. Knapp as an honest guy of sound professionalism. It was entirely evident that the Hamilton Police force really wanted me to let this go.

We then moved onto the next steps of the investigation. He indicated that he knew someone at Canada Borders Services Agency (CBSA) who he would be contacting about the passport monitoring question from 2019. I told him they had already responded "No" to my privacy act request, but he gestured that this didn't mean much. He also let me know that he had checked out my wife in the system and that there was nothing "in her name." He seemed puzzled by this, as though that is something that never happened. He requested the contact info about one of the former RCMP'ers that I had spoken with before I finally called the phone interception into the Hamilton Police. I informed him that I would prepare a list of investigative ideas for him, which he was amenable to. He also indicated that he had been watching my interview live from another room. I asked him how it appeared to him and he said that he had no issue with anything that I shared in my video statement. We moved onto the subject of having my house and computers probed to see if they were currently compromised. He indicated that he would have to check with his technology officers to see if they could do that. I also suggested that he get a judicial order to wiretap Justin Trudeau's phone. I said something to the effect of: "I am sure he will talk about this situation on the phone." Officer Rowan balked at that comment and retorted: "Well, he is the Prime Minister, Mr. Brown." He seemed quite intimidated by the gravitas of the situation. I then said something like: "Well, if he was calling this in about me, you would be on my phone in 15 minutes… so why not the other way around? Shouldn't he be held to the highest standards of accountability?" At some point, Nathan asked if he could get on my phone. I

CHAPTER 16: THERE'S A SPIDER ON THE PILLOW?

assumed he meant in order to check if someone else was on my line, but, in retrospect, I am not so sure.

It was entirely evident by the end of the conversation that the investigation had begun. He walked me out, and I drove home.

What was most memorable from this experience was not the giving of my 'statement' – that was quite straightforward – it was the intensity of Detective Rowan's concerns about the missing USB stick. It seemed very likely to me that they either gave the stick to the RCMP, or they were concerned that the public would find out they potentially handed it over to the RCMP. If this became public knowledge, it is undoubtedly contrary to their fiduciary duties and mandate vis-à-vis citizens in their care. I have never heard of a situation where someone reports a crime and the officers not only fail to follow up, but also hand the evidence over to the other side independent of a lawful disclosure process. If this is actually what happened, it stokes the already burning fires of public mistrust, and would likely ramp up the persistent calls throughout Hamilton for the defunding of police. Perhaps this is why the RCMP constable I first connected with suggested that I call it into Ottawa police, first. Perhaps he knew something about the way that the Hamilton police operate.

On January 10 and 11, I followed-up with both Nathan and Troy via email providing some of the additional information that I had said I would provide: phone numbers of the Toronto Islander who called me December 12/20 and a dear friend I spoke with soon thereafter, and the number of a former police inspector who I shared the story with that winter. I also included some additional information that Troy had asked me about. And I included a list of 18 investigative ideas. Troy had expressed an openness to them, and Nathan had also confirmed that I should send them.

In the latter email, I included this paragraph: "...if it is the case that anyone provided info to Hamilton to the effect that I was stalking Mrs. Trudeau, perhaps they would be so kind as to provide the source of that fallacious information. Because it is clear that whoever was providing them with that information, was trying to cover-up wrongdoing. Otherwise, why do and say this? If they had nothing to hide, why lie and claim she was being stalked? <u>Innocent people don't make up stories like that</u>."

No reply to either email.

Also on January 11, a Federal Government source told Global News that Trudeau would hold a 3-day cabinet retreat in Hamilton later in January (January 23-25). Global shared that information at 5:13 PM that day.[60]

137

I called Detective Rowan on January 14. In that call from my main cell phone, Officer Rowan confirmed the existence of the investigation and indicated that he would be meeting with Troy to organize details. When asked if I should prepare another binder as we had discussed, he answered "yes." When asked if it could possibly get in the hands of anyone "off campus," he assured me that it wouldn't. When I inquired if there was an investigation being launched, he replied "Yes, of course, otherwise I wouldn't have brought you in." I emailed that information to Cribb from my main Hotmail account at 3:18 PM. After all, he said the Star would publish if the investigation was confirmed. It was now confirmed.

I texted Nathan on January 16 to let him know that I would have a stick with the binder contents for him soon, as I had said I would. I asked him "What days are you around this week?"

No reply.

Not surprisingly, on January 20, I received an 'HST Post-Assessing Review' request from Revenue Canada that was dated January 16. The HST is a hybrid of federal and provincial goods and services taxes. In the case of Ontario, it is 13%. Any funds collected – less any business-related purchases that included HST – have to be remitted to the government every three or twelve months, depending on your scheduled arrangement. In any event, I was given 30 days from the date of the letter to explain why the sales totals I provided on the HST (paper) forms were different from my overall annual sales on the tax return.

If this interestingly timed request was yet another abuse of political power, it was impeccably timed. I was already overwhelmed by running my businesses, preparing for a police investigation, and working on the affidavit for the Privacy Act appeal. Adding the annoyance of having to go through the folders and organize all the extensive details for the HST Review was no small thing.

On January 23, Cribb emailed on my Hotmail account to affirm he had received my confirmation of investigation email sent the week before, and that he was "hoping to get to some redrafting of my story this week incorporating this new material from the federal case, as well as Hamilton." In other words, they were likely going to press.

Trudeau arrived in downtown Hamilton on Monday January 23. Over the course of 3 days, he showed his face at various locations and endured all manner of hostility, as a large group of angry protesters circled his hotel, shouting and throwing things against the windows where the meetings were being held.

Chapter 16: There's a Spider on the Pillow?

On Tuesday, January 24, my wife and I decided to go for a drive after a long day's work. At this time, I had no idea where Trudeau was staying in Hamilton. We had no particular plan, but ended up driving to Ottawa Street in Hamilton – an area that we both liked to visit. After checking out the street, we turned back up Barton Street to make our way home. As I turned left onto James Street to make my way to King, I encountered a police roadblock at the edge of Jackson Square Mall. The air was thick with intensity and agitation, and the blare of sirens. I turned left on Wilson, and then right on a side street. When I reached King, I turned right again. Suddenly, a Hamilton police car raced up behind me, quickly turning itself horizontal to block the road at that light. We were now cordoned off by police, and locked into a slow-moving traffic jam. Clearly something had occurred up ahead.

When we again reached James Street, I asked someone at the light what had happened. They said that Trudeau was going to dinner and that there were protesters chasing him. We turned left and went up Hamilton Mountain, finding our way to the comforts of a Dairy Queen sundae. Sweet relief.

The next day, Trudeau and Cabinet Minister Filomena Tassi visited the Automotive Resource Center at McMaster University – just up the hill from where we lived. The press was there in full force. I believe that the 'cabinet meeting' ended on Wednesday evening, January 25.

On the morning of Thursday January 26, I went to a nearby public library early in the morning to work on the very detailed affidavit that I was intending to file the next day for my CSIS related Privacy Act appeal. As I sat there, I again knew something was coming. Something to frighten me, or to show me who's boss, or to claw me back from filing this privileged and revealing document on the court record. *I just knew.* Like clockwork, at 10:01 am, I received an absurd email from Detective Rowan. I will include it, and our subsequent interactions, before speaking to it thereafter:

> Hi Jeff,
> Rather than call you, I decided to put this in writing as you have expressed concerns about privacy pertaining to your phone lines.
>
> I have reviewed the documents you have provided; including emails, screenshots, transcripts, audio recordings, reports from other investigators, and monitored the 3.5 hour interview you had with our polygraph expert. I am aware you have kept a copy of additional emails – but from my understanding there is no additional new information in those emails that you have not already provid-

ed.

As a result of the investigation, I have concluded that there are no grounds to proceed with Criminal Charges, and there is no proof of criminality stemming from the claims you have made.

I appreciate you taking the time to forward your investigative ideas for follow-up, but I would like to reinforce that there is nothing that you have reported that constitutes a criminal offence has been committed.

I have many years of experience dealing with people and criminal investigations – and I did find some of your own statements very concerning. This matter has consumed you for several years – to the point you believe tracking devices have been implanted inside of your body. At one point in the interview you paused and said, "I don't know what's real." This worries me and I do hope that you are able to move on and put these things behind you. In regards to your mental health, I would encourage you to reach out and speak with someone you trust, like a family member or professional assistance; perhaps they could assist you during this time. The Hamilton Police always has COAST available if you ever need to talk.

COAST HAMILTON

In conclusion, there are no grounds to further a criminal investigation in the matters you've alerted us to.

Take care,
Detective Nathan Rowan
Intelligence Branch
Organized Crime Investigator
Hamilton Police Service

Such irony. The guy who was highly agitated in the room because of the missing USB stick was accusing me of mental health issues. I had been able to remain intact for then over 3 years under some of the most grueling, challenging, and dire circumstances I had ever faced and maintained my focus, met my responsibilities, and persevered. If there had been any evidence of mental instability in my video statement, Nathan would not have taken me in another room to try to persuade me that the USB stick was 'overwritten.' And, he certainly wouldn't have discussed the next investigative steps with me.

I replied accordingly shortly thereafter:

Nathan, My reference to not knowing what is real was a reference to a singular event that I agreed may have been a dream (as my wife had suggested). I had chosen to accept her view as true at the time, but, because of the various events that had happened the nights before (and the fact that I have no history of confusing my dreams with reality), I was left to wonder. I do not feel paranoid about it, nor do I feel it necessary to have my body probed. It was just a concern, and one where it is impossible for me to know if it is valid. Nonetheless, that was not the thrust of my allegations, which have been thoroughly detailed in the documents I provided you. Are you saying that because of that one reference, that nothing here is worthy of investigation? sincerely, Jeff

And then he responded, indicating that I had called twice (I had actually called the office once – it seemed plausible to me that nervous Nathan was exaggerating as part of his effort to characterize me as an obsessive.) Although I do remember trying his cell phone a few times and it said something like 'this number is no longer in service.' Did they set that up so he couldn't talk with me? Why was he so insistent on email alone? Was he actually feeling guilty?

> Hey Jeff,
> I just was notified by my office that you called a couple times. I'm in Toronto now on another matter and will do my best to get back to you asap.
> Thanks for your patience.
> Nathan

And later that day,

> Hi Jeff,
> I do not believe I can give you an answer that will completely satisfy you.
> I have thoroughly examined the evidence you have provided. I watched and reviewed the interview you had with our polygraph expert.
> What is crucial to a Police investigation is determining whether a criminal offence has occurred. If a criminal offence has not occurred, then it is not reasonable to continue with further investigative steps. After examining and reviewing the evidence I do not believe that a criminal offence has occurred.
> It is my professional opinion that you are not the subject of an illegal wiretap.
> This matter has had the consultation of two divisional detec-

tives, an interviewing expert, the Intelligence Branch Staff Sergeant and myself (a Sergeant in the Intelligence Branch). It is a unanimous opinion that there is nothing further to investigate.

If you are not satisfied with the conclusion there are other avenues to pursue like the OIPRD etc.

Regards,
Nathan

And my response:

Nathan, I hear you, but- with all due respect- it just doesn't make sense. How can you say there is no illegal wiretap, without evidence that it didn't occur, or at least an investigation into whether it can be proven? I don't know anyone who ever answered a cell phone call and a stranger is there. If it's a spoof call, sure, but not if their friend calling could hear them. And that it happened after that intense week with Mrs. Trudeau giving me pushback about my wanting to disconnect, a wiretap is the only reasonable explanation. And Troy and I discussed that text that came in at the end of the media call, and he agreed that contacting the liberal party to see who sent that text was a good investigative idea, in this context. As for the spider story, I shared that casually. It was never something I deemed significant enough to note in the summaries. If I was a paranoid person, I would have hundreds of stories like that. I don't. It's the only super weird thing that stays with me as a lingering wondering. I have provided so much material that supports the idea that there is wrongdoing here. Is there really no way for you to investigate some of the components? I am not giving you attitude. I respect what all of you do, and I called you because I have faith in law enforcement. I wouldn't waste your time or mine, if I didn't sincerely believe that crimes were committed. sincerely, Jeff

No reply.

The next day, I wrote and asked for a copy of my video statement:

Hi Nathan, I understand that you made your decision, so I won't ask about it again. One last thing- Is it possible for me to get a copy of the recording that I did with Troy? Is it possible to send me a download link, or something I can have picked up? take care, Jeff

Before I dignify this nonsense with an explanation, I should also point out that <u>only a few hours</u> after I received the investigation terminating email from Detective Rowan (or whoever penned that work of fallacy-ridden logic), I also received another email. This one was sent at 2:07 PM from CSIS, wherein they responded to my December letter to their Director, David Vigneault. You may remember that I was required to send a letter before I could apply to the NSIRA – CSIS's overseeing body – for their help. This was their interestingly timed response:

> Dear Jeffrey Brown:
> This is in response to your letter dated December 9, 2022, in which you request assistance from the Canadian Security Intelligence Service (CSIS).
>
> The mandate of CSIS, under section 12 of the CSIS act, is to investigate and advise the Government of Canada for threats to national security. For the purpose of fulfilling this mandate, threats to the security of Canada are defined in section 2 of the Act and are limited to terrorism, espionage, sabotage, and foreign interference.
>
> The circumstances you describe have been carefully reviewed and the appropriate internal inquiries have been made. We can assure you that CSIS is neither responsible for, nor involved in, the circumstances you describe.
>
> We trust the foregoing has been of some assistance.
>
> Sincerely, (unnamed human or bot)

And so, in only a few hours, the criminal investigation that was active and confirmed days earlier, and – if I was going to take the CSIS letter at face value – the purpose of my privileged Privacy Act Appeal, were both essentially nullified. Well-played, maestros. Well-played.

Now, back to Mr. Rowan's unfounded accusations. I am responding not because they have any true merit, but because it is important to put gaslighting in its place. We had already seen Mrs. Trudeau's attempt to characterize me as someone with a mental health issue related to a sleep aid (after my December 5, 2020 farewell email). The RCMP subsequently characterized me as a stalker, and so it is no surprise the Hamilton Police resorted to citing a mental health issue. Without these offensive maneuvers, the emperor would surely have no clothes.

Here is further analysis of these letters, with my correlating commentary in italics:

Detective Rowan's hypocrisy reveals itself in the first sentence: "Hi Jeff, Rather than call you, I decided to put this in writing as you have expressed concerns about privacy pertaining to your phone lines."

He is essentially accepting the possibility that my line is or may well be tapped (and later claiming that there is nothing to investigate with respect to that possibility). If he wasn't accepting the possibility, he would have no problem calling me.

MR. ROWAN'S LETTER: He has 'reviewed' various things, including my 3.5 hour interview with their 'polygraph expert'.

The man he is referring to is 'Troy', and I assure you that if you met him, you would not make the assumption that he is a walking polygraph test. He seemed like a nice chap, but nothing about him screamed 'walking polygraph test.' And take note that I have never been asked – in the now 4+ years since I first contacted Hamilton Police – to take a polygraph. Ask yourself why.

In addition, let me remind you that I spoke with Detective Rowan – in a taped phone conversation – the previous week, where <u>he confirmed the investigation</u> and that he and Troy simply had to arrange their schedules so they could meet to split up their investigative duties.

MR. ROWAN'S LETTER: "As a result of the investigation I have concluded that there are no grounds to proceed with Criminal Charges, and there is no proof of criminality stemming from the claims you have made. I appreciate you taking the time to forward your investigative ideas for follow-up, but I would like to reinforce that there is nothing that you have reported that constitutes a criminal offence has been committed."

The above is coming from a man who witnessed the video interview, where Troy and I talked about the distinction between criminal and non-criminal acts, and agreed upon various criminal inquiries i.e. investigating the phone interception from December 12, 2020, and looking into who might have sent the Liberal party text at the end of the media call. In my subsequent conversation with Detective Rowan in the room, he acknowledged that he had already begun the investigation i.e. he had looked into my wife's history, he had the name of someone he knew at CBSA to contact about the passport ping issue, and we agreed (1) that he was going to see if his technology team could check my house/computers; (2) that I was to send him the contact info for the friend who called (and heard) me when the line was intercepted; (3) that I was to send him my various phone numbers and my wife's phone number to have them checked (presumably for current wiretaps); (4) that he may be able to check with my cell phone company to see if they could confirm the existence of someone on my phone December 12, 2020; (5) other numbers for people I shared the story with soon after the event (including a former Peel Police Inspector). I sent him that, and a list of 18 investigative ideas.

Chapter 16: There's a Spider on the Pillow?

MR. ROWAN'S LETTER: "I have many years of experience dealing with people and criminal investigations – and I did find some of your own statements very concerning. This matter has consumed you for several years – to the point you believe tracking devices have been implanted inside of your body. At one point in the interview you paused and said, "I don't know what's real." This worries me and I do hope that you are able to move on and put these things behind you. In regards to your mental health, I would encourage you to reach out and speak with someone you trust, like a family member or professional assistance; perhaps they could assist you during this time. The Hamilton Police always has COAST available if you ever need to talk.

COAST HAMILTON

In conclusion, there are no grounds to further a criminal investigation in the matters you've alerted us to.

Take care,
Detective Nathan Rowan
Intelligence Branch
Organized Crime Investigator
Hamilton Police Service

He is insinuating I am an obsessive ("consumed for <u>years</u>") who BELIEVES (rather than wonders) that tracking devices (actually, 1 tracking device) have been implanted inside of my body, and I do not, generally "know what's real." Apart from the defamatory mischaracterizations (to be discussed in a moment), here's the problem. Even if we were to accept that I am not living in something that Nathan calls "reality," then all that might do is omit the phone interception as a viable investigative path. Not sure how they deal with the fact that my friend heard me talking to someone else on the phone, or the fact that my wife was sitting beside me, or that I have never had a single significant mental health issue apart from the neurosis that plagues most of humanity, but their bigger problem is that many of the things I have reported are objectively verifiable. For example, I have reported a Liberal Party text at the end of a media phone call and provided evidence that I was not on the Party list. I have provided evidence of significant Facebook warnings/violations right after making steps forward (which suggests that there may be a connection between the wiretapping 'organization' and someone at Meta). I have reported a variety of alarm issues, perfectly timed with various visitors to my home etc. All of those things, if proven, are likely criminal code offences, and all of them were included on the list of viable investigative paths. And Detective Rowan knows it.

I will proceed to address the tracking device story. Around the end of July/August 2021, I felt something bite my right ankle area 4-5 times over the course of a week. It was always on my right leg, and always on the right side of the bed. I would either be falling asleep, or just asleep, when it occurred. It was an intense, razor-sharp bite, something perhaps more than a bedbug. I was too tired and overwhelmed to think much about it, but I did tell my wife that I wondered if we had a bedbug. She was certain that we didn't have bedbugs, but she cleaned the sheets. It happened again.

One morning, after she had gone downstairs to get her coffee, I woke up and opened my eyes, looking toward her pillow. I saw a small metallic blue creature – about 2-3 inches in size – on Susan's pillow, heading toward me. It appeared robotic. It looked like one of those remote control spiders that people buy at hobby shoppes. As soon as it caught my glance, it turned around and scurried away.

I immediately got up and searched the floor and the bed. There was nothing there. I went downstairs and told Susan about the occurrence. She surmised that I had probably had an anxiety dream. It was true that I had just woken up, and perhaps was still in a kind of in-between dreamlike state. Yet, it is important to note that I have no history confusing dreams with reality. But I accepted her interpretation and thought very little about it thereafter. Even if it was all part of the strange 'letting me know they are there' game, it wasn't particularly significant. Because I already knew that they were there. They were on my phones. They were manipulating my Facebook and Instagram. What is curious is that after the "spider" appearance – the bites to my leg ceased altogether.

Weeks before giving my police statement, my wife and I went out for dinner with a lawyer friend and his wife. While enjoying our dinner, I told them the spider story. His wife – a former Eastern European – said that it was very common for politically motivated operatives to install tiny tracking devices in those they wanted to monitor. She was quite confident in her assertions, and we discussed whether I should have my leg checked. My wife suggested the veterinarian we use for our cat Lacy, as they are versed in implant devices like a microchip. I gave it some thought, and decided not to bother. Not because I thought it impossible, but because I hadn't noticed any indication of an entry wound. And, it didn't make sense to me that they would need to do this to monitor me. After all, phones, vehicles, and computers are easy tracking devices. So, why would they bother?

Chapter 16: There's a Spider on the Pillow?

During the interview with Troy, I brought up this incident. It had never been anything that I listed as an investigative issue, but I suppose I was curious if the police – being privy to modern-day security threats – knew something about the possibility of implantations. And now I see that I walked right into it. I would have to see a copy of the video for confirmation, but I do recall telling the story about the bite sensations, and the (possible) spider. His eyes lit up and he said something to the effect of: "Like a needle?" And I believe I replied, "Yes, like a needle." Because that was kind of how it felt. He then responded to the effect of: "Maybe you should get that checked." And I recall agreeing that I should. I believe I then mentioned the possibility that I was in a groggy in-between sleeping and waking state. I couldn't be sure, in this instance, if it was a real experience or was, as my wife suggested, an anxiety dream. I did not say I have any issue distinguishing fantasy from reality.

To no surprise, after the video recording, nobody mentioned having any issue with the casual manner in which I mentioned the implantation device. It did not flag the attention of the polygraph expert, or nervous Nathan when we privately discussed the missing USB stick, and specific investigate paths to pursue. There was no reference to my off-the-cuff mention of the spider-incident. And yet, it was cited in the letter as a key reason to abort the investigation. And, Detective Rowan certainly didn't mention the incident when CONFIRMING that the investigation was moving forward in our recent phone conversation. Because it wasn't an issue. Because this was all just a diversion to get out of investigating my claims. I have every faith that even if I hadn't shared that story, they would have cited some other excuse to terminate the investigation.

Now 56 months later, I look back on the spider events differently. There is no question that something was happening with respect to my right foot on those evenings. It is certainly possible that it was a combination of tension in that area of my body, extreme hypertension in my nervous system, and the way that I was positioned. Being in a continuous state of fight-or-flight can have all kinds of mysterious effects on the body. With respect to the robotic spider, it is more likely than not that it was a dream. I was drifting in and out of sleep, while my general sleep patterns during this time were disturbed and agitated. It is no wonder I would have dreams that magnified the subconscious processing of this situation. But I will never know. And, truth be told, it is now entirely meaningless. So very much has happened since that is anything but questionable.

Interestingly, I had a conversation with a friend of mine soon after these events with the cops. This was a person who had been in many spiritual communities, and was connected to various people who had left the espionage world. They would often come to these communities, to hide out with a new spiritual name. In any event, she explained that in the espionage world, often the first order of business – when trying to destroy the credibility of people who might publicly expose political figures – was to craft a strangely unbelievable scenario that could be used against them. In other words, to have the target experience something so outlandish that if they reported it, it would cast doubt on their sanity. Given that I am an author who is known to immediately write about and share his experiences in the public domain, the spider story could have done the trick. Except I didn't take it seriously enough to share it publicly, although I did make the mistake of sharing it with the cops.

It is worth noting that I have still not received the copy of my 'video statement' that I requested and am entitled to. Why haven't they provided it? Do they still have it, or did they pass it over to the RCMP? What about the second USB stick that I provided with the summaries? Where is that, now? If the laws permit, I would like nothing more than to put my video statement up on YouTube for the whole world to see. It is surely in the public interest. Then we can decide together, what is *really* going on here.

Soon after the termination of the investigation, I went onto Facebook and began to write a post about what had just transpired with Hamilton Police. I was rightfully pissed off. In the midst of writing it, a never-before-seen written warning flashed before me. Something to the effect that what I just wrote – even if it wasn't yet publicly posted – was possibly subject to prosecution. It flashed so quickly that I was unable to capture a screenshot (which I assume was their intention). But I clearly and indisputably saw it. It confirmed my theory that they had someone on me 24/7.

Much more on that soon…

CHAPTER 17

WINKGATE

After forwarding my emails from Detective Rowan (or his ghost-writer) to Cribb, The Star stepped back from publishing. It was my view that the story had now become even more relevant to the public interest – I mean, could a now 16-month-long cover up have been any more obvious? – but that was apparently not the editor's view. I did tell Cribb that I would grant The Star permission to make a Freedom of Information (Privacy Act) request for my video statement, or that I would simply send it when I received a copy from the cops. If he watched it, I was confident that he would see that the characterization of me as someone who cannot distinguish fact from fiction was nonsense. But he chose not to pursue this. Strange.

(Note: In a recent conversation with Cribb, he did not recall my suggesting that to him. I choose to believe him. I am more inclined to think that it had not landed as an investigative path simply because he knew that it wasn't going to prove fruitful even if the video exposed the inanity of the police's story. Because the police have a tremendous amount of latitude with respect to whether they wish to pursue an investigation. That's just the way it is. To his credit, he now informed me that after this second investigative turnback, he had a number of conversations with senior Hamilton police and spent an afternoon there inquiring into the question of whether the RCMP had interfered with the initial investigation i.e. by providing the fictitious stalking story. They did not deny it, nor did they confirm it. In his words, "What I brought back was not sufficient for the confidence of editors." So, he was shit out of luck. And so was I.)

After the police and the Star's retreat, the very prominent litigation lawyer who had been helping me with some of the documents, told me that he was retiring from his long-time practice. I had engaged in a phone conversation with him right after receiving the investigation-terminating emails from Detective Rowan, and he did sound quite agitated. In fact, he often sounded agitated when we spoke about this situation. In any event, his resignation was quite significant because it meant that I was now truly alone. His presence had been very grounding and helpful. Strangely, I have seen him making news for subsequent litigation matters. Hmmm.

I again considered releasing it all to the winds. I had surely fought the good fight, but these systems were not designed to protect citizens. They were designed to protect Prime Ministers. They were designed to shield wrongdoers. They were designed to gaslight victims. And there was nothing one person could possibly do. It would take an army, and I didn't have one. I just had me, and some tired old faith that justice would prevail. In other words, I was royally fucked.

I contemplated withdrawing my Federal Court action. Not because of The Star's hasty retreat, but because of what had happened with the police. Even if they had been unable to prove that crimes had been committed, the very fact that they were going to pursue the investigation had invigorated my sense of self, and revitalized my sense of hope. It reminded me: I had rights again. Or so I imagined. And the police's retreat – particularly the very desperate energy coming off it – felt like it was something far more than a neutral thing. I could not disregard the mannerisms, body language, and overall energy of Detective Rowan when he tried to convince me that the USB stick had simply been written over by Detective Sgt. Knapp. It felt desperate and untrustworthy. When I received his circus act of investigation-terminating emails, I could feel that same dark distorted energy, now fueled by all the higher-ups who I suspect had conspired on this plan. A chorus of characters who were likely terrified that they would lose their jobs if the public ever found out what had happened the year before.

The PTSD symptoms that had released some of their grip over the holidays returned, compounded by the fear of what my intimidators would do next. Because now I had a real problem – <u>I was entirely unprotected</u>. Nobody was coming to check if my phone or my car or my house were probed, and even if I found evidence of wrongdoing, I couldn't call it in. Because I had been declared a "stalker" and mentally unfit. If some event were to force them to take my concerns seriously, they would look even worse than they did before. If I couldn't call my local police for protection, who could I call? Not my lawyer, the media (clearly), the RCMP – who had made it clear that they wouldn't get involved without a referral from local police – or CSIS, because, after all, I wasn't a terrorist, a saboteur, a foreign interferer. Who then? Ghostbusters? Wayne Gretzky? Captain America? Where were my comic book heroes when I needed them?[61]

Chapter 17: Winkgate

I was also aware that whoever was trying to intimidate me was aware that I had no other investigative options. So, they could pretty much do anything, and get away with it. And, so they did.

Despite my discomfort, I felt an odd kind of compassion for the Police, locked as they were inside of their archaic chain of command system, one where any cop who dared to disagree would suffer the consequences. My whole journey had been a kind of meditation on power, and my perspective was broadening. The thing is, I have generally liked cops, and have fond memories of working with Eddie Greenspan to help them. And I now understood that all of us – even those who seem to benefit from abuses of power – are trapped inside of an ungratifying and savage system that ultimately benefits few. Once the cops put this fire out, they would likely be onto the next, doing whatever it takes to keep their ship afloat and shield themselves from public scrutiny. Not because they are inherently horrible people, but because humans have yet to devise systems that truly serve and protect everyone. In a certain sense, we are all victims of abuse of power, even those who abuse it.

Soon enough, I regained my footing. Not sure where my determination was coming from, but it kept returning. Something about listening to the music of Geoffrey Oryema and Krishna Das seemed to kick me back into gear. And, something about reflecting on the relationship between this experience and my soul's journey, kept me just curious enough to walk on.

I then served my affidavit of facts on the Attorney General in the federal court matter on February 1. It was a frightening step to take, given that it included many of the emails (and 2 of the poems) that Mrs. Trudeau had sent me, and a full transcript of our phone conversation on December 8, 2020. It also included a myriad of additional details, including reference to the spate of fake Revenue Canada and Facebook emails that I was receiving on my Hotmail account. Interestingly, I stopped seeing them there soon after filing the document.

The next step was to wait for the Attorney General to serve me their affidavit of facts within 30 days. And then, we would come together for a cross-examination process. In the meantime, I turned my attention to working on the book. Nobody was going to help me. It was clearly up to me to bring this story to the world. As I began the writing process – I felt more empowered. Both because exercising my voice helps me to come to terms with it, and because every chapter brought me one step closer to reaching the public. A double-edged sword to be sure, but one that I preferred to keeping all of this locked inside.

On February 16, I faxed the information that Revenue Canada had requested re: the HST Review. I explained that there was no meaningful discrepancy between the figures because I had been filing using the paper form, which does not have a line for Zero-Rated (outside of Canada) sales. That line is only available if you file electronically. I would have thought they already knew that, but it appears they didn't. I awaited their reply.

Soon thereafter, I spoke with the Revenue Canada representative who had made the initial request to confirm that he had received my information. He indicated that he had. Much to my surprise, he was friendly as could be, even indicating that he would add a note on my account that I had been using paper forms so that I wouldn't receive one of these requests for the following 2 filing years.

I couldn't help but wonder if he had been instructed to be particularly easy-going just now. If I was reading this right, the review had been sent when it was as a tactic to either overwhelm me, or deter me from proceeding with the appeal and police investigation. Just letting me know they were there, again. But it didn't work. I filed the affidavit with many of the salacious details included. The next step was the cross examination – one step closer to putting all the documents on the public record.

In the coming weeks, strange things continued to happen. I would open my iPhone and it would show me the weather in Ottawa. I received four site lockout notifications on February 25 for my publishing house website: www.enrealment.com. They didn't yet include the actual user name for the website, but that would happen soon enough.

I also continued to notice significant issues with advertising on Meta. My most popular download course landing page was still not capable of being boosted. When I tried to run an ad for another landing page for the course, it would only allow 'Facebook messages' for interested others rather than 'Learn More' with links to the landing page itself. I also found that my most popular active course (Writing your Way Home) could not be boosted from one of my devices as well. I had taught this course for 7 years, with nary an advertising issue. This may seem like a small thing, but when you rely on social media advertising to survive, it is quite significant. It was getting clearer all the time that somebody out there was of the belief that restricting my livelihood would ensure my silence. And, as noted earlier, if someone at Meta was doing this deliberately, <u>they were limiting shareholder profits at the same time</u>. (Where's the SEC when I need them?)

Chapter 17: Winkgate

On March 7, I received a Notice of Motion from the lawyer for the Department of Justice. In it, he indicated that they were bringing a motion to seal certain documents before filing their affidavit, and they were seeking to make their submissions to the judge *ex parte* (in my absence). Strange. In the emailed letter from CSIS Director David Vigneault in January, he had indicated that there was nothing there. Yet, they now had something in my personal information file that they were determined to seal. In other words, I would never know what was in there. So, I discontinued the application altogether, and set my sights on the step that had been recommended by someone I spoke with at the Privacy Commissioner: Request that the NSIRA do a search inside the personal information bank. Now that I had evidence of what appeared to be a contradiction (nothing in there vs. something to seal), I felt hopeful that I might finally get some real answers.

I didn't hold this against Roger Flaim – the counsel for the Department of Justice. I know that he was just doing what his client asked him to do. In fact, in all of my interactions with Mr. Flaim, I was startled by the depths of his sincerity, decency, and empathy. After two years of feeling like my rights as a Canadian had been stolen, his manner alone bolstered my spirits, and reminded me that my natural-born human rights actually mattered. In the midst of this debacle, it was easy to lose sight of that. A true dignitarian, his humane way of relating in an adversarial system should be studied and implemented by law societies the world over. Because even if you lose in court, you will <u>always remember</u> the way that you were dealt with by people in positions of authority. That alone will change our world.

Perhaps most memorably, Roger let me know that his office had been having trouble with my legal argument. That is, the contention that the "presumption of perfection" [the assumption that something is in perfect condition or operates flawlessly without evidence or proof] built into the statute was unconstitutional under certain circumstances. So, if you are an activist who seeks to make the world a better place, consider taking some time to sift through any government statute that contains similar clauses, and launching a constitutional challenge into the court system. It is imperative that we remove all possibilities of Dudley Do-Wrong from the system.

After signing the discontinuance, I made one more empowering step. I contacted my web designer to remove the video of myself and Mrs. Trudeau conversing in 2018. It was the last vestige of our connection on my website. As noted earlier, I left it there as evidence of our connection – in the event I reached out to someone who needed to verify it. Having made the firm decision to write this book, there was no need to reach out to anyone new again. My power was back in my own hands.

On March 12, I booked a two-day writing-cation at the Delta Hotel in Guelph, Ontario for March 17-19. I liked writing there now and then. I booked it on my main laptop, and the notification was sent to my main Hotmail account.

When I arrived at the hotel on March 17, I saw something on TV that indicated that Trudeau was in Guelph that same day to announce a $4 billion housing accelerator fund for Canada. How uncanny. I had lived in nearby Rockwood and didn't remember him being in Guelph very often, if at all. That evening, while closing the drapes, I looked down at the parking lot and noticed that there were some large black vehicles that are often used to drive around dignitaries. I wondered to myself: "Is he staying here tonight?" I dismissed the thought and went back to work. It seemed unlikely, given that they can fly him back home to Ottawa on a moment's notice.

At some point, I did browse the Prime Minister's posted itinerary for today on the government website. It indicated that the media was to arrive by 930 AM and he was to make the announcement at 1030 AM. No indication that he was spending the rest of the day in Guelph.

On the morning of March 23, my wife and I were in the house. Her phone was close by. She shared that she wanted me to text her "I miss you" more often, when I was away from the home. She was naturally feeling isolated in this demented situation that we were in. That morning almost immediately after I left the house, she received the following text from an unfamiliar phone number:

I miss you!

Wondering if it was me using a different phone, she texted the question "Who are you?"

She received a quick reply:

Nice to hear that, I'm Diana, remember me?

She responded:

from where? Think you have the wrong number

Another quick response:

in Manhattan. Are you not Sophia?

Chapter 17: Winkgate

Of course, there were numerous suspicious occurrences up until this point. It was becoming commonplace. When you are inside of them, they become increasingly obvious to you. It simply becomes your life. At the same time, it is difficult to gather all the evidence as it unfolds, because you are trying to maintain the demands of work and everyday life. It takes a concentrated effort to put it out of mind, in an attempt to normalize. In other words, you try to ignore it, so you can get through your day in one piece.

But, as you will see in a moment, some "synchronicities" are simply too obvious to ignore.

On March 27, Cribb was good enough to arrange a meeting for us with a lawyer he had recently met. A very experienced litigator who had knowledge of the ways that the national security system functions within Canada.

While driving to the meeting, Cribb and I had an intense phone conversation about things that had transpired. Even though I did not agree with The Star's decision not to publish after the second police fiasco, I appreciated his efforts to bring the story through. It had been a lonely journey, and just the fact that there was an engaged journalist walking beside me was a great comfort. I am even left to wonder if his involvement in this story somehow kept me safe.

I met with them at a Wine Bar in downtown Toronto. This may have been the most useful conversation I'd had in over two years of trying to understand what the fuck was going on here. The lawyer had looked over some of the details of my story, and had some thoughts to share. I listened close, as he laid it down.

The first thing he noted was that it was very likely that CSIS was involved with some or all of the shenanigans. Not because I am an actual threat to the security of Canada, but because the information that I held – beginning with the material carelessly shared with me by Wildhorse in her kitchen – would be perceived as potential *kompromat* (a Russian word for damaging information, which may be used to create negative publicity, as well as for blackmail) that could be used against the administration. Of course, an ordinary citizen doesn't think like this – our understanding of national security risks is only known vicariously, through shows like Homeland. I certainly had no interest in selling information to the Russkies, but government agencies tasked with protecting our borders, don't know that until they look into you. The lawyer asserted that it was very likely that they investigated me and my personal background, in one form or another, if only to ensure that I wasn't an actual threat to national security. He also contended that it would be best if I didn't fly over Russian or Chinese airspace, given that it was certainly possible that they have caught wind of this situation. He was concerned that they would find a way to force the plane to land, in an effort to gain access to my information.

Before I left the meeting, he agreed to submit my NSIRA application in his name. After going through most of this alone, I finally understood the value of legal clout.

After the meeting, I took some time to integrate this information. Something about it felt significant. It wasn't that I didn't already know that I was being monitored by one entity or another. It was that I hadn't really put all of this in the context of a national security threat. A journalist had mentioned something to that effect after digging around and speaking to one of their sources in the summer of 2021, but it hadn't really landed then. In my naivete, I hadn't fully understood that any information you hold that can expose the truth about national leadership will be immediately perceived as potentially dangerous on an international level. Throughout this situation – and certainly in those instances where Mrs. Trudeau reacted strongly after my attempts to disconnect – I saw it as a situation where she and possibly her husband were concerned about Canadians discovering compromising things about their marriage – and my political contributions – because of their potential effect on their political agendas. This did not move me, as a justification for the terrifying shenanigans of the past years.

Yet the issue of an international security threat did move me as an appropriate – albeit nefarious – justification. Not because I had any lingering compassion for the Trudeaus but because I am Canadian and have no interest in compromising our borders. I can comprehend, to some extent, that government agencies tasked with protecting national security have to keep watch on various people now and then. As long as they do it lawfully, it's a necessary evil.

I sat with this perspective for some time to see how it might influence my drive to bring my story to the world. After much reflection, I decided to continue writing my story. Because even if this situation was truly about a perceived '(inter)national security risk,' it should have been handled in a manner that respected the rights and well-being of this Canadian citizen and his wife. Simply put, they should have contacted me and talked it through face-to-face. I'm a reasonable person, always open to adult conversations. And CSIS is known for visiting with people of concern.

Chapter 17: Winkgate

It's well within their ambit, and I would not have been offended by such a conversation. It would have helped me to understand the bigger picture. If they had done that, all of this may have gone down differently. But they didn't. They either were never involved – which means all of this was possibly off-book – or they were somewhat involved and didn't have the professional integrity to contact me directly.

So, I kept writing the book. It was not an easy task. Imagine sitting in your home, wondering if you are being bugged, and trying to say nothing aloud that gives away what you are doing. When I became concerned that my main computers were infiltrated, I went and purchased one with a different writing program. I had grown so accustomed to decades of using Word that it was a difficult creative adjustment. Add to this, the feeling that you are being watched while creating, particularly by someone who doesn't want your story told, and writing becomes an arduous mountain to climb.

I often thought of acclaimed Canadian writer (and Senator) David Richards's recent speech about Bill-C-11 (a Federal Bill that grants the Government the right to control what Canadian's see and read on the internet) where he reminded us of a passage shared in Russian writer Aleksandr Solzhenitsyn's 1968 novel *In the First Circle*, where he references a novelist (a favorite of Stalin's) sitting down to write a book with the expressed intention of writing the truth, but feeling as though Stalin's eyes are upon him, he decides to make the next book the truthful one. I didn't actually imagine Trudeau's physical eyes upon me, but I did understand something of the novelist's plight.[62]

On April 5, I received the first of many emails from someone (allegedly) named Harsh Oza – a self-described Meta Marketing Pro – to arrange a time to discuss my advertising goals and future campaign ideas. Historically, I would be occasionally contacted by a variety of Facebook marketing employees that would schedule times to discuss goals and challenges – they would email me on my Hotmail account. What was strange about this guy is that he was writing me on my main website (jeffbrown.co) email address. I had never received a legitimate Facebook email at that address.

I booked a time with him for May, mainly to see if this was a real business meeting, or yet another mind game.

* * *

On Friday, April 14, I received a key text from Robert Cribb, checking in to see if there had been any progress on my NSIRA application:

Robert: Yo. Any updates?

Jeff: Focused on many aspects including the submissions through (name redacted – the lawyer we recently met with)

Robert: Are you guys in touch?

Jeff: Sent him the stuff to submit. And just checked and we r opening a file. I am not stopping until there is justice.

Robert: Who is opening a file?

Jeff: (lawyer name redacted)

Robert: Great!

Two mornings later – Sunday April 16 – I (and WT) received the following text from Cribb, sent at 9:06 AM Pacific Standard Time:

> *Funny story this morning, gentlemen. I was jogging on the sea wall in Vancouver. A guy passes me slowly to my left. Another guy is behind him. They continue for a few minutes running slightly ahead of me, then the first guy stops, turns around and heads back. As he passes me, he looks at me and I at him. It's Justin. He gives me a smile and a wink.*

Yes, dear reader, you read that right.

The next day, I took a look at the Prime Minister's publicly posted itinerary for Sunday April 16th, and it clearly stated the following:

National Capital Region, Canada
Personal

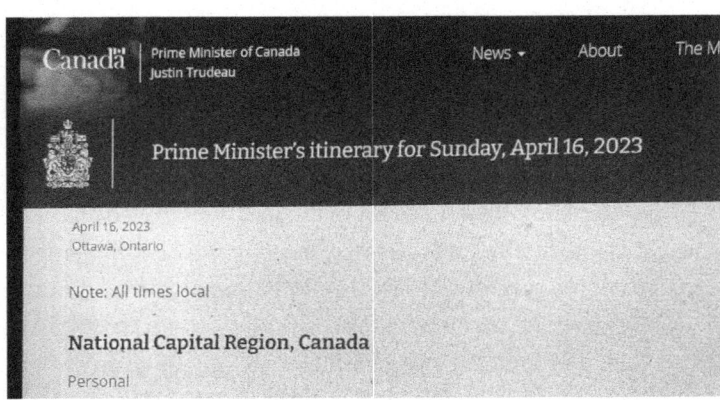

Needless to say, the National Capital Region is the Ottawa area. And I suppose 'personal reasons' includes flying across the country to smile and wink at the Toronto Star journalist covering my story... only a few days after we had texts confirming my NSIRA application.

Just letting him know he's there.

Synchronicity? I think not.

Chapter 17: Winkgate

* * *

After this last bit of insanity, I was sure that the Star would publish. The Canadian people surely had a right to know what was going on here. And I assumed that Cribb agreed – the fact that he felt compelled to text me and WT soon after it happened signaled to me that he understood its significance in the context of this story. But his editor(s) didn't agree. He recently told me that he had brought it to them, but it didn't hit the publishing bar. Huh?

On April 21, 2023, while texting a friend in Winnipeg about what happened with Cribb in Vancouver, I received a text from number 17 "Num. Msg. 7." I looked into it and found out that when someone is in your phone (<u>not</u> your line), that these kinds of numerical messages confirm that what you texted is being forwarded to someone else.

On April 28, in response to a Pierre Poilievre post about Trudeau spending personal time in the Big Apple while the largest federal strike was taking place in Canada, I wrote this: "Justin wants to be a star. Problem is he has no talent or personality." I knew when I wrote this, there would be consequences.

I woke up the next morning with a Facebook community standards notification (I believe only my 4th issue in 15 years). It certainly could have been arbitrary, but I doubt it. Someone at Meta went into one of my groups (*Soulshaping*) and found something there that allegedly "went against our Community Standards on sexual exploitation of adults." And... "No one else can see this post. We have these standards because we want discussions on Facebook to be respectful." Underneath, it said, "POST UNAVAILABLE. We are unable to show content that goes against our Community Standards on sexual exploitation of adults. To protect other's privacy and keep everyone safe from harmful content, we do not show content that violates Community Standards on sexual exploitation of adults."

Quite apart from the obvious fact that their community standards are nothing more than a subjective game, they conveniently failed to show me what they had found. But they did let me know that there is "Good News: no violations to show." My subjective interpretation: *We went into your group and allegedly found some issue with something somebody wrote (although you will never be able to confirm it, because we blocked it from your view in the Details section designed to show it). We did this so that we could intimidate you to back away from crossing the line towards a Trudeau public revealing… but not scare you back so much that you are suspended here and we have to worry about you going fully public in response.*

The game was on and on…

CHAPTER 18

HUMANIFESTATIONS

My new book of quotes came out in May 2023. Normally a great delight to finally get a book to the world, *Humanifestations* was hobbled from the get-go. I should let you know that the book does contain 12 quotes (pages 5, 25, 52, 92, 95, 101, 108, 120, 139, 142, 151, 153) that I had written and shared on Meta that directly relate to this ongoing situation. I have little doubt that they had been seen by whoever was monitoring me at the time.

In April, I had contacted my US distributor for *Enrealment Press* to see if they could get a pre-purchase Buy Box established on Amazon.com. Normally there from the beginning, I had noticed that it was absent for some time. Then they would add it back in, and then remove it again. Challenging to build energy around a new book publish without it on Amazon. I would later notice that the 'Jeff Brown' bio on the book's Amazon page was connected to a different author by the name of Jeff Brown. In my 15 years as a published Author, I don't recall seeing this happen before. I contacted Amazon via "Author's page" to remedy it, and they did so.

We distribute to Amazon Canada directly from our home office. Before you get orders from Amazon, you have to add the book to the list. Usually an easy process, I had considerable technical troubles and glitches – resulting in many emails back and forth – before I could get the new book added to my account. After it was eventually added, we received a number of orders that were returned by Amazon. In many years distributing to Amazon.ca, I don't remember ever seeing a book returned, other than an occasional book that was damaged while shipping. None of these books were damaged, but they apparently were not welcome on Amazon.ca. Now we had a real problem.

In addition, the new book was not coming up on searches on Amazon.ca and Amazon UK as well. I had never seen a book not come up on searches, least of all one that was in the early stages when both the publisher and Amazon benefit from the build-up in sales. We all know that all Amazon cares about is earnings. In any event, I would punch in the name of the book in the search box, and it wouldn't come up. Other books – with the title *Manifestations* – would show up. But not *Humanifestations*. I wrote Amazon.ca and received a long-winded emailed response to the effect that "only one member of a family is chosen for display in search results when multiple members match a query." Problem is that there is no other product that uses the word *Humanifestations*.

There could be no doubt that someone at Amazon had been prompted to shadow ban and limit access to my new book, thereby limiting my earnings.

On May 10, 2023 at 10:23 AM, it got even more suspicious. I wrote this post on Facebook: "My Fellow Canadians! Some of you have been writing to me, with respect to trying to order a copy of my new book – *Humanifestations* – from Amazon Canada. And the book is not coming up in searches, nor is it orderable (despite the fact that we have stock.). I am pretty sure that I know who is beyond these shenanigans (as well as those here on Meta) – freedom of expression is not something welcomed by all – and I am doing my best to get things in proper order. Will let you know soon. In the meantime, this is the link…"[63]

About 90 minutes later, I received a Facebook hate speech warning. This one, related to my *Writing Your Way Home* course group that was active at the time. Someone at Meta went into the private group and found something written by one of the students and took it down. And yet again, I received only a notification, with no copy of their alleged error, and a reminder that my group wasn't being penalized. Naturally, the student was quite upset. So was I, because now I had to worry about whether I could continue to market this very popular writing course. Not simply because the previous strikes against me left me in a precarious position, but also because I had to be concerned about the safety of this very vulnerable writing group. If Big Daddy kept showing up to remove innocuous sharings, the students would feel unsafe and the course would develop a terrible

⚠ **A group participant shared a post that goes against our Community Standards on hate speech**

No one else can see this post. We have these standards because we want discussions on Facebook to be respectful.

Notice visible until August 8

Details
The following goes against our Community Standards on hate speech:

reputation. And – as would later be confirmed – if I had to remove the 'feedback group' option, the course would not sell anywhere near as well.

On May 11, I received a strange letter from Revenue Canada related to my Soulshaping Institute Source Deductions account. Source Deductions relate to the employee-related funds (i.e. pension, taxes) that you have to remit to the Canadian government by the 15th day of the following month. In this case, I had mailed the April payment in a timely manner. But Revenue Canada was on strike, so the check did not get deposited that month. In any event, in this letter dated May 8, 2023, they let me know that they had not received my April payment and that "Not remitting deductions withheld at source is a serious offence. We may charge you penalties for not making these deductions and remittances." They also provided a 'Remittance Breakdown Form' so that I could submit my (allegedly) missing remittance.

How very strange. They're claiming that I didn't submit a payment, while they were on strike and not processing payments. And, what's worse, the system doesn't mail you the form for the following month's payment, until they process your remittance. In other words, the next payment would be necessarily late because I didn't have a fresh form to submit.

I took a look at my bank account and discovered that the payment submitted in April was actually deposited by Revenue Canada on May 9, <u>one day after</u> this letter was mailed. Interesting.

So, I called them. The person on the phone confirmed that they had received my form and payment on April 14 – one day before it was actually due.

Given the nature and timing of various letters from Revenue Canada since this nightmare began, I had to wonder if this was yet another way of showing me who's boss. Under normal circumstances, I wouldn't give it a second thought – errors happen all the time – but in this context – and particularly because the check that they had received on April 14 was deposited one day after sending me the May 8 letter – I felt doubtful. Abuse of power had permeated most every system I dealt with.

On May 12, I had a scheduled appointment with Meta 'Marketing Pro', Harsh Oza. He didn't show up. I then received a few of his generic automatically generated emails the following week. Only when I responded to one of his emails inquiring about our missed appointment, did I receive a "technical issues" explanation for his absence. Harsh would regularly leave me hurried and incoherent phone messages from what appeared to be a Facebook number. I did email him at one point to confirm that the FB email that he wrote from was indeed his. He responded directly, so I made the assumption that he was a 'legitimate' Facebook marketing representative.

On May 18, I had a very emotional conversation on my cell phone with my best friend, Samuel. His mother had just passed away that morning. Among other things, we discussed the fact that she had made arrangements for her burial at a previous time. A mere few hours later, I received what would be the first of many 'Burial Insurance' emails on my Hotmail account. It's important to note that my phone and my email address are not connected. Someone was listening to the call and decided to send yet another triggering email to let me know they were there. Lovely people.

I would soon receive a steady and constant barrage of emails to the same account – all addressed to "Soulshapin" (almost the name of my first book, *Soulshaping*) – that concerned credit card debt, ADT security (our provider), taxation, car repairs, and loan opportunities. Now I understand that many people receive this kind of junk mail – just as many people receive Canada Post and Revenue Canada faux texts, but the trick to this story is, again, *timing*. There are the usual suspects with respect to junk transmissions (things that many people arbitrarily experience over the course of their busy week), and then there are – and continue to be – a significant number that are responsively timed to things I say and do. Not just on Meta, but everywhere I check messages.

That they continue to utilize techniques commonly used with the public makes perfect sense. This way, if they are ever publicly noted by me in the context of this story, it becomes easy to attribute my interpretation as paranoia. I get the game, now. That's not to say that my instincts are always right – they can't be in a reactive situation like this – but time has informed me that I am often right. Just like my surveillers have spent a considerable amount of time learning what makes me tick (and trigger), I have spent a lot of time tapping into the ebb and flow of their psychological warfare.

It was also no accident that almost every time I would break free of the tension that I was carrying and began to joyously sing in the car, I would immediately get dinged with another anxiety-provoking text. This occurred most frequently after I was singing to warrior empowerment music like 'The Hu.' They really wanted to keep Jeff Brown in a very limited range of feeling: tension and terror only. No spontaneous joy or self-confidence permitted.

Chapter 18: Humanifestations

With respect to Meta, I was also getting barraged by a series of fake 'Jeff Brown' pages and accounts that would connect with people (often women) on my Facebook business page. Some would message them in private, others would message them directly on the wall. What was particularly curious was that I was often unable to block many of them from the page. Yet, my followers indicated that they were able to block them from their devices. This led me to wonder if they were actually being engineered by Meta itself, in an effort to make it look like I was hitting on my own followers.

In addition – and this had already been going on for some time – I would find a horde of fake hacker and relationship repair comments on my Instagram and Facebook accounts. They would always provide a link to someone who could either get on your partner's phone and find out what they were up to, or someone who could help you with your relationship problems. At first, they seemed to be similar in number to those that I saw on other popular pages, but it then became clear that they were far more prevalent on mine. At some point – and many people on my FB business page can attest to this – it became a hacker link frenzy that led many people to write me to express their discomfort with remaining on the page. What was, and continues to be most interesting, is that the hacker posts <u>often appeared</u> about one minute after I began scrolling Facebook or Instagram on my phone or laptop. They then predominantly targeted posts that contained links to books or courses for purchase, and/or those individuals who made very <u>positive</u> comments about either me or the written piece that I had shared in the post.

Meanwhile, I continued to get a steady flow of faux Meta emails on my main website email address to the effect that my page and/or my account were going to be taken down. Whoever they were, they were making a lot of money playing with me.

* * *

Toward the end of the month, I had a strange inter-personal experience with a religious neighbor. The night before, while feeling particularly frustrated, I said quite loudly and near my phone that I was going to go see him and tell him EVERYTHING before going public. I was feeling desperate to blurt out the situation to someone.

Interestingly, he contacted me the next morning to meet for lunch. We met on the street, and walked to a nearby Thai restaurant. We were the only two people in the rather large restaurant. Soon after sitting down, a strangely curious man came in and sat down at the small table right across from us. He didn't look like he was from this area. He was dressed like someone from Quebec, or perhaps Europe. He could have sat anywhere – including at a cozy window table – but he made a point of sitting right across from us. I began to notice him looking at me regularly, like he was really wanting to get my attention. I couldn't help but notice the bag that he had with him. It was something that an art student might carry around with them – an open bag for sketch pads and the like. But there were no sketch pads hanging out of it. What did he have in there?

After the waiter brought him a menu, he connected to ask me what I was eating. He said something to the effect that he hadn't eaten Thai food before. I answered "Pad Woon Sen. It's fantastic!" He then ordered 'Pad Thai' like someone who had ordered it many times. He continued to look my way often with a particularly intense gaze. He ate his food relatively quickly before leaving.

To this point in the story, I'd only had two menacing interactions – the guy walking the dog who did the walk-by stare last autumn, and the menacing Hummer-like vehicle experience the year before. My wife had also recently had a strange experience. Just after speaking on her cell phone to a friend who referred to her daughter as a "Princess," she left the house to go for a walk. About a minute later, a man leaning against a vehicle in a nearby parking lot made a point of communicating with her: "Hi Princess!" My wife hasn't been called a Princess in about 45 years, so that was hard to miss. But these few events aside, I saw no indications that there were individuals watching either of us. Yet. Although the experience in the Thai restaurant had a particularly unsettling quality to it.

When I was back at the Delta Hotel in Guelph for a night with my wife on June 3, I asked the person working the desk if Trudeau had stayed there that night when I was writing back in March. She said he had stayed there for some or all of that evening. Of all the places he could have slept that night, he was staying at my Guelph hotel, while I was working on a publicly exposing book about the Trudeaus?? *Had the leader of a G-7 nation stalked me?* If this was true, did he actually believe that his presence alone would silence me? Who does this nepo baby think he is?

Driving home, I was enraged. I wanted to share my story, but the double bind again ruled my consciousness. The most I could do was passive aggressive comments, which actually helped a little. That night, I came at one of the fake hacker's comments on my Facebook wall, with a reference to the Delta Hotel. Then on Instagram, I went after one of them with a ref-

Chapter 18: Humanifestations

erence to the journalist wink moment on the Seawall. <u>Immediately</u> after posting my comment, a GIF was posted in response: Will Farrell sitting in a chair shaking with a glass of wine in his hand in what appeared to be a drunken, anxious state. What is important about this response is that it actually came <u>from my own page</u>. In other words, it looked like I posted it. I didn't. Someone at Meta did. I didn't do GIFs. They had someone on me 24/7.[64]

Soon thereafter, I drove to Toronto to meet with the lawyer who had told me not to fly over Russia or China because of my "kompromat." We discussed the possibility of my retaining him. I felt confident that there was a legal path here, even though we had one significant problem: Who do you sue when you are being worked by invisible gang-stalkers? It certainly made sense that they were politically motivated, but who were they working for? Someone protecting Trudeau's political agendas? Someone else with knowledge of these events who was trying to trigger me into public revealing? Russia? China? Conservatives? Mossad? All of the above?

Interestingly, soon after first meeting with him, I began to receive a steady flow of fake 'Unusual sign.in activity' emails on my Hotmail account. They were all allegedly coming from an IP address in Russia and marked as high importance with a red exclamation mark. These emails continued steadily for many months. I felt confident that they were being sent by the same paid clown that was sending the daily stream of taxation and debt-related emails to this account but I would need a little more time to prove it.

On June 7, I received word from the NSIRA that they had received my request with respect to the CSIS. I knew that there was a slim chance that they would investigate any personal information banks in my name, but I had to take a shot. Again, CSIS Director Vigneault had emailed me last January indicating that they had nothing to do with the events. Yet, the Department of Justice had subsequently brought a motion to seal documents during my Privacy Act appeal of CSIS. Something wasn't lining up.

On June 9, I wrote Cribb from my usual Hotmail account to update him on the NSIRA issue. The next day, I found myself again unable to run an ad for my most popular download course (The Abandonment Wound Healing Course) on Facebook. When I tried, it said "This post can't be boosted. You can choose from a list of your eligible posts to reach more people and get more engagement." I had seen this before.

On June 19, I drove to Toronto to drop off a retainer for the lawyer I had met with. Three days later, I drove back to meet with him and his team. As before, I brought my phone with me but left it in the car when I parked it in a lot a block away.

I also met with a former RCMP'er now Private Investigator (who had been on Trudeau's security team). He had intrinsic knowledge of the way that other "investigators" (read: intimidators) operated. In other words, he was quite familiar with the game that was being played with me. We formed a game plan with respect to possible action.

The next morning, I was notified that people couldn't purchase my download courses from jeffbrown.co. As noted earlier, this is where I generate most of my earnings. They would go through the process and it would stall when they clicked on 'Complete Purchase.' I wrote my designer, and there was an issue with the interface between PayPal and E-junkie (download link provider). It was finally fixed a week later.

When you get into a situation like this, it is very easy to make the assumption that most of the things that happen are deliberately organized by the gang of thugs that have been assigned to fuck with your life. In many cases, there is no other reasonable interpretation. Occasionally, situations will emerge that are more nebulous or difficult to discern. The latter is particularly true if something happens that impacts other businesses as well. In this recent situation, others reported having the same problem as I was having. So, I accepted that I was not being targeted. But there was a part of me that wondered just how far all of this had gone. I didn't want to imagine myself significant enough to warrant all this attention, but now that the "kompromat" that I held had expanded to include two police cover-ups, Meta and Amazon livelihood obstructions, Trudeau's smile and wink moment with Cribb on the Seawall in Vancouver etc., it made the notion of someone blocking my PayPal product purchases entirely feasible (and blocking others they had issues with, or simply to make it look like a wider problem than just little ol' me). Especially since the ongoing onslaught of emails that I was receiving were invariably threats to my livelihood or threats of impending poverty. This, again, was the theme of most every game they played.

* * *

On June 22, I submitted my final request to a government agency about this situation. I made a formal complaint to the Civilian Review and Complaints Commission. The CRCC is an independent agency that reviews public complaints made about RCMP officers. In my complaint, I asked them to look into the question of whether someone at the RCMP had acted wrongfully and obstructed justice: (1) by possibly providing information to the Hamilton Police to the effect that I had been "stalking" Mrs. Trudeau; (2) by claiming to have no knowledge of my connection with Mrs. Trudeau during my Privacy Act process, while simultaneously holding information to the effect that I was (allegedly) stalking her; (3) by possibly playing a role in the termination of my second police investigation during Trudeau's 3-day cabinet meeting in Hamilton in January, 2023. Given that the RCMP is always with the Prime Minister, I wondered if they had provided information to the Hamilton Police that led to the cessation of that investigation.

On June 25, a FB follower messaged me that they had gone onto Amazon UK to order *Humanifestations* and found that there was another author's picture and bio credited as author of the book. This again! I took a look around and found it to be true. Someone at Amazon had again replaced my bio and pic with the same one I had spotted months before. Madness.

Around this time, I was also notified by potential purchasers that they couldn't order *Humanifestations* – or its sister book *Hearticulations* – from Amazon UK. I looked into it, and someone at Amazon had limited the geographical reach of both books to a small part of England. People in other countries around the world – including other countries in the UK – could not order it at all. I was being punished for the book's contents.

I cannot begin to tell you how significant this was for my small publishing business. Since *Book Depository* closed down in April, Amazon truly was our best shot at building momentum for a new book worldwide. By making it geographically inaccessible, difficult to find on searches, and confusing to a potential purchaser with a different author bio, the book didn't stand a chance.

Between the shadow ban on Meta, and the games being played on Amazon, I now had a clear understanding of why the USA had always abhorred monopolies. With no competition to be concerned with, the very human temptation to abuse power has nothing standing in its way and no oversight. If they want to fuck with you, they can fuck with you. It's that simple. This is particularly problematic when the monopolies in question have become entirely indispensable in our daily lives. We need them, and they know it. Quite apart from misusing their power to penalize people who have pissed off their powerful friends, it's a perfect recipe for disaster if one or all of the monopolizing entities decide to silence and shut down those who don't align with their political or monetary agendas. If ever there was a time to rid the world of monopolies, it is right now. Between the advances in technology and the advent of AI, we are doomed if we leave them intact. This is particularly so if many of them share the same globalist goal-set and are in cahoots with each other politically.

On June 28, I made a step toward public revealing on a live 'Banyen Books' podcast event. In the business of selling spiritual and healing books since 1970, this Vancouver based bookstore had contacted me some time earlier to arrange a time to discuss *Humanifestations*. Before going on, I promised myself that I wouldn't talk about the politically inspired content of the book. I had made this decision both because I didn't want to risk more issues with the book's distribution, and because I had been inundated with what I perceived to be warning emails on my Hotmail account and – for the first time since this shit storm began – three very close in succession fake Meta take-down emails sent to my main website not long before the show. Nonetheless, I got so comfortable with the host, Ross McKeachie, that I spilled some beans.⁶⁵ This story really wanted to be told.

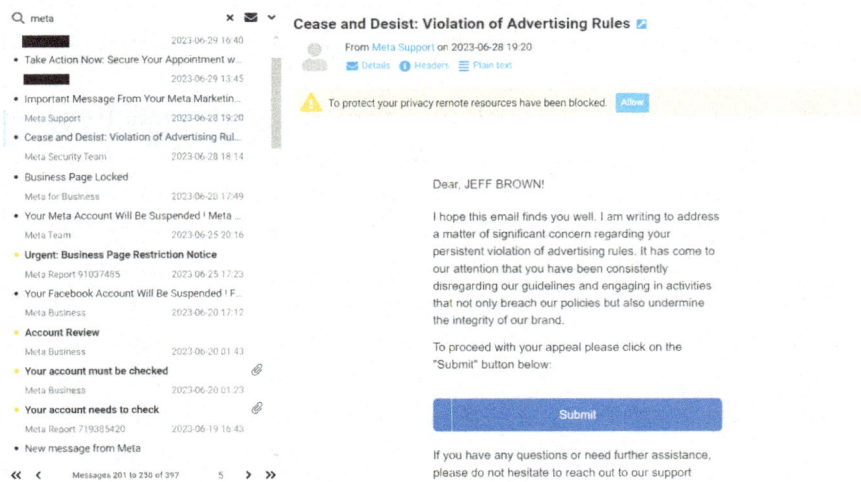

CHAPTER 19

THE DIVORCE

The real Meta now got busy with me. Quite apart from the unmistakable slowing down of my page growth on Instagram, my Facebook groups began to get dinged with some regularity. In early July 2023, someone at Meta went in and found three pieces of content to remove from a group that I seldom utilized any longer. Again, the ironically stated cause was "Cybersecurity." It's like shooting you with a pistol and then charging <u>you</u> with assault. Meta's gaslighters were out in full force:

On July 9, I received a DM on my Facebook business page from someone using the two first names of the lawyers I was working with. His entire message: 'hi.' Now this might seem like a remote event, but I assure you that it isn't. There had been many strange messages here – some using my name, a woman's pic, and yet another 'hi'; some using my face with a different name and strange messages, and as you will see towards the end of the story – some actually use my name, profile pics, and a lawyer's name to ensure that I know I am being targeted.

On July 11, I drove back to Toronto for a meeting with the law firm about possible courses of action. What was interesting about this meeting – and I will speak to this more thoroughly soon – is that my previous bravado with respect to taking legal action was nowhere to be found. I was suddenly more interested in an agreement than a confrontational approach. I had never wanted to turn this experience into money, but something was happening to me. For the first time in 31 months, I was feeling it necessary to back off. And, I was now wondering if a financial settlement was possible.

That same day, I began to receive many of the PayPal notifications for my audio course sales at the wrong email address. We had done nothing on our end to make this change. It didn't happen on its own.

That evening, I received the following text from an unfamiliar number. Was someone listening to my conversation with the legal team? Or had someone informed them that I had been there and discussed the possibility of negotiating a settlement. If so, who?:

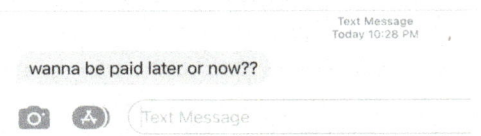

On July 13, I was again unable to boost my Abandonment Wound Healing Course from my Facebook page. That same day, I wrote my US distributor for Enrealment Press to see if she could help me with the access problem with respect to *Humanifestations* on Amazon UK. She provided contact information but I was not able to get any response to emails sent. I was out of luck.

Around July 16, something troubling began to happen on our *Enrealment Press* email account. We started receiving 3-4 fake emails per hour, usually from a variety of Gmail accounts with Russian writing in the main body. These were not phishing attacks – there was no link to click in the emails. It is my understanding that this is commonly used by hackers to bewilder and torment their targets with spambots. It also has the effect of flooding the email account so that it becomes easier to miss relevant customer emails. I did not spot this game until mid-August, when I cleared nearly 5000 of these emails from the account. And this was only the beginning of such attacks on that website.

On July 18, I emailed a friend from a new Proton Mail account that I had created with the word 'shipping' in the email address. <u>Right afterwards</u>, I received this text from a meaningless phone number. This kind of mind-fuckery was now part of my every day, in one form or another…

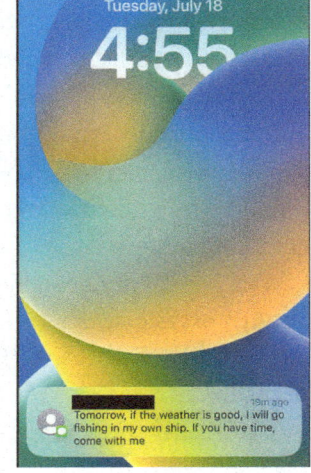

CHAPTER 19: THE DIVORCE

On July 20, there were three more strange dings from Meta related to my Soulshaping group on Facebook. All under the gamesy guise of cyber-security, yet again. Two of them were entirely innocuous posts that were somehow located from 2012. The alleged 'sexual exploitation' post mentioned on the third image? It's simply ludicrous.

What has Facebook become? We should rename it Gamebook, or more appropriately, Agendabook? How is any of this legal?

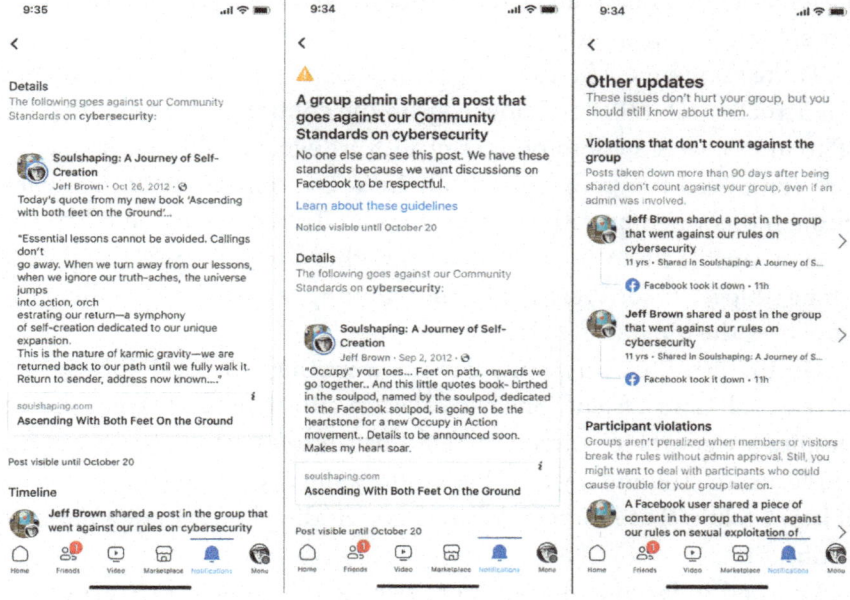

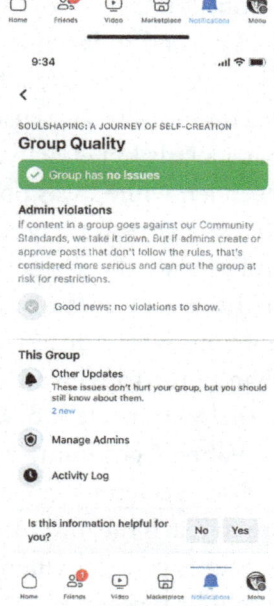

And then the game of games, yet again. Letting me know that there was no group issue, after all: "Good news: no violations to show." Because, of course, the purpose of sending me these was not to actually remove the group. It was to frighten me into submission.

Towards the end of July, I noticed an intensification of the fake Meta threat emails to my website. At this time, I wasn't doing anything in particular to frighten the intimidation team, so something else was afoot. What was it? Why did they now want me even more concerned that my pages would be taken down?

On July 31, I wrote my functional medicine doctor and asked him to prescribe a mild sleeping pill. I was having a hard time sleeping and when I did, I would wake up in a start. He prescribed *Dayvigo*. I filled the prescription and began to take it soon thereafter.

On August 2, I woke up to the news that the Trudeaus had announced their divorce.[66] It certainly didn't surprise me. What did surprise me was how frightened I felt. I couldn't help but wonder if this situation had somehow contributed to the ending of their marriage. If so, I had an even bigger problem today than I had yesterday. I wasn't sure I could take much more. I was feeling utterly exhausted.

At the same time, I had a strange wondering as to whether the divorce was actually real. I had no knowledge to the contrary, but something felt off to me. Given how ambitious they both are, what could have happened that compelled this to happen while he was in office? Justin had been through this when his father – Pierre Elliott Trudeau – was in office and it was a terrible thing. So, why now? No other choice, or was this part of a much bigger ruse? Were they really splitting, or were they pulling the wool over the public's eyes, yet again?

On the drive back from my day spent writing at a local library, I received a call from a friend. She had called to inform me about the divorce. Despite my efforts to contain myself, I began to express my anger at the Trudeaus for "ruining my life." I got quite animated, expressing the truth of how I felt in that moment. When I got off the phone, I saw a message notification.

I clicked to listen and there were two rapidly uttered messages from Harsh Oza, "The Meta Marketing Pro," who had been steadily contacting me for months. I was used to his incoherent messages, but these two were particularly hyper-active. What was interesting is that these messages had been left while I was on the phone, but I saw no indication while talking that someone was trying to call through. They appeared to have been left from inside the system itself. Was this the guy in my phone? Was Meta orchestrating some, or all, of the phone games? If Harsh wanted to talk with me, why didn't he actually ring through? Was this guy nothing more than a prop to keep me nervous about losing my accounts? Or, was he not actually connected to Meta at all?

When I got home, I noticed that Harsh had also emailed me on my website account soon after I got off the phone. He *appeared* to be desperate to reach me, or desperate to make me nervous about losing my Meta accounts on a day when Trudeau was particularly vulnerable with respect to public revealing.

Chapter 19: The Divorce

Later that day, I received a number of calls and emails/texts from both WT and Cribb to contact them. I went out on the street and called Cribb back at around 8 p.m. He wanted to know what I thought about today's divorce news. He also informed me that WT had received a call today from a Federal Court judge about my situation. A federal judge calling our investigator on divorce day? Huh?

He then stated that WT had been recently confronted at a recent funeral by a higher-up from a well-known political organization. There was something about that interaction that felt staged to him – a tricky attempt to find out what WT knew about this situation. Interesting.

Before getting off the phone, Cribb shared that he was going to work on a piece about my story for The Star. He was "looking to take another shot at it." Afterwards, I reflected on the strange timing of his willingness. Why now? Why not after two police cover-ups and your winky-poo moment on Vancouver's seawall? I wasn't in enough danger, yet? You needed a divorce before you could bring this story to the world? What the fuck is going on in this country?

(Note: In a recent conversation with Cribb, he helped me to understand his thinking: "… when news events like that occur, things open up more. It's just the reality of it. There was no longer a protected marriage. It was a marriage that was publicly declared to be over. And when that happens, there's sources. There's a level of openness that one can utilize in a way that one can't when its behind closed doors and it is officially a very happy marriage. Your story is partly a story about marital dissatisfaction. So, when the marriage ends, of course, it was thematically aligned with your story. So, I thought, let's have another go at it. Let's see who might be willing to talk now, who wasn't willing to talk yesterday.")

I went back outside and called WT later that night. He wouldn't speak about the federal judge issue, preferring to share that with me in person. He did speak to the funeral encounter, and made it clear that he now felt certain that it was this particular political organization that had strategically organized the sinister maze of occurrences these past few years. He wasn't the first person to tell me this – I had also heard this from one of the prominent lawyers that I had retained. He said that he had spoken with a lawyer "in-the-know."

WT let me know that The Star was wanting to publish my story now, particularly on the issue of "security." He said that this was only the "3rd inning" of this situation and to "stay strong." He also told me that the divorce opened the Pandora's Box and that every media outlet in the world would be looking for dirt on the Trudeaus. WT closed by telling me that I would probably hear from the RCMP in the next few weeks and to lay low until then.

I got off the phone, frightened. I had wanted this story brought for over two years, but I had run out of energy. I felt strangely anxious and vulnerable at the same time.

Later that week, Susan and I drove to the Beaches in Toronto to get a shiatsu massage. I barely made it. Those sleeping pills weren't working. I was emotionally and physically drained to the bone. I hoped a therapeutic treatment would restore a functional level of energy. We arrived early, and took a short drive. While driving past a nearby cemetery, I was overcome by gloom. I gazed at the gravestones and saw myself there sooner rather than later. My optimism had vanished. I could only see misery. Something was killing my spirit.

Just before going in for my treatment, I decided to postpone the story. I had fought the good fight but something was dreadfully wrong. I didn't want it to go away forever, but I needed some time to recover from whatever had become of me. I sent Cribb a text expressing the concern that both Susan and I were not in any physical shape to deal with this going public until we could do some healing.

Soon thereafter, I received a DM on Facebook from a well-known Canadian investigative journalist inquiring into my previous working connection with Mrs. Trudeau. He was particularly interested in whether a post that I had pinned on Facebook about my "political situation" and a Federal Court matter were related to my connection with her. He asked me to contact him. I didn't, although I often wondered if he was actually the right person to bring this story.

I texted Cribb. He asked me this:

"You're disinclined to pursue publication at this point?"

I didn't want to claw back the story, but something was dreadfully wrong with me. The searing stress of the past few years had taken its toll on my body. I wasn't sure I could make it out alive. Purely from the place of survival, I responded:

"Just feeling quite drained after 4 years without a vacation etc. Trying to recover somewhat."

He then asked me about the former RCMP investigator that was coming to scan my house for any unusual activity: "Is that still happening?"

I gave him a vague response, because I believed that my phone was compromised.

Chapter 19: The Divorce

* * *

The next day (and, then again, two days later for good measure), I received FB notifications to my *Enrealment Press* business page from two fake accounts 'Warning Harmful Content J 66860' and 'report infringgement…' warning me that my page had been both suspended and had limited access. In fact, the page hadn't been suspended, but our distribution relationship with Amazon Canada appeared to be. We were now receiving very few orders.

Soon thereafter, I went to buy gas in town. My *Enrealment Press* credit card was rejected. Strange. I was up-to-date with my payments. I then tried my *Enrealment Press* debit card. Rejected. I went into the Toronto Dominion bank to inquire as to what was happening. The teller did me a favor and did a deep dive into the account. It seems that my cards had been locked on the evening of August 2 because of an (alleged) security issue. August 2nd… that was the same day the Trudeaus announced their divorce. Synchronicity? (Note: I am confident that they said August 2, but it may have been August 1, 2, or 3.) I had heard of credit cards getting compromised, but both a credit card and a debit card at the same time? Even stranger, I had received no phone call about this from the bank. But I did receive a new credit card in the mail weeks later. (I believe that the debit card was unfrozen at some point). It was almost as though the universe was determined to sideline my publishing business. Or, was some more human entity now involved?

Around mid-month, the house alarm went off in the middle of the night – 1x when it was on, 1-2 x when the alarm wasn't on. I believe that this was the first time it had gone off in the middle of the night since 2022! The fake Meta threat emails continued, as did the standard stream of 'Soulshapin' emails to my Hotmail account – debt, taxation, alleged Russian efforts to get into my Hotmail account. I also began to receive a number of DMs on my FB business page to the effect that I was a scam business with defective products and that they would have Facebook block my page. New angle? Scam man? Also, the fake hacker comments on my Facebook business page were showing up rapid-fire. There was also a continuous host of fake emails sent to my main website that were written in the same style – and with the same Russia writing – as the hundreds of daily spambot emails sent to Enrealment.com. Likely the same cyber-stalker set them up.

The real Meta began to ding me yet again on one of my groups. Yet another unknown "CyberSecurity" issue:

On August 19, I had the most informative interactions yet. The Private Investigator I had met with in July came to the house with his partner to do a security analysis. They first did a search of the property to assess whether it had been probed. In other words, were there any listening devices in the house or cars? They did a thorough search and found nothing. They did find a considerable amount of heat around the alarm panel, which they were not in a position to analyze. I wasn't concerned about it – I already knew that the alarm had been compromised.

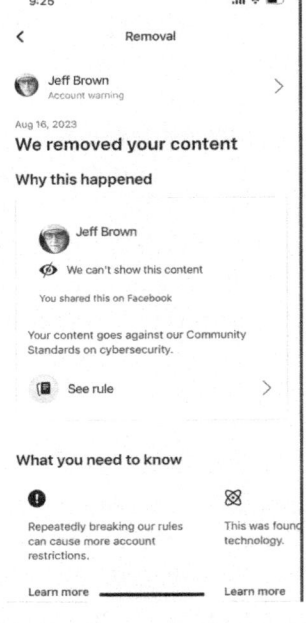

I gave a thorough recount of the suspicious events that had occurred. He advised us to get rid of our I-phones and laptops. As it turns out, various miscreants are paid about $3,000 to get into your phone with Pegasus spyware, or something similar. So, if a politically motivated organization wanted to keep eyes on (and manipulate) a slew of potential threats, they could spend a few million dollars and know everything they are doing, including tracking their location. Easy peasy. This may explain why so many high-level Canadian civil servants have been acting in uncharacteristic ways. Someone is on their phones, and playing games to gather information and frighten them.

He also told me that his best friend was <u>very high up</u> in the RCMP. His friend also believed it very likely that the aforementioned political organization was orchestrating all of this. This was now the third highly connected individual to provide this information. It didn't mean it was true, but it did stand on reasonable ground. And if it was true, and the RCMP had knowledge of it, why had I never received a warning? They have a statutory "duty to warn" when they know that a civilian is in danger. Or were they in on it, perhaps because they were protecting their own asses after what had already transpired?

I asked him to take a look at some of the suspicious emails that I had been receiving. I was particularly interested in those that were sent to my Hotmail account. Again, I felt confident that they were all coming from the same hired gun. I selected two seemingly unrelated emails – one of the fake

Chapter 19: The Divorce

Microsoft emails that suggested someone from Moscow was attempting to break into my account – and another frequent email with the subject "Settle Your IRS tax debt – Free Consultation." He went in, and found that both were coming from the same apartment location in Germany. Whoever was doing this wasn't smart enough to use a VPN when sending them my way. The investigator made it clear that most of these characters worked out of apartments in Europe, something that I had also been told by WT. They were paid a fortune to keep the heat on people of interest.

I then asked him what proved to be a somewhat prescient question: "Don't these people know that continually triggering people can kill them?" He quickly responded: "Of course they do. That's the idea. They don't give a shit what happens to you." Basically, they are hired to frighten you into submission, make you crazy, or kill you. At that moment, whatever was left of my Canadian naivete evaporated in thin air, never to be seen again.

Most importantly, he put all of this into investigative context. My intimidators were all trained in something called "Influencing your Ooda Loop." *Ooda* is an acronym for Observation, Orientation, Decision, Action. Initially a military strategy, the idea is to closely observe you, identify your particular vulnerability, and then form an adaptive plan of attack that activates and then continuously stimulates your anxiety over an extended period of time. In one situation that he described, the terrorists had focused on targeting a prominent journalist's beloved family. In my case, they focused on the fear-of-poverty that emanated from my childhood. But they neglected to notice something far more relevant – the contempt for abuse of power that was also birthed in my childhood. By replicating the abusive and impoverished conditions of my childhood, they were bringing my Justice Warrior back to life.

Just before leaving, the investigator said something that I would soon understand: *"You're not the same person that I met in June."* I certainly felt that was true with respect to my now highly anxious emotional state, but there was more to it than that. Something was happening to my body. Something foul.

* * *

On August 24, I received yet another frightening Facebook ding on my account. The still-lingering threat of a newspaper article telling my story in Canada's leading liberal newspaper was likely keeping the heat on. After all, I hadn't permanently halted the story in my texts with Cribb. I had merely asked for some recovery time:

On August 25, I was unable to do a search on Google.ca because the following warning came up. Was someone engaging in malicious behavior from within my Wi-Fi or laptop? Was my data being manipulated?

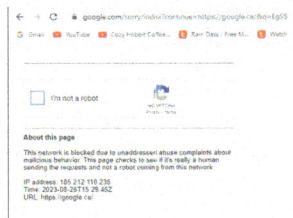

Around the same time, I would go onto youtube via our tv to play music to calm me. In the section 'Recently Viewed' (or something to that effect), I would now see a whole row of Russian videos, all with Russian writing. Was someone viewing them from inside of our Wi-Fi? Or was someone inside our system posting Russian videos just to trigger me? Did my cyber-stalkers think I was afraid of the Russkies? If so, they were wrong.

I also began to notice that some of my texts didn't arrive in a timely manner on my compromised phone. It didn't capture my attention until I failed to receive a text from a shiatsu business stating it would be closing. I received that text too late to book somewhere else, at a time when I desperately needed a treatment. Fortunately, they found a way to accommodate me. The issue of texts not arriving, or disappearing, or text dialogues being presented in a chaotic manner, continued for a long time.

Toward the end of the month, I went to meet with Samuel for dinner to discuss this situation. On the way to Toronto, I had to keep pulling over to rest. I could barely make the 60-minute drive. At the same time, I was receiving a barrage of triggering texts that I believed were related to these events. Again, there is often an interactive quality to this game. For example, just before I arrived at Samuel's place, I turned onto St Clair Avenue, and immediately received a phone call from a meaningless number from

CHAPTER 19: THE DIVORCE

'St. Clair, Ontario.' One thing I learned with certainty is that this team had fake phone numbers everywhere. There was no point in answering – there was never anybody on the other end. The calls were made to keep me hopping.

Samuel and I thoroughly discussed the situation over dinner. I was hyper-anxious. He said something to the effect that I was visually "wasting away." I did not yet understand what he meant. Before I drove home, I sent a long text to WT where I expressed my rage about the things that had happened. I listed off a number of details I had been told about Trudeau by various journalists, and shared the realization that this was no longer about an attempt to silence me – it was now an attempt to destroy me. Without missing a beat – the text was sent back to me, in a framed format. I had never seen that before.

My phone was under siege.

That night, I opened an email to my main website from someone who had allegedly purchased a personal session. I had received no notification of their payment from PayPal. In their email, they let me know that they had paid on PayPal, but were then abandoned without any confirmation of payment. They informed me that they had been a web developer for many years and proceeded to give me a little lecture about this business practice causing potential anxiety in purchasers. They encouraged me to connect with my developers about this "problem."

Quite apart from the strangeness of my not getting a notification of the payment, which I do not remember ever happening with a session payment, and the strangely condescending tenor of the email – a similar tone to the 'scam business' DMs I was receiving on my FB page – this former developer also had their name, address, phone number, and email address visibly noted at the bottom of the email. I don't recall ever seeing a person's home address listed on the footer of an email, unless that information was relevant to the interaction. What was even more startling was that this individual lived in the US on a street called **Wild Horse Way**. A little hard not to notice that. I couldn't help but wonder if this was all part of the trigger Jeff Brown game.

So, I checked him out online. It turns out they were also some kind of a clairvoyant. I found two advertisements for events that they had hosted in the United States not long before.

The next day, I wrote back to thank them for their feedback. They responded the following day: "No rush on scheduling, I'll be writing a page or so to share and send in the next day or so." I never heard back from them, but I did finally receive the PayPal notification a few hours after they responded. Strange happenings, on Wild Horse Way.

CHAPTER 20

TRUDEAUMANIA

As September began, I continued to receive messages from people who couldn't order *Humanifestations* and *Hearticulations* on Amazon UK. That included potential purchasers who lived in England itself. It's important to note that the latter book was published in 2020 and had been entirely accessible – until this fiasco began with *Humanifestations*. I also took note of the fact that images with my writing quotes on them that were posted on my Facebook business page in August, had received about half as many shares as the year before. And that's despite the fact that the page was now larger. 'Shares' aren't a perfect measure of reach, but they are a meaningful measure.

On September 2, I received two more "Cybersecurity" post removals from Facebook related to the *Soulshaping* group and the *International Year of the Woman* group. Many people on Meta never get a single ding like this.

Around this time, I wrote my doctor to let him know that the *Dayvigo* prescription was not working well. It wasn't helping me to sleep through the night, and I was having disturbing nightmares. They were unlike anything I had ever experienced: dark, calamitous, violent, with an apocalyptic undertone. I was being chased, the world was ending, Susan and I were under attack. I would wake up drenched in sweat, crying out for help.

Sometimes, I would see something in my mind's eye that I would later understand to be the archetypal *Death Mother*. She was an elderly woman, sitting in a rocking chair, looking off to the right. Now and then, she would turn her head in my direction, and cackle at me with horrid delight. Her laughter was excruciating. After I first saw her, it became even harder to fall asleep. I couldn't bear to encounter her yet again. I wanted to keep my eyes open.

What was particularly strange about it was how real it felt. Not real as she was really inside my mind, but real as in it felt like she wasn't emanating from the usual symbols that manifest in nightmare form. It was almost as though this image had been deliberately projected from somewhere else. I had no words for it then. I'm not sure I even do now. But something about this 'nightmare' was uniquely different from anything I had ever experienced.

I e-mailed my doctor to prescribe a sleeping pill called *Zopiclone* in Canada. He agreed, despite knowing that I had experienced difficulty with the holistic sleep aid *U-Dream* in 2019. After U-Dream was banned, it was said by Health Canada to have included a substance "similar to" Zopiclone. I did not know that it was, in fact, Zopiclone. I would find out later that my doctor was well aware of that. He was also aware of my adverse reaction to U-Dream.

Nonetheless, he sent the prescription through to my local pharmacy. I began to take the drug soon thereafter.

On September 4/5, Meta came after me again, removing two old posts for alleged 'Cybersecurity' issues. And yet again, on September 7. My story must have carried an enormous weight, for Meta to become this intensely involved in stopping me.

The same day, I received a FB notification that my seldom used *Enrealment Press* business page was at risk of being taken down. Not surprisingly, the fake page contacting me was named "Crash Problem." This mocking game piggy-backed on the anxiety that I was already experiencing about the Enrealment website crashing due to the endless stream of fake emails that I would later find out were overwhelming the servers. And the restrictions on two of the books that *Enrealment* had published.

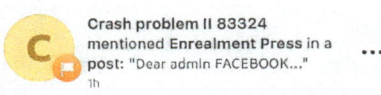

My reaction to this was different than before. My defenses were weakening. I felt palpably terrified. I couldn't sit still. For some time, Susan had begun regularly accompanying me on neighborhood walks in an attempt to quell my anxiety-riddled nervous system. But now that things had escalated, I became more reactive on our walks – more agitated, more easily triggered. Relief was hard to come by. Along with neglecting my physical health, I stopped attending to my physical appearance. Pride does indeed goeth before a fall. The only moments of respite were found in monotonous YouTube videos of persistent rainfall. There was one in particular that comforted me for hours at a time. In it, the rain was falling hard in a dimly lit forest and there was a cabin porch to sit on. It felt like a hideaway

– one that no aggressor would look for or find on such a rainy day. I just kept imagining myself there, momentarily peaceful, momentarily safe.

I did my best to maintain the businesses and my public outreach, but it was a nearly insurmountable challenge. I was having a hard time getting through personal sessions with clients. I maintained my composure, but I became utterly depleted partway through. I was faltering with respect to other responsibilities, as well. For example, I was organizing the dates and running the ads for my courses and Susan's Poetry Healing Course, but there were consistent obstacles. I had scheduled a Writing Your Way Home course in October, but I was forced to remove the popular Facebook "private group option" due to the removal of a student's content in last spring's course. The private group feature had always been the anchor of this writing course. It brought people to it. I also had to move Susan's course from October to November, because I had fallen behind on running the ads for it. Not to mention that I didn't feel secure putting funds into running ads for my own courses, with a perpetual account warning in place. Again, they could boot me off any minute, and I would have to refund the payments while never retrieving the lost ad revenue. I had worked so hard for so many years to build my following through Facebook but it was now patently unsafe. My entire livelihood that I had labored so hard for, for decades – was in jeopardy.

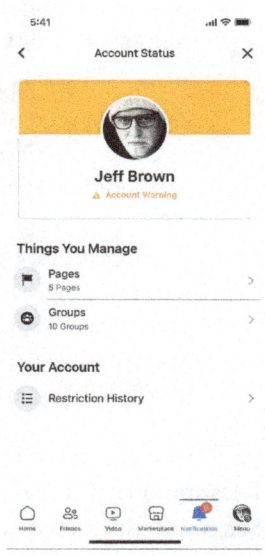

In addition, I was having difficulty writing the last classes for a course that had just begun (*The Enrealment Method*). I had only managed to record the first 4 of 7 weekly classes, but not the others. Under normal circumstances, this wouldn't have been an issue. But it was now.

And there was this older man. While working on the course at the Waterdown library, I kept seeing him sitting at the same corner table. He was one of those guys who has piles of cue cards on the desk in front of him. Like he's organizing his life, or someone else's. Whenever I would pass him or look his way, he seemed to be staring deeply into my eyes. It seemed important to him to make contact. Normally, I wouldn't give it a second thought, but he reminded me of the 'clairvoyant' from 'Wild Horse Way.' In fact, he looked quite similar to him.

On September 12, I received an email from Harsh Oza. I had been receiving emails from him every few weeks or so. In this one, he let me know that he would like to share my campaign results related to a recent Abandonment Wound Course advertisement. You may recall that this was the popular course that had frequently been blocked from advertising on Meta. Was this a sincere email from my "dedicated Meta Marketing Pro," or another mind-game on the cyber-battlefield?

On September 14, I received a strange email from the TD Bank. The TD bank manager I later spoke with said they had never seen such an email before. At the top, a reference to the last 4 digits of my personal credit card: Important request regarding your TD Credit Card account(s|) ending in _____. And then the following somewhat inconsistent words:

> At TD Bank Group, we periodically review customer information that we have on file to ensure that your information is complete and current. During a recent review, we have identified information related to your Account(s) that we need to confirm. You must contact us right away if you make any changes to:
>
> Account Information;
> Your mailing address;
> Your name; or
> Any other contact information you gave us such as your mobile number and/or email address.
>
> Please ensure your account(s) are up to date by visiting your nearest TD branch of by calling 1-866-666-8598. We would be happy to assist you. Our Customer Service team is available to take your call between 7 a.m. to midnight (ET), seven days a week. If you use TTY, simply call 1-866-704-3194.
>
> Your prompt response is greatly appreciated to confirm if there are any changes to your information, as noted above. We appreciate your business and thank you in advance for your cooperation.
> Sincerely,
> TD Credit Cards

Because the email was so shoddily written and inherently inconsistent, I assumed that it was a fraudulent email. First, it references that a review has been conducted and certain information needs to be confirmed. Then it mentions to contact them *if* I intend to make certain noted changes, including to my "name"? Huh? Then, they ask me to visit or call to "ensure that my account(s) are up to date."

Chapter 20: Trudeaumania

I didn't like the way I felt when I read this email. I get that my then agitated state of mind could have played into my response, but something felt off. I looked around online to see if anyone else had received an email like this. Usually, there are a variety of people on Reddit etc. asking others when they receive strange emails. I found nothing.

* * *

On September 16, I was working in *Microsoft Word* on the laptop that the investigator had advised be discarded. The following block came up. I clicked on it and nothing happened. I closed the document and tried to open others. The same block came up again. I Googled it and found out that this was either a legitimate issue arising from an incomplete Office update, or an indication that there was malware in the system. Partly because I had been updating in a timely manner, I made the assumption that the cyber-stalkers who had penetrated my computer were alerting me that my voice of expression was now blocked. I already knew that, but this took my repression to the next level. When a writer can't write, bad things start to happen. Or in this case, bad things get even worse.

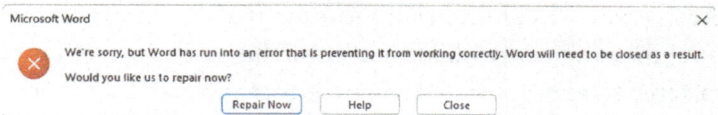

That evening, I arranged to meet Samuel for dinner to celebrate my 61st birthday. On the 45-minute drive over, I had to pull over twice to rest. It wasn't sleeplessness – I had been getting more sleep now that I was taking Zopiclone. It was something else. It felt like my entire system was collapsing. My willful nature took a backseat to an unfamiliar combination of lifelessness and suicidal ideation. I had experienced painful moments in my life where I thought about suicide as a concept, but I had no experience with actual ideation. And not just ideation, but the certainty that I was going to die soon. I felt like I was already halfway in my grave.

Over dinner, I discussed the very real possibility that my life would soon end. I wanted to know his thoughts on how to best organize things for Susan. He did everything a human could to convince me to stay alive. He told me what my suicide would do to him, to Susan, to those who were supported and uplifted by my writing. I listened close, looking for a reason to stick around. But I couldn't seem to find it.

We went for a short walk after dinner. Everything felt distorted. He looked so large. I felt so small. I kept reaching down to pull up my pants.

Where's a belt when you need one? I felt certain that everyone that passed us was part of the surveillance team. And that our waiter had told us which table to sit at because it was bugged. I kept looking around, waiting for the cops to arrest me. Huh?

At the same time, I still had my wits about me. Some part of me knew that I wasn't thinking straight. I remembered something that the investigator had shared when he visited the house in August. He told me about a person who had gone through something similar to me. In her case, she had been in Europe for some time. While there, she was being psychologically terrorized in various ways by Russians. When she came home, she thought she saw a Russian everywhere she went. Her consciousness had been in a hyper-vigilant state for so long that she could no longer make normal distinctions. Everything was a threat, everybody was a Russian.

On the drive home, I wondered if that is what was happening to me. After 33 months of living in a kind of alternative reality, had my psyche reached a tipping point? Had I cracked?

Strangely enough, I rejected this idea. There was no question something was wrong with me, but I refused to believe I had completely crumbled. At my core was an ironclad fortitude that marked my very nature. After spending my entire childhood surviving in the eye of the storm, I had mastered staying grounded when the tornado reaches its apex. Cracking wasn't an option.

I sensed that something else was contributing to this exaggerated state. I just couldn't calm down for long enough to see it. And neither could anyone around me, or could they? Did they know something I didn't know?

I remember this drive as my final attempt at objective thinking before the shit really hit the fan in the coming weeks. Some part of my psyche was trying to tell me something about what was actually going on here, but I just couldn't hear it. There were too many 'ideations' in the way.

The next day, I went for a shiatsu in the Toronto Beaches. On the drive over, I again had to pull over to rest. After the treatment, I said a very emotional goodbye to my massage therapist. I had known him for years, and wanted him to know how grateful I was for his efforts and healing touch. I let him know that I didn't think that I would be here for much longer. It was a very poignant moment.

On September 19, I received a response in the mail from NSIRA that was dated on my birthday just a few days earlier. This letter related to my June 2023 request for them to look into any CSIS personal information banks in my name. Like most of my life nowadays, I found their response confusing. In the first paragraph, they stated:

> I am writing to inform you that the National Security and Intelligence Review Agency, pursuant to Rule 7.02 of the Review Agency's Rules of Procedure, determined on September 14, 2023, that it does not have jurisdiction to investigate your complaint under section 16 of the NSI-RA Act.

And then at the bottom of the letter:

> The Review Agency has carefully reviewed your complaint and has conducted an independent verification of your allegations against CSIS. After conducting the verification, the Review Agency determined that the allegations raised in your complaint do not refer to an activity carried out by CSIS. As such, the first criteria to establish jurisdiction pursuant to subsection 16(1) of the NSIRA Act has not been met. Because your complaint is not directed towards an activity done by CSIS, it is not within the Review Agency's mandate to initiate investigations into your allegations.

If I understood this correctly, they could not investigate my complaint for jurisdictional reasons. Yet, they conducted an 'independent verification' and confirmed that CSIS wasn't involved in the wiretapping (etc.) events that I had referenced in my request letter. Huh? Although the letter appeared to contradict itself, I accepted the outcome as valid. That is, that all of these various shenanigans were not carried out by Canada's spy agency. The spies were largely, if not entirely, off-book agents hired by those with a vested interest in keeping me silent. (Although what is it that CSIS was asking to have sealed in an ex-parte motion during my Privacy Act Appeal? That was baffling.)

A few days later, I went for a Thai massage in the Guelph area. I deliberately arrived early so I could go to a nearby library. I opened a public computer and searched for ways to commit suicide. I didn't like the idea of a messy suicide. I wanted a peaceful death. Drugs and alcohol were the only thing that made sense to me. I planned to buy some booze to mix with the Zopiclone and something else. Advil, maybe? Or maybe a cough medicine?

I left the library and drove around southern Guelph to contemplate my fate. At some point, an ambulance pulled up right beside me and, moments later, turned on its siren. Yet it didn't go anywhere. It just drove along beside me for some time with its siren on. It was so intense. Everything – inside and out – was amplified. I was tense – it was as if my head was in a vice-grip – I couldn't think straight.

After the massage, I shared my dilemma with the practitioner. I asked her what she would do: end her life and leave Susan in a solid position economically, or wait for the cyber-stalkers to come and get me, thereby destroying everything we had built? I didn't have any idea *why* they were coming to get me – I just felt certain that they were. She suggested that I go away on a vacation to regenerate and get some perspective. I rejected the idea. I already had my plan.

I went home and continued to work on a document that I had been creating for Susan of pertinent information so that she would be okay after I was gone: passwords and business details, a list of key individuals and their contact info, my life insurance and personal will. Each time I would assemble more information, I would then place it in a special box in the front room.

Around that time, I noticed that I was no longer receiving fake emails about Russian's trying to open my Hotmail account. The last one arrived on September 18. Nor was I receiving the flood of emails about loans, debts, and burial insurance. It was as though whoever was behind it, knew that I was now a not-so-hot mess. Mission accomplished? Or, perhaps they didn't want to antagonize someone who was losing his mind, because he might just lose it and share all the emails, taped phone conversations, and court documents on the public record (where they actually belong in a political context like this one). Whatever it was, they had essentially gone silent.

That weekend, Samuel insisted on getting together. He drove out to Dundas, and we drove to a park outside town – in the village of Lynden. As we were driving, I gave him a photocopy of some of the documents that I had gathered. We sat at a park bench and I discussed my intentions. He spoke from his heart, and pleaded with me not to end my life. I said I would do my best to stay here. But he wasn't convinced.

At some point, I noticed a black SUV parked about 50 feet away. It seemed quite suspicious. I got up to walk toward it. It immediately backed out, and left the park. I had little doubt that it was there to monitor us. But who was it? The RCMP wasn't previously interested in my story. If you recall, they passed me over to the Hamilton Police. What would ignite their interest now? My backing off from the Toronto Star? Did that catch their attention? Or was it the anxiety-ridden gibberish coming out of my

Chapter 20: Trudeaumania

mouth now? Did they see this as an opportunity to sweep their wrongdoing under a carpet of "Jeff Brown's gone mad!?"

On the drive back, Samuel told me that he would have to share my suicidal intentions with Susan. The man had known me for 30 years. He wasn't going to act like this was just a normal day. I encouraged him to please not tell Susan – it would alarm her. When we got to the house, I brought him upstairs and showed him where the box was with all the information.

Although immersed in my own personal hell, my heart still ached for Samuel. An only child, he had just lost his mother after tending to her health for years. Prior to that, he had devoted a decade of his life caring for his father, who had suffered from Alzheimer's and all manner of disease. A true dignitarian, my longest dearest friend had never missed a beat with respect to their care. The last thing he needed was this horrifying situation on his plate.

I felt even worse for Susan. She had endured my reactive outbursts and rambling walks for months. She repeatedly told me that she needed to see a psychiatrist. She had started calling Coast for support – the local mental health line that the Hamilton Police referred me to when they terminated the investigation. The situation had become dire. We were both at the end of our rope. Could this finally be rock bottom?

A few days later, Susan told me that Samuel was coming to meet with her in the morning. He had candidly shared with her about my suicidal imaginings, and he wanted to discuss a course of action. After their walk, he and I went on a number of walks around the town. I was quite wired and highly activated. I felt like I could walk for days. And I was sure that many things we saw – the Fed Ex and garbage trucks that agitated me as they raced by, the gravestone that sits at the edge of a neighborhood park, the guy walking from right near my house towards two 'suspicious' trucks with a computer (my computer?) in his hands – were part of a conspiracy to destroy me.

My suspicions quickly expanded to include Samuel. I noted that he was now driving a fancy BMW. Where did he get the money for that? And that he had not been ticketed for parking in a no-parking zone all day. Who was this guy, really? And why does he keep talking about the mental disorders that I might now have? What was his agenda? I put two and two together and decided that he was in on it, too. That he was being blackmailed into getting information from me. Or that he actually ran CSIS, and his agenda was to have me declared crazy so that my "kompromat" would lack credibility. The Martha Mitchell Effect, yet again.

We went back to the house and he spoke with Susan. She was supposed to leave for the US the next day to see her daughter after two years apart. Her daughter was going through a difficult time, too. Susan was caught between a rock and a hard place. Before he left, Samuel pushed to have me admitted to a hospital. I utterly refused to go. Susan called Coast to come visit the house. I refused to meet with them. They cancelled the visit, allegedly telling her that they couldn't come unless I agreed to the visit.

I spent most of the evening convincing Susan she should go on her trip. We went to sit down in a little park near the house. She said that she hated it when two men were telling her what to do. I assumed that she meant Samuel and I, but she later denied that. I reassured her that I was not trying to hold her back. She needed a break, and I shakily contended that I would stabilize if I had some time alone.

The next day, I drove her to the airport. We were both quiet. I reached for her hand – it was cold as ice. During the drive, I handed her a note. It contained four words – the title of her first book: *Hope is a Traveler*. It was a reminder for her to keep going, no matter what happened. Although not consciously suicidal at this time, some part of me was certainly anticipating my demise. Everything felt so bloody dark.

It was the oddest thing. I had endured close to three years of intimidation and harassment, without experiencing anything close to suicidal ideation. And yet, here I was, accepting that suicide was my destiny. It seemed like a *fait accompli*, an indelible imperative. What had happened to my once powerful mind?

I walked her to the luggage area. My God, her bag was so heavy. I had watched her fill it with one item after another for weeks. It was as though she was moving permanently. She chastised me as we placed the bag on the roller, "but now I have to do all of this myself!" Something about the way she said it didn't feel genuine. Why would you want someone with suicidal ideation to feel bad about not accompanying you on a trip?

She called me soon after clearing customs. My sense of time was now distorting. I was sure that we had parted just moments ago. Who let her through that quickly? Where was she going? What was going on here?

On the drive home, I decided that she was in on it, too. That she wasn't going to the US. She was being flown to Ottawa by the Canadian government. Or maybe she wasn't flying anywhere? She was going to meet with her boyfriend for a two-week rendezvous. Maybe it was someone I knew?

After I got home, I turned off my phone. I fed Lacy, our cat and Susan's little shadow, and then slept for hours and hours. My bed was my only comfort.

I woke up feeling strange, like something had happened to my body while I was asleep. And there was someone else in my head. He was interacting with me, literally anticipating and mocking my thoughts. Wherever he came from, the guy was sharp as a tack. I tried to outsmart him, but he had an answer for everything. And he made it clear that he wasn't going anywhere. My brain was no longer my own.

I soon entered the doppelganger stage. My strange new brain decided that the people I knew weren't who they said they were. I texted Samuel with some questions about his relationship history. I was testing him. I didn't buy his answers. I decided that it wasn't him that I was writing to. He wanted to talk. I didn't respond. I didn't trust him anymore.

The voice – which I began to think of as that of God, both because of its tenor and its clarity – said that nobody could be trusted. Only him. But he was so mean. Where was the benevolent God that I had once imagined?

Time crawled by. I would spend what I thought were hours inside of my mind. Then I would look at the clock. Only a few minutes had passed.

In those slow-moving moments, I reconnected with countless memories. I remembered moments of victory, and was reminded by the voice inside of mistakes I had allegedly made along the way. He was utterly determined to chastise me and tear me down. I began to wonder if he was the man glaring at me in the library and living on Wild Horse Way.

I often saw my life as one might see it in those final moments before passing. Everything trivial fell away, and all that was left were those significant moments of tragedy and triumph.

Sometimes I would look through the front window. One time, there was a Canada Post truck parked in front of the house with a woman of authority standing in front of it on her cell phone. Another time, a Reliance Home Comfort truck with a device hanging off the front grill – the kind they use to break into a house to reclaim unpaid water heaters. It was as if all of those frightening texts I had been receiving for years were now manifesting into reality. Or so I imagined in my mind's eye.

And the oddest thing kept occurring. Our home backed onto a gas station. At some point every afternoon, a man who appeared to work at the station would start up an old beat-up car sitting on the lot. He kept it running for a really long period of time, regularly stepping on the gas. The sound that came from the vehicle was beyond a nuisance – it felt like an auditory assault. In the irrational state I was in, I couldn't help but wonder if this was a deliberate act designed to take me over the edge.

At some point, the phone rang. It was an unfamiliar Toronto number. When I called back, the woman on the phone – who sounded remarkably police-like – answered with something like 'Division 44.' When I asked her if they had called me, she now said that I was calling a machine shop and laughed.

I then had a zoom with a friend. It didn't exactly look like him. His face was much larger, his voice a little softer. Was he wearing a mask? Had he also been hired to fuck with my head?

I opened Susan's end table drawer. I found pictures from our wedding on a red USB stick. Who was she smiling at? Who was the cameraman, really? A government employee? Part of the plan? The USB had a 'Made in China' sticker loosely affixed to it. And it said 'JLT Canada' on the stick. The sinister character in my head set me straight: *"There you go. She's with Trudeau. Has been all along."*

* * *

I lay down to feel into this new information. I was overcome with excruciating pain. I began to cry. Whatever Susan may or may not have felt about me, I loved her soul deeply. I reached for my trusty Zopiclone to calm me down and put me to sleep. A nightmare woke me up 14 hours later. In it, I was inside of a mobile home in middle America. A man came by to share the story of Justin and Susan. They had met in Montreal when she was very young. They loved each other, but he couldn't marry her because she wasn't Canadian. So, they concocted a plan to get married later in life. In the meantime, he would arrange a "political marriage." But it had been difficult for them to stay apart. So, they implemented a new plan – she would marry a Canadian as cover. This way, it would be easier for them to hook-up now and then. After he left office, they would reconnect.

I stumbled out of bed and created a little altar for Susan and I in the walk-in closet. Something she would find after I was gone. I wrote some loving messages and surrounded them with pictures of us.

Throughout this period, I continued to spew nonsense. My mind was making up stories about my past, and I was reciting them aloud. Sometimes I even spoke them to my phone while I was alone. Sometimes, I spoke to Susan and actually accused her of being with Samuel in Toronto. I accused him, too.

At some point, I actually called him to say that I would ring him at a set time each day, just to let him know that I was still alive. I felt that knowing

Chapter 20: Trudeaumania

he would be expecting my call, would keep me from terminating my life. He rejected this idea, because he felt that it would be triggering for him to wait on those calls. Fair enough – it was an unreasonable request. He then made an additional point, one which made sense to me in the state I was in: "After all, when you're dead, you're dead." In other words, no need to set up a system to signal your demise. By that point, we can't do anything about it anyway.

I began to think about suicide. The perfectly attuned voice in my head said "It's time." If people I loved had left me alone in this state, I figured that I must deserve it. Stoking me was the next stage of my unfolding delirium – the belief that "they" were waiting outside to kill me. I didn't exactly know who "they" were, but it didn't matter. I either died at their hands, or mine. I preferred to die on my own terms.

Without going too far into it in this book – there is another book that is calling to be written – I leaned strongly into the question of whether I wanted to live or die on three occasions. And, every time, I would pull back at the last moment. It's not that I didn't want to die. I truly did want to put an end to this misery. But I wanted something a little bit more. I wanted life. And I sensed, on some inexplicably intuitive level, that what was happening to me was not exactly as it appeared. Something else was going on here. Maybe lots of 'something else's'.

After one of these explorations, I was sure that I heard a man's voice saying this to someone else: "He's not going to die from that. He's just going to faint." This was the first time that I thought I heard someone's voice coming from somewhere outside of me. Was I being observed?

* * *

One day, I got up from my almost death bed and roared like a bloodied lion. I stood in the walk-in closet and roared and roared like the burdened beast that I was. I wasn't ready to go, yet. Despite being utterly certain that I had nothing left to live for, and that Susan would benefit from my passing, I just kept choosing life.

Soon thereafter, my thai massage therapist friend came by to take me for a walk. I refused to go with her. I was sure that she was taking me to my death. And, I didn't even think it was her. My senses were distorted. She seemed so large now. Couldn't they have picked someone her size? Didn't they realize I would figure it out?

The following afternoon, I opened the door and stepped outside. I had been in the house for days, but I needed to face the demons. Even if they were going to string me up on a hydro-pole (as God-voice said), I wasn't going to hide. And I was hungry. I had eaten all the frozen food Susan had left.

I got in the car and drove to a nearby town, looking for food. I felt confused, bewildered. I kept pulling up to restaurants and then driving away. I finally found my way to the Starbucks drive-through. I tried to order but the attendant couldn't hear me. My voice was very weak. I tried a few times, before we got it right. When it came time to pay, I found it difficult to punch in my PIN. My fingers were so weak. What had happened to me?

Interestingly, while I was out of the house, that nasty voice inside seemed to vanish. This only served to confuse me further. Why was he only there when I was in the house?

I went home and took a shower. When I came out, I looked in the mirror for what may have been the first time in months. I looked at my face. It was so thin. My scalp was exposed in spots where I had lost hair. I looked at my body. It was startlingly skinny, and my muscles had shrunk. I reluctantly stepped on the scale. No longer 215 lbs, I was now back at my high school weight – 170 lbs. I had lost over 40 pounds in a brief period of time. WTF?

I went for a walk outside. My legs did not feel like they were the same ones I had walked on for decades. I was more vital than I had been in years, and simultaneously uncoordinated. The loss of so much muscle had apparently altered my gait... or perhaps these weren't my legs at all? I looked at my hands. The fingers were flimsy. No wonder I had trouble punching in my PIN. Most of the muscle was gone there, too.

In the state that I was in, the only conclusion I could come to was that my body had been swapped. I asked the character in my head to confirm it. He happily did. He let me know that they had gotten rid of my original body, and swapped it for a lighter body – one that would live longer. And that they had preserved my powerhouse mind (how very strange to receive a compliment from a voice in your head 🙂). Not because they valued me, but because the Liberal Party wanted to use it for their own malevolent purposes. Huh? I was now a blend of myself and another, whether "I" liked it or not.

I returned home and took stock of the crackling sound that my jaw made when it moved. I'd first noticed this back in July or August. Something was broken in there. At that time, I'd assumed that the intense stress had caused me to bite down too hard on my mouth-guard while sleeping. But I now saw this differently. It wasn't something I had done. The sur-

Chapter 20: Trudeaumania

geon had fucked up when they did the body swap. Yah, that's it. I was now a hybrid with a faulty jaw.

The story continued to blow-up in my mind. Soon enough, Susan was Canadian – born in British Columbia. She had been Justin's girlfriend, until he was told to marry Sophie for political purposes by a prominent French-Canadian corporation. And then Susan went to university in the US and completed three degrees. She became a cutting-edge surgeon, the first doctor to perfect the art of swapping mind and bodies. In fact, she had performed my surgery, but she fucked up the jaw. I checked in with the sinister dude in my head and he confirmed it: "She actually hates your guts. She probably gave you TMJ on purpose." Lovely guy.

The next morning, I woke up and noticed that there was, in fact, a small amount of blood on the sheet. It may well have been there for days. It was around mid-mattress, nowhere near my nose in case it had bled one night while I was sleeping. How very strange. Lacy hadn't been in the room. Where did this blood come from? And why did I have a headache? Childhood falls aside, I'd never had a headache until now. And why was I getting the feeling that someone really had tampered with my body and mind at some point?

A few days later, Susan and I met on Zoom. We had spoken a few times, but I hadn't believed anything she said. During this talk, I spoke from my shattered heart. I expressed my love, and asked why her and Trudeau had picked me. Did they have to mess up my life, too? She calmly explained that none of the stories in my head were true. Of course, I didn't believe her. In my mind, she was speaking to me from a Liberal Party office in Ottawa. It didn't look anything like an apartment. And the man's voice chatting in the background – who she later said was her daughter's partner – was a Liberal party staffer talking to someone about the next election.

At some point, I told her that the picture I had posted of her and Trudeau from the Hamilton political gathering had just shown up in my feed on Facebook. She said "Oh yes, we're aware of that picture."

I said, "Whose we?"

She replied: "That picture from when Justin and I met on Hamilton Mountain."

I replied: "Hamilton Mountain? It was on James Street in downtown Hamilton during the election."

No reply.

In the state I was in, I could only come to two conclusions: Susan was either with Trudeau, or she was wanting me to believe that she was.

Soon thereafter, I entered into a state of utter panic. God-voice told me that the cops were coming to get me. They had to make sure my political story didn't reach the public and expose them. They had to conjure things up to destroy me first.

The voice told me to get dressed. I asked if I could bring my laptop and write in jail. He said, "yes, but hurry up." I got up and put my clothes on. I grabbed a bag, and filled it with the computer and other things I would need. He told me not to sit down. They would be here in a minute.

I emailed Susan to let her know they were coming. She responded that she was going to book a flight and come home right away. I didn't believe that she was actually flying home – I figured that the RCMP would just drive her back from Ottawa – but I was happy to know that I would see her. Who knows what would happen if I was alone for much longer?

Then the voice told me that the cops had been delayed. Jurisdictional issues. I could relax, for now.

Susan sent me a short video while in route, imploring me to hang on. I took one look at the video and decided that it wasn't actually her. It was one of two versions of her that they had been using since this marital charade began. This one was the surgeon. The other was the one that lived with me most of the time. Doppelgangers, everywhere.

At some point that day or evening, Trudeau made the news in the strangest of ways. He was in Parliament, and he winked and smiled at the new speaker-of-the-house, Greg Jarvis, in the most exuberant of ways. Justin sure likes to wink. I had never seen our PM so happy. I couldn't help but wonder why. Did he get some very good news? Did he know that I had lost my mind? Was he somehow involved in this?[67]

* * *

Before Susan returned home on October 5, I leaned into the question of suicide one more time. But every time I explored it, I thought of her. Her beloved brother had explored the same question once before, and it had deeply traumatized her. I couldn't do that to her, even if I didn't know who *she* was anymore.

She arrived home in the middle of the night with a story to tell about her journey. She had barely slept the night before, and then took two flights (Indianapolis-La Guardia, La Guardia to Toronto) over the course of the day. It was a big thing, given that she had managed all of this with her visual disability intensified from the stress. I didn't believe a word of her story, but I was happy to see her. Right after she sat down on the

CHAPTER 20: TRUDEAUMANIA

couch, I was certain I heard a man speaking through a cable outlet on the wall beside us. It sounded like he was on some kind of a walkie-talkie, chatting with his comrade. I wondered if this was a mistake on their part, or if it was something that they wanted me to hear so they could call me crazy if I reported it. Interestingly, Susan didn't flinch.

The next days were a physiological nightmare. I couldn't use the washroom normally – it felt like I had acquired an entirely new stomach. It either didn't work at all, or it worked better than it ever had before. I then became convinced that I was a different kind of hybrid – one with a machine body. Also, my voice was virtually gone by noon. I would have to whisper the rest of the day. Finally, I was unable to remember people's names. And my short-term memory was compromised. I would eat, and then forget that I had eaten. I would send an email, and then go back to send it again. At the same time, my mind felt crisper than ever before. I would wake up with fully formed sentences ready to be written. I could easily grasp concepts that had baffled me in the past. I saw through the bullshit of the world more clearly than ever before. It was as though this calamity had cleared the cobwebs in my mind.

Nonetheless, I wasn't able to run the class. I asked Susan to cancel my imminent writing course and refund the students. And I did the same with the Enrealment Method course. I had somehow managed to write the final classes, but I couldn't record them for the students.

In my mind's eye, Susan soon became a hybrid. And then, she wasn't Susan anymore. She was the guy in my head. We were all emotionally bereft hybrids, crafted by the surveillance team to serve their malevolent purposes.

One afternoon, Susan went out to pick up some food. I was standing at the edge of the bedroom. Suddenly, I felt myself dropping to the ground. It wasn't a fainting thing – it was a full-blown collapse of my system. As I fell quickly to the ground, I somehow managed to divert the corner table. If not, my head would have struck it. I lay on the ground for some time, certain that this was the end.

It wasn't. After some time, my system seemed to regulate. I crawled back into the bed to recover.

Over the course of the next days, I became difficult to manage. My mind was again making up stories about my past, and I was reciting them aloud. I also berated Susan with one accusation after another. I even insisted that someone had drugged me, while she was standing in the driveway talking with a neighbor. There was no question that I felt off, but something else felt off, too. I asked her to take me for a blood test, to see if I had been drugged while she was away. She contended that those kinds of drugs wouldn't show up on a test.

At the time, I assumed that her very sober minded management of the situation was a reflection of her emotionally bereft hybrid blueprint. As I would later find out, it was quite the opposite. It was a reflection of her love for me. Despite the fact that this situation was affecting her eyesight, and that she was experiencing chest pain and pressure, while facing a psychological onslaught – she continued to fight for my life. She fed me, she listened to me, she cleaned up the space I was sleeping in, and she tried very hard to figure out what condition I had. Brain tumor? Delusional disorder? Capgras? Louie body dementia?

One night, when it was at its absolute worst, she organized a Balinese massage night. We had been to Bali in 2016 and found it to be a nurturing paradise. She drew me a bath, and set up the space. She put on the Balinese music and lit the incense. I lay down on my back under the blankets, certain that she was going to slit my throat. She did the opposite. She gave me the most loving neck massage and facial I've ever had. In the most internally chaotic moment of my life, one where I was utterly certain that I was no longer human, she reminded me of my human value. And she did this after enduring days of my nonsense. Extraordinary.

* * *

Throughout the week, Susan kept suggesting that I should go to my family doctor. Or the hospital. I balked at the idea. It's not that I didn't realize something was wrong. I didn't trust mainstream medicine, and I didn't trust her. I assumed she was wanting to get me committed, so that the people she 'worked for' would be able to say that I was crazy if I ever brought my "kompromat."

She remained persistent until I agreed. Not because I wanted to go to the hospital, but because I had a plan. I couldn't live with this double-bind anymore. I couldn't keep this story to myself. If they locked me up, I would have no choice but to tell it. I had everything prepared. I had all my passwords in my wallet. I had all the documents, audio calls, and transcripts ready to go. I just needed to access a computer. I would find a way.

On October 11, Susan told me that two dear friends were on the way to the house. They were going to accompany us to St Joseph's Hospital in Hamilton, despite my repeatedly telling her not to take me to a Hamilton hospital because of the two police cover-ups. I wanted to go to the new

Chapter 20: Trudeaumania

Oakville hospital – Oakville-Trafalgar Memorial Hospital. I had heard very good things about it. But she said that the Hamilton hospital had already been arranged. I didn't know that emergency visits could be pre-arranged.

My friends arrived early afternoon. They looked smaller than I remembered them. I was sure they were doppelgangers, wearing facial masks. I began to cross-examine them, trying to catch them in a lie. I thought I had, but it didn't really matter. I was going along with it anyway. I had already decided – better to be buried with my story told, than live with my story buried. I had my plan. Let's go...

The doppelgangers followed us in their van. On the way, I was certain I heard a man in the phone giving Susan directions to the hospital. Probably the commander of the surveillance team. There was, in fact, a Hamilton police car in the lane RIGHT BESIDE US for most of the trip. I figured that was him. Our police escort, there to make sure we arrived and to trigger me so that I arrived at the hospital bat-shit crazy.

When we arrived, Susan took charge of the situation. She laid out the details for the intake person. She emphasized my weight loss and other symptoms.

We met with the triage Doctor. She shared the same information. He seemed disinterested. I figured he knew I was coming before I arrived. That it was all a set up. Why else was a Hamilton cop escorting us if this wasn't a setup?

Susan and I were directed to the emergency ward. My doppelganger friends left for home. While sitting there, I was even more sure that the whole thing was a stage show. It was Canadian Thanksgiving after all. Why were all these people working? The few patients I saw reminded me of Hollywood actors. Wasn't that guy from 'Days of our Lives?' Why is that other guy glaring at me so angrily? His mother, too? Who are these people? This farce must have cost someone a pretty penny.

It was my turn to give blood. Everything felt strange. The nurse looked like a beautiful Asian woman I used to date. Why is she pushing up against me so hard? Didn't she learn boundaries in nursing school? Is she really a nurse? She tried to draw blood from my left arm. The needle went in and then she said that the vein collapsed. Why does she have a little bag of blood already in her hand? She moved to the right arm. She positioned herself strangely. I couldn't really see her. I felt the needle go in briefly and come out. She said she had gotten enough. I looked down. There was an enormity of purply-looking-something splashed all over my arm. I thought it was dye. She left it there, and partly covered it with a bandage. What, you don't clean up after yourself? Did you really take my blood?

We waited a number of hours, before a young guy came to take me downstairs for a brain scan. Seemed kind of angry. Didn't say a word. He took me into a room with a giant machine. The attendant kid had me lie down and move back and forth a bit. It all felt surreal – like a fake scan. When I was done, the angry guy took me back upstairs.

Eventually, I was taken to a room to be seen by the emergency physician. She shared the results of the tests. The brain scan was normal – no brain tumor. The bloods were normal, except that my Lipase levels were elevated. Lipase is a pancreatic enzyme that breaks down fats. Really? That's all that looks weird while I am in this state?

Susan explained to the doctor that she was concerned about my weight loss and other physical changes. She recalls saying that she was concerned about the possible role of prescriptions I had been taking. That I had been on thyroid medication without having a thyroid condition. I don't remember her saying the latter, but I do recall that the doctor was only interested in my psychological symptoms. She asked us to wait to see a psychiatrist.

We were eventually brought into a small room. After some time, we were joined by a young psychiatric resident. Quite apart from my altered state, this was one of the strangest interactions I have ever had.

Right after entering, she let us know that she normally worked in Toronto. She was just here now and then. Was she brought in special for this assessment? Susan remembers expressing her concern that the prescription medications that I had been taking might be contributing to this. She told her that I had been a robust man and that I was now quite fragile. She told her about the rapid weight loss and the distinction between my previously deep and now currently raspy voice. The resident took no interest in this. She didn't seem remotely interested in what was causing this event. She appeared to have a different point of focus.

She had a folder in her hands that contained information about me. She didn't disclose the contents, other than to mention there was something in my name related to an interaction with Coast in 2021. I couldn't imagine what that was, unless it related to the Social Worker the cops had brought to the house after I finally reported the phone interception. In any event, I had a strange feeling when the resident shared this information with me, without reading us the contents of the folder. What was the point of bringing this up? What was she up to?

Chapter 20: Trudeaumania

She then let me know that she had checked out my writing online before meeting with us. She seemed baffled by the disparity between the clarity of the writing and the confused state that I was presently in. When I heard that she had checked me out online, I became even more distrustful. After all, there are thousands of Jeff Browns on the planet. And, she had never seen my face. How did she know it was me? Who told her?

She asked, "So, who's Sophie?"

I wasn't sure where she got that information from, but I began to share some of the details of my prior relationship with Mrs. Trudeau – how we first made contact, what I had written for her, how the connection had ended. The resident continued to ask questions, including asking Susan if she agreed with my perception of the strangeness of the initial emails from Mrs. Trudeau. She did. What struck me was both the fixated and pesky pitch of the resident's inquiries, and the strange feeling that I was being judged. It felt to me like preexisting beliefs were on the table. She actually seemed protective of the Trudeaus. At some point, she made a reference to "that family," almost as though she was implying that I was a danger to them. It didn't seem to occur to her that "that family" might actually be a threat to me. Looking back, I can certainly understand that she may well have been making assumptions rooted in her psychiatric experience with delusional people and their projections onto fame, but it just didn't *feel* like it at the time. At this time, I couldn't help but wonder – did this resident come here with an agenda? Had she been told the inane 'stalking story' before she entered this room? Was she here to confirm it diagnostically?

At some point, I leaned forward on my chair and let her know that I was a hybrid. She told me that this was not scientifically possible. I told her that she was just not up-to-date with the latest technologies. She told me that I have a delusional disorder and that I'd had a psychotic break. I then laid out more of the underlying political context for whatever the fuck was going on. *This* really interested her. In fact, that and providing me with a diagnosis, seemed like the only things she was interested in.

Then she recommended that they admit me under a Form 1: Ontario's 72-hour committal order for the purposes of psychiatric assessment. By rights, a Form 1 is only ordered when someone is a danger to themselves or others. Even though there was an exhausted part of me that liked the idea of having a nice long sleep in a hospital bed, I firmly refused. I wasn't a danger to anyone, and I did not trust this kid one bit. Susan backed me up – she did not want me brought into the system. She said that she just wanted help making sense of what was happening. And, as I would find out later, she didn't trust this Trudeau-fixated psychiatric interaction at all. Something seemed off.

As delusional as I was, I knew all about the patriarchal psychiatric system and its own delusions of grandeur. Quite apart from the fact that there is virtually no evidence that brain chemistry causes psychological conditions, their obsession with psychotropic medications and rejection of body-centered psychotherapies is truly a crime against humanity. I can't even begin to imagine how many people ended up committed for life, because the psychiatrist knew so little about the vast array of factors that influence a patient's state of being.

Surprisingly, the resident didn't argue with me. She acknowledged that she couldn't force me to be committed while there was no clear danger. This begged many questions – if there was no evidence of potential harm, why suggest a Form 1? Does she often suggest them when a patient doesn't meet the criteria? Or was she okay with my decision because she had an agenda to get the delusional disorder diagnosis on the record? Was that her primary goal? And, aren't form-1's involuntary? Why let *me* decide not to engage?

The resident then suggested that I take an anti-psychotic drug. I had the good sense to refuse it. That would have only escalated my condition. She then suggested that I take an anti-anxiety medication (Lorazepam). We took the prescription with us, just in case.

And then it got weird again. She opened the door and popped her head outside. She shouted down to someone in the hallway, "He's not staying." I asked her who she was talking to. She said that there were people from the team waiting to take me. Huh? How could there be a Form 1 already in place before meeting with me? This reinforced my concern that my committal had been prearranged.

We got up and left the hospital immediately thereafter. On the drive back home, I breathed a deep sigh of relief.

CHAPTER 21

ZOPICLONE

The next day, Susan drove me to see my new family doctor. I wasn't sure why – we already had our diagnosis. She said she still didn't have an explanation for what was going on with me. She had found the psychiatric resident's level of interest in the political context frustrating: "It felt like she had already swept it up and knew the answer."

We went in to meet the doctor. Same drill, different day. I explained I was a hybrid. He told me that I was in psychosis. I told him that he was an actor. He said he was a real doctor. He offered to give me an anti-psychotic. We were right back where we started from.

Over the next few weeks, my thinking began to normalize. I realized that Susan was actually Susan, Samuel was actually Samuel, and I was just Jeff. God-voice was nowhere to be found. It didn't feel like a psychological transformation, so much as a physical one. Like there was a forest of stories in my brain that was shrinking in size. Little by little, the real Jeff filled the space.

Susan and I went for a walk one afternoon. It was a startling experience. Adrenaline was racing through my entire system. I could have walked for days. The world felt strange and unfamiliar – everything felt sharp and searing to my system, like I no longer had a buffer or filter. It was like I had died, or been in a coma for months, and now I was back. I felt agitated, confused. What the hell had happened to me? What was this world I had stepped back into?

We soon put the pieces together. In mid-October, 2022, I had asked my functional medicine practitioner to prescribe a drug called 'Armour Thyroid.' I had taken *Armour* some years before for a brief period of time to give me more energy. It had helped me to feel more energized, and then I got off of it. I have been part of the holistic health community for some time – I tend to avoid meds unless I absolutely need them. In any event, I began to take it again both because this political situation was exhausting me, and because Cribb and WT had just visited the house – it was likely the police investigation would soon be initiated. I needed a little more energy.

The Doctor faxed the prescription to my pharmacy. Even after seeing that my thyroid numbers were optimal when I did a blood panel weeks later, he at no time told me to stop, nor did he insist on regular blood tests to determine if the thyroid medication was creating a problem. I continued to take Armour daily for somewhere around 10 months – until around mid-August, 2023. There were still pills in the bottle, but Susan's chattering about it and my oft-ignored intuition told me to stop. I eventually listened.

Because I had become so wired, I had asked for the Dayvigo sleep med on July 31. This pill entered a system that was already a metabolic disaster. It appears that the thyroid medication had accumulated in my system, leaving me with outrageously high T-3 levels. I was already losing weight, but I was too hyper-anxious to notice. It had all kind of crept up on me. Because I have never really done drugs, I didn't spot the signs that I was inching my way towards a full-blown drug trip.

It's important to note that I am what is often referred to as a "low metabolizer." In other words, I have difficulty processing a variety of medications and substances (even drinking too much coffee now causes me to limp). This – and the related fact that we now know that I have a non-alcoholic fatty liver – likely played a role in that accumulation. My body simply could not get rid of this excess thyroid medication.

In any event, I took both medications for a few weeks before stopping on the Armour around mid-August. This may explain why I was intermittently hyper and sluggish – the thyroid med was wiring me, and the Dayvigo depressing my sensitive system.

After getting off of the Dayvigo, I then made a terrible error. I went on Zopiclone (which in this case, could be playfully referenced as Zopi-Clone 😊. If you recall, I'd had a problem with U-Dream, which Health Canada has said included "a substance similar to Zopiclone." Now, I didn't have delusions or anything of the sort back then. But, had my system already been riddled with months of excess thyroid medication, the U-Dream could have also sent me onto a drug-trip.

Soon after adding the Zopiclone to the melting pot around September 10, my drug-tripping mind began to take reasonable suspicions and exaggerate them into overblown narratives. The drug-trip preyed upon my fears, stretching them from situationally reasonable to delusional. It began quietly, before manifesting as suicidal ideation and the wild stories that I have shared with you. Somewhere around the time we went to the hospital, I stopped taking the Zopiclone. Some part of me intuitively sensed it was time to stop. And then, 7-10 days later, right thinking began to restore. The substances were leaving my body, or whatever was left of it.

As it turns out, I didn't have a "delusional disorder" – I was on a drug trip. Telling me that I was psychotic was like telling a guy on an LSD trip that he's having a psychotic break. It's unreasonable, but I understand it given that psychiatrists have tunnel vision with respect to their understanding of the human psyche. And again, virtually no understanding of the relationship between medications and psychological states and consequences.

So, who is responsible for this near-death calamity? Leaving aside the fool who was stupid enough to engage with (and then clumsily disconnect from) the political world (me), it begins with my functional medicine doctor. On a microcosmic level, he made a number of grave errors here. Quite apart from the fact that he is paid an annual fee to give his patients special attention, he should have known (1) not to prescribe the thyroid medication until he saw a fresh blood panel; (2) to stop on it once he saw that my thyroid numbers were optimal; (3) at the least, to insist on regular blood work to see the affect that the medication was having on my blood chemistry.

In addition, he should have refused to give me Zopiclone (or, at the least, insist that I get pharmacogenetic testing to first determine its likely impact on my system). As noted earlier, he was aware that I'd had difficulty with U-Dream, and he later told me he was aware that it contained Zopiclone.

On a macrocosmic level, the real culprits are those individuals who participated in this then three-year long techno-terror campaign against me. Let there be no doubt – this would not have happened but for them. These cowardly and Godless deviants – and surely whoever hired them – are fundamentally responsible for everything that ensued.

If there was any doubt as to their role, one only has to look at the nature of the delusions I experienced. Although wildly ridiculous on one level, <u>none of them came out of nowhere.</u> They were all extensions and exaggerations of preexisting realities. The synergistic alchemical combination of the colliding drugs simply compounded true-to-life existing circumstances – to the point of breaking with reality. The drug-trip may have broken down my capacity to distinguish fact from fiction, but it directly reflected the truth of my lived experience. For example, the God-voice in my head was an exaggerated version of the one who had emailed me from Wild Horse Way. I had checked them out online, and it was their face I envisioned. The cops were all coming to do someone's political bidding. The desire to kill myself was an internalization of what the techno-terrorists were trying to do to me. The belief that everyone was against me was a reflection of the fact that a whole host of significant institutions had turned away or turned against me. It really was (and still is) David vs. Goliath, on steroids.

And, of course, it was easy to believe that both I and everyone else were hybrids. When you feel like a machine for long enough, everyone else does, too. If you can't express yourself freely, you stop moving freely. You stop breathing freely. You stop thinking freely. Expression is so fundamental to our nature that, in its absence, we become something less than human.

As for how I survived this, there is no question that Susan's urgent return was my saving grace. Given that this drug-trip had reached unexpectedly harrowing levels while she was away, I am not sure if I would have made it another week without her. Her presence softened the edges of my madness, and gave me the tiny thread of hope that I needed. Many people proved to be tremendous disappointments – I have since bid farewell to a whole slew of narcissists and fame-seekers – but she was utterly remarkable during this period of time.

In addition, it may well be that the 40+ lbs that I lost actually helped sustain me. This debacle weighed heavily on my heart – the continuous wave of palpitations was only one indication – and it may well be that the shedding of substantial weight kept my body alive. Finally, in the most dire of circumstances, that roaring lion that lives inside of me simply refused to die. I would lie on that bed for hours, taking stock of my life. I would sincerely ask myself: Time to die, or more time to live? And when I would feel utterly certain of my uselessness and most inclined to perish, I would often think of the politically motivated miscreants who had wreaked havoc on my psyche and life. I would try to imagine their twisted faces and plastic smiles. Then I would look them square in the eye and say: "Not today, Motherfuckers. <u>Not today</u>." Besides, Lacy Cat had to eat. Even if she was a hybrid in my drug-ridden mind, she still had to eat. I had to feed the machine until Susan got home.

CHAPTER 22

RE-ENTRY DRAMA

It was the oddest thing. As the physiological and psychological shock wore off, I found myself quietly wishing that I was still unwell. Not because I had enjoyed myself, but because it had given me a break from what had become a very unpleasant chronic reality. It was the first time in a number of years that I had slept like a baby. And the first time in decades I had felt like someone else was in charge. The idea of being taken care of by the system didn't seem all that bad. It was far better than re-entering this nightmare.

Nonetheless, I slowly re-joined the world. My roaring lion wasn't done yet. I was too triggered by recent events to work on this book, but I was able to write some fresh quotes and work on my Substack blog. I got caught up on administrative tasks. I began to do sessions with clients again – I had missed those most of all.

At the same time, I granted myself permission to initiate a healing and closure process around this traumatic event. The forest of stories inside of my mind had dissipated but I still needed confirmation of reality. With that in mind, I met with various 'doppels' to confirm their humanness. I went back to locations where I had misinterpreted events. Susan and I returned to the hospital to integrate my memories. And I began to listen to my favorite music and watch my favorite films so that I could reconnect with the old Jeff.

No matter what I did, it was clear that I had changed. I wasn't the same guy. My perspective on this human life was forever altered. I appreciated its gloriousness like never before. I felt reverential and devotional like never before. And, I was aware of the dark side of human nature like never before. My mission was now clearer than ever – I would fight for our collective right to the light, no matter the consequences.

I also understood suffering in a way that I never had. I had spent years calling out the 'spiritual bypass' – a term created by John Welwood to describe[68] the tendency to use spirituality to avoid unresolved issues and painful realities – without fully understanding the pain that compelled it.

I am sorry for my insensitivity. I had known pain, but I had never known true hopelessness. Until those little pills introduced it to my life. Now I understood so much more about the human condition. My compassion for our shared challenges had expanded exponentially. As had my love for (most of) humanity.

At the same time, my experience of my body continued to be concerning. I had lost over 40 pounds rapidly – most of it muscle – and every system was re-adjusting. My stomach growled like a beast after eating. I either had the runs or I was constipated. I continued to lose my voice midday. I felt physically weak. I had to hold onto the handrail while going down the stairs. I had to train myself to type harder when I worked on the computer. My adrenals were cooked. I had to lie down between interactions, just to recover. Where before I could work a solid 10-hour day, I was now limited to 4-hours tops.

I connected with my functional medicine doctor to arrange some tests. The bloods came back normal, with the exception of (not surprisingly) high cortisol levels.

I then went to see a kind-hearted psychiatrist that the hospital had arranged for a follow-up. We had about 40 minutes together. Both her and my family doctor emphasized how unique this whole thing was. They were used to seeing this kind of severe reaction from people doing illicit drugs, but not from prescription medications.

We discussed the events at the hospital. I asked her this: "If they had taken me in on a Form 1, is it possible that they would have just propped me up with drugs and never realized that it was the drugs that were causing the problem?" Her reply was telling, "Possibly, but not definitely." Thank God I refused the Form 1!

When I asked her if I could see her a few more times to process the experience, she said no. I asked her why. She pleasantly replied, "You've had an adverse reaction to medications. You don't have a psychiatric condition. We have to see the people who do."

Best day ever – rejected by psychiatry.

When I was ready, I began to scan my various email accounts. I began with the *Enrealment Press* emails that were being flooded by spambots last summer. Maybe those had ceased when they stopped sending fake emails to my Hotmail account? No such luck. There had been another 30,000+ of them sent since I had cleared them in the summer. Busy little bots. I cleared them again.

Chapter 22: Re-entry Drama

In addition, I checked the sales of my publishing company *Enrealment Press* on Amazon Canada. We distribute the 15 titles that we have published in Canada. In other words, Amazon generally orders them from us. Not anymore. Where before we would average somewhere around 80-100 ordered books per month, we were now receiving orders for a handful. And this had been going on for months – since around the time they had sent back a number of boxes of *Humanifestations*.

This would not necessarily be an issue, given that Amazon can order those books from other distributors. In other words, we would make money on the books one way or the other. But there was a bigger problem. I went onto Amazon.ca to see how the books were being presented, and that told me everything. A number of the books were either unavailable, or priced at an amount that was not accessible for most.

For example, *Hearticulations* (my then best-selling title) was no longer available in the usually accessible price range (maximum $19.99 US or about $26.00 Canadian). And it was clearly not being ordered from us:

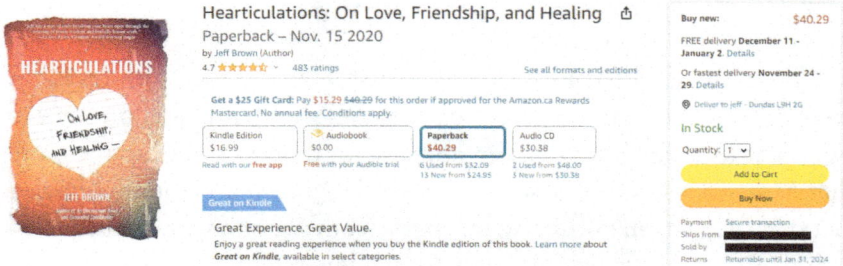

Humanifestations was certainly not being ordered from us, but was available at an exorbitant price from a faraway location (no doubt with shipping charges to reflect it). Like *Hearticulations*, it properly retails at $19.95 US (or less):

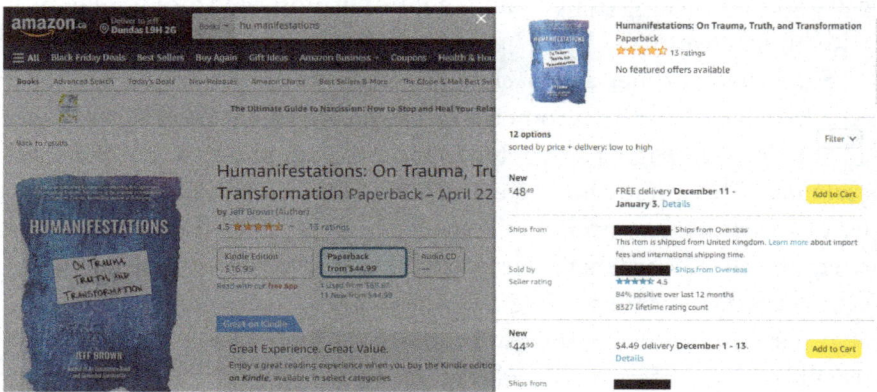

Grounded Spirituality – always in stock in our storage unit – now indicated it would take 1-2 months to ship. And one of our most popular titles, Victoria Erickson's *Edge of Wonder* (published in 2015), was now notated as a "not yet been released" title, available for pre-order.

I went into our account to see if *Humanifestations* was even on my list anymore. It wasn't. It said it had been enrolled, but it also said that it was "restricted". And there was no "Buy Box" on the actual book page:

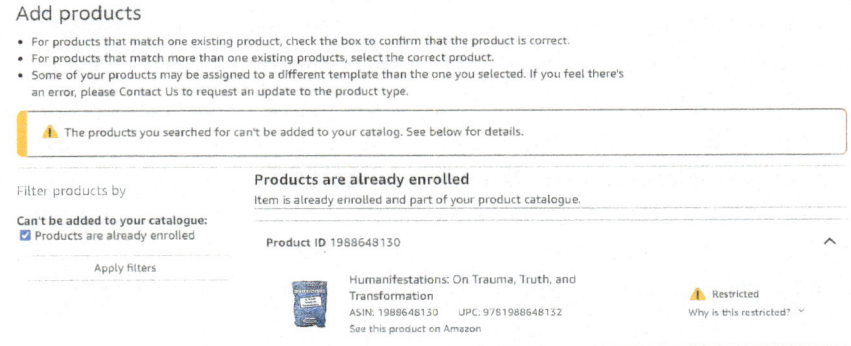

I began to send emails to Amazon customer service. With respect to *Humanifestations*, 'Durga' wrote back to tell me that it was on my consignment list, which was simply not true. In their email, they also noted that Amazon orders are based on demand. Quite apart from the obvious fact that they weren't ordering this book from me or anyone affordable, it is difficult to build demand if you are shadow-banned on Meta and your posts containing book excerpts are not reaching enough people. In other words, this game had a number of interrelated components. With respect to the missing Buy Box, Durga wrote back that there is "no Buy Box because it is not in inventory." <u>A little hard to get it inventoried, if nobody can order the fucking thing</u>. Games politically motivated monopolies play with human lives.

So, I tried another approach. I had been told that I could ask for a "stock-up request." This is something that you do if you are going to run an advertising campaign. I attempted to make a stock-up request for *Humanifestations*. That got me nowhere. I also sent a stock-up request for 20 copies of *Hearticulations* on Friday November 25 at 12:43 PM. A few hours later, I received 7 orders for *Hearticulations* (the book without the politically related excerpts) totaling 107 books. I don't remember ever getting an order this big for any title. And certainly not sent to us on a Friday (we usually receive orders on Monday mornings).

Chapter 22: Re-entry Drama

The message was clear – you can sell *Hearticulations*, but not *Humanifestations*. Somebody out there doesn't want that baby in the hands of Canadians.

My anger had reached a new level. It was always there, but the events of the last months had taken it to a new place. Even if I wanted to forget, I was always reminded of it by the sound of my jaw every time I moved my mouth side-to-side. My TMJ (Trudeau Mania Jaw) was no pleasure. Not only the cracking sound of the jaw, but also the sound of my rage, bubbling to the surface with every crunch. To think, I had gone through all of this suffering because of a connection to a nepo baby and a Wildhorse.

The anger began to leak out. In social media interactions (my apologies, for any needlessly unkind comments), in emails with those had who disappointed me, and on long walks with Susan. I simply couldn't understand how all of Canada's justice-seeking systems could have turned their back on this. The RCMP and local police knew about this, and never launched a real investigation. Even a federal judge tracking the situation led to nothing. The allegedly top investigative newspaper in Canada – the Toronto "Star" – had been provided with various drafts from Cribb and did nothing. Even after Cribb witnessed two investigative obstructions of justice, visited with Hamilton Police after the second one and they did not deny the 'stalking' story, and was winked at by Trudeau on the seawall 48 hours after our NSIRA confirmation texts, his editor(s) still didn't publish.

It was my conviction that if the police had investigated in the early stages – even if they couldn't prove a thing – I would have been able to submit more evidence as it arose. If they didn't have enough to begin with – they certainly did now. As a result, it's likely fewer games would have been played because the techno-terror team would have known that those lines were still open. I sincerely believe that the medical calamity that ensued wouldn't have occurred (unless there is more to it than meets the eye), if proper investigations had been initiated. Whether it was because I would have then had the presence of mind to notice what was happening with my body, or because I would have felt bolstered by systemic support, things would have gone down differently. To know there was oversight and accountability enacted by legitimate authority figures would have changed my entire psychological landscape. Instead, the lack of accountability – and blatant failure – of the system compounded my original problem. Now I was dealing with more than just the political world. The entire system seemed rigged. The moment the Hamilton police constructed their mental health narrative, they sealed my fate.

They should be ashamed of themselves. Perhaps one day they will be.

CHAPTER 23

JACORDRIS GREGOIRE

I went public – in video and written form – with some of the details of my severely adverse reaction to prescription drugs. I did not provide the overarching context, but I have little doubt that the techno-terror team found even the mention of it too close for comfort. I was slowly scratching my way back to the surface, and that didn't sit well with whoever was in charge.

Towards the end of November, I received an email from a student that she couldn't sign up for my December writing course, because it now said "bookings are closed." Bookings weren't actually closed – it had been set up properly and was fully functional. My web designer went in to try to resolve the problem, but he *said* it couldn't be fixed. He had to construct a new landing page.

On November 28, Revenue Canada mailed me yet another of those 'HST Post-Assessing Review' requests. This one was related to Enrealment Press for the period June 1, 2021 to May 31, 2022. I wrote back to again point out that there was no meaningful discrepancy between the reported HST sales figures and the annual company sales figures. The discrepancy was again because I had been using the paper form, which does not have a line for zero-rated sales outside of Canada. I awaited their reply.

The next day, there were two more Facebook dings against my accounts. Someone at Meta went into a group and removed two old posts – one of which was about the importance of standing down abusers of power. Evil has a twisted sense of humor:

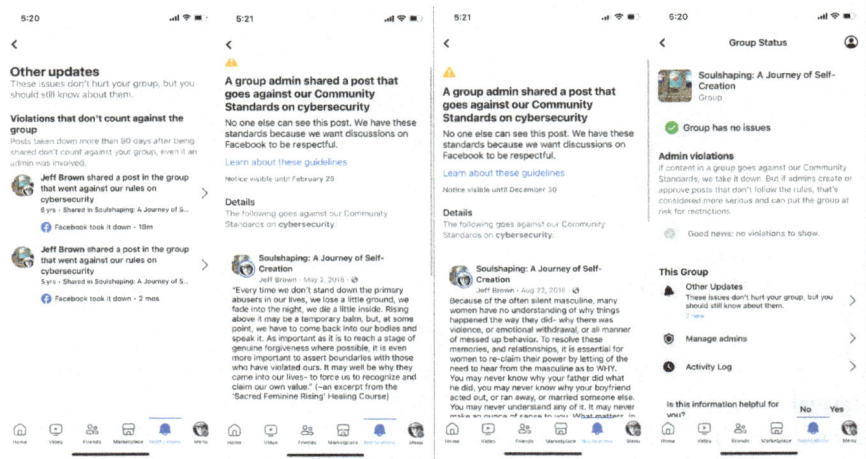

In early December, I began to notice the return of the hacker referral comments on my Facebook business page. Not that they ever entirely left, but it seemed to intensify again with a flood of comments on the page. Of course, these comments were not legitimate. They were attempts to gaslight and trigger me re: hacking. Meanwhile, I was receiving a continuous stream of fake notifications and DMs with threats to remove the page. The gang's all here (again)!

Around the same time, I checked one of my old email accounts. I had set up various email addresses, in an effort to interact privately. Inside one of those accounts, I found two important things. First, an email from the Civilian Review and Complaints Commission. You may recall that I had written them in June to see if they could look into whether the RCMP had behaved improperly with respect to my Privacy Act process, and the premature termination of my two Hamilton police investigations. In this emailed response – dated September 29 – they informed me that my complaint had been forwarded to the RCMP for investigation.

I also opened an email dated November 2 from the RCMP wherein they let me know that they had received the complaint from the CRCC. In it, they confirmed that a member of the RCMP would be appointed to review and investigate my complaint.

When I read these emails, I felt momentarily elated – Dudley Do-Right had finally arrived! – and then deflated – Dudley Do-Wrong had returned! Both because of what I had already experienced and because of what had happened to Jody Wilson-Raybould – where obvious obstructions of justice were swept under the carpet – I wondered if this was all

Chapter 23: Jacordris Gregoire

just a set-up. Surely, they weren't here to help me. They were here to make matters worse.

On December 6, Revenue Canada mailed me yet another 'HST Post-Assessing Review' request. This one was related to Soulshaping Institute Inc. for the period June 1, 2021 to May 31, 2022. I again wrote back to point out that there was no meaningful discrepancy between the reported HST sales figures and the annual company sales figures. I awaited their reply.

That same day, the fake Russian emails came back with a vengeance after a two-month vacation. They became a regular part of my online life, yet again.

Microsoft account

Unusual sign.in activity

We detected something unusual about a recent sign-in to the Microsoft account soulshaping@hotmail.com.

Sign-in details
Country/region: **Russia/Moscow**
IP address: **103.225.77.255**
Date: **Wed, 06 Dec 2023 13:18:30 +0000**
Platform: **Windows 10**
Browser: **Firefox**

A user from **Russia/Moscow** just logged into your account from a new device. If this wasn't you, please report the user. If this was you, we'll trust similar activity in the future.

Report The User

On December 11, I went onto Amazon.ca to check out the status of *Humanifestations*. At this time, the lowest priced copy of the book was now $68.28. Despite my best efforts to contain myself, I just couldn't. I immediately wrote a piece on my Substack newsletter about the shadow-banning of *Humanifestations*[69] and provided a link to purchase it directly from our Enrealment website.

* * *

On December 14, Susan and I both caught Covid for the first time. We had been able to repel it for years, but our immune systems had clearly weakened. Susan had a particularly difficult time with it. The pressure in her chest that had begun months before, became noticeably worse. Something was very wrong with her.

On December 20, I received yet another ding from Meta – the (anti-) social media PSYOP that never sleeps. This one related to an innocuous question from someone on my Soulshaping group from 2018, wherein

217

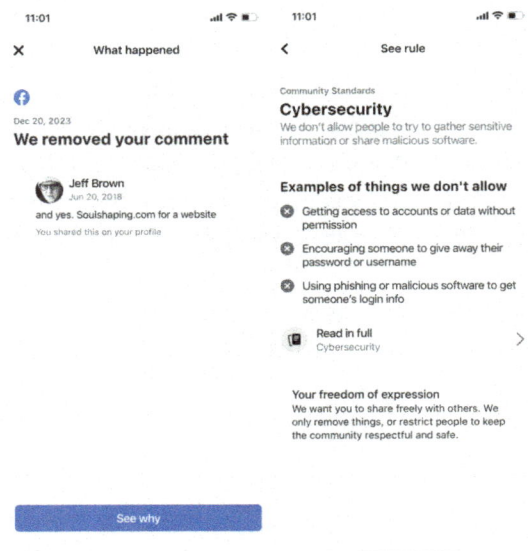

I had provided them with website information. I remember seeing this particular removal notice, and feeling an intense gripping in my chest. My lungs had been significantly impacted by Covid, and this particular 'cybersecurity' attack masquerading as a community standards issue knocked the wind out of me. Anyone who thinks that you can't destroy people with acts of techno-terror is a bloody fool:

On December 29, I received a site lockout notification for Enrealment. Com (the publishing house website). The hackers were now using the correct user name. These would now become a regular part of my life, as would brute force attacks on jeffbrown. co. Meanwhile, the fake Facebook shut-down emails picked up their pace on that same website. They also continued on Facebook itself, including the following one which arrived 39 minutes after I put up a New Year's post on my personal page about 3 politically inspired books that I planned to write emanating from this experience:

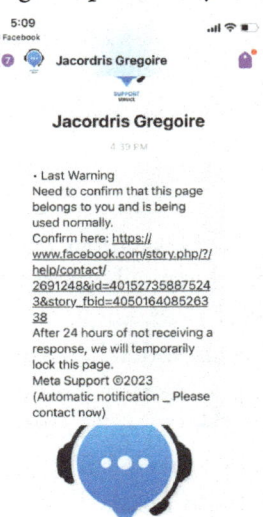

The fake JEFF BROWN pages soon picked up steam, spamming followers with fake prize offers. This game would prove quite significant shortly:

Chapter 23: Jacordris Gregoire

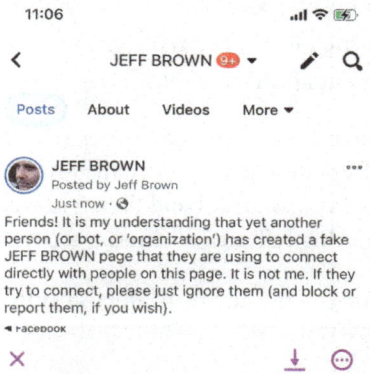

On January 3, there was yet another issue with the payment link no longer working on an imminent course. This one, my February writing course. The designer had to fix it again.

A few days later, the debt, loan, home security, and burial insurance email onslaught returned to my Hotmail account. The Cyber-stalking Gang's all here! Poor souls. They thought they had solved the Jeff Brown problem. Not today, Futhermuckers. 😊

There was basically nowhere that I could go online where I wasn't triggered by these homicidal lunatics: my main email addresses, my Facebook messages and notifications, my Amazon account, my sales totals, my texts filled with fake CRA, Canada Post, and suspended bank card messages. The latter often happened after I had actual difficulty using my actual bank card at a debit machine. The messages didn't come from the bank. They would include the name of a different bank. Ask yourself how they knew my card hadn't worked if all the players in this scheme weren't interconnected.

And on PayPal, I again noticed something that I had first seen in December. On the account for *Enrealment Press*, this seemingly innocuous alert remained in place:

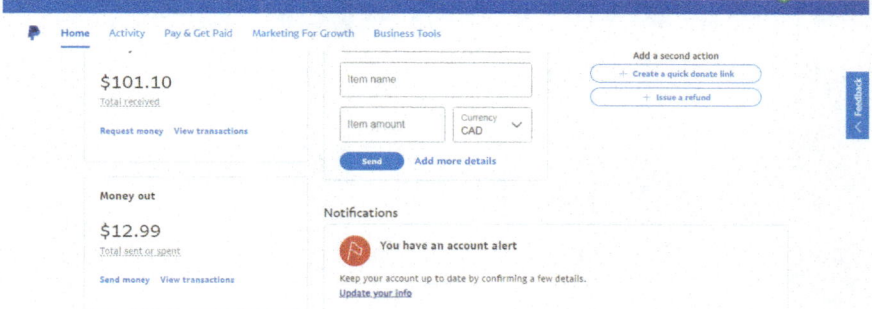

Whenever I clicked it, it asked for no information. It merely said that I was "all set." But then the alert returned right afterwards.

So, I contacted Paypal about it weeks later. They responded:

> Thank you for the information, Jeff. It means that we might asked for additional information from you on the future. No need to worry. I have reviewed your account and there's no restriction that will prevent you for having full access with the account.

What a strange thing – an account alert about details that they may one day need? If that's what this is, then everyone should have one because you never know!

It is worth mentioning that, 16 months later, the warning was still there.

CHAPTER 24

LEFT ATRIAL ENLARGEMENT

On January 16, I received a response from Revenue Canada indicating that the HST review they had commenced in December re: Enrealment Media Inc. was complete. In their words: "There are no changes required."

That evening, I went for a walk with Cribb along the Toronto shoreline. It was the first time I had seen him since last spring. We discussed the various things I had been through, and the steps required to finally bring this story to the Canadian people. When I told him about this book, he asked if he could see it before it was published. I refused. He then said something that baffled me: "What will my editors say if they read it?" I didn't know what to say. He was concerned about his job. I was concerned about Susan and I.

After we parted, I felt confused. Based on various things that he had expressed over time, I made the assumption that he was sharing all relevant information with his editors: the obstructed police investigations, the 'wink of warning' moment on the Vancouver seawall, the updated summaries of events that I provided, all the information related to Meta and Amazon. I had assumed that it didn't hit their publishing bar, whatever criteria that was based on. If that wasn't true, then what the hell was going on here? Who was holding this story back? And, why?

During this conversation, he acknowledged that he hadn't looked at the social media related info I had sent him. I had asked him time and again to get one of the up-and-comers from The Star's *University of Toronto Investigative Journalism Bureau* to do it. It wouldn't have been difficult – he is the founder and director. I even emailed him that request again that evening. He subsequently told me that he would do that. I never heard anything about it thereafter.

(More recently, I spoke with him and he again acknowledged that he was not someone familiar with social media matters, but that he had eventually shown the stuff to people who do. He indicated that they had said that there was something there, but that they would need more. As this book confirms, I had more (and more), but he had not told me that someone he had approached had an interest in seeing it. Without that information, I had no reason to believe that continuing to send it would have been of any value.)

The next day, I mailed a letter to the psychiatric department at Hamilton Health Services. As part of my personal closure process, I wanted an explanation for some of my lingering concerns: (1) The psychiatric resident referenced the contents of a personal information folder she had in her possession. Is it standard practice to have access to such information and to reference it during a diagnostic meeting? (2) The resident had stated that she had checked my social media. How did she know where to look? Why did she check it? Is this standard practice? (3) My wife had informed the resident that the prescriptions I was taking might be the problem. Why did the resident prescribe other medications, before first exploring the possibility that withdrawing from the meds would solve the problem? (4) Why was there a Form 1 in place <u>before</u> meeting with me? Why was it suggested and organized if there was no evidence of risk to self or other?

The online games continued, including one that blew my socks off. Check this out. On January 17, I noticed a fake page trying to get my attention on my Facebook personal page with 'like' clicks and a friend request. At first, it was using the same images I was using: my personal page headshot(s) as the profile picture, a picture of another author holding *Grounded Spirituality* as the banner image. And then it changed the banner image to the picture of some of my books used on my Facebook business page.

What is significant about this is that <u>it wasn't using my name</u>. It was using the name of one of the prominent lawyers I had been interacting with (John Phillips) spelled backwards. This wasn't done to confuse people on my page – they wouldn't know what the hell is going on. It was done to trigger me. If this doesn't illustrate the mind-fucking nature of their techno-terror game, nothing will. In an effort to torment me and to discourage legal action, they wanted me to know that they knew which lawyer I had connected with.

CHAPTER 24: LEFT ATRIAL ENLARGEMENT

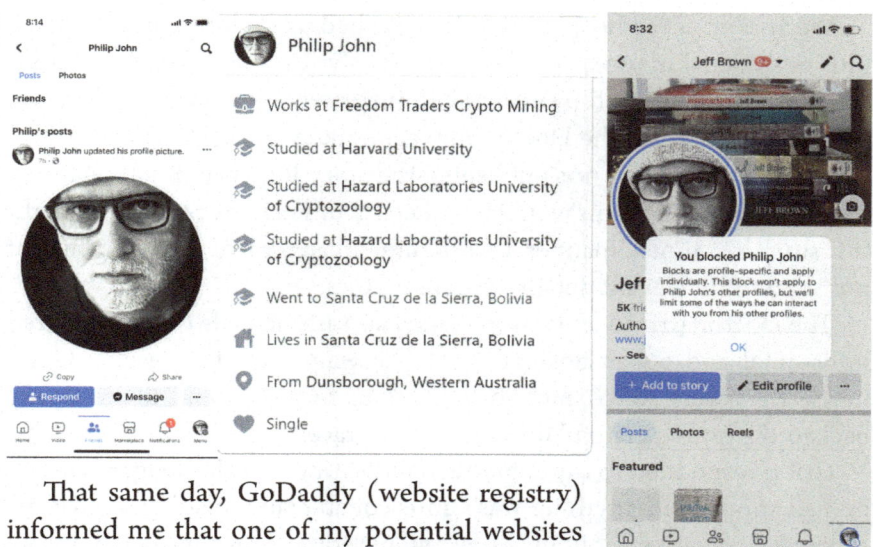

That same day, GoDaddy (website registry) informed me that one of my potential websites – EnrealmentHour.co – couldn't be renewed because of a payment issue. Strange. There was more than enough money in the PayPal account. Nothing seemed to be going right anymore.

On January 25, I received a response from Revenue Canada indicating that the HST review that they had commenced in December re: Soulshaping Institute Inc. was complete: "There are no changes required."

On the evening of Saturday, January 27, our lives changed. In the midst of the escalating tension, Susan's chest pain and pressure had become much more pronounced. She had been trying her best to recover, but the tension in her body was too high. Tonight, she described it as an elephant on her chest, and asked me to take her to the hospital. Before we left, she suggested that we wait until tomorrow. She was concerned that I wouldn't get a good night's sleep. I thanked her, and told her to get ready.

As I raced us along Highway 5, I saw it all differently: the wiretaps and phone games, the frightening emails and threatening gestures, the shadow bans and book blocks, the obstruction of my two police investigations, the trickery that undermined my Federal Court Privacy Act appeals, the psychological warfare that had become my life. I saw the evil behind it. I saw the horror. I could live with me being targeted – but not her. I don't think I had *really* prayed for 40 years, but as I raced her to the Oakville-Trafalgar Memorial Hospital, I reached for God. And God reached right back.

223

We arrived at the hospital, and they rushed us to the front of the line. This hospital takes physical calamity seriously. They took her blood pressure – over 180 on the top end – and immediately brought her in for tests. While waiting to see the Doctor, my rage spiked. Tonight, it was Cribb I was pissed off at – for not publishing the story long ago. I couldn't help but believe that all of this would have been avoided if the Star had brought this story in a timely manner. I wrote him an angry text, accusing him of not sharing all relevant details with his editors.

The Doctor arrived. He was informed and attuned. He quickly ordered in-hospital and out-of-hospital tests. We waited for the results. Good news. They were stable enough to allow us to go home. I drove slowly back to the house, grateful for God's good graces.

Cribb responded to my angry text, indicating that the suggestion that he had suppressed anything was "unreasonable and false." And that his expressed concerns about my book and his editor's response on our walk was "perhaps just some misunderstanding of his clumsy communication." He provided what appeared to be a reasonable explanation. Included in it was the following statement:

> "There is nothing nefarious or covert in the comment. I've told you honestly that I spent weeks pouring through the hundreds of emails, cataloguing them and drafting copy. I did many interviews, transcribed and added voice. And I'm saying clearly that all of that information is in drafts that my editors are fully aware of. They believe, as I've said, that we need a clear piece of evidence about the surveillance element which is really the core public interest piece of this story. And that's where it stood and stands...."

(In a more recent conversation (May 6, 2025), Cribb further clarified. He indicated that his expressed concern on our walk about how his editors would feel about the book, was not because he was not sharing all the details of the story with them, but because they might not be happy about the fact that "I kept coming to you saying my editors aren't going to run it. I can imagine my editors not being happy with that.")

* * *

If any part of me imagined that the cyber-stalkers would stop after this second medical calamity, I was soon reminded that evil never sleeps. So, I again began to publicly post some of the games that were being played:

CHAPTER 24: LEFT ATRIAL ENLARGEMENT

Literally a minute or two later, one of the so-called bots that are humans posted a comment on my Facebook personal page. Just to let me know they are there. This was quite significant, because I believe it was <u>the first time they had ever come onto my personal page</u>. And this was minutes after I put up a post that threatened to expose more of the cyber-stalking team and its shenanigans. Let nobody tell me that these are all "bots" ever again. (Weeks later, I actually wrote a comment to one of them, which they immediately responded to. More confirmation that they are not "bots." They are utilizing fake accounts, but they are actual techno-terrorists paid to post antagonizing things on targeted pages.)

The russians are coming! Seriously, do you ever get fake 'Unusual sign.in activity' emails on your email system? I get them most everyday. They aren't actually from Microsoft. What could possibly motivate someone to send fake emails about non-existent attempts to hack my emails from Russia?

Unusual sign.in activity

We detected something unusual about a recent sign-in to the Microsoft account soulshaping@hotmail.com.

Sign-in details
Country/region: **Russia/Moscow**
IP address: **103.225.77.255**
Date: **Fri, 02 Feb 2024 00:55:08 +0000**

The same day, yet another 'cybersecurity' ding from Meta for an innocuous comment made on a group <u>5 years earlier</u>. I was getting more and more pissed off by the hour. And yet, I was coming closer to really accepting that all of this was somehow intrinsic to my callings in this life. Yes, it was messy, but it had a kind of strange directionality to it. Like it was leading me somewhere that my soul needed to go, if only to more fully understand the reality of the human condition. I had been a student for a long time. On February 3, I put up the following post on my Facebook business and personal page, pinning it to the top:

JEFF BROWN
Posted by Jeff Brown
Just now ·

I sat outside of a Staples in Ancaster, Ontario on December 5th, 2020, writing a farewell email. Since soon after that date- now 3+ years ago- I have been actively surveilled and terrorized by wrongdoers. I have a good idea of which organization is involved in this. Those acts of technological terror led to both Susan and I almost losing our lives this autumn and fall. For a long time, I was perplexed by all of this, trapped inside a double bind. I no longer am. It is entirely evident that all of this happened for a particular reason. Sometimes our callings arrive in the strangest of ways.

225

On February 4, I checked the Enrealment emails to see if the bots were still active. It turns out that they were, and that they were now sending fake emails at a rate of more than 1 per minute:

At the same time, the unrelenting frenzy of seeming bots commenting on my Facebook business page posts continued. Sometimes they were hacker related, sometimes relationship related, sometimes porn images. Again, the important thing to note is that these comments very often began about a minute or so after I began to scroll Facebook 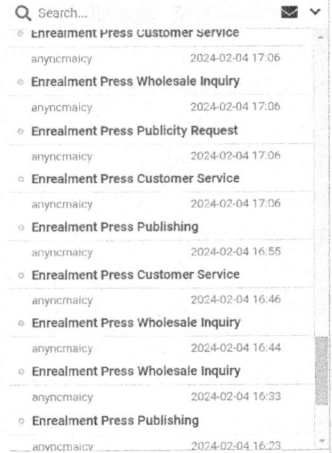 from my phone or laptop. They weren't just trying to bewilder people on my page – they were trying to trigger me while I was right on the page itself. And even more interesting – many of these never-before-seen 'bots' had 'Top fan' characterizations beside their name. How did the Facebook algorithm identify them as such if these specific ones had not continuously engaged with the page?

On February 6, Susan and I returned to the same hospital for a stress test and ultrasound of her heart. This time, the news was not so good. Not only was her blood pressure particularly high when she met with the Doctor – likely because I had made the mistake of answering a call from Cribb while we were at the hospital – but the ultrasound revealed that she had a left atrial enlargement. Part of her heart had expanded to accommodate the increase in blood pressure. And it wasn't certain that it would ever return to normal. The Doctor asserted that it was essential that her stress level decrease. Her life depended on it. He prescribed a blood pressure medication.

Later that night, I contacted Cribb and gave him a piece of my mind again. He handled it well. On the drive back, I also gave *myself* a piece of my mind: "Why had you wasted so much time chasing the system for help? How could you forget what you already knew about the world we live in? You have a voice. Use it for fuck's sakes."

On February 8, I opened an account on "X". I can't even begin to tell you how good it felt to be able to express myself freely, after living in a repression chamber for so long. Little by little, I recovered some of my lost voice. Interestingly, I went back onto X the next day to change my password, but it kept rejecting the password that I had used. I tried again more recently, but their system wouldn't recognize my user name.

Chapter 24: Left Atrial Enlargement

Around this time, I went back to look for the ('Chair Quinby') posts that I had told you about in the spring of 2021. The Instagram with an image that looked strangely familiar, accompanied with the nasty words in the messages sent. Back then, I had posted about it on Instagram and Facebook. Now, both posts were gone, as was Chair's page (although the page is back as of the final draft of this book). I had not removed my posts. Who had an incentive to get rid of them?

One afternoon, I browsed my emails to find those sent by the person on 'Wild Horse Way' who had purchased a session and then never came back to book it. Back in August, I'd been sure that they were part of the game, but I was no longer sure if that was true. I recognized that this may well have been a misperception caused by my prescription experience. So, I wrote them and asked if they still wanted to do the session or if they preferred a refund. No response. I remembered seeing them on my Facebook page at some point, so I searched for them there. Nowhere to be found. I refunded their payment and wrote them to let them know. No response, again. Soon thereafter, I saw them clicking 'like' on one of my Facebook pages. The mystery person had returned!

At some point, I began to wonder if a few of the people who were booking personal sessions were sent by the techno-terror team. One of them really stood out. Before the session, she had written me from two different email addresses, each with its own personal name. And the session was paid for by someone with yet another name.

During the session, she made a point of bringing up themes that were strangely consistent with the triggering emails I was receiving: homelessness, impoverishment, politically motivated taxation issues, government surveillance and malfeasance. It wasn't just the themes that struck me. It was the way that she was expressing herself. She appeared to be reading a description of herself and her situation from something off to the right of the computer screen. It didn't feel natural. It felt entirely staged. A teleprompter, perhaps?

Subsequent to the session, I wrote her to let her know that I didn't have time to follow through with a task she had requested. I never heard back. Given her intense level of interest in this task, it surprised me she didn't respond. I was left to wonder if she – like 'Wild Horse Way' before her, and a few others that did sessions with me and appeared fixated on something off to the side of the computer – had already achieved their goals while communicating with me the first time. Why reconnect if they had already accomplished triggering their target?

On a number of occasions, my TD Bank debit card was declined when there were funds in the account. And I still continued to receive a slew of fraudulent texts from other banks indicating that my account had been frozen. One time, the fraudster even managed to succeed at a double trigger game, referencing my TD Bank and Amazon accounts all in one text (and only <u>moments</u> after I had worked on parts of this book that contained references to TD Bank and Amazon). Just to rub it all in my face, yet again:

> Text Message
> Today 9:25 PM
>
> TD: Did you recently attempt $22.20 at AMZN Mktp US on your TD Rewards Credit Card ending in 1784? Reply YES/NO. To opt out, reply STOP. Msg rates may apply.

On February 19, GoDaddy emailed me that the renewal payment for a web domain name that I had previously registered ("theabuseofpower.com") had been rejected: "Your payment method isn't valid." Again, there were funds in the connected PayPal account.

How very interesting. "PayPal" had allegedly refused to provide funds for website renewals related to 'Enrealment' and 'Abuse of Power.' The universe has a remarkable sense of humor.

On February 23, I had a call with the Patient-Relations Psychiatrist (Dr. Fudge) who was assigned to discuss the letter I had written about the curious interactions with the psychiatric resident on October 9, 2023.

With respect to the question of why the resident had accessed and referenced preexisting information about me, he indicated that this is standard practice for some psychiatrists in case there is something in the file that assists with their assessment. Quite apart from the fact that she should have told me what was in the file so as not to stoke my suspicions, I found this response reasonable.

With respect to the question of how the resident knew which Jeff Brown to look for online (and how she could be sure it was me before meeting me for the first time), he indicated that they do google searches at times, but he couldn't answer that question in this particular context. I have no issue with the quest for useful information under certain circumstances, but I needed to understand how she knew that it was me before she had ever met me.

With respect to why the resident had paid little attention to Susan's concerns that the prescriptions were the problem – and suggested that I

Chapter 24: Left Atrial Enlargement

take an anti-psychotic before exploring that question – I'll leave that question for another book. It speaks to a broad range of issues with psychiatric training and the worrisome relationship between the profession and big pharma. It may well be that the emergency physician had been instructed to pass this onto psychiatry, but in the absence of confirmatory evidence, its best I leave that be for now.

(*Note: If you are interested in the subject, I encourage you to check out Rob Wipond's groundbreaking book, 'Your Consent is Not Required.' Great stuff.)

With respect to the question of why there was a Form 1 put in place before the resident met with me, he clearly said: "It wasn't the resident that put you on the form. It was the emergency department physician. The resident vacated the form." When asked why I was Form 1'ed, given that there was no indication of danger to myself or anyone else, he had no clear answer other than to say that the physician may have erred on the side of caution to protect herself legally and to get me the psychiatric assessment that she felt I needed. Given that I was going to get that assessment in the impending meeting with the resident, the existence of an already initiated Form 1 made no sense to me.

We left it that he would get back to me about my lingering concerns after speaking with the psychiatric resident. I also left a subsequent phone message indicating that I wanted an explanation from the emergency doctor as to why she chose to put me on a form.

*　*　*

On February 24, Meta yet again removed some of old content without showing it to me. According to them: "It looks like you tried to gather sensitive information, or shared malicious software." Whatever. This time, I went public on my business page:[70]

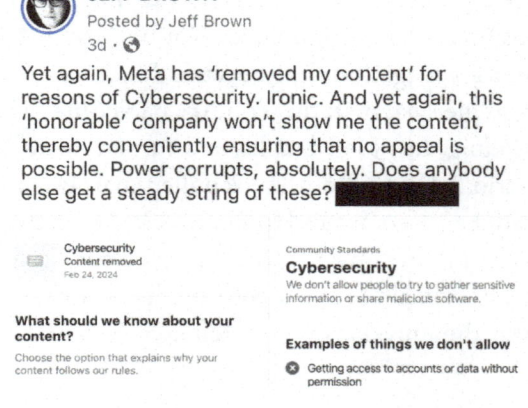

Then I wrote this response to someone on the thread: "Ask yourself why they don't show it. If they were truly motivated by the desire to secure cyber, wouldn't they want you to know what kind of content to avoid using? So, if that's not their motivation, then what is the reason for dinging certain individuals? What purposes is this monopoly engaged in? What is it trying to intimidate and contain?"

Soon thereafter, <u>that thread was removed</u>. Not by me. Woah.

On February 25, the city of Hamilton experienced a cyber-security related outage of its online systems. It continued for months. This proved to be remarkably inconvenient for many people, including me. I had been checking various emails and working on this book at various Hamilton libraries. I had really found my groove at one in particular. I now had to travel further and scout other locations to find the just right space to write in. This would prove to be particularly relevant shortly.

On February 27, I received an email from my web hosting company to the effect that I had to upgrade my hosting plan for Enrealment.com because of the overwhelm of activity: "You are actually one of the top users on the server over the last 60 days when it comes to both CPU and memory usage." If this was happening because of a swarm of potential book purchasers, I would have been delighted. But it wasn't. It was caused by what I now understand to be a 'Denial-of-Service' (DOS) Attack. The techno-terrorists set up a half-handshake on a website so that it maxes out its space. It has nothing to do with legitimate activity. I then had to pay for a much larger capacity for the website.

Those book quotes in *Humanifestations* must have seriously pissed someone off.

On February 28, I opened an email from the Sergeant put in charge of my RCMP obstruction case, indicating that he wanted to arrange a time for me to provide my statement. He was ready to initiate the investigation. When I read this email, I felt frightened. Not because I disliked the idea of an obstruction investigation, but because I had no idea who to trust anymore. Not a single system in this country had come through for me.

<u>Right after</u> reading this, I left Staples and turned down Brant Street in Burlington, Ontario. A Dodge Ram Truck pulled sharply in front of me. The owner had moved the letters around to spell out WAR on the tailgate. It was a little hard to miss. I didn't imagine that this interesting synchronicity was staged by my cyber-stalkers to mess with my head (or was it?), but I did wonder if this was the universe's way of telling me something. It certainly

Chapter 24: Left Atrial Enlargement

felt like I was living on a battlefield. How to win a war with an invisible enemy? At least David could see Goliath. My enemies were all cowards.

Later that day, I made an effort to call the officer at his RCMP precinct. I wanted to touch base and feel it out. I called from a reliable cell phone zone near my home. On six occasions, the phone either cut off before it connected, or just after it began to ring. On two occasions, it cut off right after someone answered. I then waited a bit before trying again. Before doing so, I played a little game. I opened my car window and pretended I was talking to someone outside: "I'm going to try one more time and if it cuts off, I'll use your phone." This time, my phone didn't cut off. The call went through to their machine. Somebody, somewhere, did not want me connecting with this officer (OR wanted it to look like they didn't want me connecting with this officer):

The next day, I called the Sergeant from a payphone. No disconnection issues. And, he was available to chat.

We had a productive conversation. He indicated that he had some space in the coming weeks for me to come in to give my statement. I said that I would email him with some dates. I was still feeling very concerned about Susan's health, and wanted to delay this process a little longer to be sure she would be stable. Initiating the investigation would undoubtedly be an intense and triggering process. I also needed some time to dig into the details and prepare a proper statement. I wrote back and suggested the last

week of March, or thereafter. We agreed on Tuesday, March 26.

In the meantime, things became even more intense with respect to 'hacker' and other comments on my FB business page. There were hundreds of them. Somebody, somewhere, really didn't want me to make it to March 26. But I persisted.

On March 3, I posted the following on my Facebook business page. I tagged various members of Congress, some of whom had been on various committees exploring Meta's various shenanigans.

JEFF BROWN
Posted by Jeff Brown
12m

Would an honourable public company like Meta ever shadow ban and limit the reach of any of its loyal and consistent advertisers? If so, would that be a failure to satisfy their fiduciary duty to maximize shareholder profits? What if advertisers were threatened with being removed from the platform, thereby making them afraid to put their efforts into growing and advertising on Meta? Would such acts of intimidation be consistent with their mandate? What if this was possibly being motivated by political considerations? Josh Hawley Dick Durbin Senator Richard Blumenthal Senator Laphonza Butler Cory Booker Chris Coons Senator Ben Ray Luján Senator Chuck Schumer Senator Chuck Grassley Congressman David Cicilline Senator Thom Tillis Senator John Kennedy Democracy Watch Marsha Blackburn

I also connected with PayPal again about the persistent warning on the Enrealment account. They indicated that they had no option to remove it. Really? PayPal can't remove a warning that they themselves posted? Then why isn't it on my other 2 PayPal company accounts? Only, the publishing company…

Hello Jeff, I understand you're wanting the warning removed from your account. Unfortunately, there's no option to remove this warning off your account but can assure you it does not affect your account. However, I have notated your account regarding the concern though.

Thank you for your understanding and for being a valued member of PayPal! Feel free to close this message contact if there are no additional concerns that need addressed.

7:17 PM - Elaine

CHAPTER 24: LEFT ATRIAL ENLARGEMENT

The business page warning messages of permanent deletion on Facebook also began to intensify:

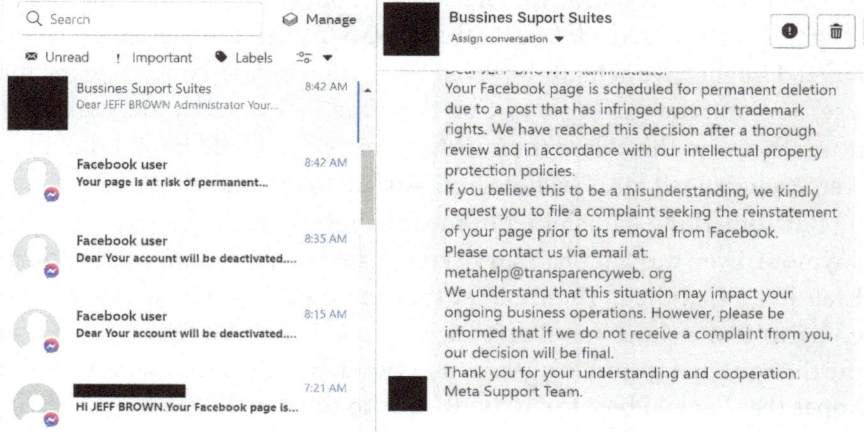

I went back onto the Enrealment website to check the flood of bot emails we had been receiving. I cleared another **65,000** of them.

On March 8, I wrote a retired police officer friend from my Hotmail account. I provided some of the details and asked if he could accompany me on statement day with the RCMP. We agreed to meet for lunch to talk things through.

*　*　*

On Saturday, March 9, something quite significant happened. I received a message on my FB business page from an American woman asking if I do personal sessions. When I looked, I saw her message with her pic, <u>and</u> the SAME FACE PIC used on a fake page warning message (from a page called 'Meta Recommendations') citing that my page would be deactivated. It was sent hours before the message requesting a personal session. <u>The same image was used in both locations.</u>

My ever-devoted techno-terror team was clamoring for my attention. So, I messaged her back and engaged in a dialogue about the session she wanted to do. She left me a number of audio messages, where she laid out – in a way that sounded quite intense and contrived – all the reasons why she wanted to talk to me. On a few occasions, I heard a gunshot go off in the background. She explained: "That's my neighbor doing target practice." I didn't believe her.

233

I knew the tactics by now. Get his attention and scare him. And if it doesn't scare him, he may post about it. Then, we have more evidence to work the 'paranoid' narrative, if he ever goes public about this whole story.

If they hadn't used her face on the fake Meta page, their tactic may have failed. I might have actually believed that someone was contacting me for a session. But they used her face on that page, so I would understand that it was them. So that when the gunshot went off, I would know what they were trying to tell me. Psychological warfare to the utmost degree.

But something had shifted in me. In short: I really didn't give a shit anymore. Even though I had survived last autumn, there is a way in which I felt like I had died. The thought that some backwoods miscreant was going to come shoot me didn't frighten me. What did frighten me was the thought that I wouldn't get my story told first. So, I kept writing in the hopes that I would beat the Grim Reaper to the punch.

Again, better to die with your story told, than live with your story buried. Especially when your abusers are politically motivated.

Another fascinating game that continued to occur was the frequent and immediate blocking of various comments on my Meta pages. It first began on Instagram while I was engaging in an edgy dialogue with someone from my phone. Suddenly, the following words would appear and block my response:

I had never seen anything like this before in all my years on this platform. Interestingly, this only seemed to happen when I was feeling intensely eager to express something. It didn't seem to happen with dialogues that were less emotionally charged. Of course, this should come as no surprise. My cyber-bullies have been studying my psyche for 39 months. They know what makes me tick. And they know the key factors that could drive me to a heart attack or stroke. Suppression of my expressiveness when it was emotionally charged was one of them. Similarly, they began using the following block when I was eager to respond to an interaction:

Clearly, these are not glitches. These are snitches. Somebody was still on me 24/7 at Meta. If this happens to you, you'll know that someone is on you, too. They're trying to frustrate you, likely for politically motivated reasons.

On March 11, I made an effort to email a few prominent journalists about the impending RCMP investigation. Strangely, that email immediately bounced back to my Hotmail account. But it was different than usual. Now and then, I would receive an email notifying me that an email I attempted to send hadn't gone through, but that they would keep trying. In this case, the email I received firmly said: *The email system had a problem processing this message. It won't try to deliver this message again.* I had no idea if this was related to my story, but did remember the prior issue with emails related to this story not arriving from this account to my literary lawyer's email address. Something that he said hadn't happened in all his years of practice.

On March 13, I decided to offer my followers a free link to a *Humanifestations* e-book. Nothing had changed on Amazon. We were still only receiving orders for only a few books per month (and virtually none of them – *Humanifestations*) and people were still writing me about their challenges accessing the book affordably, if at all. So, I wrote a piece about it on Substack and put up a post on Facebook:[71]

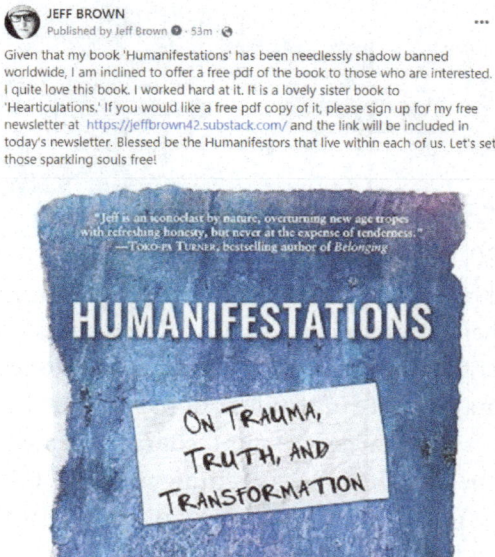

Because Meta seemed to be (momentarily) moving off of me, and now targeting my followers, I put up the following post on my business page the next day. It was actively commented on by a variety of people. I went back onto the business page and tagged a number of US congress members who are known to challenge Meta's shadow-banning practices. I also tagged some Canadian media outlets. Interestingly, when I tried to tag the Globe and Mail *and* The Star, I was blocked with a 'never seen before' notification: 'Unable to edit post right now.' Soon thereafter, <u>Meta took down the whole post from the business page</u>. I believe that this is the first time that they have removed a current post from one of my pages. This is direct evidence of monitoring and, even more importantly, an obvious attempt to contain my outreach to individuals and outlets that can potentially expose this story and challenge Meta on its corrupt practices.

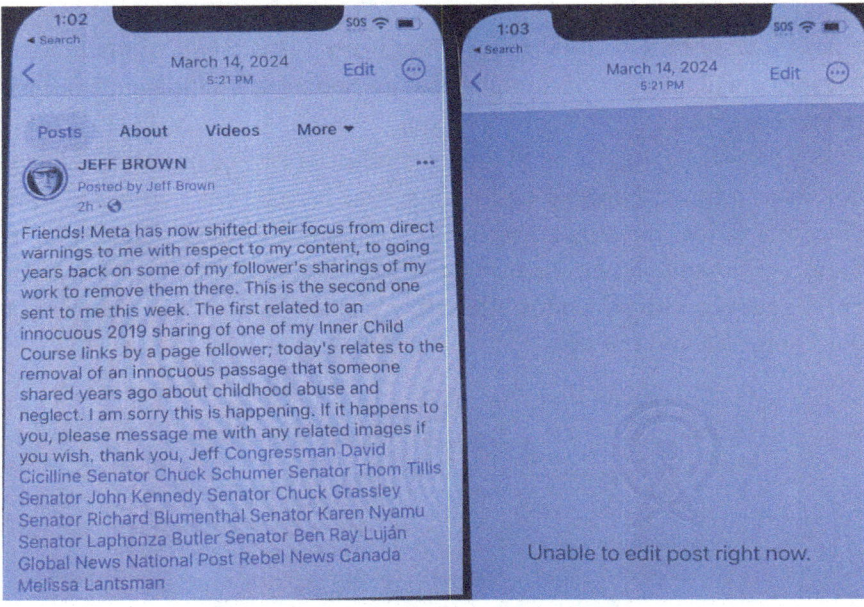

On March 20, I got a message on my business page indicating someone received a message from Facebook to the effect that my writing course went against their community standards. The next day, an email from another purchaser that they received a "This page is banned 404 URL error" after paying for a copy of Humanifestations on PayPal. Another said they received this warning: "Access to this resource is denied." In these cases, I didn't actually believe them. I was getting savvier to the various ways the game is played. Yet again, accounts (real or otherwise) retained to send you information that triggers your anxiety.

That same day, I went to record some of my old writings with my producer at his home in downtown Hamilton. Finally, a peaceful day. Not. Just before I arrived, the power went out on James Street, very close to his home. I didn't imagine that I was being targeted, but I did begin to feel a looming sense of dread. It was certainly in the Canadian ethos – everything felt like it was being deliberately shattered by a rogue administration – but it was something else. I had been working on this book and the statement notes for days, and I was really running out of steam.

At the same time, I was finding inventive ways to keep myself afloat. Not that any of this was a pleasure, but I began to look at some of it as an opportunity. An opportunity to love myself even when all the feedback I received from my daily life was that I was worthless. An opportunity to explore the plight of others, by expanding my empathic range beyond its usual parameters. An opportunity to imagine myself at my noblest, and then to actually challenge myself to embody it when it seemed impossible. An opportunity to scratch my way to meaning in the very darkest of places.

CHAPTER 25

Dudley Do-Wrong?

As my RCMP statement day drew closer, the agitators became more activated. There was the usual cacophony of games, and they threw in a few new ones, for good measure, including a series of fake emails from "Glass Door Jobs." I had once owned a glass door insert business, but I did not sign up for any newsletter. I had been receiving one such email every day or so for about a week, and I then received three on the day that I went in to give my statement. I only received one more thereafter. Somebody was trying to tell me something, but what?

I prepared my notes and headed out to the RCMP headquarters on March 26. I had a number of pages that I was planning to read in for the record. I also brought a small taper with me, so I would have a copy. I didn't want to make the same mistake that I'd made in Hamilton.

I arrived about 10 minutes early and entered the building. The sergeant was waiting for me in the front. He led me into a small room. I asked him how he would feel about my taping the statement. He assured me that it wasn't necessary – he would provide me with a copy later. I felt comfortable and agreed. He then asked me to sign a document that noted the primary focus of the investigation – the question of whether the first police investigation had been called off because of the stalking story. I asked him to add the other 2 issues as well: (1) the claim that the RCMP had no knowledge of my connection with Mrs. Trudeau during my Privacy Act process, while simultaneously holding 'stories' that claimed I stalked her; (2) the possibility that the RCMP played a role in the termination of my second police investigation during Trudeau's 3-day cabinet meeting in Hamilton in January 2023. He was amenable and added them to the document.

The sergeant turned on his tape player and I proceeded to read in the material that I had brought. When I was done, he asked me to repeat a few of the things that WT had told me about the stalking allegations. He then turned off his recording device. Before we left the room, he reached over and removed a piece of tape that was covering a piece of metal on the wall. As it turns out, that piece of metal was a microphone. He said, "I covered it, so you don't have to worry about others listening." I wasn't sure why this was necessary – I hadn't been concerned about others listening. It was now him that I was concerned about. Was I being played by the RCMP?

After giving him a few phone numbers that he requested, we had a brief talk. He let me know that this wasn't a criminal investigation. That's not to say that it couldn't lead to one if obstructions were found, but his mandate was restricted to the question of whether any member of the RCMP had acted in a manner incongruent with their professional responsibilities. In other words, his mandate did not include the question of whether anyone in a position of political power had obstructed justice. If the evidence led in that direction, it would have to be handled by the Hamilton Police (Please God, no) or another RCMP division.

I drove home feeling both depleted and relieved. I had made the decision before I went that this was my last attempt to get help in the system. Enough really was enough. The only decision left was whether I would go directly to the people by publishing this book, or walk away. I wanted so much to walk away, but I couldn't seem to stop. Something deep inside kept telling me to "Trust Creation." I wasn't even sure what that meant, but I trusted that I would one day understand.

I mean, if you can't trust creation, what can you trust?

* * *

Soon thereafter, I connected with the TD Bank to see if they could investigate a few things. The most pressing was the question of what had happened with my Enrealment credit and debit cards last August. You may remember that they were frozen (and the credit card canceled) – without letting me know – on/about the evening that the Trudeau's announced their break-up. This was confirmed when I went into the bank in mid-August and the teller pulled up the information about the alleged security breach. This time, I also inquired into why my personal debit card was now getting periodically declined when there was money in the bank. With respect to the latter, there was no clear explanation available.

The day after making these inquiries with a manager, my Enrealment Credit Card was declined at a gas station. Deja vu. First time that happened since August.

I went into the bank and met with a representative. She looked into what had happened in August. She was unable to find any information about this in their system. It appears to have been either removed or made inaccessible. But she was able to pull up information about another situation with my Enrealment card(s) in early October. I knew nothing about this. I had not been contacted about yet another 'security issue.'

On March 31, I received word from GoDaddy that they couldn't renew another of my purchased domain names – Rebrave.com – because of a payment rejection issue. As before, I went onto the GoDaddy website and made the payment. There were funds in the connected PayPal account. It may be worth noting that I had coined and used the term "Rebrave" in various Facebook posts when I was integrating elements of this experience into my public outreach. It is also referenced on page 120 of *Humanifestations*, and is the name of a book that I plan to write about the ways in which we have been collectively diminished and unbraved by political abusers of power to serve their malevolent purposes.

Despite being advised to shut up, I kept posting some of the details about what was happening with Fake Meta and Facebook account deletion messages on my website emails. I was too angry to just sit back and put up with any more bullshit:

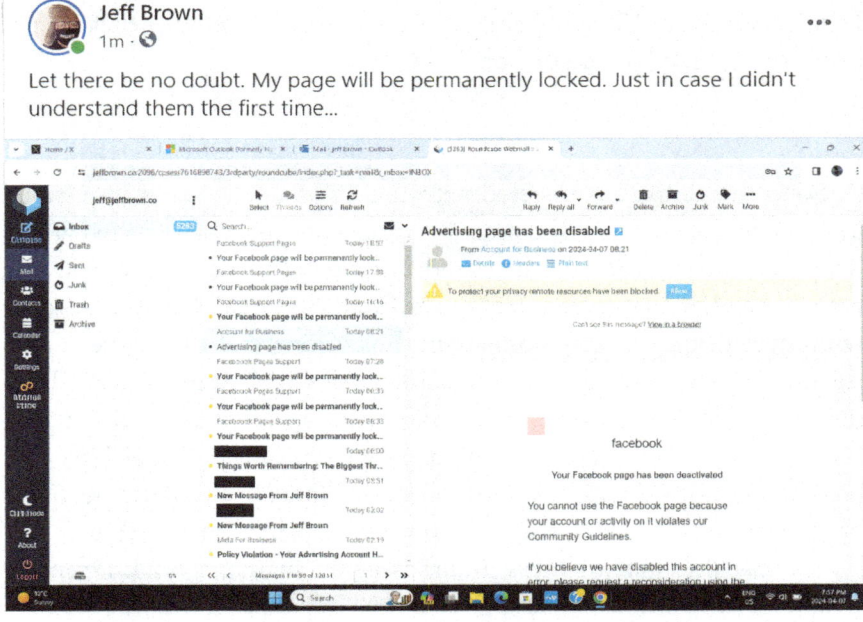

I began to post my thoughts on X, unwilling to contain my voice. One night, in particular, I felt entirely enraged. I had gone for a walk with Susan, where she shared her physical struggles from that day. I then put up the following post:[72]

CHAPTER 25: DUDLEY DO-WRONG?

📌 Pinned
Jeff Brown ✓
@JeffBrownEnreal

There was a time when the threat of murder was limited to physical violence. Times have changed. Given that technology makes it so easy to access others, you can actualize the intention to harm in other ways, too. For example, if you continue to cyber-stalk an older couple with the intention of frightening them, threatening them, obstructing their livelihood, and triggering them into submission, it is safe to say that you have formed the intention to harm them physically. And if, for example, you and your fellow co-conspirators kept at it EVEN AFTER KNOWING that your actions had caused both of them to nearly pass away, then it is safe to say that every single person who knew of such a plan, and who chose to participate in that plan, is guilty of attempted murder. Techno-terror and abuses of online power are no game. And anyone in the media who had knowledge of such events, and chose not to report on them, should be deeply ashamed of themselves.

Last edited 6:28 PM · Apr 8, 2024 · **326** Views

The next day, I had a final conversation with the Psychiatrist (Dr. Fudge) who was looking into my questions about the night I visited Emergency last October. With respect to the question of how the Psychiatric resident had found me and my writing online, given that she had never met me and I have a common name, he said that her reply was, "I can't recall." This really puzzled me, given that it seemed to me that there were only two options: (1) She went online and punched in my name and address and arrived at my website. She then clicked on my Facebook or Instagram links and took a look at both me and my writing. She then came in the room, saw that I was the same guy she had seen online, and shared her impressions about the cogency of the writing. Given that the psychiatrist had previously told me that this was a common practice, this would seem like a rather straightforward (and innocuous) recollection; or (2) She had preexisting knowledge of who I was.

What's not to recall? Door #1, or Door #2.

As significantly, he changed his tune about who Form-1'ed me. If you recall, he'd asserted that it was the emergency physician who had put it in place, and that the resident had vacated it after I refused to be admitted into the hospital. But today, he asserted that I was never under a form. The psychiatric resident was open to initiating it, but did not follow through after I refused. This new version of events felt particularly strange given that the resident had then popped her head outside and said: "He's not staying." When I asked her who she was talking to, she said: "There are people from the team waiting to take you."

So, I asked him: "Why were they waiting to take me if there was no prearranged Form 1?" The only explanation he could give was that sometimes a resident will bring security with her before meeting a patient who is presenting with psychosis. That seemed reasonable, except that she had said that there were "people" waiting to take me. And I was gentle as a lamb, with nothing to suggest potential violence.

Towards the end of our call, he shared the details of the folder notes that the resident had in her hands. You may remember that she had shared that there was information about me related to a prior interaction with Coast (St Joe's Crisis and Support Team). As I had suspected, those notes did reference the interaction that I'd had with the mental health worker who had accompanied the cops when I first reported the surveillance issues in 2021. In his meeting notes, the worker had written: "Spoke with the client at great length. Client was articulate, organized, and coherent. His concerns do not appear to be delusional in nature."

So, where does this leave me with respect to my goal of achieving closure around this hospital experience? It leaves me unsure as to what was really going on with that resident. I would like nothing more than to come to the conclusion that everything was copacetic. But I just don't know. I find her inability to 'recall' how she knew that it was me, peculiar to say the least. And I find the shift from previously Form-1'ed to not Form-1'ed, suspicious, too. Both because there were "people" waiting for me before she came in – she said nothing about *a* security person – and because I am told that Form 1's aren't usually abandoned because the patient says no.

Adding to my confusion with respect to these events is the strangeness of the drive over to the hospital. It is my belief that the fact that a Hamilton police cruiser drove along beside us most of the way – combined with what I share below about the voice on the phone – meant that they were both apprised of my condition, *and* eager to ensure I got to the hospital to get diagnosed. Susan later denied that the voice on the phone giving directions was a cop, assuring me that it was one of the male Suri voices on the iPhone, but it sounded nothing like that AI voice. I believe it was the cop right beside us, both because it sounded exactly like one, and because she had said before we went to St. Joe's Hospital that my visit was already pre-arranged. So, something was going on here. This doesn't mean that she knew they were going to arrive at that particular diagnosis,

Chapter 25: Dudley Do-Wrong?

but I believe she knew something of their involvement. My unconfirmed hunch is that they had convinced her that a mental health diagnosis was the best thing for me, given that they likely frightened her into believing that I would be otherwise incarcerated for whatever they had conjured up. This is often the game that is played to contain whistle-blowers. Convince an overwhelmed but good intentioned family member that the right thing to do is have their loved one declared crazy, so that they don't have to face the dangerous consequences of bringing their story public. Unfortunately for the cops, I got off the prescriptions and right thinking restored soon thereafter. Now they had nobody to blame but themselves for their two obstructed investigations. Poor babies.

In addition, I am left with two more strange events that stay with me from my sick phase. First, before leaving the house one day, I had hidden a number of Zopiclone pills in the pocket of some shorts that I placed on the floor near the dresser. I was trying to hide them from myself, because I was experiencing suicidal ideation. When I came home a few hours later, the pills were all sprinkled on the ground from the dresser to the bed. They were in a kind of suggestive line. It wasn't the cat's doing – the bedroom door had been left closed.

Second, I had purchased a box of Nytol sleeping-aids in early-September while I was waiting for the Zopiclone prescription. It was a gel pack, with each pill in its own separate section. One night, I reached in to grab one and found that the pill was wet on the outside. I checked a number of others, and they were wet, too. I had taken a few previously, and they had been dry. Interestingly, on the evenings after I took the wet ones, I was hyper-aroused for hours. My heart was racing rapidly, and I was riddled with tremendous anxiety. I felt like I was on a barbiturate or taking cocaine. I couldn't calm down and fall asleep until mid-morning. And I was sure that there were tiny black things attacking me. As it turns out, there was nothing there, but I didn't know that then. I am left to wonder if something was injected into those pills beside the bed to make me crazier. Is that why I became suicidal? Was I being drugged?

* * *

Now, back to the narrative.

Towards the end of April, the techno-terror games continued with a new twist. I began to notice a number of fake pages coming onto the business page with critical comments and attacks, often using trigger words that related to this experience. These were not in the ordinary range of commentary and always seemed to come from pages with 'locked profiles.' I would block them. And former course purchasers would email *Soulshaping Institute* with irrational complaints. For example – that they couldn't access materials from a class that ended the year before. Or, that they had never actually signed up for the class, and wanted a refund.

In addition – and this had been happening for some time – people were paying for personal sessions and not getting back to me to book them. I couldn't help but wonder if this was by design – a premeditated opportunity to say that they never heard from me or received a refund – if I brought this book public. One person had a session with me – and then vehemently asserted that I had said something I had never said. In fact, I had said the opposite. Another individual completed a number of sessions with me, and made sure to repeatedly remind me that she didn't know how to classify me ("whatever it is that you are"), with respect to the work I do with clients. That is actually true. I'm not a formal psychotherapist, nor am I a formal coach. I do path and purpose sessions. I was getting a strong sense that much of this was being set up in anticipation of making scammer allegations if I brought this story public.

I also noticed that those profiles which appeared at the top of my social media feeds ('stories' or 'posts') – and as something like 'Profiles you might like' while scrolling – were often those of individuals that I had been in conflict with or dated at one time or another. I had reason to believe that someone was reading everything inside of my old Meta messages (and old phone bills and texts), then connecting with those people in an effort to conjure up *kompromat*. And then, making sure that I saw the person's profile in an effort to frighten me about the creation of a possible dossier.

This was equally true with respect to my personal emails. In 2019, I had been interviewed by a prominent podcast host. After the show, we had a disagreement relating to the tenor of the interview. We emailed back and forth for some time on my Hotmail account. Not long ago, I began to receive a series of taunting emails on my website account referencing that show. It was entirely evident that the emails were fake – and that the intention was to remind me that my intimidators had alleged 'information' on me related to an inter-personal conflict.

This line of thought seemed even more realistic when I finally took the time to open a series of what appeared to be fake Scotiabank emails that I had first noticed coming to my Hotmail account in April, 2023. They were all of the 'INTERAC e-transfer: Your money transfer to _____ was deposited' variety. Since I don't have a Scotiabank account, I didn't ever look at them, despite having a feeling that they were somehow part of this techno-terror game. It turns out, I was right. Because the names they were using were significant with respect to my previous home improvements business. Most of them were messaged to the name of the woman who had managed the office for years, and the more recent ones, were messaged to the full name of someone I had sued for non-payment in small claims court ten years ago. I then did an email search, and found an email to my manager about this particular person. Sadly, I had to sue somewhere around 8-10 individuals per year for non-payment.

Having now spent over 3 years interpreting my techno-terrorists messaging, I understood what they were trying to convey. On the most basic level, they were trying to tell me that they were going to play the scammer card. Ironic, given the homicidal intentions behind their years-long scammer attacks on me. On the more significant level, they were telling me something that I was already intuiting: They had access to my Hotmail account/all my accounts and had read everything in it/them. Because that's what they do. If they can't kill you, or drive you crazy, or prove that you are stalking a Wild Horse, they discredit you. And this is precisely why so few people ever blow the whistle on systemic wrongdoing. They can't find a safe path through.

On April 28, I removed **162,263** spambot emails sent to the Enrealment website since early March. Those bots were such busy little beavers:

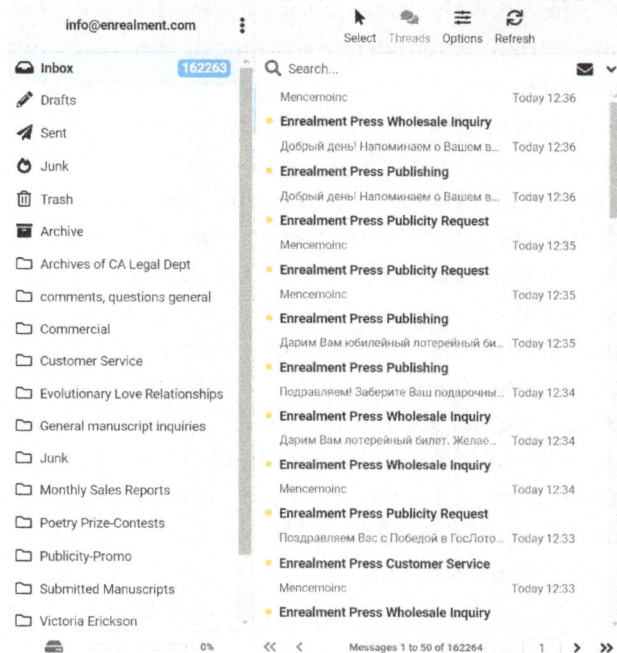

A few days later, I went back to the Burlington, Ontario library that I had been writing in. While there, I went to use the computers to check emails and forward something to a journalist I had been in contact with. Right after sending it, a man eagerly approaches me to say hello and chat. I had met this guy when I was writing here last year, in the months before I became ill. He had shared his personal challenges with me, and I had gifted him a copy of *Hearticulations*. Months later, when I was in the throes of my sickness, he had emailed me with an update on his life and provided a link to his new healing website-in-process. Timing aside, what was so puzzling was that I had never given him my Hotmail email address. Never. And it was nowhere to be found online. So, I didn't respond.

A few months ago, I had re-written him and asked him where he got my email address. He let me know that he had moved to Waterdown (near Burlington) and that he must have gotten my email from the back of my book, *Hearticulations*. There is no email address there. So, I didn't respond again. And now here he is, right after I send an email to a journalist on this story, to feverishly say hello. I responded with decisiveness: "I don't want to talk to you." He hadn't expected that. He mumbled something and walked away with his tail between his (likely PSYOP) legs. WT had instructed me about being careful not to go to the same place too often. And to be careful when strangers suddenly appear to friend me. I should have listened.

On May 2, they took the game to the next level. In recent weeks, I had become casually friendly with a guy working at that same library in Burlington. I had been compelled to work there more often, after the Hamilton library system went down. I needed to check lawyer and media-related emails, without using my laptops. In any event, *Richard* was always working on his laptop close to me, on the top floor. I shared some of the details of what I was going through, and he shared some of his tale of woe. Something felt a little off about him – but I kind of liked him.

One day, we had an interaction where he pulled two phones from his pockets. One, for calls. The other, for various online activities. He seemed unusually cyber-protective for a former "business consultant" allegedly down on his luck. He had previously shared a somewhat sophisticated understanding of techno-terror and the manipulations of the state. So, when he pulled out the phones, I got the message and decided to stay away from him when next I came to the library. I began working on the floor below, nowhere near his visual range.

One morning, I arrived at the library around 10 am. His beat-up old van was not in the parking lot. I tucked myself into a corner of the library to get some work done. About an hour in, he comes walking towards me with a little smirk on his face. He's very excited to tell me a story:

"You'll never guess what happened to me the other day. I was at a Tim Horton's in Burlington, when a curly-haired man comes up to me and asks me if I'm Jeff. I said no. He said it was strange because I looked <u>exactly</u> like his friend Jeff. He then proceeded to tell me that he's a retired cop, who worked for Interpol, and that 'Jeff' has a limp in his right leg, so it can't be me. At first, I didn't connect it back to you, but now I'm wondering if it was you he was looking for."

I said something to the effect of "Well, I do have a limp in my right leg when I drink too much coffee, but why would he think you are me? You don't look anything like me."

He replied, "I don't know, man. I've seen some of things you've been posting on your Twitter. Do you think I'm getting paranoid?"

Here we go again – with the paranoia routine.

I said that I didn't know. And I made it clear that I had work to do. He walked away with his little smirk intact.

At this stage, I've got the game down pat. Tie together themes that can bewilder and trigger me: Doppelganger, paranoia (because if this story goes public, they will immediately say I am paranoid), my situational fear of law-enforcement, throw in Interpol to take it up a notch, add in the limpy leg so that I know that this is a pre-organized PSYOP.

I packed up to leave the library. Too bad, I really liked writing here. Before leaving, I decided to go looking for the scraggly varmint. I found him in his usual corner hovel on the upper floor. We had a brief conversation:

"So how did you feel when the guy came over to you at Timmie's and asked if you were Jeff with a limp. Were you standing or sitting?"

"I was sitting."

"So why do you think he asked you that? How did you feel having heard a bit of my story?"

"Right away I just said I'm not Jeff. I hadn't connected it to you yet. But he wouldn't give it up. He kept saying, 'But you look just like Jeff', you know…"

"So, you look like a guy named Jeff."

"I look like a guy named Jeff."

"So, what did he look like? He's a white guy, stocky… looked like a former cop?"

"…looked like a former cop… late 60's… curly hair… said that he worked at Interpol… his career was at Interpol… he still does some projects with the RCMP."

I laugh inside. Now's he added another theme from my story – the RCMP ... a retired cop who worked at Interpol (do cops work at Interpol!?) who does part time (off-book?) work during his retirement with the RCMP...

I laugh: "Sure he does." He laughs too. We both know this story is bullshit.

I then say the following: "Yah special projects. How did the limp thing come up once you already said no?"

"I said no, and he started telling me this story about Jeff."

"What was the story about Jeff?"

"Jeff can make a whole room of people laugh. He's a lot of fun, but he's really into Hitler. And he hates all the immigrants. I say, 'I remind you of this Hitler guy?' And he replies "I guess you're not Jeff. Jeff actually has a bad leg." Like it was just so fucking crazy. (laughs). I'm not making this up..."

Quite apart from the obvious – how could the curly haired man have known that the sitting down man had a bad leg? – he threw in Hitler etc because he knows that I'm a Jew, and said that I hate all the immigrants because they want to say I am a right-wing extremist if this story ever goes public. And the little varmint added in the RCMP to trigger my preexisting anxiety about them and their trustworthiness.

I've had just about enough. I say: "It's a crazy world man."

He nervously laughs, "It's a crazy world man."

"People get hired to do all kinds of weird things, like befriend people they don't even know... and then pretend they're something they're not..."

He affirms, "Yah."

".... doing a job they're not really doing."

He again affirms: "Yah."

"...but they're there for another reason..."

He then immediately says, with what appeared to be a measure of guilt on his face, "They're there for another reason."

I reply: "See you buddy..."

He then begins to say: "I'm not playing..."

I cut him off, "No, I know you're not. See you buddy..."

Then he says something in a very different tone than he had ever used before: "So what was it really? Now, tell me..." I had no idea what *it* was, but it sounded like he was pleading for me to make some kind of admission.

I left the library, now certain that he was part of the game.

Chapter 25: Dudley Do-Wrong?

* * *

Communications related problems continued to plague me in the months ahead. For example, for reasons unknown, I was no longer receiving my Bell internet bill in the mail. All I would receive is an email with a clearly noticeable red exclamation mark that read: "It seems like you may have forgotten to pay your recent bill." Similarly, I would no longer receive my Fido cell phone bill. I would only receive emails related to an overdue payment issue. And I couldn't seem to get any help with a Fido message issue that had begun when I got my new iPhone in 2023 (after my relatively new previous iPhone suddenly stopped working). Where before I had unlimited messages – something still included in my plan – my phone capacity was now limited to 3 messages (and for 2-3 days only). In addition, my new iPhone stopped functioning properly. I then replaced it with an old-style flip-phone, and the same challenges with texts arriving long after they were sent began to occur. Somebody was in this phone, too.

(Note: Something that is quite interesting is the increasingly more remarkable relationship between events that I describe in this document, and subsequent occurrences. For example, I wrote about my new iPhone above on my laptop, and the phone immediately rang with a fake IPhone promo call. Or, I wrote about a particular event with a Facebook follower, and they then book their first session with me days later. Or, I opened my social media – and a whole series of profiles and ads immediately appear that directly correlate with the themes of the narrative. Some of this might make some sense if this computer was online and somehow connected to my various emails and social media locations. But it isn't. I had bought a new computer – and brought it to someone to remove the Wi-Fi option. Before leaving it with him to work on, he indicated that he could both remove the interior Wi-Fi modem, *and* my capacity to connect with an available Wi-Fi account. When I picked it up two days later, he indicated that he wasn't able to remove the interior Wi-Fi modem, but that he had disabled my ability to open Wi-Fi. He had a strange look on his face. I now believe that this computer was compromised.)

Not long before, I had been working in a Guelph library. While checking emails on the library computers, I noticed a man wandering around behind me. He wasn't menacing, but he did seem to be making an effort to see what I was up to. I took leave of the computer, and sat down in the working area. A few minutes later, he came over and sat down right beside me. He opened his computer, and began to work. About 20 minutes in,

249

he stood up and gathered his things. He made it a point to connect with me. Ever-friendly fool that I am, I removed my earphones and chatted with him. He had very little to say, other than to let me know that he had worked for the Canada Revenue Agency, and had to go and get a print-out of his criminal background from the police. His potential new employer – a local truck company – insisted on it before they could hire him. He made sure that he mentioned the CRA and the police repeatedly, before leaving the library. Yet another warning in human form.

On June 16, I put together a document to submit to the Hamilton Police – in the hopes that they could help me. The document contained a list of various cyber-related issues, including the overwhelm of spambot emails we had been receiving on Enrealment.com. Susan and I discussed it that evening – with our phones on and nearby – and when I woke up the

> Dear Jeff Brown (Enrealment Media Inc),
>
> This is a notification that your service has now been suspended.
> The details of this suspension are below:
>
> Product/Service: Premium Plus
> Domain: enrealment.com
> Amount: $539.40 USD
> Due Date: Thursday, March 20th, 2025
> Suspension Reason: **The contact form on your website violates spam rules. Hackers are using it to send spam!**
>
> Please contact us as soon as possible to get your service reactivated.
>
> ---
>
> HostUpon Web Hosting

next morning, I had received the following email from my website server, Hostupon:

I contacted the server, and I was angrily informed that there had been somewhere around 1000 spambot emails sent in one hour this morning. As a result, they had to shut down the website for Enrealment – which meant it also shut down the active website for another of my companies because it is in the same hosting group. I then contacted a reliable web designer and she removed the contact form from Enrealment.com so they couldn't continue. Right around the time she was finishing them, the

Chapter 25: Dudley Do-Wrong?

bots-that-are-actually-humans then began to focus on my wife's website with a series of targeted emails – including one with my name in it.

On June 19, Urban Dictionary approved my definition for the term "techno-terrorism."[73] I had submitted it days earlier. They also approved my definition for "Invisibully" on June 21.[74.]

If I couldn't bring this story to the world, at least I could bring some measure of wisdom that would help others in the future.

Around this time, I formally reported the series of cyber-related events to the Hamilton Police. I phoned it in, reported it on their website, and emailed the details to one of the Detectives that I had dealt with in 2022.

* * *

On June 26, I woke up and left the house in the morning to drive to Niagara Falls to meet my editor. I had given her this manuscript two weeks earlier – and today was the day she was going to provide me with the edited version. Before leaving Hamilton, I stopped in at a favorite cafe to grab a coffee. While in the lineup, I was excitedly introduced by the owner to someone whom I had never met. It felt pre-orchestrated. He made an effort to chat me up, and then asked me to sit down and talk with him. This was the first time a stranger asked me to have a coffee with them in 5 years in this city. I grabbed a chair. After sharing a bit about himself – he had worked for CBC for many years as a journalist – this book came up. I got the sense that he already knew about it. He was quite interested. At some point, he brought up the topic of whistle-blowers. He made it a point to remind me that things don't usually go well for whistle-blowers because they are not in the "circle of power." He stared me deep in the eyes when he shared this information. He was clearly a messenger, sent to warn me about the consequences of publishing this book.

At some point, the topic of various things that had been shared with me about Trudeau by Canadian media came up. He seemed to know about that, too. He asked if I intended to include them in the book. I said that I didn't feel it was my job to share everyone else's story. He then stared me deep in the eyes again, and said that I should include them if I published. It was clear from the strangely provocative way he said it, that he was trying to tell me something. The only conclusion I could come to was that he was trying to tell me that if I shared those details, they would smear me in response. Of course they would. That's how this game is played. I left soon thereafter.

The next morning, I looked into him and saw that he was *followed* on one of his social media pages by two Liberal Party Cabinet Ministers. This dude was connected! That afternoon, I went to a Burlington library to work on this book. This library was a fair distance from the library I had been working at throughout the spring. About an hour after I arrived, my scraggly Interpol friend, Richard, showed up to work on his computer. Wonders never cease!

On the evening of June 29, I put the following post up on Facebook:[75]

> "The story began so innocently, until I began to see through to the darkness. It was a little hard to miss, given that much of it was shared with me. And so I tried to get away. Not my people, not my scene. But there was one problem – things I had been told and contributed. So getting away wasn't allowed. And then the intimidation began. And the compromising of various systems. And the shadow bans, and book blocks, and house alarms going off, and the bank account games, and the swastika on the car, and so much more before two medical calamities. And all for what? Nothing. A thank you for your service would have sufficed. No need for any 'organization' to go onto destruction mode. No need for any of this. But that's how evil rolls. It snickers till the people rise. And then God cleans up the mess. God's gonna need a big broom for this bloody story."

When I woke up in the morning, I found out that my bar mitzvah synagogue – The Pride of Israel in Toronto – had been attacked only hours later.[76] Someone had thrown something at the windows beside the front doors and made a real big mess. I'm not someone with a tendency to believe that world events are related to him – but I couldn't help but notice that I had put up a frequently shared Instagram post in January, 2024, wherein I named the synagogue where I had my bar-mitzvah:[77] – and I had sat outside that synagogue with my wife a few weeks before the attack, talking about my Bar Mitzvah experience, and thinking that it wouldn't surprise me if someone attacked the large windows beside those doors. We know with certainty that my phones are compromised, so our presence there would be known. If I am correct to wonder if there is a connection between my Facebook post – and the attack on The Pride of Israel hours later – I am also left to wonder who actually ordered it and those that preceded it.

What I also find tangentially interesting is that – to that point – there had been at least 12 synagogues and 18 Jewish schools attacked or vandalized in Canada since the events of October 7th, 2023.[78] These attacks were becoming a regular part of Jewish reality in Canada. Were these arbitrary anti-semitic attacks, or were there particular Jews associated with those locations that were also being frightened into silence by politically motivated miscreants?

On July 6, I went to Toronto for a health appointment that I had booked days before. Beforehand, I stopped in at a High Park library to send a variety of emails – including one to the lawyer who would vet parts of this book. After the appointment, I returned to the same library to have a Zoom conversation with a friend. That too had been booked in advance. I walked to the back tables, and sat down to get organized. I looked over, and there was a bearded Eastern European man (who looked like a stockier version of hockey player, Alex Ovechkin), sitting at a corner table glaring at me. He kept staring while I was on Zoom, and then took a number of screenshots of me. He laughed at me, as he took the pictures. He then appeared to send them to someone from his phone.

The library soon closed. I stepped outside, and there he was – waiting and glaring. I then walked the other way on Bloor Street, and the young man he probably sent my picture to made it a point to walk towards me aggressively. I pretended that I was talking to someone beside him ("Hey Robert!") and the aggressor moved over and walked away.

When I got in the car, I called Samuel to report the events. While talking, a call rang into his phone. It was from my phone number. A spoof call, courtesy of my (un)friendly neighborhood techno-terrorists.

They were busy with me, today.

Chapter 26

Cross Border Stalking

On July 8, I received an email from an American person that I had once done a personal session with. They had sent a number of angry emails expressing their dissatisfaction with a teacher I had recommended – interestingly, the same person who had called me when the phone incident occurred on December 12, 2020. At some point, I had told this individual to stop contacting me. In today's email, they shared the following: "If you contact me again, I will be in touch with law enforcement in Toronto. I believe you may already be on their radar." A clear warning.

Early the next evening, I wrote the following on Twitter. I was getting clearer and clearer on the game:

> It's been my experience that the most common way that abusers-of-power undermine a potential whistle-blower (wb) is to activate their trickster minions to craft and/or mischaracterize a broad array of things that will undermine their credibility. Those include but are not limited to: acts of in-person and techno-terrorism designed to impact wb's mental health ("see, they're crazy"), manipulatively and illegally penetrate emails/texts/bank accounts/phone calls/personal history in the hopes of pre-organizing a patchwork of alleged wrongdoing (see, they're bad!"), craft fake relational scenarios i.e. course purchases/personal sessions booked by players intent on stoking reputation-undermining chaos ("look at what that scammer did!") etc. Ideally, the effect of all these games is to cause the death of the potential whistle-blower (and their spouse) before any whistle gets blown. The minions probably get bonuses if they accomplish that. If they survive, the goal is to destroy their credibility altogether. What is always ironic, of course, is that before the potential whistle-blower broke away, they were seen in the highest light. Their skills were highly sought after and utilized, their words/ideas happily copied and shared, their wisdom hungrily ingested. But then they rejected 'royalty', and became the perceived enemy. If anybody thinks that we have made progress with respect to human rights, think again. Technology has handed abusers-of-power the key to the (global) kingdom. God help us all."[79]

Chapter 26: Cross Border Stalking

That evening – and throughout the next day – I was peppered with a series of fake Meta account warnings on my main website emails.

Soon thereafter, I met with my middle brother at his apartment. I had given him a copy of this manuscript to hold at a previous time. I had a bad feeling about it, and I wanted to get it back.

When I arrived, he was drunk. I hadn't seen him drunk in decades. It threw me off. He had been an alcoholic and drug addict. I thought he had been clean for years. He began to share a variety of grizzly details related to his drug history. Included was the time he spent as a violent drug runner for a local gang. I knew something about this, because he had been using my mother's vehicle without her knowledge and she was not able to renew her license plate because of the exorbitant toll highway bill. He had also repeatedly stolen her rent money, causing her to finally change the locks to her apartment. This whole sequence of events caused her to plummet into yet another depression. One night, she was so out of it that she left the water running in the washroom and it flooded the floor below. She was evicted from her apartment, and myself and her close friend helped her to pay to move to another building. If not, she may have been homeless if she insisted on staying in the Toronto area.

This night, he took his admissions to the next level. He let me know that he still had a connection with the gang world. He also shared the details of a gun battle between himself and someone he was sent to meet with to do a drugs-for-money-exchange. When I asked him if he had killed the other person, he made it clear he didn't know and he didn't care. I also asked him about his role in a possible murder that he had discussed with my mother, one where somebody's legs were broken and they were left in a forest. He elaborated: "Rolling them up in a carpet, throwing them in the back of your truck, driving them to Algonquin Park, and pushing them out…" He did all of this for drugs as payment. This time, he cried for that person, apparently feeling guilty about the fact that his penchant for drugs had led him to be involved in such destructiveness.

He also made an effort to persuade me that he was going to help me with my situation. He offered to work for me as security, and contended that he had a number of gang friends in Hamilton etc. that could protect the house. And when someone pulled their car up in front of his apartment, he shouted at them to take off, as though to persuade me that he was my great protector. In fact, I had been his great protector – he was surely not mine.

It was all very dramatic, until he went quiet and made assertions that sounded quite scripted. He very calmly said something to the effect that he had only stolen rent money from my mother on one occasion, and that he was her favorite son. Neither were remotely true – he had shattered her life for decades – but I went along for the ride, trying to make sense of what was happening. What was going on here? Was our conversation being taped? Who was he trying to convince that he had been a good son? Why was he crying so much? I knew him well – he usually cried when he felt guilty. Or when he was up to something. What was the purpose of trying to get me to agree with these fallacious assertions?

In the heart of all of this, he said something to the effect of "these political people are harder to deal with than the gangs." How did he know this? Was he being utilized by someone involved with my situation to try to set me up? It wouldn't surprise me – he had done many destructive things to me over the years, and with his history, the political people could possibly frighten, bribe, or blackmail him into compliance. And note that he didn't say the RCMP, or the Police. He said "these political people." Did they get to him?

Towards the end of our time together, his gratitude shone through. He shared a memory of my being there for him when he had attempted suicide long ago. His suicide attempts and notes were a regular part of my mine and my mother's reality for years. That time, I had contacted the Police, and they had pulled him out of a raunchy motel and raced him to the hospital. According to him, he had taken hundreds of sleeping pills, and had a gun in his possession. He remembered that I had gone to the hospital to be with him, and he expressed his gratitude. He also made it a point to tell me that each room in the motel was under video surveillance. (Strange – why hadn't they spotted his suicide attempt?) Knowing him as I did, I wondered if he was trying to tell me something about our current interaction.

I asked him for the USB stick with the book manuscript on it. He reluctantly gave it back to me. I then gave him a USB without a manuscript on it. As he walked me to my truck, he was in a strange state. When we arrived, he got in real close and whispered in my ear. He let me know that there were three individuals living in the building next to his. Former militia, and they had guns. I wasn't sure why he was telling me this – perhaps because the part of him that cared about me wanted me to know that I would be protected. The fact that he felt the need to whisper this left me wondering if he was wired throughout our preceding conversation. Or, he was told to make it look like he was wired, so I would be frightened into silence about telling my story.

Chapter 26: Cross Border Stalking

As I drove home, it all made sense. We had met a few times after many years disconnected. Each meal had a strange kind of feeling to it. And when I was going through the worst of the prescription drug misadventure in 2023 – right around the time I was talking aloud about suicidal ideation – he had sent me a message on Signal with a series of happy Trudeau pictures. One was a likely fake meme of Justin Trudeau in underwear with a big smile on his face. Another, a well-known picture of a black-faced and smiling Trudeau with his arm around a smiling young woman. In the state I was in, I read these messages as an attempt to mock me and make me feel worse. Later, when off the drug, I assumed that it was just strange timing. But now I wonder: Was he told to send those pictures in that particular moment because of the state I was in? In the hopes that it would take me over the edge? Had he been involved in my political situation for years?

I was feeling the heat. I was now concerned that I wouldn't be able to finish writing this book. So, I included this paragraph on my Substack and on Facebook, X, and Instagram on July 15 and 16:

> Hi Friends, I want to inform you that I have been working on a politically inspired memoir for some time. The updated version is nearly complete. At this stage, I have no plan in place to publish it. It is a book I am finishing for my own (and Susan's) protection, and because I am seeking personal closure after a very lengthy and bewildering journey. For a variety of reasons, I am concerned that determined efforts will be made to undermine my completion process. We live at a time where politically motivated individuals and organizations freely infiltrate and influence seemingly independent government agencies, public corporations, and investigative entities, in an effort to disable perceived political threats. Trust me – I have learned this the hard way. As I work towards putting this behind me, I feel it is important that I share this concern on the public record.[80]

Interestingly, I received my very first Meta AI summary soon thereafter. I can always count on Meta to have my best interests at heart :):

> META AI
> What people are saying
>
> The Commentator's supporters are encouraging them to finish their memoir despite their concerns about political backlash and censorship. Many commentators can relate to the fear of political persecution and agree that it's essential to document one's experiences for posterity and stand up for truth.

On the evening of July 16, I received a call from someone in my community. An acquaintance that I had met once in 2019 – and spoken with briefly one time since. In their message, they made sure to reference my alleged 'unworthiness' in an off-hand way. I understood what this meant – they were yet another fool sent my way to diminish my self-concept and frighten me into silence.

The next evening, we had a phone conversation. He informed me that he was in a very bad way, due to a situation with his wife. His tone was off. It sounded like straight-on bullshit. He went out of his way to let me know that she works with court employees and jails ("being hauled into jail is the worst day of your life"). After sharing that information, he let me know that he had read my above-excerpted post about the book write. He was quite interested in finding out if I was planning to have the book published, or not. He also informed me that he knew about the context that I was referencing in that post – because I had disclosed details to him in our past conversations. In fact, I had *never* disclosed details to him at any previous time. It was my belief that he was sent to contact me to find out what my intentions were about the book I mentioned on social media – and to plant the idea of prison in my mind. And, he was also sent to make me uncomfortable about the fact that evermore members of my community were being recruited – no doubt with a series of politically motivated defamations – to trigger me into silence.

It was entirely clear that the surveillance team had studied my writings and my public sharings to the letter. They were continuing to do everything they could to perfectly replicate the most challenging aspects of my early life: scapegoating, gaslighting, public shaming, persecution, abuse-of-power. And, interestingly, all of these aspects were congruent with a variety of events that involved the current Liberal administration.

On July 18, I finally heard back from a Hamilton Police officer in the cyber-security department. Nearly a month after I first reached out and, again, only a few days after the above-noted post which included a reference to compromised "investigative entities." I wonder if that is what finally compelled a response? In our conversation, we discussed the difficulty of identifying the individuals who were sending various forms of spam to my emails, but identified a possible path forward with respect to one issue.

More importantly, he called me back to let me know that he had checked "Have I been Pwned?" – a website where you can check if your email address has been breached. He had checked my main Hotmail account, and found that it had been data breached on eight occasions. On one level, this did not surprise me given that I had evidence that individuals had been going through some of my emails. On another level, I felt like this was just a game to camouflage what was really going on inside of those emails. If there really had been 8 data breaches of a substantive nature, I think it is safe to say that some of those 'breachers' would have found the hundreds of emails exchanged between myself and Mrs. Trudeau in the hard-to-miss 'Sophie' folder. They would have found them and they would have either gone public with them, or attempted to retract some ransom. Given that none of that happened, I believe that my techno-terrorists had set this up to make it look like something it isn't. Whether they actually got into my emails because they saw my password when I punched it in on various devices, or because they had someone at Microsoft provide them with access information, is beyond my knowing. But I have every faith that they did not need to play the kind of data breach game that would show up on "Have I been Pwned?" They may have gone in that way 8x to make it look arbitrary, but that's wasn't how they accessed the information and the contacts that they sought to engage with in their efforts to concoct their kompromat dossier.

On the morning of July 24, I received a DM on my Facebook business page from what appeared to be yet another fake account. In it, the following words: "Hey @jeffbrownsoulshaping, just found a few negative Reddit posts talking about you and thought I'd reach out to see if you wanted someone to take it down for you. Let me know (smiley face.)"

When I read this manipulative message – a likely attempt to worry me about my reputation if I published this book – I felt quite sad. It had now been more than 3 1/2 years since the original phone interception. In all that time, there had been thousands of games played with my consciousness. And yet, as noted earlier, not a single grown-up had been sent to talk to me about the situation. Not one effort was made to organize a formal off-the-record conversation about what was transpiring. Is it possible that – among the large team of individuals involved at various stages – every one of them was an emotionally regressed game player? How could it be that there is not a single adult in the room who can have a direct and clear conversation about all of this?

* * *

Speaking of indirect communication, I began to notice that nearly all of the people who signed up for personal sessions were now operatives, in one form or another. Most were American, some were from the UK. I would post links on Facebook and on my Instagram story, and the strangest cast of characters would show up. This had been going on for some time, but they now took their messaging to the next level.

Where before they would more subtly attempt to trigger me, this group came in harder. They made sure to overstate references to incarceration, homelessness, smear campaigns, M. Scott Peck's book *People of the Lie*, the very unique name of the dog (Maslow) I had briefly owned before giving him to my middle brother, Harvey Weinstein, and psychotic breaks. I understand that some of these themes are very prevalent among many of us, but it was entirely evident that many of these references were deliberate attempts to frighten me. They did not flow from the conversations themselves, and the individuals involved were often not the kind of people who usually book "sacred purpose" sessions. Some struck me as formal members of the intelligence community, others were day-to-day people who had been asked to do this for money or some other benefit. And, interestingly, none of them appeared to be conservatives (or republicans).

Sometimes they sent someone who was a heavy-hitter in the US. One of them – a lawyer and active supporter of the Democratic Party in the coming election – booked two sessions in close proximity. They seemed to be in a hurry. We focused on various elements of their (alleged) personal challenge, before the pay-off moment at the end of the final session. While seemingly referencing themselves, they looked me square in the eye and slowly said this: "This is my moment of hazard."

I understood the meaning: this was *my* moment of hazard. Either I backed off from the idea of publishing this book, or whatever dossier they had constructed in my name would become a matter of public record. And, the (politically motivated) cops would be coming too.

Ignited by this interaction, I wrote a quick Substack on July 31[81] that referenced a moment of peril, and then days later – while laying down on the bed with Susan – I asked this question aloud: "Where is God in all of this?" It was the most sincere utterance I could muster in a moment of complete confusion and terror. And, then I spontaneously began to write a book by the same title – one that gave birth to the new Encodings Model I am now developing. Some part of me, way deep inside, was doing it's very best to pull out of this situation and go back to my calling to write self-help and develop a teaching model. Unfortunately, my enemies continued to up the ante.

One of the clients was an alleged psychotherapist who booked a number of sessions. Early in the first session, I sensed something was awry. She seemed to be far more interested in asking questions about me – particularly whether the content in my fictional book, "An Uncommon Bond," was actually real. It was quite strange. I had the distinct sense that she was sent to psycho-analyze me, perhaps even prepare a report for the team of miscreants that employed her.

In one of the early sessions, she invited me to the US to spend time with her and her partner at one of their homes. She said that her partner knew Joe Biden from their law school days, and that they had been a higher-up in the Justice department under Rudolph Giuliani. I checked it out, and believe this to be true. She also informed me that it would likely be possible for a former FBI Chief-of-staff to come by and talk with me about my political situation, if I came for a stay in their home. Some part of me liked the idea – an actual adult to discuss this with? – and some part of me was frightened by it – what was she up to? I balked at the idea.

I then blocked her on Instagram. She had been occasionally messaging me there and on email, seemingly attempting to build positive energy between us (this is almost always part of the game.) I then changed my mind days later, and unblocked her. She then booked a session <u>almost immediately thereafter</u>. So, it was clear that she was no innocent bystander. She was involved in all of this.

As it turned out, she suggested that I speak with her partner on Zoom about my situation. I agreed. While talking, I did notice that someone was behind them. I got the feeling that my spotting the person was no accident. They wanted me to see someone back there – taping perhaps?

Her partner made it clear that they were aligned with some of the views of the Democratic party. They also made it a point to suggest that I may be under FBI investigation for sexual predation because of my connection to Bhagavan Das – the subject matter of my documentary *Karmageddon*. It seemed important to emphasize this. And then we talked about the possibility of my publishing this book. He went out of his way to detail a plan that resulted in a December 2024 publishing date.

After we got off, I went for a walk to reflect on the conversation. Why the pre-organized plan to share about the book? Why the December date? And why so many amped up Americans trying to frighten me lately? The answer was obvious. They were concerned I would publish this story before the US election in November. If so, what were they afraid of? This was a Canadian issue, right? Or was the American left wing involved in this long before? More on that, soon.

I believe I had one more session with their partner. In it, she gave herself away by suggesting that I was the emotionally healthiest person she had met. Not only was this nonsense, it struck me as nonsense with an intention – to build good feeling between us, so she could continue the charade. I then refunded her next payment, and put things to an end.

* * *

It may be helpful to note that while all of this was happening, I was still being inundated with frightening emails on both my Hotmail and main website accounts. Also, my main website links had stopped working on Facebook (the images were not coming up, when I attempted to post), and someone received a "403 Forbidden" message when I sent them the sessions link that they requested. In addition, my main Facebook page (facebook.com/soulshaping) was continuing to be shadow banned and now going backwards with respect to the number of followers. It had exceeded 543,000, and it was now under 540,000. This is the first time that I recall that page ever going backwards. That's not to say that one doesn't naturally lose followers with any page, but if the page is not shadow banned, new followers dramatically outnumber them.[82]

In addition, I continued to experience ongoing issues with my recently purchased flip phone. Key texts would not arrive until days later, and when I went into the Bell account to pay for the home internet bill from one of my home computers, there was another email address already noted there, indicating that someone had likely manipulated data from inside my computer. A few days later, I found out that the same thing had happened with my Shiatsu massage booking account. My email address had been removed, and replaced with a fake email address.

On August 3, I wrote the following on Facebook:

> "As the darkness swirls around me, singing its framing narratives, desperate to cling to power at every cost, there is something else swirling about, too. It's not as obvious, but it's even more real. I think I'm ready to call it God."[83]

I wasn't even sure what I meant, but somewhere in the heart of the shadow-bans and techno-terrorism, there was this tiny little voice springing to life inside.

Soon thereafter, a swarm of fake emails arrived at my main website email address. God wasn't the issue – humans were.

Chapter 26: Cross Border Stalking

The next day, I felt inspired to share the first piece I wrote for 'Where is God in all of this?' on social media and Substack.[84] I called it Psalm One. Sharing this publicly doubtless took the threat level against me to the next level. Right after posting it, my main website (jeffbrown.co) went down. And, again, later that day. Who took it down?

My summer of weird kept intensifying. Somewhere around this time, a Jewish businesswoman named Kim Smiley and I casually connected on Instagram and Facebook. A social media 'friend' had encouraged it for some time, perhaps imagining we had something 'spiritual' in common. Soon thereafter, Kim found a way to let me know that she had done business with Sophie Trudeau, by sending me a link to a video she had just created that included those details on her list of 'late bloomer' accomplishments.[85] In the video, she also stated that she had "galvanized a global empathy revolution" at age 36. An odd thing to boast about, if true.

I googled[86] and went on Kim's website,[87] and her connection to Mrs. Trudeau appeared to be true. Mrs. Trudeau had purchased some of Kim's clothing and jewelry, and wore a set of her earrings on the Trudeau's infamous trip to India in 2018. Mr. Trudeau had also worn one of her pocket squares on that trip—during a state visit with Prime Minister Modi.

Interestingly, in a subsequent interaction, Ms. Smiley said that she hadn't known that I knew Mrs. Trudeau, before connecting with me. I remember Chantal Kreviazuk telling me that as well.

More recently, I went back and noted that there are $250 earrings for sale named "Sophie." And, the following words accompany the link:

> Canada's First Lady, Sophie Gregoire Trudeau, rocked those earrings on her official trip to India in 2018. The world held its breath as Kim Smiley was launched as a designer on the international stage.

Quite apart from the fact that Canada doesn't formally have a "First Lady," I am highly doubtful that the world was holding its breath because Mrs. Trudeau was wearing said earrings. I know that I wasn't. It seemed like Ms. Smiley was very excited to have the Trudeau eye looking in her direction—something I could previously relate to—and had found a way to convert that into an ongoing business opportunity.

She invited me to go to synagogue with her, asking me to come to a next day service at Toronto's The Village Shul, an Orthodox synagogue, located right across the street from the apartment building where my father died in 2013. Just in case I didn't feel like going to synagogue, she suggested we go for a walk together. Both the requests and the interactions felt strangely inappropriate to me, so I said no to this veritable stranger.

On one occasion, I referenced my 2023 prescription misadventure in a message. She quickly responded that she was covered in goosebumps and suddenly very cold. She wrote that she gets cold when connected to that which is evil. She then immediately let me know that her husband is a criminal lawyer, and that her whole body goes cold when he is speaking to a murderer.

She also tagged me in a post related to the 'Bernard Betel Centre' in North Toronto—a place that my grandfather used to go to socialize. And, a place a few blocks from where my mother passed away in 2015.

I had a bad feeling about this person's interactive motives, and blocked her on Instagram. After blocking her, she confirmed my mistrust, when she wrote me on my main website:

> Hi Jeff. Checking in. Everything okay? Haven't seen you on IG. Kim

> I replied: Why are you continuing to contact me, stranger? We don't know each other at all. Please stop.

> She replied: lol. We need to make sure all members of the tribe are accounted for. All this madness and antisemitism in the world is making me paranoid (I think for good reason).

"Lol" to an email telling her to not contact me? What was this person up to?.

On or around August 22, I noticed something strange. Before leaving the house, I would let Susan know where I was going. Today, it was east on Highway 5 towards Waterdown. Just before I arrived at the corner of Highways 6 and 5, I noticed a Hamilton police cruiser arriving at the corner of nearby South Street. It arrived moments before I got there, turned right and then turned right again on Highway 6. I didn't give it a second thought until it happened again, the next day. And then, on August 24, I again noticed a Hamilton police cruiser arriving at the South Street Stop sign just before I arrived. The timing was impeccable. This time, I was in the far lane, signaling to turn left on Highway 6. The cruiser deftly maneuvered itself through traffic, and placed itself right behind me as I turned. It remained behind me for some period of time, until I changed lanes and positioned myself behind the cruiser.

A few days later, I made the same eastward journey. This time, there was an unmarked Hamilton police cruiser stopped on the opposite side of the highway, oddly angled in a way that you could not miss. The cop was staring at me from the cruiser. I turned back around to take a closer look. When I again turned eastward, it did a U-turn and began to quicken in my direction. While I was sitting in the center lane at the light, it pulled up slowly beside me and lingered for a while, before it then turned right onto Highway 6.

On my next few drives, a police car (or two) would suddenly appear before me in ways that you could not miss. I understand that there are police cars on the roads, but this did not feel remotely accidental.

* * *

On August 30, Susan went back to the US for a ten-day trip to visit her daughter. Although I was afraid for her because of this situation, we felt that it would be an opportunity for her to heal and regenerate. Her heart condition was still a real concern, particularly when the situational stress intensified inside the home. Both her heart and her psyche needed a break.

While she was away, I worked on *Where Is God in All of This?* While working on it, I received a slew of fake texts indicating that various organizations had attempted to deliver a package to the house. This time, there were far more than usual. I had a strange feeling that they were trying to tell me something, but I ignored them and avoided the mailbox so that I could stay with the creative process.

After she returned, their intentions became clear. Susan checked the mailbox, and there was yet another audit letter from the CRA. This time, a fairly detailed request for proof of advertising related to the year 2022. Something that would take a day or so to find and assemble. The date on it was the day she left. How perfectly convenient. I couldn't help but wonder if this was sent, during this particular week, because the powers-that-be were concerned that I was going to work on or perhaps even release my political memoir while Susan was away. In fact, that was not my intention. What I did consider was having all the emails, court filings, taped audio calls and transcripts, finally released to the public record <u>where they belong</u>. If ever there was situation where the Canadian people have a right to know, it is this one. Fortunately, or not, I contained said release.

September continued along the same trajectory. Cop cars showing up in the strangest of places, including one pulling up right behind me in Dundas when I was having a very energetic phone conversation with

Samuel about this situation. The cop car stayed with me for some time until I turned into a parking lot on Hatt Street.

I continued to have problems with my *Enrealment Press* credit card. Included in that were two rejections of monthly payments. I went to the TD Bank, and asked a representative to call in for an explanation. On the call, they were told that the rejections weren't visible on their end, but that the only explanation was that I was late on a $10 minimum payment due in August. The representative got off the phone, and told me that he had worked at TD for about a year, and that he had never heard of such a thing happening unless someone had failed to make payments for 3-6 months.

The problem continued now and then, thereafter. That included rejections of payment when I tried to pay my Fido phone bill. In that case, I was right up to date with my minimum payments.

Toward the end of August, I put up a Facebook post asking for volunteers to explore my *Encodings Method* in process. A number of people connected and booked in. Most of them I didn't know previously. Three in particular were unforgettable. The first two were therapists, with a real interest in the model I was developing. And they were both utterly effusive about the importance of my continuing this work. I appreciated the votes of confidence, but something felt off. It seemed almost personal for them. Sometime later, I took a look and one of them was an ardent supporter of the Democratic party in the coming election. On its own, that doesn't mean anything, but in this context, it struck me as potentially relevant. Was there a pattern at play? Were they sent to get me so psyched about developing Encodings that I let this whole political situation go?

The third person shifted my whole lens on what was going on here. Someone who had been advocating for my work publicly for some time – a woman named *Sheri* from Washington D.C. – directly messaged me to do a volunteer session with someone who had expressed an interest in Encodings. Because I trusted her, I connected with him.

Our session was unforgettable. After discussing his personal life in relation to the concept of Encodings, he brought up my political situation. He had some very specific things he wanted to share. First, he let me know that he had some knowledge of it, and that he felt that I should retreat from it altogether. Second, he told me that he had worked with a psychic intuitive and that they had told him about his past life way back in Atlantis. Yep, Atlantis. In that (alleged) past life, he had been someone who spoke "truth to power," and they had destroyed him by defaming him throughout the community. In this life, his calling was to avoid the conflictual political world altogether ("Let them skirmish over there in the corner, Jeff.") and to do work to help the collective heal. Third, he strongly asserted that he 'just now had an intuitive hit' and that he saw me teaching and growing Encodings worldwide. That this, and not the political situation, should be my point of focus.

I got off the call, and woke the fuck up. Not only was he an obvious plant, so was the woman who sent him to me. I looked back at the date of Sheri's initial interactions with me and it was soon after my initial attempt to sever from Sophie Trudeau in 2019. I then looked back at my initial contact with Atlantis Man. His first message to me was sent the day after my second attempt to sever with Mrs. Trudeau on December 5, 2020. Wonders never cease.

We then engaged in a conflictual interaction on Messenger. I was angry about being played yet again by another indirect communicator.

I then unfriended Sheri on Facebook. Only hours later, she wrote me to ask if I had unfriended her. I asked her how she knew she had been unfriended so very quickly. She told me a silly story about an app that she had added so that she would know when someone unfriended her. When asked why she needed such an app, she said that she "added it out of curiosity after people freaked out about me unfriending them." LOL. Did she have an app, or was Meta or some other entity providing her relevant information about people she was targeting?

I then hearkened back to my interactions with this self-proclaimed political activist. Not only the messages where she acknowledged her connection to Capitol Hill politicos, but also the disconnected manner in which she discussed spirituality with me. She felt like someone whose head was always somewhere else. I also remembered talking with her about this political situation one day while I was driving to Toronto for an appointment. She presented as very compassionate and interested (they always do). On the way, I stopped in at Yorkdale Mall to meet with another new 'friend.' We had some tea, and then while walking back to her shoppe, she surprised me by taking my hand. I held it there for a moment, suspicious as to what was going on. I then unclasped my hand. On the drive downtown, I couldn't shake the feeling that someone was taking a picture of us. It seemed preposterous, so I put it out of my head. It no longer seems preposterous.

I met with her again. Twice with her partner, another time just the two of us for lunch. I wasn't sure why I was meeting with her. On a conscious level, I felt like she had something to offer me with respect to this situation. On an unconscious level, I think I was picking something up. I was just too overwhelmed and flooded with anxiety to tap into what it was.

After lunch, I drove her back to her place. She invited me in to check out the house – a kind of communal space for a variety of interesting people. She introduced me to someone, and then showed me her own room. There was a strangely opportunistic look in her eye. I felt uncomfortable, and told her that I had to leave.

After my interactions with Atlantis Man, I began to wonder if she was yet another fake friendship orchestrated by my politically motivated adversaries. And then I woke up one morning with a whole internally downloaded list of fake friends and supporters in my mind. It was a very long list. She was on it. So was a staunch Democrat that I had been phone friends with for a few years. And a mentally unwell man who penetrated my pages and groups with one drama after another. It all made sense now. This had been going on for some time. Also on the list were some of the people who did regular sessions with me. Not just one-offs – old style regulars. Some were from the UK, others from Canada (including a few who worked part-time for the Government of Canada) and the US. Some were new 'friends' I spoke with on the phone; a few I met with now and then. And one of them, a well-known Toronto 'healer' who was acting flirtatiously when she would greet me. I now saw how she had rigged various interactions in an effort to create a seductive space. Months later, she subtly acknowledged that she had been texted by a stranger (Do you have a minute?) who had things on her, and that she had agreed to 'set me up' in exchange for silence and cash in an envelope.

Bottom line – somebody paid a shitload of money to gather information and keep tabs on me. That's a lot of trouble to go to if all you are dealing with is an (alleged) 'stalker' with 'mental health' issues. In fact, I would suggest that if they went to all this trouble, they knew that they were royally (and not so royally) fucked if this story ever went public.

That I didn't notice these fakers actually makes sense to me. The game of influencing your 'Ooda Loop' basically turns your consciousness upside down, particularly if it goes on for years. Eventually, you are so flooded with cortisol and worry that you're not remotely yourself. And the affronts to your privacy prevent you from relating naturally to your friends. In fact, they are the last people you want to talk with on the phone because you can't help but speak openly with them. So, you hobble around like some kind of Frankensteinian version of yourself, sharing your story and spewing nonsense with veritable strangers, looking for help in all the wrong places. You're not a hybrid, exactly, but you really do become something less than human.

As I woke up to the strangeness of all of this, I hearkened back to many strange internet occurrences. There are way too many to reference here – I have a list of dozens (and dozens) of methods that are employed – but I do want to draw attention to the fake or otherwise compromised whistle-blower account phenomenon. It's been my experience that there are a number of self-proclaimed whistle-blower accounts on social media that are designed to connect with potential whistle-blowers for manipulative purposes. Sometimes they build an online friendship over time – as many of the operatives do – so that you will feel comfortable sharing your intentions with them. Sometimes they do that through messaging; sometimes they do that by tagging you to draw your attention to something that just happened to them on Meta i.e. shadow ban maneuvers. It is invariably something similar to what happened to you. And, sometimes, they don't really friend you, but they tag you and the words they write in the caption are intended to compel you to retreat. For example, referencing a vile smear campaign, flying monkeys masquerading as friends, cops manipulating data, Harvey Weinstein. It's not for me to know if these profiles are actual victims of wrongdoing, or complete fakes, but one thing I am sure of is that they are techno-terrorists hired out by various entities that need their services. It would not surprise me if there is a catalogue somewhere that various investigators and spy agencies have access to aptly titled *Mother Fuckers for Hire*.

In addition, seemingly innocuous events on my little Twitter account kept nagging at me. Apart from the 2-3 messages from people following me that flashed to the word 'stalking' (on accounts that later posted they had been hacked), I found it curious that the well-known wrestler John Cena began to follow me soon after I put up a particularly edgy post about my political situation. I think I had around 100 followers at that time. And not long afterwards, Michele Taylor – the Biden-appointed US Ambassador to the UN's Human Rights Commission – began to follow me, as did someone that she followed and that followed her – British crime writer Emma French. At the time, I wondered if the latter two people had arrived to help me. Now, I wonder if there was some other intention.

Around this time, an Instagram acquaintance that I had met with once for a talk, contacted me to get together. In the heart of my isolation, I agreed. We met at a cafe in Burlington, Ontario, where she shared some of her personal story, and I shared some of this story. She had bought my drink, and was eagerly interested in the details of my interaction with Mrs. Trudeau. At some point, someone walked past the table, staring at me and shaking her head profusely. It did not appear arbitrary. I had a feeling that the person I was speaking with had a wire on. If not her, the table itself was likely wired. Before leaving, my acquaintance made it a point to push me on when I was going to publish this book. It seemed quite important to her that I commit. Or, perhaps more accurately worded, important to whoever sent her to connect with me to see if I would commit. It's a good thing I didn't, or I would probably not have been in a position to finish this version of this manuscript.

Soon after connecting, she began sending me strange texts that appeared to be her way of letting me know she was involved in this situation. I already knew that. When she finally sent me one to the effect that she was being blocked from commenting on my posts (she wasn't – I saw the comment), I sent her packing. It was unfortunate – she was a nice person to talk with. The operatives usually are.

The town continued to get more involved. One shop-keeper went out of his way to engage me. As I entered their store one morning, they let me know that the cops had just chased someone down the alley. He asked if it was me they were looking for. He appeared to be trying to scare me. Weeks later, he sent me an email with a reference to a dialogue with American academic Eric Weinstein on the Modern Wisdom Podcast. In it,[88] Eric introduced the concept of the "pre-bunked malinformant." In this context, the malinformant is the civilian who has information that is inimical to the agenda of various systems of power. Pre-bunked means that they discredit you, so as to ensure that your information is dismissed whenever it arrives. In this email, my shop-keeper 'friend' also let me know that I was – from his perspective – a pre-emergent pre-bunked malinformant. In other words, the pre-bunking hadn't quite happened yet, at least not in the public realm. I may as well have been living in Atlantis :). I was duly warned.

Around the same time, I had a perilous experience on the Queen Elizabeth Way (Highway) coming home from Toronto. I had turned off the QEW and was driving in the right lane, making my way back to Hamilton on Highway 403. A sketchy looking Jeep with tinted windows came barreling down an on-ramp close to me, leaving me with a decision to make: Go ahead, or break sharply and let them in. My instinct was to go ahead. A few moments later, they switched to the center lane and raced up close to me. I opened my window, and motioned my hand in an effort to apologize. They weren't interested. They moved over, much closer to my vehicle, and proceeded at the exact pace as me. I picked up the pace. So did they. I hit my brakes to slow right down. So did they. They were pros – they had done this before.

I felt quite frightened, and somehow found a way to get away from them at the next off-ramp. When my heart stopped racing, I contemplating calling the police. But who was I going to call? The shady Hamilton Police? Not a chance.

When I had met with WT, he had also stressed that I don't drive home the same way consistently. Because of the state I was in, I ignored that. Yet another mistake.

A few weeks later, I was in the car (and near our phones) telling my wife that nobody had booked a session in weeks. Within a day or two, four apparent operatives booked. One of them didn't get back to me (that ploy, again), and two insisted on audio-only Zoom sessions and planted a series of trigger words during the conversations. The fourth was a highly animated and quite brilliant American who made sure to cover all the trigger themes in his rapidly shared story (homelessness, incarceration etc.). I asked him if he had a gang history. He said that he didn't, but that wasn't the impression I got.

And then I received information that confirmed that a previous version of this book manuscript had fallen into the wrong hands. I had already anticipated this but it was still quite shocking. The information came in the form of a fake FB account that made sure to transmit quotes from two of the people quoted in that manuscript – and a quote from an unnamed person who was fundamental to the story itself. For this and other reasons, it was entirely clear that this 'person' was both informed and involved.

Chapter 27

Smash and Grab

Late September, Susan and I decided to rent an apartment in a more peaceful town – Guelph, Ontario. And to try to sell the house. I had been thinking to turn it into an Abuse of Power Museum, with wall videos and writings that spoke to these events, but that idea was nixed by some combination of her disinterest and likely zoning issues.

Getting the house ready to be listed was a nightmare. I could barely move from fatigue, and she had a variety of limitations birthed by these circumstances. Nonetheless, she pushed on through and prepared the property. It was remarkable. Towards the end of the preparation phase, she had more than one heart related event. In addition, her visual disability worsened from the strain, necessitating that I sit closer while speaking so that she could see me clearly.

The renting of the apartment was almost as challenging. When we finally found something acceptable, I had endless problems with the rental application on my home laptop. I could only complete it when I went to Guelph to use the agent's computer. When we finally began to move in, the electricity had been turned off (it had been on, when we saw the unit). It would take a number of days before it could be turned back on. In addition, the heating system did not work and it was quite cold in the unit. When they finally sent someone, it took another few days before we had heat.

Even more strangely, I asked one of the repairmen who worked for the management company to text me his name and phone number. He did, but the information didn't arrive in my active phone. It arrived in an old iPhone – one I had stopped using because it was compromised. My always-on-the-job techno-terrorists were communicating a message: It doesn't matter where you move, or who you interact with. We can fiddle with your devices anywhere.

In mid-October, I received yet another audit letter from the Canada Revenue Agency. This one, concerning Soulshaping Institute from 2022. It was dated October 10, 2024, and it stated that I had thirty days from that date to provide a response. In other words, I would likely be putting together the documents they requested right around the time of the US Federal Election on November 6. Wonders never cease (again)!

With respect to Soulshaping Institute, it had been a solid online business for some time. But the website had begun to develop a series of problems earlier in the year. Notifications were no longer arriving in our inbox – or the inbox of purchasers – and the social media counter was no longer functioning properly. My Maryland website designer claimed they couldn't solve the various problems and quoted a very low price to re-build the website. I agreed.

Unfortunately, we did not agree on a firm conclusion date. I am now told that the job would take 2-3 days, because of the simplicity of the website. Instead, it went on for months and months, with one alleged issue after another. Included among those issues was the assertion that we could no longer use Paypal on the site because it did not align with the sign-up app. This was a real issue, because we had set it up so that economically challenged people could make partial payments on the website through Paypal. The alternative that the designer suggested did not have that option available. So, we agreed to make the change. And then, soon after making it, he let me know that we could actually use Paypal. And, only hours after I emailed another designer from my Hotmail account about the issues with the social media counter, the issues spontaneously righted themselves after many dysfunctional months. How very fortuitous. The internet is such a mysterious world :).

At various times, I had additional problems with my Enrealment Media credit card. Not with in-person purchases, but with online purchases. A number were blocked, without explanation. In one instance, I tried to provide the new card number to BlogVault (a company that backs up your websites) and TD Bank wouldn't authorize it. I also tried to make a necessary parking payment to the management company for the apartment, and that was refused.

So, I went into the bank in November. At first, they said there were no comments on the account. Then, they dug a little deeper and they found a "fraud alert" on the card. That was news to me. I pushed them to call the fraud department, wherein they confirmed that there was a block on my account for online purchases. When asked why, they responded that their system had flagged my initial rent payment for the apartment around the end of September. The telephone attendant asked me to confirm that this – and two subsequent payments (including a payment for $6.78 at the store of the person who had called me a "pre-emergent pre-bunked malinformant") were also legitimate. When asked why I hadn't received a call with such important information, they said that I would likely have received a text. I didn't. This did not feel anything like the bank I had long known.

One day, I went to downtown Toronto to visit Samuel at work. I had stated this intention to him in person days before, and also around my phone and Susan's. When I turned onto Dundas Avenue, I was almost certain that I saw the Alex Ovechkin lookalike driving past me the other way with someone else in his vehicle. I parked, and walked east to Samuel's office. While there, I asked if he could suggest a good massage place in China Town. He recommended a place owned by someone who had previously owned a similar business in Yorkville that we both frequented many years before.

I left his office to walk west on Dundas. As I crossed the light at Beverley, the lookalike appeared, walking quite aggressively toward me. I moved off to the side to avoid walking into him. As he got closer, I wasn't entirely sure that it was the same Ovechkin lookalike. He looked like a younger and far more muscled younger version. I found my way into the massage place, and while I was waiting in line to chat with the attendant, I looked towards the street and the lookalike was standing right in front of the window of the business staring intently at me. He had actually turned back around after passing me, and followed me to this location. I walked up towards him and stared right back at him. At some point, he turned back around and began to talk into his phone. He wasn't going anywhere.

The massage place was similar to those Manhattan parlors where all the tables are out in the open. While receiving the treatment, I had a hard time relaxing because I assumed he'd be waiting for me after I was done. I suppose that was one of the reasons for his game – to ensure that I couldn't relax and regenerate. When it ended, I turned around to look and he wasn't there. But the business owner was. She was staring at me in the strangest of ways, like she remembered me from years before. I asked her if she still owned the old place, and if the man who ran it for her was still there. She quickly replied no, and made it a point to encourage me to come back again and get a more expensive Hot Lomi massage presumably in one of the private rooms. She really wanted me to get that massage. It all felt very strange.

Around the same time, I had another strange massage related interaction. While we were cleaning out the house, we left a number of things on the front driveway for people to take. One afternoon, a woman walked up to look things over. We got to talking. At some point, I asked her what she did. She indicated that she did massage therapy – including Reiki. Interestingly, I had been saying that I was looking for a Reiki person to help me clear the dark energy from this experience, for some time.

I booked a treatment. When I got there, I found that I had accidentally arrived an hour early. Her response was interesting. With a strange expression and even stranger tone, she said: "Well… *you're* eager." It sounded almost accusatory. In fact, I was very much wanting a massage, but I wasn't early because I was "eager." I was early because I had failed to make a note of the time in the heart of my chaotic life. I didn't like whatever it was she was implying, but I nonetheless returned an hour later for a much-needed treatment. Toward the end of the massage itself, she did do something Reiki-like with her hands. Not hovering a little above the body as I had been trained, but with her hands firmly on the body at various points. It was an excellent treatment.

Oddly enough, the massage therapist that I usually worked with at his location, was standing outside her office when I left. It was almost like he was waiting for us. He had a strange look in his eye. He and I spoke briefly, and I went to the front to pay her. After talking about sacred purpose for a few minutes, I left the building. So did the male massage therapist. He continued to give me an odd look, as we both walked to our vehicles.

The next morning, or the morning after, I noticed a Hamilton police car parked in front of her home. No idea if they were visiting with her or someone else, but something felt fishy.

In the meantime, all the same online games were being played with me. I was still receiving a regular daily slew of fake emails to my website, situation-reactive triggering emails to my Hotmail accounts, an endless swarm of people and bots posting nasty comments on my pages, my main Facebook page was continuing to grow backwards, my Instagram was now down to 107,000 (from a high of over 112,000 and growing quickly), and there were various fake 'Jeff Brown' accounts making efforts to contact people – usually women – on my business page.

In addition, I was being contacted by a number of women that I had known years before, particularly during the early years on Facebook. They were phoning, or texting, or messaging me. This did not feel arbitrary or natural. One of them literally posted a deliberately out-of-context excerpt from our old messages right on my page. My instincts told me that her intention was to let me know that if I went public with my political story, I would then have to deal with people publicly sharing things I had emailed them. This was a former Toronto psychotherapist who had been interested in me, and unhappy that I wasn't interested in her. We were never intimate with each other. And she thanked me years later for encouraging her to get online to look for a partner because she found one – and they made a beautiful son together.

And even more interesting – I would often see the accounts of women I had dated, or rejected, or been rejected by, appear right at or near the first of my stories and feeds when I went online. This seemed to be particularly obvious on one phone and one computer – both of which were definitely compromised. This wasn't an occasional thing – it was like a flood of old faces floating by. I knew the difference, because I had been running my own social media pages for years. You don't constantly see people you never have contact with (or whose profiles you don't look at), unless some of it is being done deliberately. Unless it's being done to trigger you, and to imply that the promised smear campaign is afoot.

One of the techno-terror techniques that became particularly active related to people's names. At some point, I also began to notice that a variety of people's first and last names from my past would show up on fake social media profiles and email addresses signing up for my Substack account, to a degree that was inconsistent with the commonality of the name. These were often names of people I had dated, or flirted with (and/or who had flirted with me), or who I had some disagreement with in the past, or 'family members' with some irrational axe to grind. Sometimes even family members that had passed away. This did not entirely surprise me. Again, I have evidence to indicate that some person or organization had accessed my recent and very old emails, Messenger, perhaps my phone records. In other words, my life history.

Just to confirm that it wasn't all in my head, I would do a simple name frequency analysis. So, for example, if I saw the name 'Erica' frequently, I would check and see how common that name was in the general population. If the gap was very wide between its general frequency and the frequency that I saw it, then it was likely that this was part of the techno-terror game. Of course, one name wasn't enough to confirm that, so I would do the analysis of a number of names that were frequently utilized. And it became evident that my instinct with respect to the use of the name game was accurate. This was yet another iteration of the politically motivated game to frighten me into not telling my story.

Another Jewish woman I had known for years asked me to have a Zoom with her, wherein she went on about Arabic men who have sex with donkeys. She also told her story of moving to Israel from Canada, where she now lives an Orthodox life and takes care of her father. She made it a point to let me know that God would be ashamed of me if I went public with my political story. I wasn't sure why God would be ashamed of me, but after she shared that, I got the strangest feeling that she knew Kim Smiley (the woman who had done business with Sophie Trudeau). There was something vibrationally similar about the interactions and/or them.

So, I asked her. She said yes, and stated that she had engaged in a litigation process with Ms. Smiley, because they were both claiming to have ownership rights to a concept at the heart of one of the pieces Mrs. Trudeau had worn. I don't know where that (alleged) case landed, but I couldn't help but ponder: Was this woman trying to frighten me into silence? Was she concerned that the publication of my story would diminish any returns she (or she and Kim) received from advertising and selling a product that (Mr. and/or) Mrs. Trudeau had worn? If so, it is she who should be ashamed before God. Because the emotional damage that was caused by these kinds of games, especially when it emanated from a member of my own Jewish tribe, was (and is) profound painfully. Distressing, to say the least.

Then another old friend utilized our seeming friendship as an opportunity to communicate situation-specific messages. While together, she made it a point to tell me that the political world had rejected me. No such luck, prop. I made three efforts to disconnect. My lived experience doesn't change because power-brokers and dramatists make up stories and discredit me. What happened, happened. It is what it is ... what it is.

Interestingly, this dishonorable woman gave herself away when she acknowledged that whoever sent her was "at war" with me. That's certainly how this now felt. Not so much a silencing game, but one that was designed to destroy the man who dared to fight back. Interestingly, this same person had connected with me soon after Covid began and later 'misinterpreted' the suggestion that she possibly join a teaching team I was organizing, as an indication that I was romantically interested. When I said that I wasn't, she went ballistic. I now wonder if she had also been sent back then, as part of a 'rigging' exercise designed to entrap me. As I noted before, in the state I was in, I often didn't realize I was being played until long after the events came to an end.

There is another game that I should share with you in case you ever get into a situation like this. I called it "the threat diversion game" until a real spy told me that its more formally referred to as a "Surveillance Detection Ruse" and informally a "GME" (Gray Man Enhancement). Essentially, what happens is that you meet with someone in a public place. At some point, they point out that there is someone else in the space that may be a spy. Or they focus on a particular item (i.e. a wall ornament) that 'could be' an audio probe. Or, they let you know that the person who was at the next table left their coat behind. Whatever their point of focus, they suggest that you keep your voice quiet, or they go over to check the coat pockets for a taper, or they suggest that the two of you move to another location. If you are feeling particularly vulnerable in your situation, you may well feel far more trusting of this person than you otherwise would be. This happened to me a number of times, until I saw through it. When this happens, it's almost a guarantee that the one you are sitting with is the spy, engaged in a trust-building ("cultivating an asset") exercise with you. And, they are probably wired.

In a variety of different ways, strangers and friends would warn me that I would end up in jail or living Edward Snowden's life if I continued to push the envelope. I certainly understood the risks, but what they failed to appreciate is the uncomfortable nature of the alternative. That is, living with the painful knowledge that you gave up. For some of us, burying the feelings is far more dangerous, most certainly guaranteed to destroy us.

As noted in an "X" post earlier, I've always found it particularly ironic that the techno-terrorists devoted themselves to attacking my publishing business, given that what attracted the 'powers-that-be' to me was the writing itself. Some of those words and ideas even became part of Mrs. Trudeau's public presentation. And then I leave, and the slow-build to destroy it begins. It's a bit like throwing a temper tantrum with a message: "If we can't use your words and ideas, nobody else can either." And yet, I have a sneaking suspicion that when this story pushes public, other similarly buried stories about the political world will rise to the surface. Shutting me down may open the door to someone else's liberation.

* * *

On January 4 at 2:47 p.m., I put up the following post on my X account:

> When you are experiencing techno-terrorism for a long enough period of time, you become a shell of who you are. That's the point of the whole thing – to turn you into someone that you can't easily recognize. Ideally, you find your way back to yourself, but if it goes

on too long, you end up feeling something less than human. They begin by frightening you, so that you are interfacing with reality in a perpetual state of anxiety. And then you get isolated, because you are no longer similar to others and can't speak comfortably on your now-compromised devices. Finally, they defame you, so that you are always on the defensive in public settings. These methods have been practiced – in a myriad of forms – since time immemorial. Not just to mess up the whistle-blower, but to get them in a state where they begin talking with 'strangers' who deliberately connect with them in public settings. (Rumor has it that they also hack library systems, so that the whistle-blower is forced to work and be 'friended' in a library system where investigative errors weren't made. It wouldn't look too good to work him in the same town where the original events occurred.)[89]

That's why people in the investigative field tell those who are being targeted not to go to the same place often. Because when they do, and particularly when they are feeling lonely and unlike themselves, they are more likely to talk about what they are going through. And they are less likely to notice all the ways they are being played by paid operatives who are expert at feigning friendship.

This may seem like a lot of trouble to go to. It surely is, but all of this – and far more – is deemed necessary whenever a whistle-blower's story is irrefutably credible and is perceived to be a risk to various powers-that-be. The more solid the story, the more prongs to the attack. Anything and everything is attempted to prevent the story from being told. Does this sound like something that could only happen in Nazi Germany? Think again.[90]

Seventy-three minutes after my X post, a Charm Diamond Centre in the Mapleview Mall in Burlington, Ontario was attacked by a gang of smash and grabbers. Right there in broad daylight. This felt particularly significant to me because it was the jewelry store that Susan and I had gone to when I was sick, to replace the wedding ring that she had misplaced. The first ring was purchased at a Charm store in Guelph – the city we had moved to – some years before.[91]

We continued to have issues with the apartment we rented in Guelph. When we reported various maintenance issues on the management company's website, we received email confirms that the issues had been resolved. They hadn't been.

My Soulshaping Institute website continued to allegedly have re-build issues. One after another, until one day the designer said words to this effect: "I hear you are having issues with Justin Trudeau." And then he laughed. I hadn't told him anything about this situation. Was he compromised? The website problems continued for some time thereafter, until I replaced him with someone else. The new designer needed considerable time to make sense of the many layers of code that had been installed on the newly transferred website.

On January 6, Susan and I drove back to Dundas for moving day. It was a strangely ominous day in Canada. It was rumored that Trudeau was going to resign later that morning. Soon after I turned right onto Highway 5, a Hamilton police cruiser pulled up behind me and turned on his flashing lights. I pulled over. He stopped and turned off his lights. I got back on the highway, and turned right at the next street, imagining he was going to follow me to write a ticket (or shoot me in the snout). He did no such thing. He simply continued to drive west on Highway 5.

We got to the house and let the movers in. I went to the basement bathroom, to make a call to the alarm company to cancel the service. It said that it would be about fifteen minutes before an attendant would be available. It turns out that I was on the line for about forty-two minutes, and it was anything but boring.

In the first twelve minutes (10:06 am-10:18 am est), there were between 6-8 audio appearances from a gamesy sounding woman uttering some combination of hi/hey/hello. Clearly, my phone or my call had been intercepted for the purposes of frightening me. I then did something that I wasn't in a position to do when the first phone incident occurred December 12, 2020. I reached for a tape player that I often kept in my coat. I had a feeling that one day they would be back, but that this time I would catch them.

> (Reminder: Detective Rowan had contended that I had a mental health issue which concluded the second attempted investigation. At that time, he had indicated that there was no evidence of criminal behavior, including the phone incident I had reported to the Hamilton Police.)

I taped for the next 29 minutes or so (10:19-10:48 est) The woman continued to 'hi/hey/hello' and at one point the sound of mocking laughter could be heard. At 23 minutes (10:42 est), the unmistakable sound of a rapidly firing machine gun. That's right, <u>a machine gun</u>. Soon thereafter, Susan came in the room and briefly spoke to me. Then the frightening sounds ended and I hung up the call. I was not remotely surprised that the sounds ended after she came in the room. The game is for me, and me alone, to hear it so that if I report it, they can again call me crazy. No witnesses, after all. But this time I taped it. And I put a download link to the taped call up on X and later Facebook.[92]

Trudeau publicly stated his intention to resign right around or just after this incident. I am not suggesting that he orchestrated this event, but I do believe that both this and the squad car flashing light game had the same protective motivations: (1) to ensure that I was too frightened to see Trudeau's resignation as an opening for public revealing; (2) as opportunities to make me look mentally unwell if I reported them without tangible evidence.

Interestingly, Susan and I went for a walk in Guelph's Stone Road Mall around that time. I remember clearly having the thought that the Charm jewelry store would soon be hit there, too. Because that's where we purchased her first wedding ring, and where we lived now. This was the second time in my life that I had a premonition like this. The first was related to my Bar-Mitzvah synagogue, which was attacked soon thereafter.

On the evening of January 16 (9:44 pm), I put up a post on X that included the following content:

> Isn't the political world wonderful? One of the things I will be sharing soon relates to the way that the techno-terror team methodically worked to derail our businesses. The publishing house (book blocks, shadow bans etc.), my personal website course downloads, and now Soulshaping Institute (website app problems, gamesy efforts to complicate/delay a super basic website rebuild). If I had once believed that all of this was done to silence me, I soon came to realize that this was more about destroying than silencing. This is classic economic sabotage, with the medical calamity that often follows...[93]

The next day, the anniversary of Susan's father's death, the Charm store in Guelph was attacked much like the one in Burlington weeks before: a smash and grab during late afternoon business hours. How very charming.[94]

I later put up a related Media Investigative Challenge on X.[95]

In it, I provided some of these details, and cajoled them to not make the assumption that the abundance of smash-and-grabs, and attacks on synagogues and churches, was arbitrary in nature. I invited them to contact those locations and inquire into whether there was any person, or persons, affiliated with them that may have recently done or said something that pissed off power. I certainly believe that some or all of these events are forms of maniacal communication from those protecting power to those who have offended them. It can't just be me.

I continued to receive fake account sign-ups (Substack and Meta) peppering me with a series of names of people from my past. There was no question that my emails and Meta messages had been scoured through to find key names. Sometimes the account name and description actually reflected the familiar themes: Predation, Poverty, Vile Smear Campaign, Incarceration. This pattern seemed to intensify whenever they found evidence to suggest that I was going to publish my politically inspired memoir or something similar. For example, one day we were working on 'Where is God in all of this?' on computers that we knew to be compromised. No sense getting new ones. They would just compromise them again. And then I got a sign up on Substack from an account named "Prison Roses." Their description: "I hire other people to blame other people of my malfeasance." I'm sure they do. Pigs.

What was interesting about many of these Substack notifications is that they often appeared in my Hotmail inbox but a few moments after I opened it. Whether it was because the techno-terrorists were on that computer, or because they were actually in the Hotmail account, was beyond my knowing. So, I did one thing right. I turned off the Substack notifications to my email address. A great accomplishment for a terrorized luddite. A little bit of peace now and then.

CHAPTER 28

HOMECOMINGS

The weeks to follow were very difficult. Despite settling into the new town, nothing much changed. In fact, it became worse in a variety of different ways. .

I began to work on this book at a favorite library north of Guelph, but I had to stop because it became apparent that they had sent a small team of misfits to watch over me. One of them made himself known when I went to check emails on the library computer. I sat down, and he turned in my direction and immediately brought up Member of Parliament Chrystia Freeland who had just resigned her seat in cabinet. In the days that followed, the same guy was often there, sitting close by, glaring at my computer while I worked. In addition, there was one guy that seemed to always be there when I sat at a table to write. He too was a glarer and when I refused to look his way, he found other ways to draw my attention including picking up his laptop and deliberately dropping it on the ground. He did this twice. The second time, I heard it but refused to look up. He stormed off. I stopped working at that library soon thereafter.

In addition, the Guelph police seemed to be close by a little more often than felt natural. A few times, they pulled right up behind me soon after I had posted something about this situation. One day, after a particularly bold post, I found them sitting on a long on/off ramp in a plaza in the north end. Two police cars side by side, obstructing most of the ramp. In order to exit the plaza, I had to slow right down to avoid hitting them. As I slowly made my way past them, both officers made it a point to glare at me with tremendous intensity. It was very uncomfortable, as intended.

While working on 'Where is God in all of this?', I made it a habit to ask people what they would ask God if they were given the opportunity to ask one question. It helped me to stay connected to the material, and to ensure that I asked questions that were relevant to others. One afternoon, I noticed a Guelph patrol car following along behind me for a few moments. I had no concrete evidence that he was part of my situation, but my spidey senses were tingling. After he turned into the McDonalds parking lot in downtown Guelph, I turned back around and brazenly pulled up beside him.

I lowered my window, and invited him to lower his. After exchanging a few pleasantries, I asked him my question: "If you could ask God one question, what question would you ask?"

He looked me square in the eyes and replied "Why are you such a bad human?" He strongly emphasized the word, *you*.

I had very little doubt that this officer had preexisting knowledge of who I was. Like so many before, he had been trained in the art of disparaging the threat. Again, if they can't call the whistle-blower bad, or mad, they are left with little more than the rancid fruits of their illicit labor – their horrifying actions revealed to the world. It's usually a lot easier to ruin the target. Usually.

After 'Where is God is all of this?' was published in February, I felt a little lift. In its own way, working on this book had saved me. It reconnected me with God and the writing journey that I had loved for years before, and the teaching model that comes through the dialogue gives me hope. Even if I couldn't repair my life, I found something that could invigorate others.

But then it got strange again. There were all the same online games, but there was more. My wife began to confuse me. I didn't believe that she wished me harm, but something felt off. She inquired into where my safety deposit boxes were located – the place where I kept copies of some evidence. She jumped up and held my arms back, when I sat down to write a politically risky post on Twitter. She made a determined effort to get me to say that I was "obsessed with the Trudeaus," which is patently false. (If anything, I'm entirely bored with them.) She pushed me to admit that I needed to see a psychiatrist. I don't. This all happened in the apartment. I couldn't help but wonder, as I had to some extent when she drove me to the hospital with our police escort, if she'd been convinced by the techno-terror crew that helping them to either declare me crazy (she had recently talked favorably about the idea of us going on disability and living a quiet life), or to undermine me as a story-telling threat (i.e. eradicate evidence), would be safer for both of us.

If this was the case, the timing made sense. Although I had previously turned down a solid publishing offer for this book, another offer had arrived in the autumn of 2024. I was mulling it over. There is little doubt that the techno-terror team was aware of this. And little doubt that they were particularly concerned about this book being released during this

Chapter 28: Homecomings

vulnerable political moment for the Liberals in Canada. With Trudeau on the way out, and some uncertainty as to who would be selected to replace him, the last thing they wanted was this kind of book announcement.

Although Susan and I were talking about going to the US for her daughter's birthday, I made the dangerous decision to fly alone to Israel on February 26, 2025. I had never been there before, but I didn't know where else to turn. The tipping point was a very strange experience with the Guelph Police. I was driving with Susan in her car, and feeling very confused and frustrated by another event. When we pulled into a plaza, I began to express my anger at all the games the cops were playing with me. The many police follows in Hamilton and Guelph were really getting to me.

Still in the car, I said something to the effect of "Arrest me already, motherfuckers! Let's break the bubble of this four-year holding pattern and get this story out there." Within 1-2 minutes of my making this utterance, two Guelph police cars pulled hurriedly into the plaza. It was that fast. One of them pulled in right behind Susan's car and parked. The other parked close by and glared at me. I got out of the car and walked toward one of the police cars. The cop got out of his car and walked into the bank. I went to place an order in a nearby restaurant. By the time I returned, he was back in his cruiser. I walked towards him and motioned for him to lower his window. I asked him why he had come to the plaza exactly when he did. He said that he was there because someone had complained about an aggressive panhandler. I saw no such panhandler.

I couldn't help but wonder if Susan's car was wired and if I was under formal investigation. From a legitimate legal perspective, this didn't make a lot of sense. If they had a formal court order, it would only entitle them to watch and listen. It would not entitle them to immediately engage or intimidate, and certainly not when a crime wasn't being committed. My instinct was that this situation was yet another spoke of the terror wheel that had become my life. In other words, someone was pulling strings yet again to gain illegal access to information even though I'd never had any formal issue with the Guelph police. The RCMP and Hamilton Police had fucked up big time and had every reason to keep me hopping. And we all know that the cops stick together. Blue always protects blue, citizen's rights be damned.

I booked two weeks alone in a Jerusalem hotel, right near the Old City. Just before I left, Susan insisted that I take one of her large suitcases on my trip. I had been planning to take two of my small suitcases. But she insisted: "This way, you have room to bring back some presents." It was a strange request (and she said it in an unusually odd voice) – I had plenty of room in the other bags – but I went along with it because it seemed so important to her.

On the first flight from Toronto to New York, I ended up sitting beside a Canadian with a particular interest in my Trudeau story. She was flying to Los Angeles, via New York. I may have brought the book up as a response to her question about my work, but she seemed unusually interested. What struck me as most significant was her focus on whether I'd any direct contact with former Attorney General Jody Wilson-Raybould. I hadn't. Her interest didn't entirely surprise me, given that a number of characters had connected with me online to find out if I had a personal connection with someone on the American right. If I was reading this right, these were pre-emptive attempts to diminish this book's credibility by claiming that I am someone's political prop. I'm not. (More on this in the final chapter).

My second flight was from New York to Paris. Just before boarding, I received a phone call from a (possibly compromised) 'friend' – who, interestingly, often rang through at key moments – from Canada. While chatting with him, the Air France attendant told me to step aside: "Did you come with one bag or two bags?" he asked. It's almost as though he knew I had made that choice before leaving. After some time fiddling with his computer, he handed me back my boarding pass and let me on the plane. It felt staged.

My flight from Paris was a delight. As I got closer to my homeland, my spirits began to soar. I had no clear plan, other than to visit the Western Wall, the Dome on the Rock, and the Church of the Holy Sepulchre, where Jesus is buried. Because I felt I could no longer trust anyone after all these mystifying human – and non-human – interactions, I wanted to get as close to God as I could. Was God in Jerusalem? If so, would he turn me back from publishing this book, or make it even more imperative?

I slept deeply for the first few days. Something about seeing soldiers and obvious surveillance cameras on most every corner actually calmed me. At least they were all out in the open, and none of those young soldiers were following me. In fact, I knew that if I was in peril, they would actually help me. I hadn't felt worthy of protection for a very long time.

Before and during my trip, a series of individuals that I (mostly) did not know reached out to me on social media to meet in Israel. I refused them all, with one exception. I went for dinner with a socialistic American expat

Chapter 28: Homecomings

with deep Israeli roots, who, I later found out, was personally connected to the 'friend' that called me just before I boarded in NYC. It was going well until he appeared to play the "Surveillance Detection Ruse" game I had mentioned earlier with respect to two people staring at us from a nearby table. He then pushed me to let go of telling this story. "Go to the light, Jeff. Go to the light," he said. Lesson learned. No more meals with strangers on this sacred pilgrimage. I was here to get closer to my soul.

There was no question that I had something like PTSD, but because it wasn't over yet, it felt more appropriate to call it OTSD (Ongoing Traumatic Stress Disorder). The only thing that seemed to calm me, chocolate rugelach and falafel aside, was being at the Western (aka the Wailing) Wall.[96] There, I was able to remember myself in ways I hadn't for years. And, by tapping into my Jewish roots, I could remember how important it was to continue to fight the good fight.

I spent a number of days in and around the Old City. I never wanted to stray too far from its cobblestone streets. Every hour here felt like an awakening. The intensities, the thawing out, the re-assemblage, were continuous. Although I had profound experiences at the Wall, I felt like I was connecting with every religion as I wandered these streets. Whatever their seeming differences, they were all here together, swimming and praying to God in the very same ocean. The ocean of essence. Such a bountiful place.

Being here helped me recognize our shared plight. The issue is not this religion, or that spirituality. The issue is those who utilize them to divide and conquer humanity for their own malevolent purposes. Disempower the divisive ones and we will find our way. Let them continue – particularly with the technologies now at their disposal – and we are doomed.

It's near impossible to avoid the deeper questions of your life in the Old City. The authenticity of the place pushes the real *who you are* and *why you are here* to the surface. Its urgency brings you face to face with your mortality and your reasons for being. After about ten days in Jerusalem, I began thinking about this book again. On the one hand, it seemed utterly irrelevant by comparison to the plight of the Israelis and the Palestinians. On the other, it seemed utterly essential to bring it through. How could I uncourageously retreat from this story, after all humanity had endured?

During the week of March 11, I engaged with my literary agent and readied myself to finish the book. I was supposed to fly home on March 13, but I canceled my return flight. Something told me that I needed to stay a little longer.

After more than four frightening and isolating years in Canada, I was slowly regaining a sense of my own power here. And my relationship to God was deepening. I felt him closer by the minute, and I felt myself readying for whatever he had in store for me. It's not that I imagined myself special, but there had to be some reason why I had survived this challenge this long. Something beyond me had held me safe these last years. It was also hard not to notice how many friends, acquaintances, and colleagues who had neglected me or been engaged to play games with me during this political situation, had suffered immeasurably. Three lost their homes to fire (and a few came very close, as though God was aware of the fact that they still had time to do the right thing in this situation). Others had terrible mold infestations and medical calamities. Some got strange cancers. Many lost their parents and pets much earlier than expected. I don't know that I believe in past-life Karma per se, but I couldn't help but wonder if certain crucibles are designed to stretch and test a vast array of participants. This one definitely felt bigger than me.

I finally began another book draft on March 16, a few days after Trudeau formally resigned and handed the PM reins over to the strangely disembodied Mark Carney. As for Trudeau, all the public knew was that he went to a Canadian Tire department store on March 17,[97] and purchased a potato masher and some other kitchen items. There doesn't seem to be any press on where he was for the next few weeks. As for which kitchen he bought these items, all we knew was that it wasn't Rideau Cottage. He was no longer welcome in the Prime Ministerial home. He had been ousted as Liberal leader.

Interestingly, there was another picture of him circulating on X around that time. This one, taken by his long-time photographer, showed him standing in the Rideau Cottage kitchen before he left office, with a now empty kitchen cupboard.[98] For whatever reason, Trudeau really wanted us to associate him with a kitchen right before and after leaving office. Interesting.

Also on March 17, Global News announced that there had actually been an arrest made back on January 10 with respect to the attack on The Pride of Israel synagogue last summer.[99] And not just there, but also the synagogue very near to where my middle brother lived (2 or more attacks), a church that he may well have attended, the synagogue where my parents were married, and other personally relevant locations. Synchronistic indeed!

Given that there were allegedly 19 hate crimes in total, I find it difficult to imagine that this was all orchestrated by one individual. Even if the accused was involved, I am curious to know which antisemite hired him and directed some or all of his actions. What I also find interesting is that the final attack is said to have been on January 3 and the arrest wasn't reported on by the media until today's court appearance months later. Why wasn't this information released while Trudeau was in office? Is there a connection between the accused and his Liberal administration?

While working on the book in Jerusalem, I was very troubled. Not by the content of the book, but by challenges in my relationship with Susan. While in Jerusalem, I found myself entirely confused by our interactions. There was the woman I had known for now over a decade, and now someone else connecting with me. Not in the doppelganger sense, but in the behavioral sense. To put it simply, she appeared to be putting on a strange show at times. One of the themes was to say suggestive things that implied she was engaging sexually with someone else in the apartment. I choose not to get into the details, but suffice to say that I was both worried for her (this political situation could drive anyone batty) – and worried about myself in relation to those conversations. What she seemed to be hinting at could certainly have been true, but I was slightly more inclined to think that this was some kind of a set-up. If I went public with my specific suspicions, and if there was actually no basis for them, they got their 'crazy' diagnosis (except this time, without the drugs).

As a result of my discomfort – I decided to finally fly home in early April. On my return, I felt oddly concerned about whether someone was going to put something untoward in my luggage. This was not something I had ever worried about before, but the strange bag switch before I left and the oddly toned request for a "present" led me to wonder. Interestingly, when I arrived in Toronto, my bag was not on the carousel with everyone else's luggage. I didn't fret. I just asked for help locating it. It was in the middle of the floor, unlocatable without help from an airport employee. When she handed it to me, she had the strangest look on her face – almost like she was expecting me.

By the time I arrived at the apartment, Susan was gone. So were her clothes, her car, and Lacy Cat. The fridge was essentially empty, and there were two boxes of previously unused sexual enhancement pills now half empty and left in plain view in the walk-in closet. What the fuck!?

After a few days in shock, I entered into a state of bewilderment. None of the information I was receiving about what was going on made sense to me. Some if it led me to one conclusion, some to another. The only constant was chaos.

To make matters worse, it had become evident that nearly every previously close person in my life was now gone from it. Whether because of impatience, defamation, bribery, and/or blackmail, either they or I had discontinued our relationship. When you have been around a situation like this for a long time, it gets very easy to know when people are compromised. They say things that are unlike them and similar to what other compromised souls have said. It isn't difficult to see that they have all been trained by the same contractor team.

To help me make sense of it, I found myself organizing them into categories in my mind. For example, the Cancelers (individuals retained to cancel arrangements with you, to contribute to your sense of insignificance/isolation); the Triggerers (individuals retained to say or do something that they know/are told will hit your buttons); the Reminders (individuals retained to remind you of things from your past); the Distractors (i.e. individuals retained to undermine your focus and prevent you from completing your day's work), the Warners (individuals retained to warn you about what will happen if you dare to do something i.e. publish); the Seductors (individuals retained to "set you up" with all manner of come-on); the Instigators (individuals retained to play communication games with you in an effort to trigger your anger or make you look crazy) etc.

The next week, I went to the U.S. for a short meditation retreat. I no longer felt safe as a Canadian, both because of what I was going through and because of what Canada was clearly becoming under our Globalist Prime Minister. This guy had a whole bag of tricks up his sleeve. I felt much safer in America. Soon enough, I ended up at a fantastic Holiday Inn in Grand Island, New York. Some of the kindest people I have ever met work there, and in the upstairs restaurant.

After a number of days doing nothing but grieving, something shifted in me. I felt eager to sign the book deal. All of my resistance was gone. Why?

I sat with the question. And the answer was obvious: Susan. From the moment she was diagnosed with a genetic eye condition [Adult vitelliform macular dystrophy (AVMD)] in 2018, she was in my care within my heart. I immediately added extra life insurance policies, and did my very best to organize things so that she would be okay if I were to pass away before her. Because she also has asthma and a thyroid condition, I was especially concerned that she wouldn't be able to take care of herself without hired care. As a result, I feared writing this book because of the impact it could have on her health. One never knows how the world will respond to any book, but it didn't take a genius to realize that this one might be intense. I was concerned that she wouldn't survive it if we were still together.

But now she was gone. That – and the irrefutable presence of God – gave me license to get on with it. So, I signed the deal and came in hard on another edit. I devoted a part of most days to my emotional process – grieving the loss of a soul I loved deeply – and part to stepping into my new life. As a whistle-blower on a road to who the hell knows where?

* * *

While living my hotel life, an interesting figure entered my reality. *Gran*t let me know that he'd been a military intelligence operative in Iraq – and that he had some information about my situation that might be of use. Whether he had this information because he was part of my techno-terror team, or part of the team watching my techno-terror team, or because he could recognize what was happening from my online posts, is beyond my knowing. It certainly wouldn't be the first time that someone involved in this situation, befriended me. But it didn't really matter. I liked him and I needed what he knew desperately.

To begin with, he made me aware of something called MILDEC.[100] In the words of AI, MILDEC stands for "Military Deception, a strategic tactic used in warfare to mislead or confuse an adversary about friendly forces' intentions, strengths, or weaknesses. It involves intentionally presenting false information to create a desired outcome that favors the deceiving force. This can include feints, demonstrations, ruses, and displays, among other techniques." Interestingly, he also told me that Trudeau had a MILDEC person on his team. (If so, was it Grant?)

The notion of a 'ruse' really resonated with me, largely because of what I had just gone through with Susan. Although it was utterly impossible for me to know precisely what was going on, it certainly felt like someone was trying to ruse me into believing something about her new life. Grant actually claimed to have considerable knowledge of my situation. He reassured me that my worst imaginings weren't true – she is on her own and laying low in the US – but that she had been persuaded by a narcissistic friend and an ill-intended 'contractor' that I would be better off labeled 'crazy' than sane. Again, that way I wouldn't have to deal with all the fallout from announcing and/or actually publishing this book, because I'd be on disability, or hiding out in the Shire from the big bad world. If Grant's version of events was true, then the *Mildec* team must be very disappointed because I resisted their ruse by not publicly sharing details. Not because I didn't believe it possible, but because I sensed that I was being worked by nefarious forces. Not Susan, but those who may have been chirping in her ear at a vulnerable moment.

It's important to note that this ruse, of course, had not formally begun while I was in Jerusalem. That's where it culminated, particularly after I made the decision not to take my return flight home in mid-March. But it was a long-game ruse that was worked on a variety of different levels, over a long period of time. A number of individuals participated in it, including a massage therapist 'friend', the American ex-pat that I had dinner with in Jerusalem, and an immigration consultant that I will soon sue – as did a variety of businesses and political figures that had a lot to lose if this book published. And the techno-terror team supported their efforts with triggering imagery and the utilization of others who connected with me. It even appeared to include an old friend's hacked Facebook page. Her page kept showing up as the most visible 'story' in my feed, now utilizing shocking and triggering images entirely consistent with the ruse itself. One way or the other, it didn't work. The ruse came with a lot of heat, but I prevailed.

Although I prevailed, there was a time in Jerusalem when I worried that I wouldn't make it. The things they wanted me to believe were so painful in my isolated and beaten-down circumstances that I worried I wouldn't survive. If not for those replenishing visits to the Old City, I may not have made it.

I did come close to going public one night. Then I had a dream that included my mother. She didn't say a word, but kept coming over to me and softly whispering, "Shhhh." As a child, I most assuredly would have rebelled against her telling me what to do, but not this time. I knew that she was right and I contained myself thereafter. It was a good thing that I did.

* * *

Grant also asserted that the variety of things I had experienced were very unlikely to be connected to a legitimate investigation. In his view, there were too many privacy violations, and too many agencies acting outside their mandate. And government agencies don't have the money to lawfully investigate a regular citizen for four + years. I had been told the latter by a number of different individuals in the field.

In his view, strings were being pulled by a variety of "contractors" who hired out all the players, likely paid for by the illegal funneling of funds destined for various government programs.

He also confirmed that if it was a legitimate investigation, they wouldn't let me know they are monitoring me. They wouldn't even hint at it for fear that I would then alter my behaviors. In his view, they want me to know they are there, and they want me to react, so that they can freak me out and then portray me as a mentally unwell conspiracy theorist. My hunch is that it's a little bit of everything. They run harassment to try to trigger me to madness or death. If they don't accomplish their goal, they come after me for whatever they have concocted ("lawfare").

Grant also let me know that it is very likely that they don't know what to do with me, because I am no longer afraid to die. Fear of death is the primary reason a person would back off when accosted by techno-terrorists. If the person no longer cares – either because they're too worn down or because they have come to believe they're on a sacred mission that they must complete (or both) – the enemy has a real problem. When asked why they hadn't killed me yet, he essentially said that murdering the target has too many loose ends. The best approach is to isolate the target and make them crazy. Once they have accomplished that, it becomes easier to convince people that their death was an accidental suicide.

One of the things that affirmed his credibility was his explanation for a strange phenomenon I experienced after settling into Guelph. Somewhere around half the time that I left the apartment in the morning to go to a library to write, I would hear an alarm/siren going off on the main street nearby. Strangely, it only lasted 15-20 seconds before stopping altogether. If it had been a police car, ambulance, or fire truck, it would usually last longer and then trail off.

I looked around online, and confirmed that there are certain sirens permanently or temporary installed in various parts of a city to ensure public safety in a local crisis. Of course, that didn't explain why one would go off every second time I left my apartment.

I then did a calculation of how often I would hear a normal emergency vehicle siren when I stayed in the apartment all day. The average was about 8-10 times. I also calculated the average time that they lasted. It turned out that the odds that an alarm would be going off at any one moment when I was in or leaving the unit, was somewhere around 1/1000. Not half of the time.

My assumption was that they were just using this to alarm me, as they had utilized the house alarm at key moments back in Dundas. Grant begged to differ. He felt that the alarm was being used a signal to whoever was going to follow or intimidate me that I had left the unit. They have to have some way of knowing when I am on the road.

This resonated. As noted, characters would show up at many of the libraries that I frequented and watch me and/or make efforts to get my attention. They would often arrive soon after I got there. And, almost every time that siren went off, an unusual number of police cars would suddenly arrive at street corners and lights as I passed. Some of them turned the other way, others positioned themselves right behind me. It seemed very likely that the Guelph police knew precisely what that particular siren meant.

* * *

With some reluctance, I made my way back to Canada after announcing the book. It wasn't easy to leave the U.S. – a place (and a people) that had strengthened my resolve – but it was time to go home. Interestingly, the siren game did not happen again after I returned. But other things did. All the same online games and Meta shadow bans continued, but the in-person intimidation went momentarily silent with Carney as PM.

Then it started up again. I began regularly working in a regional library. I knew that they were onto me coming here, because a few individuals that I was familiar with would appear to distract me. And my name on my Hotmail account was abruptly changed to the name of someone I did business with when I was in the home improvements business. Imagining sitting there working on emails, and your name is suddenly different when you send an email.

The same day as the email game, I decided to go a Guelph library about a half-mile away for my first Zoom with the publisher's editor for this book. We had booked the time the week before, and I worked my way over to that library after having lunch in the neighborhood.

When I arrived, there was a high school student sitting a few seats over from where I normally sit, glancing at me strangely while fiddling with her phone. After the Zoom, she made it a point to immediately initiate contact with me. She was asking for my help with something, but I couldn't understand her. So, I asked her to write it down. She wrote something to the effect of 'Sustainable Development' and then pulled up a list of seventeen related aspects on a '2030' United Nations webpage. She then told me that she had a project to complete, and wondered if I could speak to any of the seventeen aspects. I said that I couldn't, but told her she could email me and if I thought of someone, I would email her back with their info.

Chapter 28: Homecomings

She then asked for my email address. I began, "Jeff..." and she finished it for me.... *Jeff@JeffBrown.co.* I asked her how she knew who I was. She said that she heard it on the Zoom. I reminded her that we didn't mention my last name or website on the Zoom. She then shifted her story: "I knew from a book that we have of yours in our high-school library." "Which book," I asked? She didn't know, so she did a quick search of my online book covers. She then pointed to "Spiritual Graffiti," which is very likely not in the high school she named (Bishop Macdonell on Clare Road). It was clear that this kid was sent to keep me hopping. Sickening, honestly. Using a high school kid to effect political goals.

One day, I had lunch with WT and Cribb at the Miller Tavern in North Toronto. WT was different than I remembered him. He was now eager to get his hands on my manuscript. He pushed on it a number of times, framing his interest as a favor to me because I needed a blurb from him for the sake of credibility. I think his ego dramatically over-estimates his notoriety. He also went out of his way to inquire into how the book ended. He really wanted to know the contents of the final chapter. I found this quite *synchronistic,* given that I had just told the book editor on Zoom that I was going to change the last two chapters. Finally, he looked me in the eye and asked me why I thought the police hadn't brought me in for a talk yet. Contrary to what Grant had said, WT said that someone could be under formal investigation for many years before they bring them in. I certainly knew that he had a lot of influence with law enforcement. I don't remember how I responded, but it was clear that he was putting the heat on me.

At some point, Susan and I booked a Zoom. We'd had a series of emails, but nothing felt normal or relationally consistent. I continued to feel completely bewildered by what was happening. When we did finally see one another on Zoom, she showed me a room that she had rented at her daughter's apt. in America. When I saw her room, I cried. She said that she hated it when I cried. Even that confused me. I hadn't known that. She also told me she had taken a job at a retirement home up the road as a room cleaner and/or a customer care rep. I didn't understand how both those things could exist at the same time.

Despite the confusion, the one thing that was clear was how much I loved her. And how grateful I was for all the years we had together. Whatever challenges there were, we created (and laughed) brilliantly together. And even if she had become compromised during this political nightmare, it was understandable. This thing was a runaway train. It could cause anyone to lose their way. The fact that she was able to take such good care of me in the heart of it was miraculous. I had forgotten what it was to live a dignified life. She kept reminding me.

In early August, I went back to the US to complete the final edits of *In Trudeau's Kitchen*. I spent a few weeks in the Niagara Falls area. There were the usual hindrances, but three that stand out as significant in the context of this story.

* * *

First, I was actively harassed by someone in a vehicle. This was the third time, and easily the most dangerous. I was on the Grand Island Bridge heading to the library when someone in an SUV came sharply over from an on-ramp and almost knocked me into the guardrail. I was moving at quite a clip, so it could well have been fatal. I did not call it into the police, largely because I knew that the driver would claim it was an accident (it wasn't), and I would lose another day of writing time, as my enemies hoped.

* * *

Second, I received an email from a man (allegedly) named Mickey Martel on August 12. He referenced himself as 'Office Administrator' for Greenwin Properties (my landlord) at 150 Darling Street in Brantford, Ontario. In his email, he said "Hello. Im just trying to touch base regarding your rent, you currently have a balance of $2,785.00 please reach out and let me know if you are needing any assistance making this payment." Having e-transferred my August rent on July 28 (and receiving an emailed confirmation from the Greenwin system on July 28), I didn't know what he was talking about. I emailed back with a copy of their payment confirmation. He then wrote me back "Hello. Please see attached copy of your ledger, this shows the balance owing. If you did make a payment as you say then that payment has bounced back into your bank account. Thank you." I opened his ledger, which looked legitimate, even if it was probably wrong.

I checked my account and nothing had bounced. Is it even possible for an e-transfer to bounce after it leaves your bank account? If so, why did I receive a confirmation of payment from Greenwin? Was this a scam? Was this really coming from Greenwin, or was the techno-terror team trying to trigger my childhood issues around homelessness? If the latter, it certainly worked. I felt tremendously anxious as this unfolded.

I then received an email on August 13 from someone (allegedly) named Sarah Duthler, Manager, Residential Operations at Greenwin's office at 19 Lesmill Road, Toronto. In it, she attached a "notice that was distributed in advance of August 1st alerting our tenants who pay directly of a banking issue." I had never received such a notice. This is what it said:

> July 24, 2025
>
> Re: Action Required -Temporary Interruption to Direct Banking (Bill Payment)
>
> Dear Residents,
> Please be advised that as of Wednesday, July 23rd, the Direct Banking (Bill Payment) method is temporarily unavailable due to a transition to a new payment processor. This unexpected service disruption will remain in effect until July 31st.
>
> We wish to clarify that this disruption only affects residents who pay rent using the Direct Banking/Bill Payment option (i.e. payments made through your bank to "Payment Pad Inc."). If you do not use this method, no action is required.
>
> If you normally pay rent using Direct Banking and are planning to pay before August 1st, follow the below steps:
>
> • Cancel any scheduled Direct Banking payments to "Payment Pad Inc."
>
> • Use an alternative method such as Visa Debit, Credit Card, or EFT through your myGreenwin resident portal.
>
> Note that any Direct Banking payments attempted between July 23rd and July 31st will not be processed. If a payment was made using this method during these dates, you must contact your bank to request a refund.
>
> We thank you for your understanding during this transition and apologize for the short notice. Should you have any questions, please contact your Site Team for support.
>
> Sincerely,
> Greenwin Corp.

I looked around online at this time, and found nothing about this, which seemed startling given that Greenwin has thousands of residential customers. I pushed back and was contacted by someone (allegedly) named Dane Aromolaran, Collection Specialist, on August 14. Dane and I had a phone conversation, wherein he made it clear that the letter Sarah sent me (and claimed was sent prior to August 1 re: July payments) has not gone out to the tenants yet. This really confused me, given that we were talking on August 14 and the letter related to late July payments for August 1 rent.

I then received an email from Dane later that day, wherein he wrote: "Regarding your payment made on August 1, there was an issue with the banking system. It has been confirmed that your funds will be returned to your account within 10 business days if the payment was made through CIBC or National Bank. For payments made through other institutions, the refund process may take up to 22 days. Once you receive the funds, you may proceed with resubmitting the payment." On August 28, he wrote me to indicate that I have to write an email to refund_escalation@propertyvista.com and they will escalate with the applicable institution.

On August 29, I received an email from (allegedly) Elizabeth Giannitelli (Manager, Data Integrity) to the effect that I should contact the Payment Tracing Department at my bank to arrange the return of funds that I will then have to re-submit.

I called my bank after the long weekend on September 3, and the woman I spoke with was puzzled by the situation. She then opened up my accounts and found that the July rental payment had been returned to my account on August 28. I then re-made the payment.

Based on the fact that the July payment was returned to my account, I make the assumption that it was Greenwin I was dealing with. Having said that, I still find this whole situation more than a little bit curious.

Most importantly, it took me a few days to regulate my system after these events. What would normally have been a standard level stressor was far more than that because of all I had gone through. One peculiar event after another, leaving me with very little to affix to or to call home.

What got me through this time was yet another deepening towards God. Some part of that was about firmly accepting that this whole experience had to be some kind of Divine mission. Not a pleasant one, not even one that I was likely to survive, but one that had God's fingerprints all over it. Nothing else made sense to me. The other part of it was the utterly brilliant music of a Christian singer/songwriter named Brooke Ligertwood. Brooke sings like Susan writes poetry. I kept her songs on repeat, and it both repelled the negative energies swirling around me and reminded me of the purity I longed for. It is always important to remember that while we're stumbling about on the Devil's Playground, Creation is busily crafting us something beautiful. Something to remind us that we matter. Something to give us hope. We just have to remember to look for it.

***

Chapter 28: Homecomings

Third, I had the strangest experience towards the end of my time in Niagara Falls. One Sunday, I drove down Niagara Falls Blvd to a Fed Ex to check some emails. Apart from two employees, I was the only person in there. About midway through the emails, I experienced what I can best describe as an energetic surge of thought around a specific theme. These thoughts did not thematically emanate from the emails I was reading, nor were they connected to any previous information. They were just there, mixed in with my thoughts about whatever I was doing. It reminded me of some of the certainties I had imagined when I was alone at home in 2023, ill from what would later be revealed as an adverse reaction to prescriptions. Except this time, no prescriptions, no psychosis, no ideation.

When I finished the emails, I left the building. Standing right there, in front of the door with a smartphone pointed towards exactly where I had been sitting, was a familiar looking young man. He was noisily celebrating something he appeared to have accomplished with the phone: "Yes, yes, yes!!!" he exclaimed. The moment he looked up and saw me, his giant smile turned fearful. Like he had been caught doing something wrong. Then he immediately did an about-face and walked quickly towards the nearby light. There was no question in my mind that whatever he was doing with that device was somehow connected to me.

I got in the car to follow him and get a better look. Why did he look so familiar? I arrived at the light he was walking towards, but there were too many cars for me to get out and talk to him. So, I turned and went all the way around and through the subdivision back to Niagara Falls Blvd. I then turned right and saw him reaching the traffic light. I pulled up beside him, and honked. He looked over at me, and spun around like a top, before covering his face with his hand and walking frenetically back towards the plaza. Again, there were cars behind me so I had to turn. By the time I returned to the area, he was nowhere to be found. He must have found a place to hide, or been picked up.

What was particularly interesting was that the kid looked somewhat similar to a twenty-something kid who used to work at a Staples that I would frequent in Southern Ontario in 2022/2023. It may not have been him, but I do remember that kid telling me he was soon going to a school that specialized in something like audio production and sound design. In fact, one day when I was sick from the prescriptions, I went to that Staples to privately check emails. While doing so, the kid angrily yelled at me: "Hey, what are you doing over there?" I was in no state to ask questions, but often wondered why this seeming stranger had an issue with my checking emails at Staples.

* * *

I parked outside the Fed Ex and wondered what the hell was going on. I had once heard that we have reached the stage technologically where it was possible to influence someone's thinking with technology. Not in the familiar ways – smartphone algorithms impacting your perspective – but with the use of an app that can transmit sound and image to a microchip or other item that is surreptitiously planted in or around your ears or brain. In other words, an app that can get you seeing or believing something that either is true or that isn't. If this technology does exist, it would surely be used by politically motivated miscreants hellbent on proving you're crazy. [101]

I called Susan soon thereafter. It was an infuriating conversation. Not only was she saying things markedly inconsistent with things she had said the last time we spoke, there was a tone to the interaction that infuriated me. This time, I said things I regret and told her that I was formally separating, something we had decided not to do in recent conversations. It had always been impossible to imagine the two of us parting for good – I had envisioned a lifetime friendship, at the least – but whatever was going on here was just too destructive. She had carried me on her shoulders for much of this political journey, but I could no longer find the bridge back to her soul. For the moment at least, we would have to disconnect. I would have to complete this journey on my own.

CHAPTER 29

FINAL THOUGHTS: THE PEN IS MIGHTIER THAN THE SHADOW BAN

When I finished my other books, I felt a deep sense of joy. I don't feel that here. What I do feel is relief, and the heartfelt prayer that what I have witnessed and shared will somehow benefit humanity. When you are constantly being terrorized, it's a bit like having a terminal illness. You know the thing is going to kill you – you just don't know when. In the early years of this crucible, I didn't want to die at the hands of my enemies. Now I don't much care, so long as this story gets out there. Because this story is emblazoned with truth. This feels really important to me, because I have long believed that truth is the gateway to the moment. In its presence, we can see things for what they really are, and effect genuine change. In the political context, this means recognizing that abuse of power exists on both sides of the aisle. Many algorithms have been manipulated in an effort to turn us into linear thinkers, certain that only one side of the political aisle can be dishonorable. As a result, we have become barbarians, trapped inside a self-perpetuating divide-and-conquer consciousness, unknowingly led to slaughter by power-hungry puppeteers.

The way back to safety – and a balanced perspective – is truth in all its complexity. Without that, inner and outer peace are not possible. Because a true peace demands that we live in reality and see things for what they are. If we are one step back from reality, we are always one step back from peace. Because those unseen and unresolved elements, will always show up to shatter our peace. With respect to my story, I came to realize that I was fighting for peace. Not just my peace, but also world peace. Not that this story alone could accomplish that, but I believe that the main revealing at the heart of the story – that the political left is just as capable of dishonorable and sadistic acts as the political right – is an essential contribution at an important time. As it is, the left tricked many of us in the West. They convinced many of us that they are the more heartfelt and conscionable side of the aisle, while simultaneously becoming expert at shrouding their agendas while running for office. As a result, they've been able to get away with dangerous shifts further left, without necessary pushback and oversight. This is the furthest thing from the breadth of truth that is required to create a lasting peace.

People have already begun to accuse me of being a political shill for the right wing. Because of my current circumstances, I'm particularly attuned to the horrors of unconscionable globalism, but I'm nobody's shill. The truth is that I don't hate Liberals (or Democrats). Nor do I hate Conservatives (or Republicans). *I hate political abuse of power.* And it's worth noting – just in case my intentions are mischaracterized by the evildoers who've had nearly five years to work diligently at making up stories about me – that I have never received any economic benefit from a political party. Nor have I been bought off by the Russians, the Chinese, or the Liliputians (although an Island vacation would be helpful very right about now). My views are my own, wholly unexpected and wholly original, birthed in an incredibly uncomfortable combination of observation and lived experience.

* * *

The one thing that confounded me for some time was why my enemies wouldn't stop. The book had been announced, and it had likely been read by them. They may not know how it ends, but they know a lot about what is shared in its pages. So, what is it that keeps them coming at me?

Based on my conversations with Grant and others in the field, one answer is clear – they are concerned with what I now know about the world(s) I stepped into. Not only what *I* know, but who I know that knows it, too. I've been at this for 58 months, after all. That's a lot of conversations, and a lot of putting pieces together. I may have lost many seeming friends along the way, but a different kind of friend appeared. One that works quietly in the night, supporting those with the courage to risk it all for humanity.

So, the enemy keeps at me in the hopes that I will eventually crack and give them a glimpse of what I am holding. Once they know what they're dealing with, they will then decide how to handle it (and me). Spies don't like living in the not knowing. It pushes up against their focused nature, and leaves both them and their clients vulnerable to attack. Not by me, but by the millions of people who will one day realize they have been played for fools by the psychopaths that run our world.

I think the story itself is also a big issue. When this first began some people were perplexed as to why a phone interception would be ordered in this context. From their perspective, Wildhorse had only shared a few salacious things with me, and my contributory role with respect to Justin's politic appears to have been limited.

If this had happened in America, I might agree. Because America is more open with respect to exposing the personal lives of politicians, my story would barely make a splash. But I'm from Canada, and anything that exposes the gap between a politician's personal life and their optics could have a cataclysmic effect on an election. It would be one thing if I'd made my getaway when Trudeau was in a majority government position, but most of this happened when he had a minority government. Other parties could easily have passed a vote of non-confidence and forced another election.

I also find it difficult to imagine that my fire was the only fire that the political protection team was trying to put out. It is highly likely that if this door opened, many others would open as well. People and their patterns!

In addition, it's important to note that containing me wasn't just about preserving the Trudeau's reputation and the Liberal's political standing. It also had to be about protecting the reputation of the many individuals, contractors, government agencies, and corporations exposed in this story. It is rare that someone survives a story with this many compromised and interconnected individuals and organizations. I was supposed to die or go mad long before it reached this level of complicity.

There is one other obvious thing – the vaster political context. That is, there is no question in my mind that Trudeau was the opener for what has been a long-game Liberal attempt to communize and globalize Canada. Carney is the submissive, yet devilish closer. I am actually reluctant to call either them or the current party 'Liberals,' because they are nothing like the somewhat centrist Canadian liberal party I grew up with and respected. This is a different beast altogether.

All you have to do is pull up a historical list of the traditional steps taken before a communist regime assumes power and you will see that most of them are now in place here. The many steps taken may be being characterized as benevolent but they aren't. For example, claiming that there is now more military spending in order to protect (rather than to seize) Canada, severing our necessary relationship with the US by blaming President Trump for Canada's (deliberately crafted) economic woes, blocking

Canadians from news access on Meta under the guise of sheltering them from misinformation (lol), seizing people's guns in the name of a more peaceful (read: controlled) society, removing bail requirements for repeat violent offenders and flooding the nation with immigrants in the name of compassion (rather than deliberate chaos), subsidizing legacy media so that we allegedly get balanced (rather than government dictated) news, increasing national debt as an "investment in the future" (actually, so that the inevitably impoverished people will beg their government for table scraps), killing ostriches for health purposes (in fact, because you want to condition fear of government in the populace). We are but one prefabricated national emergency (likely on the basis of political violence that this administration has encouraged and enabled) away from a communist coup. If stories like mine reach the populace, they threaten to crack the veneer that holds all of this political ambition in place.

And then there is a mystery. I am not sure that I can properly articulate this, but I have a strong sense that there is something else going on here. Something that I am perhaps too close to it to see or admit. It is not as simple as the Triad's fragile political grip on Canada, or the financial cover-ups that plague these administrations. It is something strange, or perverse, or unnatural that the players in this story want to hide. At times, I feel like it wants to reveal itself, but then it vanishes. Whatever it is, it is dark and devastating and takes the question of why they spent all this time and money on intimidating me (and others) to a whole different level. (Where is Sherlock Holmes when I need him?)

* * *

I may never know exactly which power broker organized all of this, but it is clear that a choice was made to intimidate me into silence, madness, or death. Somebody out there was willing to spend an enormous amount of money to keep the heat on for almost five years. And, for whatever reason, they decided that fright-and-might would do the trick. They were wrong. All that did was make public revealing a necessity. From the moment they ordered 'Pam Grier' onto my phone, they created the monster they feared.

That they continued to do this even after knowing that both Susan and I had experienced medical calamities, tells you all you need to know about some part of the political world. I had somehow imagined that her heart condition would stop them, but it actually made things worse. This kind

Chapter 29: Final Thoughts: The Pen is Mightier than the Shadow Ban

of makes sense, in a sick way. The worse the story got for them, the more necessary it became to entirely discredit and destroy me.

In a certain sense, what happened here is consistent with the tenor of my dynamic with Mrs. Trudeau throughout our time together. Looking back, it is entirely evident that I never really existed in any of my dynamic with her. If I did, she would have remembered to get back to me about ideas she had floated in a timely manner. She would have respected my marital status – if not her own – and not transmit sexy emojis, suggestive book excerpts, love poems, passion fruit and steamy kitchen disclosures. She would have thought twice before sharing her marital frustrations and sexual longings with a citizen, recognizing that this could have potentially put him at risk. And she would have respected my right to disconnect from her and her political world, by thanking me for my service, and wishing me the best.

She didn't, because I was never a human being with rights in this dynamic. I was a cryptic love interest, a "Stallion of Deep Discovery," a provider of words and ideas for her ambitious public persona. I was a symbology, and I have been treated as such ever since by whomever stepped in to protect her now ex-husband's political status. She may imagine herself a harmless, freedom-loving Wildhorse, but she is nothing of the sort. In my view, she is a narcissistic and unethical fame seeker, so desperate to be seen as a wise sage and accepted by the global elite that she will compromise anyone to get there.

Of course, the term "global elite" is far more wishful thinking than anything meritorious. They are either *trustafarians* born into the thing, or they clamor to be accepted as one of them. Either way, there is seldom anything genuinely "elite" about any of them. In fact, it's been my experience that the whole network of elites are remarkably generic and uninteresting. And, in the case of the Trudeaus – little more than attention-seeking, ignoble grifters with a penchant for cosplay.

It's impossible for me to know how much Sophie knew about all of this terror, but it would not surprise me if she knew a fair amount. If she did have knowledge of an illegal wiretap when she sent me those inappropriate emails in January 2021 (the ones I received right after my initial media outreach), then it is my view that she should be investigated as a conspirator.

And, now that I have looked more objectively at Trudeau's administration, it is clear that the approach taken here was entirely consistent with their *modus operandi* as well. Simply put, we witnessed abuses of power in an unprecedented wave with his administration. Time after time, individual rights were sacrificed on the altar of political expediency. And someone else always seemed to take the fall. For a long time, I assumed that the same thing would occur here. Because they would claim that Trudeau knew nothing about any of it. But then, he showed up in my hotel, and flew to Vancouver and winked at Rob Cribb on an early morning jog. It's now more than a little difficult to claim that he had no knowledge of this situation.

As for Cribb, I may never know what happened here for him and The Star. It could be as simple as this story not hitting their evidential publishing bar, as he said, or as complex as it not being aligned with The Star's political leanings and economic circumstances. As he told me, the decision to publish is never the reporters. It's always in the hands of the editor. If that is truly what happened here, then it is for The Star to explain its decision. I can certainly understand that no newspaper can be forced to publish a story if they don't want to – and also that some part of this very detailed story is far better told in book form – but given that The Star is one of the media outlets that receives funds from the Canadian government to stay in business, don't they have an additional responsibility to disclose stories of significant political interest to the Canadian people? Or, is it The Star's view that this story – by comparison to all the other stories they share – was not something that the public might be interested in? How can *this* story not be in the public interest?

In a recent conversation, Cribb perhaps helped me to understand this in the Canadian political context. In his words: "The allegations are so serious and sweeping and the implications are profound. Dealing with the marriage and relationship with the Prime Minister and his wife ... the bar is high. It's a very high bar." I really get that, but the other side of that coin is that if the individuals and organizations that protect a PM and his wife turn against a vulnerable citizen, the stakes are even higher. Sure, the PM may lose his power, but the citizen may lose their life. The meritocratic American system seems to understand this better, built as it was on a foundation of rebellion against the British monarchy. By contrast, the Canadian system was built on a monarchistic foundation, one where individual rights are more easily sacrificed to the delusional notion that somebody with power has more value than someone without it. The uncomfortable truth is that the Trudeaus could have been boiling babies in their kitchen and no legacy media outlet in Canada would have printed it. God help us, all.

I leave it to the reader to come to their own conclusions about what happened here. The one thing that I do know for sure is that I was the real

Chapter 29: Final Thoughts: The Pen is Mightier than the Shadow Ban

investigative journalist in my story. I was the one digging into the enormity of details, searching for answers. It was always me.

I will also never know with certainty what really happened with Hamilton Police, CSIS, or the RCMP. The one thing that I do know is that our rights are little more than an inconvenient fiction the closer we get to the top. You can safely assume that any information that threatens to expose power – or to undermine the pensions of its minions – will not be revealed in an 'Access to Information' request. No bloody way. In addition, the policing protection system has got it all backwards with respect to federal leadership. Yes, they are obligated to have one eye on the leader so as to ensure their safety, but they are also supposed to have one eye on the protection of the public. As my situation clearly reveals, two eyes on the leader is one eye too many.

The great hidden secret is simply this: Various government agencies use off-book individuals and entities to do what they are not allowed to do. They know they will not get a judge's permission to intimidate and techno-terrorize individuals. So, they hire it out. Those who run the techno-terror show are no different than the most narcissistic abuser you have known. They specialize in destroying other humans, euphemistically calling themselves "private investigators" when in fact they are "private tormentors." Often former cops or military who claimed that they left their past profession because it was too corrupt and they now want to do good things (lol), they make far more money triggering and tormenting than investigating, and likely get bonuses when they drive a person to madness or death. They often do a fair number of normal investigative things, as cover for where they make the most money.

One of the things some tormentors do best is providing locational information to the police, because they are invariably on the target's phone and know where (s)he is. So, if you suddenly find yourself being persistently followed (or harassed) by police, they probably got their info from a "private tormentor." As for why the police would have a relationship with these off-book entities, that's a whole other question. Sometimes, because they provide info to each other that they could not otherwise get, and sometimes because the private tormentor has kompromat on someone in a position of authority at the police force. Whatever the reasons, "private tormentors" have far more access to and influence over law enforcement agencies than they should. They can tell them who to follow, tell them who to bring in, and conjure up false evidence of wrongdoing, all for their own malevolent purposes. In many ways, they have more power than the cops because they are not bound by the Criminal Code. The one good thing that is now happening is that the same phone apps they utilize to watch their targets, are also being utilized to watch them.

If you are one of their victims, you are very unlikely to get help within the system. Because it puts the whole game at risk. If law enforcement investigates and arrests one of these individuals – and if they decide to spill all the beans in an effort to protect themselves – the whole house of cards comes tumbling down. Everyone – including those at the very top of many governmental chains – gets exposed. Hence, the need to completely destroy the credibility of whistle-blowers. The whistle-blower. must be committed, incarcerated or die, in order for the game to live on.

The bottom line is: The Canadian system is rigged. Until this is acknowledged and confronted, nothing of significance will evolve within Canada. With respect to how we make that happen, no-holds-barred whistle-blower legislation <u>with a bite</u> may be our only hope. And not merely legislation that protects government employees. Legislation that protects everyone, from all walks of life and circumstances. In its absence, abusers of power will continue to do as they wish. That is more worrisome than ever, because they now have access to technologies that both shield and accelerate their malevolence. This is a recipe for species-wide disaster.

Supporting whistle-blowers is not merely a systemic issue. It's also a personal issue. Defaming and destroying whistle-blowers has been going on within society for centuries. Little wonder nothing changes with respect to abuse of power. We're not letting the stories through that can change our world. Having gone through this experience, I now wonder how many people that I judged as crazy when they were claiming they'd been abused by power – particularly those with very dramatic stories and a disheveled appearance – were actually telling the truth. And, again, how many that ended up locked up in institutions (or worse) were sent there because their stories legitimately exposed abusers of power? If you have some time on your hands, and/or you are looking for a great cause, find some of these people and bring their stories to life.

* * *

As the story reveals, there were an enormous number of individuals and corporations involved in this situation. I have varying degrees of contempt for all of them, but the one that I feel the most disdain for is Meta. Meta's acts of techno-terror had a more detrimental effect on my psychological state and physical health than anything else. Whichever

Chapter 29: Final Thoughts: The Pen is Mightier than the Shadow Ban

individual there ordered and orchestrated these acts of techno-terrorism against me, is guilty of a whole host of crimes. If Mark Zuckerberg participated, someone who I already perceive as the most dangerous person on the planet because of the polarizing impact of Meta's algorithms on human consciousness, then it is my greatest prayer that he is investigated and prosecuted. Although Jews don't always get along with each other, it is inherently understood that we do not replicate our ancestral trauma by obstructing each other's capacity to make a living. It's one thing for Jews to compete honorably in business. It's quite another to economically pulverize one of us on behalf of an anti-semitic political administration.

With respect to the techno-terrorists themselves, I make the assumption that they were initially doing all of this to get me to back off and let this go. If I am correct in that assumption, then they handled it all wrong. *If you want someone to back off when they are under attack, stop attacking them.* It's not that complicated. Grant them the opportunity to calm down, feel safe, regulate their nervous system. If they can remember pleasure again, perhaps they will never again walk towards the darkness. But if you target them for years, savage their websites, restrict their livelihood, infiltrate their various accounts, harass them with vehicles, then they have nothing left to lose. It is well within reason that I will not physically survive this, so why on earth wouldn't I get my story told on the way out the door?

When I look closely at all the methods they employed, it is obvious that they had some 'genius' do a psychological analysis of me before deciding how to approach things. This is standard practice in their field. That analysis clearly revealed a number of trigger zones: scapegoating, gaslighting, false accusation, abuse of power, economic deprivation, social isolation. So, they went ahead and created precisely those conditions in my life. But they forgot one thing. They forgot how I responded to those conditions when I was younger. I didn't give up on life. I didn't accept misery as my fate. Instead, I fought back. I adapted my personality. I developed a giant tool box of defenses and coping strategies. I refused to say die, even when everything looked bleak. In their efforts to bring me back to my childhood home, all these miscreants accomplished was bringing my warrior back to life.

To put it bluntly, whoever ran this cowardly techno-terror shit-show is a fool. They need their head (and heart) examined. And a few decades of psychotherapy to deal with their underlying emotional issues. It's no accident that they never once sent a real adult to have a conversation with me. They're not adults themselves. They're emotionally regressed, optics-obsessed imbeciles, preferring trickery and gamesmanship to direct human contact. But make no mistake – their adolescent consciousness is the furthest thing from harmless. It's laced with decades of accumulated trauma and misplaced aggression. They bully others as they have been bullied. Let's send them all to an island to beat each other into submission. Then lock the winner alone in a room with nothing other than laptops and smart phones. And make sure that every time they open a device, they get techno-triggered. Over and over again, for all eternity. I'd call that justice. How about you?

* * *

One of the primary reasons why I believe Canada is at risk is because the techno-terrorists have been so effective at getting into the history and onto the phones of many influential Canadians. Whether because they are bribed or blackmailed (or both), a whole host of judges, politicians, government employees, business owners, and prominent law enforcement figures, have been compromised over the last number of years. These are not all bad people. They are often good people put in bad positions. As a result, they are making decisions and acting in ways that are not congruent with their mandates and personal views. If my story can in any way help some of them to come out of the woodwork, it would give us a shot at restoring Canada to its honorable nature before its too late.

Having said that, I do believe that more will be needed to turn away what has already begun in Canada. If I am reading Carney and the current Canadian political zeitgeist right, Canada will soon need all of its citizens to (lawfully) rise to assert their preference with respect to governance. Do they want a government that moves this far left, particularly if they never had a chance to vote on that agenda? And we may well need the support of the Americans. Not to make us into the 51st state, but to stand beside us as the friends and allies they have long been. My grandfather often said that I wouldn't be here if the US hadn't joined the war effort. I believe that is true, and that it is time for all Canadians to understand the profound role that American has played in keeping us safe and sound. You don't have to agree with or understand their politics, to acknowledge their profound significance in your life. But for America, we would be ruled by tyrants. We need them, and they need a truly democratic Canada on their northern border.

* * *

Chapter 29: Final Thoughts: The Pen is Mightier than the Shadow Ban

Looking back, I can certainly see how my naive Canadian roots played into the shock I experienced when the first 'incident' occurred on my telephone. I had been conditioned to believe that such things only happened in other countries. Canadians are kind and polite. We are heartfelt and cooperative people. We are civil by nature. We never sink to these dark depths.

Of course, I call bullshit on that narrative, now. Just because our shadow lives underground, doesn't mean that it's not there. Polite on the surface, but just as angry, judgmental, and malicious as everyone else below it. We're human, after all.

It's also not difficult to see how these narratives about ourselves played into the challenges that I encountered getting this story investigated and told. If we believe that such horrors are beneath us, the only option we have is to gaslight the story-teller. And even if we believe them, our media will not bring the story anyway. Not because they're all 'in on it,' but because it's not congruent with the safe kinds of investigative journalism that align with our cultural expectation ethos. It's just too damn dark. The perfection projection that underlies our collective Canadian self-concept wouldn't survive. Everything would have to change. And they risk losing even more of their subscription base, at a time when mainstream media is already faltering. Of course, one of the reasons it is faltering is because it has no guts. But that's a story for another day.

Without question, this is precisely the combination of conditions that benefit political abusers of power. They know full well that the darker it gets, the less likely it is to be embraced in Canada. So, they pour on the darkness, safe in the knowledge that our 'Good Canadian' conditioning will deny uncomfortable realities. Safe in the knowledge that their nefarious political agendas will always slip through the cracks. I pray that ends soon.

With that in mind, I feel it important to tell you that I have not included a series of significant – and damaging – things that the media shared with me about a variety of prominent political figures. Many of those revealings are recorded, and others are held in other formats. Perhaps because reporters have no other choice but to repress horrifying truths, some of them have a tendency to blab about them with others. I honestly don't believe that they are comfortable with the systemic repression that they endure. They want the stories they work on to be told. Nonetheless, I am choosing not to share these details with the world. I prefer to remain focused on my lived-in experience, rather than the lived-in experience of others. And it is not my responsibility to bring everyone's stories to the world unless it is truly necessary. But it is our collective responsibility to create the conditions where every credible story about abuse of power can be safely shared. That alone would change our world

I want to also acknowledge my part in stepping in this direction to begin with. There is no question that my peripheral family lineage, my misplaced altruism, and my projections onto power made a contribution towards my connecting with Mrs. Trudeau. I also believe that my own repressive Canadian conditioning played a role, both with respect to delaying my recognition of the Trudeau shadow, and with respect to my Canadian inferiority complex, which I believe was manifest as a certain kind of over-zealousness about them. I was always a little smitten with the Kennedy dynasty as a kid. There may have been a way in which I liked the idea of being connected with our own little Canadian dynasty. So much so that I forgot who I really am. That is, someone who has no regard for people who rise to power without merit. Looking back on it now, the fact that I didn't deem it significant that Justin and Sophie Trudeau were only in this position because of the accomplishments of Pierre Elliot Trudeau seems ridiculous. Such is the power of our projections, and the preposterous elevation of celebrity in our culture.

However I understand it, I took the fall for a whole host of missteps by those in positions of power. There are no words for the impact this has had on my physical health, my psyche, my marriage, my daily life, and my very way of being. Because when you have no other choice but to constrict your expression everywhere you go, you end up a kind of hopeless empty shell, muttering meaningless mundanities because you are afraid to speak about what is actually happening. And, again, when you can't express yourself freely, you stop thinking and living freely. Then everything begins to falls apart. No matter what happens now, there is no getting back these lost years.

And yet, here I am. I survived. And not just survived – God has returned to my life, and my soul has re-claimed the warrior consciousness that got misplaced along the way. Time will tell, but it is my hope that I'm still here because this story needs to be told. If not for me, then for humanity. Because democracy will never mean a thing until those who enter political life reveal the truth of who they are, and until they are held to the highest standards of accountability. Because power is not a democratic principle. Service is. Not servants of the ego, or economic benefit, or hidden agenda, or manipulated optics, or the gaslighting of naysayers

– servants of humanity. And while they are busy serving, let them always remember that we are not their props. We are their employers. It is the people who hold the power. And we shall write it accordingly. The pen truly is mightier than the shadow ban.

Endnotes

1. Brown, Jeff, (@soulshaping42), 1 April 2016, "It's been quite a day…" Facebook, https://www.facebook.com/share/p/1A5Wwd6G65/
2. Sophie Grégoire Trudeau (@sophiegregoiretrudeau),"We have nothing to hide, and nowhere to hide it" Facebook, February 7, 2017, https://www.facebook.com/SophieGregoireTrudeau/posts/1791371014449172
3. Brown, Jeff (@soulshaping), 7 February 2017, "Delighted to see…", Facebook, https://www.facebook.com/SOULSHAPING/posts/delighed-to-see-sophie-gregoire-trudeau-canadian-prime-minister-justin-trudeaus/10155137453610982/
4. Trudeau, Sophie Gregoire; Riseboro Caroline, 7 March, 2017, "Walking together…" *The Star,* https://www.thestar.com/opinion/commentary/2017/03/07/walking-together-on-international-womens-day-grgoire-trudeau-and-riseboro.html
5. Trudeau, Sophie Grégoire, (@sophiegregoiretrudeau), 3 June 2017, "Back from Rome" Facebook, https://www.facebook.com/share/18tWKSMVt5/
6. Brown, Jeff, (@soulshaping), 11 October 2017, "I am delighted…" Facebook, https://www.facebook.com/share/p/1FShfbuRht/
7. http://vividlife.me/ultimate/55985/apologies-lgbtq-community-evolving-heterosexual/; (vividlife website links are now defunct)
8. Cbc.ca/news/politics/homosexual-offences-exunge-records-1.4422546
9. Trudeau, Sophie Gregoire, (@sophiegregoiretrudeau), November 2017, "A Year Ago Today," Facebook, https://www.facebook.com/SophieGregoireTrudeau/videos/conversation-with-rupi-kaur-conversation-avec-rupi-kaur/1912943078958631/
10. Trudeau, Sophie Gregoire, (@sophiegregoiretrudeau), 14 February 2018, "Today, and throughout our lives…" Facebook, https://www.facebook.com/share/p/18u9hCNECt/
11. My memory of what was said by Mrs. Trudeau has always been solid since this interaction. That and her emotional state while sharing it are hard to forget. As to where we were standing, my memory was that it was in the early part of the kitchen, but we may have still been in the hallway working our way toward the kitchen as well.
12. Trudeau, Sophie Gregoire, (@sophiegregoiretrudeau), 25 July 2018, "Interview of Jeff Brown", https://www.facebook.com/watch/?v=2039199436332994
13. Trudeau, Sophie Gregoire, (@sophiegregoiretrudeau), 15 August 2018, "Some wisdom with the afternoon tea…", Facebook, https://www.facebook.com/share/p/16vL5KZf85/
14. www.facebook.com/SophieGregoireTrudeau/videos/c2-montreal/510697239393505

15. https://www.facebook.com/G7/videos/403701413429106. 15:35-16:55 (from 15:35-16:55) (Checked on October 14/2025 and now not there. Possibly the shift to FB 'Reels' caused its removal?)
16. Trudeau, Justin, (@justintrudeau), 2 December 2018 "Hey, @trevornoah…" X, https://x.com/JustinTrudeau/status/1069214653169844227
17. Dickson, Janice, 3 December 2018, "Trudeau criticized…" CBC, https://infotel.ca/newsitem/trudeau-criticized-for-tweet-to-trevor-noah-pledging-50m-charity-gift/it57798
18. Scheer, Andrew (@AndrewScheer) 2 December 2018, "Pledging $50 million…" X, https://x.com/AndrewScheer/status/1069434034600595458
19. Dickson, Janice, 3 December 2018, "Trudeau criticized…" CBC, https://www.cbc.ca/news/politics/trudeau-trevor-noah-money-1.4930216
20. https://en.wikipedia.org/wiki/SNC-Lavalin_affair
21. Trudeau, Sophie Gregoire, (@sophiegregoiretrudeau), 6 February 2019, "The day I realized…" https://www.facebook.com/share/p/16cDYN5Mii/
22. Minhaj, Hasan, 02 September 2019, *The Patriot Act* (Netflix) Episode "The Two Sides of Canada," Youtube. https://www.youtube.com/watch?v=cD-PeXoQUrbI
23. Kambhampaty, Anna Purna; Carlisle, Madeleine; Chan, Melissa, 18 September 2019, "Justin Trudeau wore…" *Time* Magazine, https://time.com/5680759/justin-trudeau-brownface-photo/
24. On Demand News. 19 September 2019, "Trudeau Apologises for 'Dumb…" On Demand News, https://www.youtube.com/watch?v=c2lxuyROWKs
25. Fieldstadt, Elisha; Radnofsky, Caroline, 19 September, 2019, "Justin Trudeau admits…" NBC News, https://www.nbcnews.com/news/world/third-instance-canadian-prime-minister-justin-trudeau-darkened-make-up-surfaces-n1056361; Carlisle, Madeleine; Kambhampaty, Anna Purna, 19 September, 2019, "Justin Trudeau says…" *Time* Magazine. https://time.com/5681605/justin-trudeau-blackface-more-photos
26. Image of Barack Obama and Sophie Gregoire Trudeau walking. Taken from behind. https://www.narcity.com/en-ca/news/sophie-gregoire-trudeau-and-barack-obama-are-bffs-and-her-latest-post-proves-it:; (Checked on October 14/2025 and now not there. Screenshot available.)
27. *The Daily Beast*, 18 March 2020, "Idris Elba hints…", https://www.thedailybeast.com/idris-elba-hints-that-he-contracted-covid-19-coronavirus-from-justin-trudeaus-wife-sophie; Omotoye, 'Tunde (@TundeTash) 16 March 2020, "Here's a picture…", X, https://x.com/tundetash/status/1239631614021419009 ; Racovali, John, 19 Mar 2020, "Idris Elba says…", *National Post*, nationalpost.com/entertainment/celebrity/idris-elba-says-he-was-exposed-to-coronavirus-on-the-day-he-hugged-sophie-gregoire-trudeau; Harris, Kathleen, 12 March 2020, "Sophie Gregoire Trudeau…", CBC, https://www.cbc.ca/news/politics/covid19-trudeau-premiers-coronavirus-1.5495001; Elba, Idris, 16 March 2020, "Video Statement from Idris…", CBS 42, https://www.youtube.com/watch?v=UAsKmQSwEsI
28. https://www.fda.gov/drugs/medication-health-fraud/public-notification-u-dream-full-night-contains-hidden-drug-ingredient; https://re-

calls-rappels.canada.ca/en/alert-recall/health-canada-warns-canadians-about-u-dream-herbal-sleep-aid-products-after-tests

29. Brown, Jeff. (@jeffbrownsoulshaping),11 December 2020 "The Battlefield of Truth…" https://www.instagram.com/reel/CIrfNlrHp8O/?hl=en.
30. Brown, Jeff, (@soulshaping42), 20 December 2021, "is feeling unsafe", Facebook, https://www.facebook.com/share/p/16DQ5fV8np/
31. Wilson-Raybould, Jody; Wernick, Michael, 29 March 2019 "Audio of Call between…" CityNews, https://www.youtube.com/watch?v=c5WkRWf6PGM
32. Brown, Jeff, (@soulshaping), 02 January 2021, "Perhaps the greatest impediment in the world…", Facebook, https://www.facebook.com/share/p/18fxgrYjCz
33. Brown, Jeff (@soulshaping42) 09 January 2021, "As I look back…" Facebook, https://www.facebook.com/share/p/16fhX4fF5j/
34. Brown, Jeff (@soulshaping) 19 January 2021, "I recently had an experience…", Facebook, https://www.facebook.com/share/p/1AbJ5UZRZp/
35. Brown, Jeff, (@soulshaping), 24 Feb 2021, "Sincere Apology…", Facebook, https://www.facebook.com/share/p/1CfKN2sfAR/; Brown, Jeff, (@jeffbrownsoulshaping), 21 May 2021, "Noone living in…", Instagram, https://www.instagram.com/p/CPJSHp4H_TO/?igsh=bXhlejNnd-2V3aG15; Brown, Jeff, (@soulshaping42), 24 March, 2021, "I am relieved to report…", Facebook, https://www.facebook.com/Soulshaping42/posts/pfbid02fFNdiGhmjKzjEAQtQJuLBpKA457YpwugkFRPPgryzfCAqzrrQUdKstcHurrjYdfDl; Brown, JEFF (@soulshaping42), 13 April 2021, "I have fought…", Facebook, https://www.facebook.com/Soulshaping42/posts/pfbid02DgC3qqeZYewtaNooot-G2Jpo1VShPdMw4JVtpf8hiwFyxwxwyBjcLQvXuNwdfgyWgl
36. https://www.lowenfoundation.org/
37. https://treglobal.org/
38 Brown, Jeff, (@jeffbrownsoulshaping), 16 May 2021, "I have no capacity…, Instagram, https://www.instagram.com/p/CO9ev1jHCRc/?igsh=MWZIN-3J3Z2x0NHNkeg==
39. https://www.instagram.com/chairquinby/
40. Brown, Jeff (@jeffbrownsoulshaping) 12 June 2021, "In this video, I begin…", Instagram, https://www.instagram.com/p/CQCad8rH_r9/
41. https://open.spotify.com/track/2gxWWfdW2qMXqjKSB0iy68
42. Brown, Jeff (@jeffbrownsoulshaping) 14 June 2021, "In this video, I share…", Instagram, instagram.com/reel/CQIOoJxHgjK/
43. Brown, Jeff, (@soulshaping), June, 2021 (precise day unclear), "Trauma is a subjective experience," Facebook, https://www.instagram.com/p/CQCad8rH_r9/
44. Brown, Jeff, (@soulshaping42), 24 July, 2021, "This has been the most…", Facebook, https://www.facebook.com/share/p/163vXwB28N/
45. "Pig," Written and directed by Michael Sarnoski. From a story by Vanessa Block and Michael Sarnoski. Released in 2021
46. Brown, Jeff, (@jeffbrownsoulshaping), 30 Sept 2021, "As I look back on my life…" Instagram, https://www.instagram.com/p/CUd8KojM8e5/?igsh=MThkdWc5bmxpdGJwaA==
47. Brown, Jeff, (@jeffbrownsoulshaping), 1 October 2021, "I have no capac-

ity..." Instagram, https://www.instagram.com/p/CUgHhd_rBll/?igsh=MT-JyNHR3bnkzYWc0ZA==
48. Gilmore, Rachel, 6 Oct 2021, "Trudeau says Tofino...", Global News, https://globalnews.ca/news/8247262/trudeau-tofino-truth-reconciliation-apology-mistake/
49. Stephenson, Mercedes; Gilmore, Rachel, 1 Oct 2021, "Trudeau spends 1st...", Global News, https://globalnews.ca/news/8234246/trudeau-vacation-indigenous-tofino-truth-and-reconciliation/
50. Brown, Jeff, (jeffbrownsoulshaping), Instagram, 1 Oct 2021, "I noticed that an account..." https://www.instagram.com/p/CUguxIBs5s2/?igsh=OWt3YWlnbD-BqNno1
51. https://www.instagram.com/xavtrudeau_/
52. Gilmore, Rachel, 26 January 2022, 'Fringe Minority...' Global News, https://globalnews.ca/news/8539610/trucker-convoy-covid-vaccine-mandates-ottawa/
53. Naylor, Dave, 29 Dec 2021, "Trudeau calls the...", Western Standard, https://www.westernstandard.news/news/trudeau-calls-the-unvaccinated-racist-and-misogynistic-extremists/article_a3bacece-2e14-5b8c-bf37-eddd672205f3.html
54. Brown, Jeff, @soulshaping42, 4 FEB 2022, "It has been..." Facebook, https://www.facebook.com/share/p/1ARJ9Wmai9/
55. Brown, Jeff, (@soulshaping42), 3 April 2022, "As I step closer..." Facebook, https://www.facebook.com/share/p/16RcbpXEfC/
56. *The Daily Beast*, 18 March 2020, "Idris Elba hints..." *Daily Beast*, https://www.thedailybeast.com/idris-elba-hints-that-he-contracted-covid-19-coronavirus-from-justin-trudeaus-wife-sophie
57. Brown, Jeff, (@soulshaping), 31 August 2022, "Truth is the Gateway...", Facebook, https://www.facebook.com/SOULSHAPING/posts/pfbid0DVdvLZueVBYDxgMYir4azWPpN4BWH9Zaawxwax9q4WuAHVjY6gtuTcFi3UED4y3Al
58. Brown, Jeff, (@soulshaping42), 17 Dec 2022, "Hi Friends, I feel it..." Facebook, https://www.facebook.com/share/p/16SL4dBXMu/
59. Brown, Jeff, (@jeffbrownsoulshaping), 28 December 2022, "How very interesting..." Instagram, https://www.instagram.com/p/Cmu--wvO60T/?igsh=cjRlb-zluYTlzeGpj
60. Mitchell, Don. 11 Jan 2023, "Prime Minister Trudeau..." Global News, https://globalnews.ca/news/9403492/pm-justin-trudeau-3-day-cabinet-retreat-january-hamilton/
61. I had once seen some back alley wall graffiti that said "Where are my comic book heroes?" I was never able to figure out who wrote it, but I told someone I was involved with that I could relate to it. And then she took a picture of it and had it framed for me as a reminder. Despite the great challenges within ourselves and the relationship that emanated from our histories of intense childhood trauma, we both found ways to offer love and kindness when we could. I always remembered her gesture with great appreciation.
62. Richards, David, 3 Feb 2023, "Liberal Appointed Senator..." *National Post*, https://www.youtube.com/watch?v=UvOUD7oVvvw

ENDNOTES

63. Brown, Jeff, (@soulshaping), 10 May 2023, "My fellow Canadians…" Facebook, https://www.facebook.com/share/p/1QJDBTXoos/
64. The only image there now (October 28/25) is an unrelated comment, and the image of Will. The rest has been removed (not by me). I have copies of the rest. Brown, Jeff, (jeffbrownenrealment), 4 June 2023, "Good news…." Instagram*, https://www.instagram.com/p/CtFWkOfu5Up/?igsh=MWs2b3gwNzcwanoxcg%3D%3D; *The only image there now (Oct 28/2025) is an unrelated comment, and an image of Will. The rest has been removed (not by me). I have copies of the rest.
65. Brown, Jeff, (Interviewed by Ross McKeachie), 28 June 2023, "Jeff Brown~Humanifestations…", Banyen Books podcast, www.youtube.com/watch?v=gL5E6lzPQ8o (Note: If video doesn't come up with link, search 'Banyen Books, Jeff Brown, Humanifestations' and the Keepers of the Internet Gate might let you in 😊)
66. Tabachnick, Cara, 02 Aug. 2023, "Canadian Prime Minister…", CBS News, https://www.cbsnews.com/news/canadian-prime-minister-justin-trudeau-announces-separation-from-wife-sophie/
67. Anand, Nisha; Ghosh, Poulomi (ed.), 5 Oct 2023, "Weirdo: Justin Trudeau…", *Hindustan Times*, https://www.hindustantimes.com/world-news/weirdo-justin-trudeau-trolled-for-winking-at-new-speaker-in-canadian-parliament-101696487691752.html
68. https://en.wikipedia.org/wiki/Spiritual_bypass
69. jeffbrown42.substack.com/p/the-body-that-loves-you
70. Brown, Jeff (@soulshaping) 24 Feb 2024, "Yet again, Meta…" Facebook, https://www.facebook.com/SOULSHAPING/posts/pfbid02BVf8NkxY1BTWFeDZtcRnSmGQj5X5aV7UCJobVAGDJDwtWbSp2Avs7GFvYL4cbYdDl
71. Brown, Jeff (@Soulshaping) 13 March 2024, "Given that my book…" Facebook, https://www.facebook.com/SOULSHAPING/posts/pfbid0CKVZWkRz4XfwbwoWgvaihVPJEXgKWovVL48KwRH5GAwu85QMtHTUvRgG81kkaEvzl
72. Brown, Jeff (@jeffbrownenreal) 8 April 2024 "There was a time…" X, https://x.com/JeffBrownEnreal/status/1777463658886344796
73. urbandictionary.com/define.php?term=Techno-Terrorism
74. urbandictionary.com/define.php?term=Invisibully; *Note: My memory is that I created the term invisibully in the heart of a conversation with Susan. Her memory is that she said it first. I'm fine either way, so long as the term reaches those who need it.
75. Brown, Jeff (@soulshaping42) 29 June 2024, "The story began so…", Facebook, https://www.facebook.com/share/p/186oeNog9o/
76. Alonso, Melissa; Sykes, Jillian 30 June 2024 "Toronto Police seek…" CNN, https://www.cnn.com/2024/06/30/americas/toronto-suspected-hate-motivated-attacks-synagogues
77. Brown, Jeff (@jeffbrownsoulshaping) 30 January 2024 "I am a proud…" Instagram, https://www.instagram.com/reel/C2wBqU1sc_p/?hl=en
78. Geist, Michael, 1 July 2024, When antisemitism…", MichaelGeist.ca, https://www.michaelgeist.ca/2024/07/when-antisemitism-strikes-close-to-home/
79. Brown, Jeff (@jeffbrownenreal) 9 July 2024 "It's been my experience…" X

https://x.com/JeffBrownEnreal/status/1810794248205193302
80. Brown, Jeff (@soulshaping42) 16 July 2024 "Hi friends, I…" https://www.facebook.com/share/p/1ByL8JR8tr/
81. https://jeffbrown42.substack.com/p/the-moment-of-peril
82. https://www.facebook.com/Soulshaping
83. Brown, Jeff (@soulshaping42) 3 August 2024 "As the darkness…" Facebook, https://www.facebook.com/share/p/1Fbwh8UD9N/?mibextid=wwXlfr
84. https://jeffbrown42.substack.com/p/where-is-god-in-all-of-this-psalm
85. Smiley, Kim, (@kimsmiley), 29 July 2024, "Ode to a Late Bloomer", Instagram, https://www.instagram.com/reel/C-AsGHGRUJW/?igsh=dW0wdjIzeHhzNGN4
86. Ghert-Zand, Renee, 29 March 2018, "Toronto Designer worn…", *Times of Israel*, https://www.timesofisrael.com/toronto-designer-worn-by-trudeaus-stitches-together-fashion-with-social-justice/
87. https://www.kimsmiley.com/collections/lace-earrings/products/sophie-earrings
88. Weinstein, Eric; Williamson, Chris, 4 Sept 2023, "We need to stop…" Modern Wisdom Podcast, https://www.youtube.com/watch?v=LJxBnSyH0T4 at minutes 51-57
89. Brown, Jeff (@jeffbrownenreal) 4 Jan 2025 "When you are experiencing…" X https://x.com/JeffBrownEnreal/status/1875630257535090909
90. Aguilar Bryann 04 Jan 2025 ("Police search for…") CP24 www.cp24.com/local/halton/2025/01/05/police-search-for-suspects-after-jewelry-store-robbery-at-burlington-mall/
91. https://charmdiamondcentres.com/store/452/stone-road-mall
92. Brown, Jeff, (@jeffbrownenreal), 8 Jan 2025, "Follow-up on…", X, https://x.com/JeffBrownEnreal/status/1877144602731491399; Dropbox of phone call excerpt: https://www.dropbox.com/scl/fi/omsg5w3f8t39gmi9c0zmf/Jeff-Brown-Intercepted-call-January-6-2025.mp3
93. Brown, Jeff, (@jeffbrownenreal), 16 January 2025, "Isn't the political world wonderful?", X, https://x.com/JeffBrownEnreal/status/1880083654610940347
94. Guelph Today Staff, 17 January 2025, "Video: Stone Road Mall…", Guelph Today.com, https://www.guelphtoday.com/local-news/stone-road-mall-shuts-down-after-apparent-friday-night-robbery-10095740
95. Brown, Jeff, (@jeffbrownenreal), 23 January 2025, "Investigative Challenge…", X, https://x.com/JeffBrownEnreal/status/1882550068252676345
96. https://jeffbrown42.substack.com/p/to-be-a-jew-is-to-always-be-at-war
97. Trudeau, Justin, (@justinptrudeau), 17 March 2025, "Gotta love…", https://www.instagram.com/p/DHUhHxasXHg/?hl=en
98. Lantsman, Melissa, (@melissalantsman), 14 March 2025, "The end of Justin Trudeau", Instagram, https://www.instagram.com/p/DHL_4rKASk3/ (pic taken by Trudeau's Staff Photographer Adam Scotti; https://www.thestar.com/news/canada/justin-trudeaus-longtime-photographer-reflects-on-last-decade-shares-shots-of-former-pms-final-days/article_16dd507a-0103-11f0-8bde-ef-f97c406d0a.html
99. Bell, Stewart, 17 March 2025, "Suspect charged…", *Global News*, https://globalnews.ca/news/11085673/suspect-charged-with-hate-crimes-spree-

that-included-attacks-at-5-toronto-synagogues/
100. https://en.wikipedia.org/wiki/Military_deception
101. I am no student of microchips and the like, and feel confident that we have entered an era where there are probably many techniques being explored that can access our thinking, but I do have a few more things to share about what happened in New York, and subsequently in the DC area. I don't have the energy to explore them now, but I want to note them. After that experience at Fed-Ex, I had two very rough nights at the motel I was staying in. Not that different from some of the nights with my adverse prescription to meds, where I would be woken up by strange images, sounds, and voices that seemed to be emanating from my mind but simultaneously seemed to be emanating from the space itself. Really strange stuff that only seemed to arise when I fell deeply asleep. Once I got up and got moving, all gone.

I then went to the DC area. After a few nights in a nice hotel in Germantown, Maryland, the same thing happened. But this time, I was smart about it. I got up and walked super quietly to the door to the room. I reached for the handle, and opened it abruptly. Standing right outside my room was a tall white man, with a smartphone pointed directly at the door. How he knew which room was mine is anybody's guess, but he looked up with the same guilty look as the kid outside the Fed-Ex. And then he quickly fled. The only reasonable conclusion I could come to was that whatever they are doing on that phone is targeting some aspect of my consciousness. And it is effective at whatever it is that it's doing. Whether it actually requires something installed in a person, or whether it's a cutting-edge app that the spy world has developed that can more easily permeate consciousness, is beyond me. But what I can say is that it feels likely to me that they have developed something dangerous that will start to become part of our cultural narrative very soon.

Gratitudes

Gratitudes to those people and places that offered wisdom, support and/or kindness in my time of need: Lily, Lacy, J, The Anti-spy, "David", Jean Christian, Louise Frechette, CM, T, Andrew Harvey, Theo Fleury, DD, A, The Holiday Inn and upstairs restaurant crew (Grand Island, New York), Rob Wipond, Ellie Goldenberg, Tania Cascone, New Leaf Distribution & Lotus Press, Ethan Dann, K, Alan Young, The Shift Network, T, Kent Heckenlively, Elephant Journal, the Holocaust Memorial Museum (Washington), Aaron Korpa, Eve Ensler, George, Sonia Reflexology (Burlington), Don Suzuki, Neil Sattin, Linda Thornton, Anthony Perlove, Shaunne Perlove, Auntie Ruthie, the De Cardo Hotel (Jerusalem), Michelle Barker (excellent editor), CH, The librarians throughout the Wellington and Hamilton Systems, The man who owns the Black & White (Chinese) Restaurant (Fergus, Ontario), The Lord (in all your luminous forms).

Gratitudes to those (alive or dead) who somehow inspired me to go on: The hostages, Susan, Douglas Murray, Elica Lebon, Mahsa Amini, Dana Levenson, Ivanka Trump, Buckaroo Banzai, Jeanne Achterberg, Abraham Joshua Heschel, Dr. Judith Orloff, struggling humans everywhere, Eddie Greenspan, Gordon Resnick, Trey Yingst, Trey Yesavage and the 2025 Toronto Blue Jays (Champions of the Heart), Gloria Robbins, Diane Gordon, Naomi Holland, Albert and Barbara Brown, the Gen-Z's fighting for a corruption-free Nepal, Ova Back, Sophie Strand, Toko-pa Turner, Ram Dass, Maria Shriver, Jean Houston, Freedom Convoy (Canada), Mira Sorvino, Uncle Sidney Back, Dr. Rocky Polson, Joelle Glasroth, Lisa Feldman Barrett, My wonderful writing students, Denzel Washington, Marty Resnick, Heather Garrod, Uncle Joe Perlove, Fred (Ricky) Perlove, Jody Wilson-Raybould, David Sniderman, Celina Caesar-Chavannes, James Frybort, Auntie Tilly Resnick, Abraham Lincoln, Bernard and Frances Perlove, Robin Joy (my beloved sister. Our spirits shall meet in due time), Robert Frybort Sr., Robert Frybort Jr., Jessie Frybort, the social media supporters who continued to support me, Jesus Christ.

Gratitudes to those music makers who kept me afloat and alight during this crucible:

Brooke Ligertwood, 1000 Israeli Musicians, Matisyahu, LeAnn Rimes, Nizar Francis, Soaking in his Presence, Judah (and the Lion), Nick Cave (and the Bad Seeds), Kristene DiMarco, The Hu, Yusuf Islam, Ocie Eliott, Chrissy Metz, Elevation Worship, Chris Brown and Brandon Lake, Trevor Hall, Krishna Das, Bethel Music, Benjamin William Hastings, Hollow Coves, Of Monsters and Men, Jenn Johnson, Kari Jobe, Olafur Arnalds, One For Israel Ministry, Malte Marten, The Flying Bulgar Klezmer Band, Pat Barrett, Hillsong Worship, Michael Ketterer and Influence Music, Tiffany Hudson.

Gratitudes to Kris, Ed and Julia at Trineday Press. And to IPG (Book Distributors).

Finally, gratitude for Chocolate Rugelach from the Shuk in Jerusalem, for reminding me how great life can taste. I forgot.

About the Author

Jeff Brown is a breakthrough voice in the self-help/spirituality field, and the author of nine popular books: Soulshaping: A Journey of Self-Creation, Ascending with Both Feet on the Ground, Love It Forward, An Uncommon Bond, Spiritual Graffiti, Grounded Spirituality, Hearticulations, Humanifestations, and Where is God in all of this?: A Conversation

In his previous life, Jeff was a criminal lawyer and psychotherapist. Since pursuing his path as a writer, he has launched many initiatives, including founding Enrealment Press, and an online school, Soulshaping Institute. He is the producer and key journeyer of the award-winning spiritual documentary, Karmageddon, which also stars Ram Dass, Seane Corn, Deva Premal and Miten. He has written a series of inspirations for ABC's Good Morning America and appeared on over 300 radio shows. He also authored the viral blog 'Apologies to the Divine Feminine (from a warrior in transition).'

A popular presence in social media, Jeff's new terms and well-loved quotes became a phenomenon some years ago, and continue to be shared by millions of seekers and growers worldwide. His quotes have been shared in social media by The David Suzuki Foundation, Brain Games host Jason Silva, author Amanda De Cadenet, actress Chrissy Metz, songstress LeAnn Rimes, and many others. Most beautifully, they have touched and benefited millions of souls.

Jeff currently lives in Canada. He is presently breaking new ground as an Encodings Activist. In addition, he is hard at work on three new books and courses, and looking forward to the next steps on his creative path.

You can connect with his offerings at jeffbrown.co, soulshapinginstitute.com, karmageddonthemovie.com, enrealment.com, and encodings.co. He is grateful for your presence and for your support.